Consumer Behaviour

SAGE has been part of the global academic community since 1965, supporting high quality research and learning that transforms society and our understanding of individuals, groups and cultures. SAGE is the independent, innovative, natural home for authors, editors and societies who share our commitment and passion for the social sciences.

Find out more at: **www.sagepublications.com**

Consumer Behaviour

Applications in Marketing

Second Edition

Robert East, Malcolm Wright and Marc Vanhuele

◆SAGE

Los Angeles | London | New Delhi
Singapore | Washington DC

Los Angeles | London | New Delhi
Singapore | Washington DC

SAGE Publications Ltd
1 Oliver's Yard
55 City Road
London EC1Y 1SP

SAGE Publications Inc.
2455 Teller Road
Thousand Oaks, California 91320

SAGE Publications India Pvt Ltd
B 1/I 1 Mohan Cooperative Industrial Area
Mathura Road
New Delhi 110 044

SAGE Publications Asia-Pacific Pte Ltd
3 Church Street
#10-04 Samsung Hub
Singapore 049483

Editor: Matthew Waters
Editorial assistant:
Production editor: Vanessa Harwood
Marketing manager: Alison Borg
Cover design: Jennifer Crisp
Typeset by: C&M Digitals (P) Ltd, Chennai, India
Printed by MPG Books Group, Bodmin, Cornwall

Library of Congress Control Number: 2012940757

British Library Cataloguing in Publication data

A catalogue record for this book is available from
the British Library

MIX
Paper from
responsible sources
FSC® C018575
www.fsc.org

ISBN 978-1-4462-1122-9
ISBN 978-1-4462-1123-6 (pbk)

Contents

Praise for the previous edition

This book provides a wonderful (and very unusual) balance between areas of marketing that are often at odds with each other (or, worse yet, unaware of each other) [...] I recommend it to any student, researcher, or manager in marketing.
Peter Fader, Frances and Pei-Yuan Chia Professor, and Professor of Marketing,
Wharton School, University of Pennsylvania, USA

This textbook is exceptional for the amount of relevant research that is presented and explained. Students who have read and understood this text are likely to be much more of use to industry.
Fergus Hampton, Managing Director, Millward Brown Precis, London, UK

A serious, thoughtful consumer behaviour text, that focuses on substance rather than what's fashionable in academic circles.
Professor Byron Sharp, Ehrenberg-Bass Institute, University of South Australia

About the Authors

Robert East is professor of consumer behaviour in the marketing department of Kingston Business School, London and adjunct professor at the Ehrenberg-Bass Institute of the University of South Australia. He trained as a social psychologist and is a postgraduate of London Business School. His research has mainly focused on word-of-mouth patterns, where his new evidence has shown that some widely held beliefs are mistaken. As a teacher of consumer behaviour, he has been keen to deliver knowledge that is useful to students while not over-simplifying the subject. This book reflects both his iconoclastic research and his commitment to a curriculum that is both intellectual and useful.

Malcolm Wright is professor of marketing at Massey University, New Zealand, and adjunct professor at the Ehrenberg-Bass Institute of the University of South Australia. He applies empirical principles to marketing problems and has made interrelated discoveries about brand loyalty, the use of probability scales, new product forecasting and optimizing the advertising budget. He has also published many articles critically examining the foundations of popular marketing knowledge.

Marc Vanhuele holds a PhD from UCLA and is associate professor of marketing at HEC Paris. He has taught in MBA, Master of Science, executive and doctoral programmes on the topics of market orientation, consumer behaviour, pricing and communication. He also serves as consultant to consumer goods and market research companies. His research focuses on two different areas: how consumers deal with price information, and how a new use of marketing metrics can help managers to make better decisions.

Preface

Readership and Scope

We have designed this book to support courses in consumer behaviour at master's level. It is also suited to more advanced teaching at first-degree level. Our intended audience is those who see consumer behaviour as a research-based discipline that addresses problems raised by marketing and consumer policy. The problems we explore are found in all advanced and emerging economies and, for this reason, we believe that the book will be useful throughout the world.

This new edition continues the themes of the 2008 edition and, in addition, has one new chapter on Consumer Group Differences (Chapter 6). This covers cross-cultural comparisons and some segmentation issues. The remaining chapters have been updated with additional material, reflecting changes in the field in recent years, but their structure remains essentially as before. The book is selective in the research it covers, dealing in some detail with the areas chosen. As before, the chapters are quite short and are intended to support students who will also be reading original research papers. In updating and revising the book, we have found that we can often simplify and clarify the text and occasionally omit some elements that no longer seem so relevant. The result is a book that is easier to read and no longer than the previous edition.

Consumer Behaviour: Applications in Marketing stresses well-researched aspects of consumer behaviour that are of widespread importance. Following the Introduction, we describe the patterns of customer purchasing that are usually observed in market economies and the way these patterns can be explained and applied in marketing. We then look at research that has illuminated our understanding of consumer decision-making and show how this understanding can be used by marketers and public policy-makers. The last section of the book deals with the observed consumer response to market intervention and covers research findings on price, promotion, word of mouth and advertising.

Approach

Most textbooks in consumer behaviour are extensive and well illustrated, but may present the subject in a rather uncritical manner. Often, the treatment illustrates fashionable topics rather than providing evidence that helps us understand long-standing marketing problems. Such books do not make sufficient call on the expanding research in our field and, when they do cite research, may give limited attention to the uncertainties or opposing views that persist in our discipline. In practice, there are competing findings and explanations in all areas of consumer behaviour and marketing, and we have tried to recognize these and discuss their relative merits.

This touches on a problem familiar to those who teach business students. Some of these students find arguments from evidence to be quite unfamiliar and may instead provide accounts of current business practice as though these were conclusive. Our approach opposes such uncritical thinking. We believe that those who learn to use evidence as students acquire a technique that will serve them well as practitioners.

One hazard of research-based texts is the sheer weight of evidence. We have tried to emphasize the most recent work and key papers on topics while also acknowledging those early researchers who first identified problems in consumer behaviour – problems that are usually still current. We therefore make no apology for some of the more ancient citations in this book, as these help to describe the origin of current thinking.

As subjects become more fragmented, textbooks acquire importance as integrators of different perspectives. In scientific consumer behaviour, we can discern two rather different approaches to research and application. On the one hand, there is the tradition that dominates in the large conferences of the *Association for Consumer Research*. Put baldly, this endorses theorizing and hypothesis-testing, often within experimental designs, and tends to emphasize explanations in terms of the beliefs, preferences and the culture of consumers – a cognitive orientation. In contrast to this is the approach of those who belong to the *marketing science* grouping, who place emphasis on behaviour, measures rather than concepts, generalization from an accumulation of findings, and on the use of mathematical models rather than psychological theories for explanation. Textbooks have generally emphasized the cognitive tradition. We give more space than usual to the marketing science orientation; in particular, we emphasize behavioural explanations, the role of habit and the modelling of market patterns and market change. However, we also provide a full treatment of the techniques and theory that underlie the cognitive approach to consumer behaviour.

Consumer behaviour is a changing field. New research is giving answers to questions of major importance and, in due course, will give rise to a new breed of professional marketer. All three authors are active researchers and use their own research in this book; we hope that, in doing so, we manage to convey the excitement that new discoveries arouse.

Exercises

Good education gives students the confidence to use and criticize ideas. We try to enlarge this confidence through practical exercises that help the reader to apply and reflect on ideas about consumer behaviour. The exercises require self-appraisal, calculation, observation, measurement of attitudes and the use of computer programs. In many cases, they are quickly done and the reader will benefit by doing them as they occur.

Plan of the Book

The book is divided into four Parts. Part 1 (Chapter 1) introduces the reader to explanations for the different forms of consumer purchase. Part 2 (Chapters 2, 3, 4, 5 and 6) focuses on patterns of purchase; we cover customer loyalty and brand equity, the recurrent features of mature and changing markets, and relevant differences between cultures and consumer segments. Part 3 (Chapters 7, 8 and 9) focuses on decision-making; we deal with methods for predicting and explaining decisions, the way that decisions can be biased and the post-decision effects relating to satisfaction and quality. Part 4 (Chapters 10, 11, 12 and 13) focuses on the responses of consumers to conditions that affect consumption. These are price, the retail environment, social influence and advertising.

Acknowledgements

A number of people assisted us in the production of the previous edition: Dag Bennett, Brian Birkhead, Walter Carl, Cullen Habel, Kathy Hammond, Bruce Hardie, Paul Marsh, Jenni Romaniuk, Deborah Russell, John Scriven, Byron Sharp, Mark Uncles and Jim Wiley. For the present edition, we are particularly indebted to Kathy Hammond, Magda Nenycz-Thiel, Cathy Nguyen, Francesca Dall'Olmo Riley, Jenni Romaniuk, Deborah Russell, Jaywant Singh, Mark Uncles and Melissa Vignardi. Finally, we appreciate very much the influence of our students. With them in mind, we have tried to be relevant and clear.

Companion Website

Be sure to visit the companion website (www.sagepub.co.uk/east2e) to find additional teaching and learning material for both lecturers and students.

For lecturers:
- PowerPoint Slides
- Notes for Lecturers
- Example Questionnaire
- Sample Course Programme
- Software Notes
- SPSS Data Files

For students:
- References

Part 1
Introduction

1 Ideas and Explanations in Consumer Research

LEARNING OBJECTIVES

When you have completed this chapter, you should be able to:

1 Explain why it is important to study consumer behaviour.
2 Discuss the limitations of a common-sense approach to consumer behaviour.
3 Compare and contrast different approaches to decision-making by consumers.
4 Discuss the effects of the consumer environment on choice.
5 Explain how markets are usually classified.

OVERVIEW

In this chapter, we show that findings about the way in which consumers behave when they buy and use products and services can be quite unexpected and that research is needed if we are to answer the questions posed by marketers and regulators. Then we describe three ways in which consumer choice can occur. Following this, we introduce some classifications that are commonly used to describe different types of marketing and consumer research.

SECTION 1: THE SCOPE OF CONSUMER BEHAVIOUR

How do people buy and use goods and services? How do they react to prices, advertising and store interiors? What underlying mechanisms operate to produce these responses? If marketers have answers to such questions, they can make better managerial decisions. If regulators have answers, they can design better policy. It is the role of consumer behaviour research to provide these answers.

In this book, we provide an up-to-date account of the main issues studied by consumer behaviour researchers, our current understanding based on these research findings, and show how our understanding can be applied to marketing problems. Knowledge has grown rapidly in some areas, and we have reflected these advances by describing some work in more depth. In such cases, we explain why an issue is important, how it is investigated and what the findings are. This approach culminates in *empirical generalizations*. These are general findings, based on evidence, that have stood the test of repeated investigation. Such general findings summarize the state of our knowledge and are useful to practitioners and researchers alike. All too often, popular pronouncements on marketing issues contain little evidence of this sort and it is our purpose to reverse this approach.

Where our knowledge is still sketchy, we have tried to indicate doubts about the evidence or its interpretation. Such uncertainty propels research and, as a result, creates new knowledge. Though not always welcome to students, doubt is part of good education. Students who see the uncertainties in consumer research should be more sceptical of unsupported opinions and may be better placed to interpret and adapt to new findings when these emerge. Each of the authors is an active researcher and has struggled to understand the complexities of consumer behaviour over many decades. We hope that this sharpens the account that we give. Inevitably, we have omitted some fields of knowledge; in particular, we have left out some topics that are well covered in more introductory consumer behaviour texts.

In this chapter we introduce some general ideas about consumer behaviour and marketing, which are explored further in following chapters. In Section 1, we look at the sort of *question* raised by marketing and the *answers* that are provided by consumer behaviour research. Section 2 of this chapter will discuss models that provide descriptions of *consumer decision processes* and Section 3 will focus on some of the *classifications* and *explanations* that we use to describe different types of consumer research.

Questions and Answers

There is a close affinity between marketing and consumer behaviour. In a sense, marketing is a customer of consumer research. Marketers want answers to a number of problems raised by their practices, and consumer researchers can provide these answers. Examples of marketing practices are:

- the use of price incentives
- the use of particular colours, music and aromas in the retail environment
- launching new products using existing brand names (brand extension).

Often, the direction of an effect fits common sense; for example, consumers buy more when the price is dropped. However, the benefit of a discount depends on the *amount* of extra sales generated by, say, a 10 per cent price cut and here common sense does not supply an answer. For informed action, we need to conduct systematic research, which allows us to measure the size of any effect. Evidence is gathered using the methods of market research, psychology and the social sciences. Using such methods, we seek answers to questions such as:

- How much do sales change when the price of a product is cut by 10 per cent? What happens to sales after a discount has ended? Why do these effects occur?
- How much do colours, music and aromas affect consumers' behaviour in a store? What underlying mechanisms explain any effects we see?
- When a new product is launched under an old brand name, how much does the old name affect purchase of the new product?

Another set of questions comes from legislators and regulators, who have to set rules that affect marketing. Examples of their questions are:

- How do consumers react to product benefits such as increased energy efficiency or high nutritional value? What explains their behaviour?
- Do childproof packs save lives? How are such packs used?

Sometimes, marketers give little attention to the explanation for an effect. An example is the identification of specific groups who are very heavy buyers of a product. If such people can be identified, they can be selectively targeted. This type of empirical approach can work well but explanation still helps. If we know *why* some groups buy a product much more than other groups, we may be able to design communications that capitalize on this and also predict other products that these groups will want.

In any applied subject, practitioners need to use their judgement when evidence is lacking. Those who have to take decisions cannot delay action until problems have been fully researched. However, it is important that practitioners do accept new evidence when this becomes available. Some apparently sensible practices may need to be adjusted because of new findings. For example, it has been assumed that the childproof packs for medicines decrease accidental poisoning, but this may be illusory. Viscusi (1984) found evidence that child-resistant bottle caps were associated with an *increase* in child poisoning, possibly because parents left medicines accessible when they thought that a cap was childproof, or because the child-proof closure was so much trouble for adults that they left the container open. Viscusi's work suggests that packs should carry more specific advice about use and possibly be redesigned so that they are less likely to be left open. More generally, this type of work reminds us that common sense does not replace empirical tests.

SECTION 2: CONSUMER DECISION MODELS

The traditional approach to problems in consumer behaviour employed a comprehensive model of the purchase decision process. Such models were often the centrepiece of

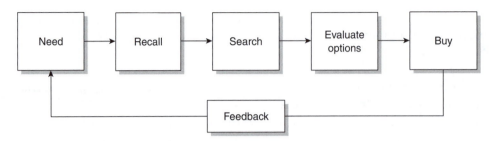

Figure 1.1   Is this how you choose?

undergraduate consumer behaviour texts and were expressed with boxes and arrows representing all the components and connections of an elaborate rational decision. In these models, the consumer is supposed to attend to product information and process it into their memory. The consumer retrieves the memory when a need emerges and, after further search and evaluation of all relevant alternatives, a purchase is made. After this, post-purchase evaluation may create satisfaction or dissatisfaction with the chosen product and this can result in a review of needs for later decisions. Figure 1.1 shows the basic form of such a model.

These days, there is less enthusiasm for such models. One problem has always been that they are hard to test because it is difficult to find satisfactory measures for all the components (Ehrenberg, 1988). Another problem with comprehensive models is that they overstate the rationality of how consumers choose. If there is plenty of time and the decision is important, then *sometimes* people will discover all the alternatives, evaluate them and select the one that seems to be the best, but we know from our own experience that we often simplify the process. Sometimes, we choose first and justify our behaviour afterwards, if we justify it at all. Thus, although rational decision models might suggest what people *ought to do* (normative), they are a poor guide to what people *actually do* (descriptive). In practice, managers want to know what people actually do since it is this behaviour that they seek to influence.

Textbooks now give more attention to 'partial decision models' where the rationality of the process is incomplete; also, it is accepted that much repeat purchase occurs automatically as a habit. Often, this range of decision making from rational to automatic is related to the degree of *involvement* with the product. People are likely to be more involved and give more thought to the choice when they are buying something for the first time and it has important outcomes. To explain decision-making in more detail, we focus on three models of consumer decision, which have different implications for managers (see Box 1.1). The models are:

1   **Cognitive**, treating purchase as the outcome of rational decision-making processes.
2   **Reinforcement**, treating purchase as behaviour which is learned and modified in response to the opportunities, rewards and costs present in the consumer's environment.
3   **Habit**, treating purchase as already learned behaviour, which is elicited by particular stimuli in the consumer's environment.

Box 1.1	Models of consumer choice

The cognitive model. This assumes rationality. The decision rests on beliefs about alternatives, which are investigated and compared. Marketers can influence cognitive decision-making by providing information that leads the consumer to prefer or reject alternatives.

The reinforcement model. Choice is controlled by factors in the environment that reward and facilitate some alternatives more than others.

Marketing influence is achieved by changing the consumer's situation. However, what is rewarding to some persons may not be so to others and this limits influence.

The habit model. Choice is controlled by managing stimuli (brand name, logo, pack features, etc.) that have become associated with a product as a result of past purchases. Sometimes this is called stimulus control.

The Cognitive Model

When consumers make an important purchase for the first time, they may reflect on alternatives and discuss pros and cons with others with the intention of securing benefits and avoiding costs. This model, sometimes called *extended problem-solving*, has always had its critics. Olshavsky and Granbois (1979: 98–99) noted:

> for many purchases a decision never occurs, not even on the first purchase … even when purchase behaviour is preceded by a choice process, it is likely to be very limited. It typically involves the evaluation of few alternatives, little external search, few evaluative criteria, and simple evaluation process models.

It is quite hard to find behaviour that fits the elaborate sequence of extended problem-solving. Beatty and Smith (1987) found that people did not search much before the purchase of durables and Beales et al. (1981) found that few people in the USA consulted *Consumer Reports*. Carefully thought-out decision-making is only likely for first purchases but these are quite rare, even in consumer durable markets, since most purchasers are either buying a replacement for an existing product or making an additional purchase. In a study of white goods purchases in the USA, Wilkie and Dickson (1985) found that two-thirds of the purchasers had bought the category before and Bayus (1991), quoting US industry sources, found that 88 per cent of refrigerators and 78 per cent of washing machines were replacements. In these circumstances, a carefully thought-out comparison of brands is likely to be the exception rather than the rule.

But, when it does occur, is a carefully thought-out decision likely to result in the best choice? When people attempt to be rational about a first-time choice, they may make mistakes because they lack experience. However, they are likely to make a better choice than those who abandon any rational processing and plump for an alternative (see Box 1.2).

Box 1.2	When pension is converted to an annuity

People build up pension funds over their working lives and then convert the accumulated investment into an annuity when they retire. They may use their pension company for the annuity or search for better value from another company. According to Hargreaves Lansdown, a large financial services firm in the UK, the majority of people buy their annuity from their pension company. Since annuity rates across pension companies can vary by as much as 15 per cent, this careless choice can mean that many retirees lose income that they could have enjoyed for the rest of their lives. The most likely explanation for this behaviour is that the retirees had a very poor understanding of the issues and they plumped for the company with which they were familiar.

The tendency to simplify decision-making is also observed in industry. One study of investment decisions in British industry revealed that these were often made first and then justified later. Marsh et al. (1988) found that faulty financial analysis and lack of coherence with stated strategic objectives were common in major acquisitions and that the company rule books were often ignored. More generally, industrial decisions often fit a 'satisficing' model (Simon, 1957). Simon describes how executives tend to accept the first option that is good enough to solve a problem; this means that there is little comparison between alternatives. Klein (1989) found that many decisions in operational settings follow a pattern that is consistent with Simon's ideas. Typically, people assess the situation and generate a prospective action based on this assessment. Then, they evaluate this action to see whether it will provide a solution. If it fails, they generate another prospective action and evaluate this, but they do not usually compare prospective actions.

When the satisficing model applies, the order in which products are evaluated is important since the first satisfactory solution will be the one that is adopted. This means that more prominent alternatives have a better chance of selection (see Box 1.3). Managers and marketers may be able to use this fact to their advantage by keeping awareness of their brands high in consumers' minds.

Box 1.3	Diagnosis

Even in medicine, decisions may be simplified. Often, the symptoms are assessed and a preliminary diagnosis is made, taking account of common illnesses; then other symptoms are checked to see whether they confirm this diagnosis. Only if these other symptoms fail to support the first diagnosis is a second one considered. This procedure may lead to the over-diagnosis of common illnesses.

These examples of decision-making in industry and medicine suggest that the simplification of choice is the norm rather than the exception and we might expect consumers to follow much the same pattern. For example, if the freezer needs replacing and a preliminary inquiry establishes that there is an appropriate model in a convenient shop, consumers may complete the purchase there and then. If the shop does not offer a suitable freezer, they may then turn to other stores and look at other models.

Although satisficing may not result in the optimal solution, it may use time efficiently when this is scarce. However, when the outcome of the decision is important, consumers and managers would make better decisions if they considered a second alternative before deciding.

Influences on Decision-Making

It is easy to fall into the trap of assuming that decisions are made by people acting on their own. Many choices are made in groups and, even when people decide on their own, they are often influenced by word of mouth from other people. At other times, people may base their decisions on information received through the mass media (e.g. advertising, newspaper, television and Internet comment). People are particularly likely to seek advice on matters that are obscure or difficult to test in other ways; this is common when the recipient of the advice is choosing for the first time or acting under changed circumstances, such as when they move home and need to find service providers such as a dentist. In later chapters on word of mouth and advertising, we consider in more detail how these influences may affect choice.

Since advice affects consumer decisions, marketers need to take account of this process. For example, advertising can include information that is easily passed on in conversation, and the design of the ad can reflect the process of giving advice. However, word of mouth is under consumer control, not marketing control, so normally marketers can only affect it indirectly.

Exercise 1.1   Decision-making

Identify an important purchase that you have made, for example a holiday, electronic device, financial investment or education course.

- Were you clear about what you wanted?
- How much investigation did you do before purchase?
- Did you consider one option and move on to others if it was unsuitable, or did you keep several alternatives in mind before choosing?
- Did you use the Internet to search for others' opinions?
- Did you consult friends or relatives?

In retrospect, you may be able to see defects in your decision-making process. Often we lack enough prior experience, time or motivation to fully compare the options.

Purchase as Learned Behaviour

A person's environment controls behaviour in two ways. First, the environment makes some actions possible and other actions impossible to perform; for example, some physical items can only be bought if they are stocked by retailers and available to you either by post or to purchase at the store. Second, when actions lead to positive outcomes they are more likely to be repeated and, conversely, negative outcomes make it less likely that the action will be repeated. These reinforcement effects on behaviour have been examined in *learning theory*; this is a systematic description of the relationship between initial behaviour, its outcomes and subsequent behaviour. Learning theory is relevant to both the reinforcement and habit models.

Reinforcement

Early research in learning theory was done by Thorndike (1911), who confined a hungry cat to a cage and placed food outside. The erratic movements of the cat eventually released a simple catch and the cat escaped. The cat took less time on subsequent trials and eventually it released the catch immediately when it was placed in the cage. Thorndike called this *trial and error learning* and it has some relevance to consumption. People entering new markets are faced with a range of brands and may make near random trials of alternatives until they come upon a brand that they like.

In Thorndike's work, the cat's actions were driven by the outcomes: gaining food and freedom. Skinner (1938, 1953) called such outcomes *reinforcers*. Skinner defined a reinforcer as an experience that raises the frequency of responses associated with it, while a punisher reduces the frequency of such responses. Reinforcers may be rewards or reductions in cost while punishers may be costs or reductions in reward. Reinforcement has most effect when it occurs at the same time as, or just after, the response. Skinner placed emphasis on the way in which reinforcement changes the frequency of the response, but reinforcement also strengthens the association between stimulus and response and this is important for the habit model. Figure 1.2 illustrates the effect of reinforcement.

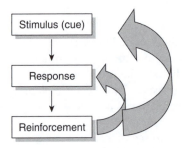

Figure 1.2   Reinforcement learning

The principles of reinforcement are applied in many sales promotions, such as discounts that offset the cost of a product. Skinner also introduced the idea of *shaping*, the process whereby behaviour is gradually shifted from one form to another by selectively reinforcing those performances that show change in the desired direction. Shaping is sometimes apparent in sales techniques where the salesperson moves the prospect towards the sales goal by reinforcing shifts in the preferred direction with nods, agreement and approval. Products also shape us. We become more expert at using computers and cars, partly because of the reinforcers that such products deliver; as a result of this, we may seek more sophisticated models.

Learning can be reinforced each time a response is produced, i.e. *continuously*, or it can be reinforced *intermittently*. Learning is faster if the reinforcement schedule is continuous but the final effect of a given amount of reinforcement is greater when it is used intermittently. This helps to explain why people are prepared to lose money by gambling on fruit machines. The cost of playing a slot machine is a fairly continuous punishment but the machine rewards intermittently. Over time, the gains are less than the losses, but the effect on behaviour of the irregular reward is greater than the effect of the regular cost.

Both stimuli and reinforcers can lose their effect if they are used too frequently. Stimulus satiation, called *desensitization*, helps people to put up with recurring unpleasant experiences. An important effect of desensitization in consumer behaviour is the way in which people get used to conditions that are inadequate or unpleasant and, as a result, may not complain or demand compensation. Examples of this are the way people tolerate litter in streets, overcrowding on public transport and being kept waiting 'on hold' on the phone. Similarly, consumers may put up with defective goods because they have grown used to the defects. Examples are the continuing use of lumpy mattresses, broken refrigerator shelves and inadequate carving knives. The job of the marketer is to overcome the inertia in these situations so that the consumer sees the problem afresh and seeks a solution.

Stimulus Control: Classical Conditioning

One type of learning, called classical conditioning, was studied by Pavlov (1927). Pavlov noticed that dogs started to salivate at the sight of the person who fed them. The older dogs showed this most and Pavlov thought that, over time, the salivation reflex that normally occurred at the presentation of food had become associated with a new stimulus, the dogs' handler. Pavlov set up a series of experiments to demonstrate this process of classical conditioning using the sound of a buzzer as the conditioned stimulus instead of the dogs' handler. Figure 1.3 illustrates this process.

Classical conditioning has considerable relevance to consumer behaviour. Packaging, brand names, colours, smells, music and the contexts of purchase and consumption may become associated with the buying of particular products. Some advertising is clearly intended to forge associations between brands and particular stimuli that can be used in further advertising and at the point of sale, e.g. McDonald's and the big 'M' sign, 'i' and phone, pod, pad, … and, more generally, all logos and their respective brands and companies. The idea here is that the conditioned stimulus may help in identification and add to

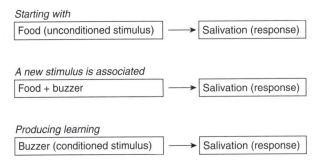

Figure 1.3   Classical conditioning: Pavlov's experiment

purchasing tendency. It is also noticeable that, to compete in some markets, manufacturers have to adopt the colours and pack shape that are conventional for that type of product. The power of such associations is revealed by a trip to an unfamiliar country. The absence of familiar features makes the high street confusing. A simple task, like posting a letter, requires investigation and effort in order to identify the colour, shape and location of the post box.

A stimulus that is associated with a rewarding product may induce a more generalized tendency to buy other products that appear similar. A direct application of such generalization in marketing is the use of an existing brand name for a new product. By this process of *brand extension*, some of the buying tendency (often termed *propensity* by marketers) that consumers have for the old brand may attach to the new brand. For example, Mars used the positive consumer propensity towards the brand when introducing Mars ice-cream and this was helped by the similarity in the appearance of the ice-cream and the confectionery bar.

Habits of Purchase

The cognitive and reinforcement models emphasize the *modification* of consumer behaviour and thus may explain the *changes* that occur in our purchasing. However, much consumption has a settled form; people buy the same brands and use the same stores over long periods. This habitual aspect of consumption is of great value to firms.

We say that people have a habit when they regularly produce much the same behaviour on encountering a particular stimulus. In the case of supermarket goods, important stimuli are the colour, size and shape of the pack. Williams (1966) found that colour positively affected buying behaviour most, followed by size then shape. Response to such stimuli is automatic, so that no conscious thought is required when we pick a laundry detergent brand in the supermarket. Habits sidestep cognitive decision-making and leave us free to concentrate on other problems where experience does not provide us with a ready response. However, even in novel situations people may trade on already acquired habits. Consider the person who is about to buy a car for the first time. Most first-time car purchasers are familiar with cars, have been to car showrooms before, may have bargained for goods before, may be knowledgeable about the ways of salespersons and may understand credit arrangements. Thus, even first-time car purchasing may draw on previous learning, some of which may have become habitual. Viewed in this way, even complex and novel behaviour may call upon behaviours in a habit repertoire.

The habit model of consumption excludes planning before action but does not imply that consumers never think about their habitual behaviour. People may reflect on their actions *after* purchase either because of discussion with others or because their purchase outcomes were exceptionally good or bad. But this is unusual; generally, habit restricts experimentation and, as a result, consumers may be unaware of improvements in products from which they could benefit. This suggests that, although habitual purchase is frequently satisfactory, it is not always the best solution. Exercise 1.2 draws your attention to habits that you may have which do not always lead to you choosing what best meets your needs.

Exercise 1.2   Habits

It is hard to detect habits that work against your own interests but consider two areas:

1   Taking sugar in tea and coffee are habits that add to body weight and contribute to tooth decay. When people give up sugar they get used to it fairly soon and after a few weeks may prefer unsweetened tea or coffee. Is this not a habit worth changing?
2   If you make a regular journey to work, is the route optimal? People can discover journey improvements after years of using a less suitable route that has become habitual.

How should marketers present new brands in markets where purchase is strongly habitual?

When purchase is habitual, a new brand must be marketed in a way that disrupts habit and provokes a review of past purchase. This is not easily achieved. Advertising may be ignored, while discounts and free samples may be used by consumers without much effect on later purchase. Most of the time, consumers carry on buying what they have bought before. But that's why marketers need to understand what types of marketing interventions work best for different customer groups in different environments.

How Free Are Consumers?

It is often claimed that the consumer is king but this may exaggerate the flexibility of action that consumers have. To be free you should be able to choose from more than one option without pressure, and be able to reject all options if they are unattractive. Many choices are controlled by the consumer's environment rather than by reflective thought by the consumer, and this casts doubt on how much freedom of action consumers can exercise.

The constraints on consumers are considerable and are not just environmental. Consumers may *lack knowledge* of alternatives when these are not displayed. Sometimes, people *have to use* products; they must put petrol in a car and laundry detergent in a washing machine and the fact that they have a choice between near identical brands is often, to them, a matter of indifference. Freedom of action is also affected by *limited access* to goods and services, by *physiological dependence* on products like cigarettes and alcohol and by *psychological dependence* when the consumer is a compulsive purchaser or gambler.

People do many things that they would prefer to avoid, e.g. going to work on congested public transport and waiting for flights in airports. In many areas, such as education, medicine and legal advice, the opportunity to influence a service by withdrawing custom or complaining is effectively limited by the continuing need to use the service. There are other areas where a lack of money prevents people from doing the things they might wish to do; large houses and luxurious cars are possible for only a few. For these reasons, we are sceptical of claims about the almost unlimited choice available to consumers and how much autonomy they have. However, the growth of the Internet has raised access to knowledge about goods and services and has assisted purchase; this may lead to a genuine increase in consumer choice.

Decision-Making on the Internet

The increased use of the Internet and the facilities that websites offer may change the rationality of choice. The ability to compare prices online generally drives down the average price of goods and services bought online. The proportion of UK shoppers who say they often consult the Internet before making a purchase is 78 per cent in 2011, unchanged from the previous year (Nielsen, 2011a). However, they seem to be making more purchases on the Internet. According to Nielsen, the proportion of shoppers claiming to use the Internet most days has increased from 50 per cent to nearly 80 per cent in the five years to January 2011, and those claiming never to use it has fallen from 25 per cent to just 7 per cent (see Figure 1.4). In the UK, the two leading sites for shopping are Amazon and eBay, each with a unique audience double that of the operator in third place. Grocery shopping via the Internet has doubled in the four years to 2011 and is now 5 per cent of total grocery shopping in the UK.

The Internet makes it easier to compare prices and specifications, and can take some of the effort out of shopping. Search engines such as Google.com assist in the identification of sources and products, while chat rooms and blogs often provide user comment on different brands. Comparison sites such as Shopping.com show the prices charged by different suppliers. Other sites, such as Uswitch.co.uk, can compute the best value among service providers and may facilitate transfer to a new provider. Websites for those buying houses, shares, books and many other items aid choice by providing easy comparison between alternatives. For example, an Australasian buyer can use a site such as realestate.com.au to specify properties by location, price and type, and can then inspect pictures of interiors. This helps to focus attention only on those properties that meet the needs of the buyer. A subscriber buying shares through a Web-based stockbroker such as Hargreaves Lansdown (hl.co.uk) can see the past return on specific shares over different periods, and can compare this performance with other shares and with standard indexes. On Amazon.com, customers can read reviews of a book before buying and be provided with

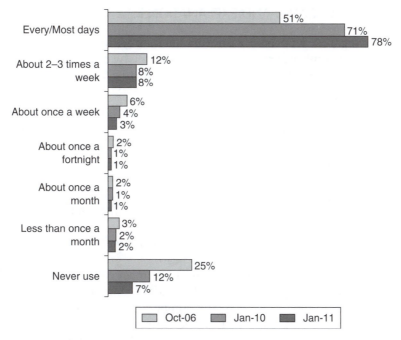

Figure 1.4   Five-year changes in the use of the Internet by UK shoppers (Nielsen, The State of the Nation, 2011)

information on new books that are related to their previous purchases. On airline sites such as ba.com, a traveller can pick travel times that are cheaper. Quite clearly, the Internet *can* be used by consumers to assess alternatives better, but how much do consumers do this to improve their choices and lower their costs?

A study by Zettelmeyer, Morton and Silva-Risso (2006) suggests that Internet customers may bring down the price that they pay for cars by an average of 1.5 per cent; this may seem modest but it accounts for 22 per cent of the dealer's gross margin. However, consumers who use the Internet may be more price-sensitive and these people might also drive a hard bargain in an offline context. Also, it appears that even Internet customers rarely secure the lowest price. According to Shopping.com, 80 per cent of Internet customers pay more than they have to. It seems that use of the Internet to obtain better value is restrained by loyalty to particular websites. Once they are familiar with a site, consumers may return to it later because it is easy to use and saves time. A consumer might agree that a book might be cheaper elsewhere but still use Amazon because of convenience – this convenience can be seen as considerable, as often customers allow trusted sites to store their credit card and delivery details, so purchasing really is a single click. Similarly, buyers normally use one online grocer because of the trouble of getting to know another site. In short, habits take over.

This evidence presents a somewhat confused picture. The Internet *can* assist people to make better decisions and buy more cheaply, but the technology may discourage experimentation when goods are regularly bought. In addition, there are some sectors, such as groceries, where choice limitations and delivery cost may raise the price that is paid online.

SECTION 3: CLASSIFICATIONS AND EXPLANATIONS

Disciplines must organize and classify information in order to explain it. Marketing is no exception and uses a number of classifications, some of which are shared with other subjects. We start with one distinction that is so ubiquitous that we scarcely notice it. This is the use of comparison in the assessment of evidence.

The Principle of Comparison

Any judgement rests on implicit or explicit comparison. When we say 'that's cheap', we are comparing the price that is presented with some standard. The standard might be given by another brand that is physically present, or it might be an internal standard that we have built up from experience. Such comparisons are fundamental to human judgements. We make sense of any raw data by comparing it with objective standards, or with personal or social norms. Comparison also occurs in the scientific assessment of findings. To illustrate this, consider Table 1.1.

This table shows the ratings that owners gave to their car compared with the best alternative that they could have purchased instead. The data come from an Internet survey of 495 owners conducted in the UK in 2003. The numbers show that 64 per cent of respondents thought that their car was better than the best alternative and 9 per cent thought that it was worse. This seems to show great confidence among respondents in their choice of car. Our finding reflects a general phenomenon called the endowment effect: objects are rated more highly once they are owned (Kahneman, Knetsch and Thaler, 1991a). However, the assessments shown in Table 1.1 are difficult to justify. When there are many alternatives, which are difficult to fully compare, it is quite likely that another brand would have been better than the one chosen. Thus, there seems to be an optimism bias in the assessment of possessions which is revealed by making the question comparative. In Chapter 8, we study these judgemental effects in more detail.

Sometimes, the standard of comparison that people use for judgements has an objective basis: for example, the average price of a basket of goods in the different supermarket chains or the fuel economy of different cars. But notice that consumers have to discover and accept such standards if these are to affect their judgements. Standards may be affected by marketing communications but, mostly, people appear to acquire price or

Table 1.1 How owners rated their current car

Rating in comparison to the best alternative make that could have been purchased instead	Current car (%)
Much worse	1
Worse	8
The same	27
Better	38
Much better	26

quality norms from experience. Such internal norms will be based on observations, discussions with other consumers and information from the media and are likely to be quite stable. In these circumstances, what changes when marketers are successful in modifying consumer behaviour? Usually, marketing activity alters the immediate perception rather than the internal norm. When the price is cut, and more people buy, it is because the new price is seen as cheap, compared with the norm.

Categories, Brands, Variants and SKUs

Classifications are also made on the basis of the context in which decisions are taken. We call anything a customer buys, whether good or service, a *product*. Then all products are divided into *categories* such as soup, wine, mobile phone airtime suppliers, cars and hotels. Within a category there will be a number of brands available for consumers to choose from. Brands are easily recognizable entities – such as Apple, Toyota and Disney – and customers can become attached to one brand rather than another when making repeated choices. Sometimes there are sub-brands, e.g. Volkswagen has Polo, Golf, Passat, etc. The branding is signalled primarily by name, but also by logo, and the shape, colour and design of the pack or product when this has a physical form. Advertising may attach other associations to the brand, such as cartoon animals and musical themes. In many cases, a company name is synonymous with the brand, e.g. BP, but in other cases, the company owns a variety of brand names, e.g. General Motors, Procter & Gamble and Unilever each manage many brand names (e.g. Unilever owns Ben & Jerry's, Bertolli, PG Tips, Dove, Lynx and Timotei among other brands). Variants are subdivisions of the product type so the Volkswagen Passat is available as a saloon or estate, and Heinz soups are available in different flavours.

In business, the term SKU (stock keeping unit) is used widely. This is a unique combination of brand, variety, pack size, etc. that is required for manufacturing or filling the shelves. The SKU is coded so that automated systems can specify it in production scheduling and stock control. Manufacturers and retailers often analyze consumer choice at the level of the SKU.

The consumer's preference to buy varying quantities of a specific brand from a specific outlet at a specific price point controls the profit that is made by the brand owner, retailer and other suppliers; marketing activities are therefore coordinated to promote brand or sub-brand preference. This means that the branding must be distinctive enough for consumers to distinguish one brand from another but, at the same time, the brands in a category often have features in common which help the consumer to recognize what they are buying when they search for the product on a shop shelf or on a website. As a result, brands often share characteristics such as pack size, colour and shape. In fact, one brand does not have to be physically different from other brands in a category. For example, at one time Volkswagen, Seat and Ford offered SUVs that were almost the same except for the name badge and the price. Similarly, there may be no detectable difference between the granulated sugar offered by two different manufacturers; consumers know this, but this does not stop them from regularly buying one brand rather than another. Often, each brand will cover much the same range of variants. Sugar brands will offer granulated, castor, icing and Demerara variants; soup brands will have much the same range of flavours; and car brands will be available in SUV, sports, saloon and estate forms. In fact, the differences between the variants of a single brand are often much greater than the differences between the corresponding variants of different brands.

The use of sub-brands can raise problems in the car industry when a new model comes out. Should the sub-brand be retained because of the value that consumers attach to it (brand equity) or is a new sub-brand needed to emphasize the novelty of the new model? Volkswagen retains sub-brand names, Citroën has tended to abandon them but has recently resurrected the DS name which was first used in 1955 on a model still revered by motoring enthusiasts (DS sounds like déesse, French for goddess).

In many categories, the brands compete only with each other for the customer's attention, e.g. Colgate versus Aquafresh toothpaste. However, in the food and entertainment fields this is less true. A frozen meal brand competes with home cooking and restaurant meals, as well as with other brands of frozen meals. Similarly, beer competes with wine and ten-pin bowling competes with the cinema.

Other differentiators beside brands are used to distinguish one market offering from another. An interesting example is provided by wine. French wine has traditionally been branded by the producer, sub-region and region, e.g. Château Cheval Blanc is a St Emilion production in the Bordeaux region. There are many other producers, and this produces a complex choice for the consumer. By contrast, Australasian wine is sold more on the basis of grape variety. Although there are many varieties of grape, a small number dominate the field (e.g. Cabernet, Chardonnay Malbec, Merlot, Shiraz, Pinot Noir, Reisling, Sauvignon and Tempranillo) and several of these varieties are grown in each region. This marks major differences between wines and provides an easy 'handle' for the consumer. When the grape variety has been chosen, regions like the Barossa, producers like Penfolds, and the year of the vintage may be used in the choice process of the more discriminating buyer.

Goods and Services

A familiar grouping of categories is into goods and services. A good has physical form, e.g. a can of soup or a bed, or in business-to-business (B2B) markets, aluminium sheets or bus wheels, whereas a service is intangible and is used by the recipient as it is created, e.g. a haircut, a visit to the dentist, professional advice or a phone call. Thus the essence of a service is that it exists in time and must be consumed at that time if a loss of sale is to be avoided. By contrast, goods, such as frozen peas, can be stockpiled by the consumer and supplied when there is demand. Most service products incorporate a goods component, e.g. the meal is consumed in a restaurant and your phone call is made from an electronic device such as a phone handset or a computer.

Goods can be subdivided into classes such as groceries, electronics and fashion, or in B2B markets, electronic components, food commodities, etc. Similarly, services divide into classes such as telephony, transport, surgery, entertainment and financial services. The fact that there are textbooks devoted to the marketing of services suggests that this is substantially different from the marketing of goods. One difference is that, because they are delivered over time, services can suffer problems of uneven demand, leading to inefficient use of resources and delay and frustration among customers. We cover research on the consumer response to delay in Chapter 9. There are also differences that arise from the interaction between the service supplier and the customer; Keaveney (1995) found that a large part of all service switching occurred because of failures in the face-to-face service encounter and this has no parallel with goods. Most goods can be examined before purchase and this helps consumers to assess how well they fit their needs. It may not be possible to examine services in this way and, as a result, those who are thinking of adopting a new service provider may seek advice from existing customers whose word of mouth provides a proxy for personal experience.

In other respects, goods and services are similar. Our three models of consumer decision-making apply to both, and so does the distinction between repertoire and sub-scription categories that we discuss below.

Vargo and Lusch (2004) have suggested that services rather than goods are the funda-mental product form since goods are made by the service of workers. This new 'dominant logic' in marketing has echoes in the work of early economists, particularly in Marx's theory of value, first expounded in *Capital* (volume 1 was published in 1867), which relates value to the labour input. At the time, economists argued that the value of goods was defined by an exchange process; it is what others are prepared to give for the goods and no amount of labour input will raise the price of something that people do not want. The character of transactions may have changed and become more cooperative but, in our view, such exchanges remain the basis of value. Marketers must be concerned with profitable trading and, for this reason, we are sceptical about making service fundamental in marketing.

Repertoire and Subscription Categories

Categories can be divided into those that are repertoire, where consumers commonly pur-chase more than one brand over a fairly short time such as a year (e.g. most groceries, restaurants and airline flights) and subscription, where consumers mostly use only one brand at a time (e.g. current bank accounts, dentists and refrigerators). Research by Sharp, Wright and Goodhardt (2002) shows that most categories fall clearly into either the repertoire or the subscription division. In repertoire categories, we can measure a type of brand loyalty called *share-of-category requirement* (SCR). This is the percentage of category purchases that a cus-tomer gives to a specific brand over a period. For example, if a person buys instant coffee on ten occasions in a year and five purchases are Maxwell House, the customer's SCR for Maxwell House is 50 per cent. By contrast, loyalty in subscription categories is shown at the time of repurchase when the customer either retains the brand or switches to another.

Market Concentration

In many categories, there are relatively few brands. Laundry detergents, toothpaste and mobile phone airtime supply are examples. In other fields, such as wine, cheese and biscuits, there are a great many producers, none of which commands a large market share. In some other fields, such as supermarkets, fashion stores, chemists and investment

INTRODUCTION

advisers, a few large chains compete with many smaller suppliers in Western markets. When a few producers command a large part of the category, we describe the market as *high concentration*. Usually, large suppliers are more profitable because of economies of scale in manufacture, distribution and advertising. Retailers feel compelled to stock more familiar brands because of demand and this helps the manufacturer (the brand owner) to maintain the price paid by the retailer.

Consumers are not necessarily disadvantaged by high market concentration. The large scale and efficiencies of big producers mean that product development can occur and the wide distribution of big brands ensures that consumers can easily find the larger brand. One concern is that high concentration may reduce competition but it is not difficult to find high levels of competition in concentrated markets. For instance, the worldwide cola market is highly concentrated, yet both Pepsi and Coca-Cola remain fiercely competitive suppliers.

Market Share

Ehrenberg (1988) has explained that many aspects of aggregate consumer behaviour can be seen as an outcome of market share. For example, the average SCR loyalty for a big brand tends to be higher than that for a small brand (i.e. the evidence is that in general the bigger the brand the more likely that it is that customers will buy it again compared with the customers of smaller brands). In Table 1.2, we illustrate how another variable, the share of recommendation, relates to market share in the mobile phone category in data gathered before the advent of smartphones.

Table 1.2 shows that the share of brand recommendations closely follows the market share of the brand. There is no mystery about this. As we saw earlier with regard to cars, people are usually happy with the products that they own, and East, Romaniuk and Lomax (2011) found an average of 71 per cent of recommendations related to the informant's main brand. So, the bigger the brand, and therefore the greater the number of users, the larger will be the share of recommendations. For this reason, managers need to take account of market share before they assess the word of mouth about their brand. In Table 1.2, Motorola is doing well because the rate of recommendation is ahead of market

Table 1.2 Market share and share of recommendations of mobile phone brands (unpublished UK data gathered in 2005)

Brand	Market share (%)	Share of recommendations (%)
Nokia	40	40
Sony-Ericsson	25	21
Motorola	14	20
Samsung	10	11
Siemens	4	2
Others	7	4

Exercise 1.3	Do big brands get more, or less, negative word of mouth?

Recommendation is positive word of mouth. What about negative word of mouth? Develop ideas about how negative word of mouth is produced. What will be the resulting relationship between market share and the share of negative word of mouth?

When you get to Chapter 12, you will see our evidence on this topic.

share. If the rate of recommendation was assessed without taking account of market share, Nokia would come top, but we can see that its performance is just average for its size.

Consumer Segmentation and Causal Relationships

We often compare population segments: those who retain a brand versus those who switch, heavy TV viewers versus light viewers, high recommenders versus low recommenders, men versus women, etc. If we have evidence about the consumption habits of different segments, we can target those that appear to be most likely to purchase the category or most open to switch brands. Consumer segmentation is an approach that is very popular in marketing; it can work well even when we do not know why the behaviour of one segment differs from another. For example, a method used by those trying to harness word of mouth is to try to identify those consumers who give more advice than others (the *influentials*). Once they have been identified, the job of the marketer is to recruit them on behalf of a promoted brand.

However, in consumer behaviour, we want to explain behaviour, preferably by finding causes for it. Why is it that one segment is more active in giving advice to others than another segment? We can investigate how segments differ with respect to possible causes. As the picture of the different factors underlying recommendation builds up, a new strategy becomes available to marketers. Instead of identifying a segment that gives more word of mouth, marketers can try to influence the factors that cause word of mouth and this can be done *without* identifying the influentials.

Behaviourism and Cognitivism

Does a change in thinking cause a change in behaviour, or does a change in behaviour cause a change in thinking? The answer is that we can find support for both processes. In psychology, the primacy of behaviour is called *behaviourism*. This approach was developed by Skinner (1953). The traditional behaviourist rejects the idea that thought and feeling are the initiators of action. Instead, action is explained by reference to the environmental circumstances that act on a person. This fits the reinforcement and habit models of consumer decision-making.

In traditional behaviourist research, it used to be believed that thought and feeling are *effects but not causes*; like ripples on the surface of a pond they indicate the fish's movements but do not move the fish. If this account is correct, we can use people's thoughts and feelings as indicators of their potential behaviour but not as explanations for it. Such narrow behaviourism is usually rejected today. One reason is that it is difficult to describe action without taking account of the thoughts and feelings that lie behind it; words become insults or praise only through an understanding of the motives of the person uttering them. The traditional behaviourist position is not subtle enough to deal with this complexity in the nature of human behaviour.

Opposed to behaviourism is the view that thought and feeling can produce change in action directly. This is *cognitivism* and it lies behind rational accounts of consumer decision-making. In its strongest form, experience is interpreted and used to change attitudes and knowledge, which then control behaviour. From a cognitivist perspective, behaviour may be modified by communications that change attitudes and knowledge. Some support for the cognitivist position can be found in the way public information campaigns change behaviour (for example, anti-smoking advertising, featuring the hazards of smoking, has been shown to be effective; see Chapter 13).

There are also examples where behaviour precedes attitudes that support behaviourism. Clare and Kiser (1951) asked parents of completed families about the number and sex of the children that they thought were desirable. There was a strong tendency for parents to prefer both the size and the sex mix of the family that they already had; for example, if they had two girls they stated that they felt two girls was what they would like if they were to have their family again. At the time of the study, there were no ways of controlling the sex of offspring, so the preference for the same sex balance can only be explained as a product of experience.

In many other cases the causal direction between attitude and behaviour may be in doubt. The preferred number of children is a case in point. Parents might have had two children because they wanted two; or, having had two children, they might have come to prefer this number. Such alternative explanations can often be seen in the social sciences. For example, Marx argued that it was not ideology that determined social relations but that social relations determined ideology. This is the sociological equivalent of the primacy of behaviour over attitude and it is contrasted with Hegelian philosophy favouring the primacy of ideas. Sometimes Hegel's account fits; paradoxically, Marxism itself was a revolutionary ideology that created change.

Some studies in consumer research show the effect of prior behaviour. Bird and Ehrenberg (1966) found that two-thirds of those who have used a brand at some time express an intention to buy it. A declining brand has a long tail of past users and, as a result, a larger number of consumers state that they are going to buy it again, compared with a growing brand with the same share. There is also evidence that brand attitudes follow the purchase of groceries. Dall'Olmo Riley et al. (1997) found that brand attributions (e.g. that 'Persil washes whiter') may depend on recent purchase. Sandell (1981) examined the relationships between brand attitudes and purchase using consumer panel data and found that individual attitudes were aligned with purchase immediately after buying, but that, over time, people's attitudes reverted to the pre-purchase pattern.

SUMMARY

Key questions for consumer behaviour come from marketing strategy and consumer policy. In order to answer these questions we need an understanding of how consumers make decisions. When people face difficult and involving choices, the cognitive model of choice may describe the process of decision-making, but the process is often simplified, even when the decision is difficult. When action is steered by the environment, the reinforcement model provides an explanation of how purchasing or consumption patterns are learned: consumer action is constrained by the opportunities available and directed by the rewards and costs that are present. Once actions such as brand purchase are learned, they may be induced by specific stimuli, such as brand name, and the habit model can apply. To change the behaviour of consumers, the influencing agent (e.g. advertising, promotions, word of mouth, etc.) must either alter the beliefs and values involved in a complex decision or, where the context controls behaviour, modify the consumer's environment. Learning principles help us to explain some marketing practices, such as brand extension.

The growth of the Internet suggests that people are able to make better choices (more suitable brands, lower prices) but it is not clear yet how much this occurs.

In this chapter, we also introduced some of the ways in which data are organized to create meaning: the use of comparison, types of category, brands and variants, goods and services and market share.

Additional Resources

For an early challenge to comprehensive models of consumer behaviour, read Olshavsky and Granbois (1979).

Part 2
Consumption Patterns

2 Customer Loyalty

LEARNING OBJECTIVES

When you have completed this chapter, you should be able to:

1 Report the different terms and measures that have been used to describe customer loyalty.
2 Explain how different ideas about loyalty developed.
3 Explain how customer loyalty is divided between brands in repertoire categories.
4 Describe other habitual features of consumer purchase.
5 Discuss and criticize the main ideas in favour of encouraging retention in consumer markets.
6 Show how design features of loyalty programmes trigger differences in consumer behaviour.
7 Report research on the associations between different forms of loyalty.
8 Report on the reasons for defection in services.

(Loyalty schemes, which are really forms of retail promotion, are also covered in Chapter 11.)

OVERVIEW

There are three types of loyalty behaviour that consumers can show. First, when they buy several brands in a category, consumers can give a high share to one of them. Second, they can continue to buy a brand for a long time; this is retention. Third, they can give positive advice about a brand and, by this action, recruit new customers. These three forms of customer loyalty – share, retention and recommendation – ensure a continuing revenue stream to the brand owner and reduce the need for the parent company to promote the brand. Marketers therefore want to find and keep customers who exhibit these forms of loyalty and, where possible, they want to encourage this behaviour. Marketers are also keen to understand why customers switch away from a brand.

A second aspect to loyalty is the feeling that customers have about brands. We talk of being satisfied by or liking a brand, being committed to the brand and, in the case of business and service suppliers, trusting and being dependent upon them.

This subject is quite complicated. We have a common term, loyalty, but it has many different forms and one form of loyalty may have a strong or weak relationship with another. Also, the measure of loyalty that we use depends on the category. We use repeat purchase to show retention in consumer durables and duration as a customer to show retention for utilities and other services. In some fields where consumers have a portfolio of brands they regularly buy we can use both share and retention to show the loyalty of customers (e.g. to grocery brands, stores and airlines). To explore these issues, we approach the subject historically, show how different measures of loyalty originated, and examine some of the evidence associated with each form of loyalty.

SECTION 1: BRAND LOYALTY IN REPERTOIRE CATEGORIES

The Development of Panel Research

Research on brand loyalty, as a share of purchase, began with a paper by Copeland (1923) in the first issue of the *Harvard Business Review*. Copeland discussed a phenomenon, which he called brand insistence, which occurs when a consumer refuses to substitute one brand for another. Copeland was concerned with repertoire markets like groceries, where consumers often purchase more than one brand in a category. In these markets, brand insistence is an extreme form of share loyalty and is now called sole-brand loyalty.

Initially, research into this field was held back because there were no sound methods for measuring brand purchases. Retrospective surveys of purchase may be used but consumers can easily forget some of the purchases that they have made. To reduce this recall error, Churchill (1942) advocated the use of panels of consumers, who agreed to make regular reports about their household purchases. The methods for measuring purchases by panel members have evolved. Initially, members were asked to provide weekly reports of their household's purchases, usually by keeping a diary of daily purchases. An alternative form of measurement was the 'dustbin' method where the consumer retained all wrappers and agency staff counted purchases from the wrappers. But all wrappers may not be kept, so this method is also fallible. When bar codes became universal, panel members were given a bar-code reader and they used this to record their purchases when they brought their groceries home. Home scanning panels are still used worldwide by companies like Kantar (formerly TNS) and Nielsen. An alternative method is used by Information Resources Inc. (IRI) in the USA. They provide the checkout scanners in the stores of a number of communities where they conduct research. When panel members use a store they show an identification card and the store scanner sends data on their purchases directly to IRI for processing.

The first regular panel was run by a newspaper, the *Chigago Tribune*. Brown (1953) used data from this panel and found that brand loyalty in a household fitted one of four patterns:

- Sole-brand loyalty.
- Divided brand loyalty (polygamous).
- Unstable loyalty (switching, between brands).
- No brand loyalty (promiscuous).

Brown classified people on the basis of runs of purchase of brands in each category. Thus AAAAAA shows sole brand loyalty, a mix such as AABABA indicates loyalty divided between brand A and brand B, and AAABBB might indicate unstable loyalty with a switch from A to B, though it is not possible to distinguish true switching from divided loyalty without an extended period of measurement. It is now clear that divided (or multi-brand) loyalty is the usual pattern of grocery purchase (see Box 2.1).

Box 2.1 | Reasons for divided loyalty

Why do people buy more than one brand in a category? There seem to be two sorts of explanation for having a portfolio of brands – which we call genuine and apparent.

Genuine portfolio

This may occur because:

1 There is little brand awareness and the consumer does not remember previously bought brands.
2 The category is one where consumers appreciate variety (biscuits, cereals, wine).
3 Customers buy discounted brands, which spreads their range of purchase.

4 The brand that the customer wanted was not available.

Apparent portfolio

1 The panel collects data on household expenditure. Members of a household may prefer different brands. Individually, they could be 100 per cent loyal but, as a household, they could show divided loyalty.
2 A household may buy different brands in sub-categories such as biological and non-biological detergent. The household could be 100 per cent loyal in each sub-category. We need to remember that the product groupings in the minds of consumers may differ from the categories used by market researchers.

Share of Category Requirement

Cunningham's (1956) share-of-purchase approach is now standard and is illustrated with invented data in Table 2.1. In the table, the last three numbers of row 1 show that, over one year, Household 1 devotes 50 per cent of purchases to Brand A, 30 per cent to Brand B and 20 per cent to Brand C. These percentages are the share-of-category requirement (SCR) measures that were introduced in Chapter 1. Another measure that is often used is

Table 2.1 Hypothetical brand purchase data for one category (assume only three brands in the category)

House-hold	Jan	Feb	Mar	Apr	May	June	July	Aug	Sept	Oct	Nov	Dec	Total purchases (all brands)	% over year A	B	C
1	A	B	B	A	C		A	C	B	A		A	10	50	30	20
2	B	C		C	A	AC		C	B		C	C	10	20	20	60
3	AA		AB	B	AA		AB	A	A	A	B	AB	15	67	33	0
4	C	A	A	B	C	CC	A	A	AC	B	A	A	14	50	14	36
5	AB		AB	A	B	C	A	A		A	A		11	64	27	9
6	A			A		A				A			4	100	0	0
7	A		C	C		A		AB		AC		A	9	56	11	33
8	C	C		A	A			A	C	A	C		8	50	0	50
9	A		A		A			B		A			5	80	20	0
10			A			A						A	3	100	0	0
Mean													**9**	**64**	**15**	**21**

Purchases of Brands A, B and C in each month

first-brand loyalty. This is the share given to the most heavily bought brand (e.g. Household 1 has a first-brand loyalty of 50 per cent). We see in Table 2.1 how purchase patterns can vary and that some households buy very little.

The last three columns give the SCR loyalty to brands of each household and the means at the base of these columns give the average SCR per brand; Brand A, with a score of 64 per cent, is more popular than Brands B and C.[1]

Exercise 2.1   Market share and average SCR

How do average SCRs relate to market share? Are they the same or different? Think about this before looking below.

The average SCRs per brand are quite close to market share. Purchase frequencies differ across households and light buyers tend to focus on market leaders (like consumers 6 and 10 in Table 2.1). This means that the average SCR of brand leaders tends to be a little above their market share. Fifty-one of the 89 purchases in Table 2.1 are for Brand A, which gives it a market share of 57 per cent, slightly below the mean SCR of 64 per cent for Brand A.

Another measure is the average first-brand loyalty in a category. What is the average first-brand loyalty in Table 2.1? This is 50 + 60 + 67 + 50 + 64 + 100 + 56 + 50 + 80 + 100 divided by 10, which is nearly 68. Figures of 50–70 per cent for first-brand loyalty are common for grocery brands.

Customers who buy a brand only once in a period must have an SCR of 100 per cent; when the brand is bought twice, the SCR cannot be less than 50 per cent; and when it is bought three times, the minimum is 33 per cent. These small-number effects mean that customers who rarely purchase in a period tend to have higher SCRs than average and, conversely, those who are sole-brand loyal are often light buyers. When more cases are obtained by gathering data over a long period, the small-number effect disappears and then light buyers are found to be somewhat less loyal (Stern and Hammond, 2004).

Loyalty Proneness and its Correlates

Cunningham (1956) also wanted to know whether the loyalty that a consumer showed in one category was related to their loyalty in another; he called this *loyalty proneness*. In his research, Cunningham found little evidence of loyalty proneness. Among 21 correlations between share loyalties for individuals across different categories, the highest was 0.3. East et al. (1995) found correlations averaging 0.46 between share-loyalty measures across four grocery categories in a survey. This evidence indicates that it is realistic to average a consumer's loyalty scores across a range of categories to obtain a score for individual loyalty proneness. Using this method, East et al. found that a customer's share loyalty to grocery brands was correlated with their store loyalty (measured as share), total supermarket spending, lack of interest in discounts and household income.

The association between brand loyalty and store loyalty that East et al. found has been noted in other studies and a number of explanations have been offered. One possibility is that loyalty to retailer brands (own label, private label) explains the effect because the customer who buys more of a particular retailer brand has to do this by shopping with that retailer. However, Rao (1969) and East et al. (1995) both found that the correlation persisted after removing store-brand loyalty, and Flavián, Martínez and Polo (2001) support this view with their finding that brand-loyal customers bought fewer private label goods. Another explanation is that those who use a wider range of stores (low store loyalty) have a wider range of brands to choose from and this would tend to reduce their brand loyalty. A third possibility is that the correlation between brand loyalty and store loyalty may be explained if these forms of loyalty are habits, and that some people are more habit-prone. This explanation is supported by the finding that those with high brand and high store loyalty are more likely to show another habit by having a routine day for supermarket shopping (East et al., 2000). Habit proneness could relate to personality or lifestyle. Habits, by their nature, tend to exclude new experience but they may save time and effort (see Box 2.2).

Box 2.2	The habits of Gilbert & George (from the *Observer Magazine*, 28 January 2007)

The artists Gilbert & George wear the same tailored suits day in, day out, and follow the same routines 365 days a year. They get up at 6.30am and go round the corner to a café for breakfast (they do not have a kitchen at home). They then work till 11, when it's back to the café for lunch, after which they put in	a full afternoon until Paul O'Grady's show comes on ITV at 5pm. … Dinner is taken in the same Turkish restaurant in Hackney every night. …They are often asked about these routines and complain that no one ever seems to grasp that they stick to them, not for show, but to save time.

Other Habits

Purchase habits also apply to brands that we routinely *do not buy*. Most of us will admit to avoiding certain brands and service providers. Research by Hunt, Hunt and Hunt (1988) has thrown light on the way consumers hold grudges against such brands or providers. Hunt et al. find that grudges persist for a long time and usually begin with an emotionally upsetting experience as a customer. Grudge-holders often give negative word of mouth about the offending product when talking to others. Such brand avoidance could have dire consequences for a manufacturer but, despite this, it has received little systematic study.

Beside brands, there are other product differentiators, and consumers can be loyal to pack size, price level, country of origin, flavour and formulation characteristics. For example, Romaniuk and Dawes (2005) found that, although people bought a variety of different wines, they tended to have a consistent pattern of preference for price tiers. Singh, Ehrenberg and Goodhardt (2004) have illustrated regular patterns of purchase with regard to other category divisions. The point that we emphasize here is that no emotional commitment is needed for such effects. We argue that most patterns of purchase, including loyalty, reflect habit rather than deeply felt commitment.

SECTION 2: THE RISE OF RELATIONSHIP MARKETING: CUSTOMER LOYALTY AS RETENTION

Relationship marketing (RM) has been described as 'attracting, maintaining and enhancing customer relationships' (Berry, 1983: 25). In a business-to-business (B2B) context, RM is an industrial philosophy that replaces the competitive transaction between buyer and seller with a more cooperative relationship[2] (Grönroos, 1994). In a cooperative relationship, partners learn to trust each other and to reveal more detail about their needs to the other, which improves the quality of mutual support. Relationship marketing has also been applied in the business-to-consumer (B2C) field, particularly by those concerned with services. As in B2B, some service relationships (e.g. dentist and patient) can be characterized by trust and cooperation but this does not apply so well when the business is larger. There is still interdependence between a large firm and its customers but any initiatives are likely to come from the firm and to be automated with the help of the customer database. Firms call this customer relationship management (CRM). Much of the CRM conducted by large firms is designed to increase sales by exploiting customer purchase habits and this has little to do with cooperation. Most firms follow good-practice rules so that their customers can trust them to deliver consistent quality goods and services, but it does not go much further than that. For their part, customers can be quite calculating. For example, they may participate in loyalty schemes because they get a discount on purchases, or gain other benefits, rather than because they like the firm.

In relationship marketing there is more emphasis placed on retaining existing customers than attracting new ones. CRM can help here; for example, when a sudden lack of spending indicates that a customer has switched supermarkets, customized vouchers can be issued that may bring the customer back. Most firms are keen to see increases in satisfaction among customers because this is thought to retain customers. This emphasis on retaining customers is based on the idea that it is more expensive to acquire customers than to retain them. So, instead of losing a customer and gaining another, it is cheaper not to lose the customer in the first place. A review by Rosenberg and Czepiel (1984) suggested that the average company spends six times as much acquiring a customer as keeping a customer. The 'six times as much' rule has now become an item of marketing folklore; the reality is that the relative cost varies with the category. For example, supermarket customers are acquired at little cost whereas credit card customers are expensive to acquire because they must be checked with credit agencies and offered financial inducements to switch.

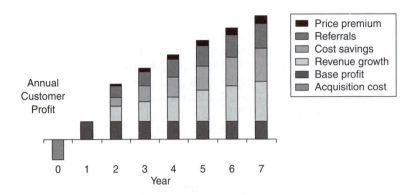

Figure 2.1   Factors in customer lifetime value (adapted from Reichheld, 1996b)

The idea that customer retention increases long-term profit was given added impetus by Reichheld and his associates in a series of papers (Reichheld and Kenny, 1990; Reichheld and Sasser, 1990; Reichheld, 1993; Jones and Sasser, 1995; Reichheld, 1996a). These ideas were brought together in a book by Reichheld (1996b). Reichheld suggests that the value of a customer grows with the length of time that they remain a customer (called customer tenure). The reasons for this are illustrated in Figure 2.1. Reichheld argues that, for each added year of tenure, the profit from a customer rises as the acquisition cost is amortized, and as the customer spends more (revenue growth), becomes easier to deal with (cost savings), introduces more new customers (referrals) and is more tolerant of higher prices (price premium). Also, and not shown in Figure 2.1, the longer customers stay, the more likely they are to remain in the following year. This means that those who are currently long-term customers are likely to give more profit in the future than current short-term customers. An admirable feature of Reichheld's work is that he is very precise about the potential effects of customer retention so that others can test these claims. Reichheld's own evidence tends to be based on case studies. Case studies serve well for teaching about management practice but, as evidence, they are not as valuable as systematic studies that are set up to test a hypothesis. Case study evidence is often already available when marketers begin to hypothesize and they may unintentionally focus on the evidence that fits their theory. Below, we review Reichheld's claims.

Customer Tenure and Profitability

We now review five assumptions for how customer loyalty might be turned into higher profits.

First, do long-term customers spend more? East, Hammond and Gendall (2006) reported on 17 services where customers were asked how much they spent and how long they had used the supplier. Examples of services were supermarkets, credit cards, dry cleaners, fashion stores, mobile phone airtime and car servicing. Of the 17 studies, only three showed a statistically significant positive association between tenure and spending:

credit cards (UK), outdoor clothing (USA) and mobile phone airtime (UK). The average correlation between tenure and spend for the 17 studies was 0.09. This shows that, usually, there is no substantial association between tenure and spending that would justify management attention. In a few categories, long-term customers may spend significantly more than new customers, but such cases need to be established by research and not assumed by managers.

Second, are long-term customers cheaper to serve? Long-term customers become familiar with company procedures and need less 'hand holding' but they may also exploit company services more. Dowling and Uncles (1997) first expressed doubt that long-term customers were cheaper to serve. Later, Reinartz and Kumar (2000, 2002) found that long-term customers in one firm made more use of the free services available, thus raising their cost to serve. They also found that loyalty programme costs increased with tenure. It seems that total costs do not routinely decline with tenure.

Third, do long-term customers refer more new customers than recently acquired customers? Long-term customers may value their providers more for two reasons. First they may *learn* more about the merits of the supplier's offering over time, and second, as those who dislike the supplier switch, the more appreciative customers remain. Despite these effects, Smith and Higgins (2000) and Fournier, Dobscha and Mick (1998) have illustrated how relationships can sometimes sour over time. Also, a brand may be salient when first acquired but may then become so familiar that consumers give it no thought and therefore do not talk about it. This loss of salience is more likely when the category does not change much (e.g. house insurance) and/or is frequently used (e.g. credit cards). When there is change, for example in the merchandise of a fashion store, the brand might be recommended again whereas a relatively unchanging product, for example motor insurance, does not merit a second recommendation.

In their review of previous evidence, East et al. (2005a) found either no association between recommendation rates and tenure (e.g. Kumar, Scheer and Steenkamp, 1995; Verhoef, Franses and Hoekstra, 2002) or a negative association (e.g. East, Lomax and Narain, 2001; Wangenheim and Bayón, 2004). In their own research, East et al. reported evidence from 23 studies on tenure and recommendation rates (shown in Table 2.2). They found that the overall association between tenure and recommendation was neutral (−0.01) but that individual associations ranged from significantly negative to significantly positive. The significant negative associations were for cheque accounts, credit cards and car insurance. The significant positive associations were for car servicing and main fashion stores (data for this latter category were gathered in Mexico). Car servicing is infrequent so it takes time for a new customer to be reassured about the quality of work. Car servicing was one of the service categories mentioned by Reichheld and, in this specific case, the evidence supports the assertion that long-tenure customers recommend more. Notice that East et al. studied credit cards and car servicing twice in the UK (with different samples); the pairs of studies gave similar results and this makes the work more convincing. Overall, East et al. (2005a) do not support Reichheld's claim that long-tenure customers normally recommend more than short-tenure customers. The association depends on the category and may be positive, negative or neutral.

Table 2.2　Correlations between customer tenure in 23 service studies (from East et al., 2005a)

Service (country)	Customer tenure and recommendation
Cheque book service (UK)	−.44*
Credit card (UK)	−.39*
Car insurance (UK)	−.36*
Credit card (UK)	−.28*
Main supermarket (UK)	−.09
Mobile airtime (UK)	−.04
Motor insurance (UK)	−.03
Dentist (UK)	−.03
Dry cleaning (UK)	−.02
Internet provider (UK)	0.02
Leisure centre (UK)	0.04
House contents insurance (UK)	0.04
Main supermarket (Mexico)	0.06
Main fashion store (UK)	0.07
Car insurance (Mauritius)	0.07
Favourite restaurant (UK)	0.08
Email (UK)	0.10
Hairdresser (Mexico)	0.12
Search engine (UK)	0.13
Main fashion store (Mexico)	0.18*
Car servicing (UK)	0.20*
Car servicing (Mauritius)	0.20*
Car servicing (UK)	0.25*
Mean	−.01

*Significant at $p < 0.05$

Fourth, are long-term customers more price-tolerant? Price tolerance is particularly exploited by providers of financial services. For example, firms may allow the interest paid on accounts to drop without telling the account holders. In addition, mortgage, insurance and credit card offers to new customers are often better than those to existing customers. These tactics rely on customer inertia and may produce short-term profit for the bank if a large proportion of existing customers do not notice the changes but, when customers do take note, they may be irritated and switch providers in order to get introductory discounts themselves. This behaviour can be very damaging to long-term profits. Reichheld makes it clear that this sort of exploitation of customers is likely to be detrimental in the longer run. However, in other fields there may be no long-term price premium. In three B2C companies that they studied, Reinartz and Kumar (2002) found that long-tenure customers did not pay more than short-term customers for the same goods. They also found that

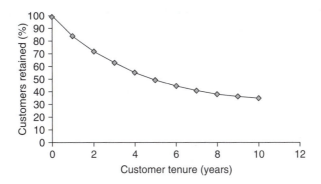

Figure 2.2   Normal customer survival pattern (adapted from Reichheld, 1996b)

long-tenure customers were *more* price-sensitive and that these customers expected better value when compared with recent customers.

Fifth, do defection rates decline with tenure? In general, this is true. Reichheld finds that a company typically loses about 15 per cent of its current customers in the first year and 50 per cent over five years. If we follow a cohort of customers and examine them over a period, we find that fewer and fewer customers defect each year and that the decay curve levels out, as shown in Figure 2.2. A study by East and Hammond (1996) estimated defection rates for a range of groceries and found an average of 15 per cent defection in the first year. In the second year, defection halved. This means that the customer's prospective lifetime value increases with tenure. However, there must come a time when changes in life stage (and even death) mean that customers no longer need the category and defection may then rise. In addition, there are some products and services which are only used for a limited period, for example disposable nappies and crèche facilities, and here we would see a different pattern from that shown in Figure 2.2.

In conclusion, Reichheld's claim that customer loyalty translates into long-term profit is more a plausible hypothesis than a fact. Each of the potential sources of the profit increase from loyal customers has been challenged by more recent research, and companies should examine to what extent loyal customers may be an advantage for their particular business.

The Strategy of Customer Retention

The evidence summarized above indicates that the benefit of customer retention in consumer markets has been exaggerated and that the benefits from retention differ substantially between categories. One implication of this evidence is that customer acquisition may bring more advantage, relative to retention, than is conventionally recognized. We need more evidence of the relative cost of sales gains through customer acquisition and retention and we also need more evidence on how increases in market share come about – are such increases due primarily to acquisition or retention of customers? Two relevant studies are by East and Hogg (1997) and Riebe, Sharp and Stern (2002). East and Hogg found that, when Tesco overtook Sainsbury in 1995 as the leading UK supermarket, the Tesco gains came equally from increased customer acquisitions and reduced defection. Sainsbury lost customers because of reduced recruitment, not increased defection. Riebe et al. found that increases in drug prescription among doctors came mainly from the acquisition of new prescribing doctors. Sharp (2010) also argues that brand gains come mainly from customer acquisition and presents evidence from several studies to support his view.

There are a number of other points that are relevant to the retention versus acquisition argument. First, it is quite difficult to reduce defection. Reichheld's calculations suggest large gains in profit if customer defection is reduced from 15 per cent to 10 per cent but a one-third drop in defection is a substantial amount. Reichheld did give some examples where defection averaged only a few per cent a year but, in services where there is a specific location for service delivery, a large part of the defection occurs because of the relative inaccessibility of the service. For example, East, Lomax and Narain (2001) found that 43 per cent of the defections from a main supermarket were because the customer had moved home or because a more convenient store had been built nearby. This sort of customer loss is very difficult to counter.

A second point is mentioned by Reichheld but is sometimes forgotten by those who espouse his arguments. This is that the customers who are retained by a successful marketing intervention or service improvement are not necessarily typical of the other customers of the service provider. Customers who defect are obviously more mobile; when these customers are retained through a marketing intervention, they may be more likely to defect later.

A third point is that it is in the nature of loyal customers that they stay put. They may not need incentives to stay; if this is so, investments in rewards and product improvements may give little return with this group. Similarly, it may be very difficult to prise away the loyal customers of competitors. This leads to a paradox of loyalty. The most loyal customers may have the highest value but they may not be the best segment for marketing intervention because of their inertia. So which customers should be targeted when we have evidence of their loyalty? Should you target your high-share customers, who cannot increase their share much and also may not be willing to change their habits?[3] Or medium-share customers, who can increase their share and may be more changeable? Or low-share customers, who can increase their share substantially or may change easily, but also may be prone to change again away from your brand later? This is a complicated problem which requires category-specific research.

Although customer retention is emphasized in relationship marketing, this evidence shows that customer acquisition may be more important. Reichheld (1996b) does not ignore customer acquisition. He gives the example of the MBNA credit card organization. This company managed to acquire high-spending and high-retention customers by the careful design of the service and by well-chosen targeting. It is also well accepted that not all customers are profitable. Company costs can exceed returns on small-spending customers and sometimes retail facilities are so overstretched that more profit is made when some customers defect.

| Exercise 2.2 | Brand switching |

Consumers switch for many reasons which may vary across categories. Your own experience may be a guide. If you have switched banks, mobile phone companies, doctors, hairdressers, supermarkets or alcoholic beverages, why did you do this? Choose two categories in which you have switched your main brand:

1   List the key reasons for your switch.
2   Identify four things the supplier could have done to try to retain you.
3   Evaluate how effective each of these supplier initiatives would have been in your particular case.

Loyalty Programmes

Many B2C companies now have loyalty programmes. These programmes have been introduced for different reasons. Some companies saw a genuine interest in rewarding their most loyal customers, and business books like *The Loyalty Effect* (Reichheld 1996b) encouraged them in this direction. They often had to open up their programme to less loyal customers, which in some cases increased the costs up to a point where the expected gains from the overall programme were erased. Other companies felt forced to imitate their competitors for fear of losing customers. In some industries, loyalty programmes increased the overall costs for all players without real effect on loyalty (a zero-sum game). Overall, recent academic research suggests that loyalty programmes only generate small effects (Verhoef, 2003) or no effect (DeWulf, Odekerken-Schroder and Iacobucci, 2001; Mägi, 2003) on purchase behaviour. But these programmes nevertheless exist and should be optimized. Drèze and Nunes (2011) developed a programme of research to examine how insights from consumer behaviour can help marketers design and improve their loyalty programmes.

In most loyalty programmes rewards can be earned repeatedly (e.g. discount certificates at a retailer, free nights at a hotel chain, free tickets on an airline). Consumers work towards the goal of obtaining the reward and, once the reward is obtained, have to build up their reward credit again. Drèze and Nunes (2011) examine what happens to consumption behaviour after a reward has been obtained. One might expect a post-reward reset and deceleration in purchases after the consumer attains the reward. Using a large-scale dataset from a frequent-flier programme, the authors show that, instead, success is followed by an increase in effort to reach the same goal again. Interestingly, this effect is only obtained when success requires perseverance. Successes that come too easily, when small rewards are frequently obtained, do not have this effect. Creating larger rewards with greater purchase requirements leads to more overall effort. In a subsequent experimental study, Drèze and Nunes show that the consumer's self-perceptions of efficacy play an important role. Some form of self-learning takes place in the process of goal attainment which affects action designed to secure the second and subsequent rewards. Overall, this work shows that cleverly designed loyalty programmes really can stimulate purchases.

A loyalty programme can also be designed to give consumers additional incentives to purchase, without additional cost. In a field experiment at a professional car wash, Nunes and Drèze (2006) randomly distributed two types of loyalty cards. For the first type, eight car wash purchases were required for a free car wash. With the second type of card, ten purchases were necessary but, as part of a special promotion, two free stamps were given such that the number of required new purchases was also eight. The respective redemption rates were 19 per cent and 34 per cent. Framing the task as already begun apparently enhanced the effort to reach the reward goal, although the distance to the goal was no different between the two groups. Consumers in that framing condition also accelerated their purchases: they left 2.9 fewer days between washes.

Another design feature of loyalty programmes is that they can have a hierarchical structure with different tiers to give the 'best' customers (supposedly, the highest spenders) a special status. Companies have to decide on the number of tiers they want to introduce (a single tier is an option) and, in the case of multiple tiers, on the number of customers they want to admit to each. Drèze and Nunes (2009) show, in a series of experiments, that the desire for tier status can drive behaviour. Companies face the trade-off of making as many customers as possible feel special, without disenfranchising the very best customers by diluting their special status. The authors show that a three-tiered programme is more satisfying than a programme with two tiers, and this applies to all customers, not just those qualifying for elite status. The size of the top tier can be increased without decreasing the status perceptions of its existing members, as long as a second tier is added. Adding a third tier enhances self-perceptions of status of those in the second tier. (Note: other aspects of loyalty programmes are considered in Chapter 11).

SECTION 3: COMBINATION DEFINITIONS OF LOYALTY

So far we have described loyalty in terms of share, retention, recommendation and satisfaction. We have not combined these different forms of loyalty into a more complex definition. Most marketing scientists use a single behavioural definition, usually share or retention (see East et al., 2005a). By contrast, most of those who have theorized about loyalty suggest that loyalty is not behaviour alone, and many feel strongly that attitude should appear in the definition. For example, Jacoby and Olson (1970) defined loyalty as the biased (i.e. non-random) behavioural response (i.e. purchase), expressed over time, by some decision-making unit (e.g. household, person), with respect to one or more alternative brands, which is a function of psychological processes (decision-making, evaluation).

Customers who stay with suppliers because of unthinking habit or simple convenience are not regarded as loyal according to this definition because a feeling about the brand is required in addition to behaviour. Oliver (1999: 34) emphasized the role of feeling as well as behaviour when he described loyalty as 'a deeply held commitment to re-buy or re-patronize a preferred product/service consistently in the future, thereby causing

Repeat patronage

		High	Low
Relative attitude	High	True loyalty	Latent loyalty
	Low	Spurious loyalty	No loyalty

Figure 2.3   Forms of loyalty (adapted from Dick and Basu, 1994)

repetitive same-brand or same brand-set purchasing, despite situational influences and marketing efforts having the potential to cause switching behavior'. Also, Day (1969) suggested that 'true' or intentional loyalty occurred when there was a positive attitude to the brand and he distinguished this from 'spurious' loyalty where purchase of the brand was not supported by any commitment. Another widely quoted paper by Dick and Basu (1994) used Day's distinction and divided customers into four segments in the typology shown in Figure 2.3. True loyalty occurs in the top left-hand quadrant of Figure 2.3. Latent loyalty covers those who would like to buy the brand but who have not been able to do so in the past because it was not available, too expensive or because they had no need for it. Spurious loyalty occurs when consumers buy the brand but regard it as little better than others. In this typology, 'relative attitude' means that the attitude measure includes a term such as *compared with available alternatives*. Then, if a brand gets a high score, it is because it is rated much higher than the nearest alternative.

So should we see loyalty simply as behaviour or as behaviour with attitude? Ryanair and Wal-Mart can make profits from customers who use them regularly but may not like them. Indeed, for brands in some utilitarian categories like bleach and sugar it is difficult to generate much feeling. But when loyal behaviour is supported by a liking for the brand, retention may be greater and more profit may be made. There are brands like Harley-Davidson which are clearly liked a lot by their owners. Fournier and Yao (1997) studied how consumers experience their relationships with their favourite brand(s) of coffee from the perspective of interpersonal relationship theory. In-depth interviews with eight consumers show that the strength and character of loyalty relationships with brands can vary widely even if, on the surface, there may be not much difference in behaviour. For some consumers, their favourite brand is like a partner and provides sense and structure in their life. Even brands with a small share of use (SCR in our jargon) can play a very significant role in some people's consumption routines.

Definitions relate to the type of explanation that the researcher seeks to make. In Chapter 1, we introduced *segment comparisons* and *causal relationships*. Dick and Basu's typology allows researchers to make comparisons between the four segments with respect to retention, share, recommendation and overall profitability, though we have been unable to find research that does this. Pritchard, Havitz and Howard (1999) used the Dick and Basu typology to show a number of differences between travellers who were classified according to the four segments but the authors did not investigate behaviour

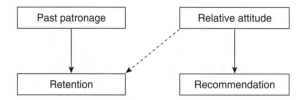

Figure 2.4   Consequences of different forms of loyalty

such as recommendation and retention. Macintosh and Lockshin (1997) also found significant differences between customers divided according to the Dick and Basu typology, but they investigated *intention* to repurchase rather than actual retention, and intention to repurchase may not relate closely to actual retention. Combination definitions of loyalty may be useful if retention and recommendation differ across segments, but we need to see evidence on this matter.

East et al. (2005a) investigated whether relative attitude and past patronage both predicted later retention and recommendation. For supermarkets and cars, they found that greater relative attitude was associated with more recommendation but had little relationship with retention. They also found that customers who bought mostly from one supermarket or who had bought the same make of car on the last two occasions (high past patronage) were somewhat more likely to retain the supermarket or buy the last make of car again at the next purchase, but that the level of past patronage had no effect on word of mouth. Figure 2.4 summarizes these relationships with the dotted line indicating a weak relationship. We conclude that retention and word of mouth have largely different causes. One simple way of explaining the relationships in Figure 2.4 is that 'like correlates with like'. Past patronage and later retention are alike because they are the same measure at different points in time. Relative attitude and recommendation are alike because the reasons that people have for liking a brand are likely to be much the same as the reasons they give when they recommend it.

Research studies have generally shown a weak positive association between satisfaction and retention. Crosby and Stephens (1987) found that life assurance renewal was slightly greater when customers were satisfied with the provider. Kordupleski, Rust and Zahoric (1993) found limited evidence that satisfaction increased retention in company research by AT&T. Reichheld (1993) reported that between 65 per cent and 85 per cent of customers who defected were satisfied with their former supplier. Ennew and Binks (1996) did not find clear evidence of a positive association between retention and service quality (the latter is usually closely related to satisfaction) and Hennig-Thurau and Klee (1997) generally found moderate associations between satisfaction and retention in a review of studies in this field. Against this weak evidence we can find a few stronger findings but these are where *dissatisfaction* has caused customers to switch. Andreasen (1985) studied ten patients who reported serious problems with their medical care and found that six of them switched physicians; Bolton (1998) found that dissatisfaction with a mobile phone airtime provider led to switching if the users had recently adopted the service and lacked knowledge of the supplier's longer-term performance. Winchester, Romaniuk and Bogomolova (2008) show that defection is indicated by prior negative beliefs about the product. Overall, the research evidence indicates that satisfaction with a brand or supplier provides a limited prospect of increased retention but dissatisfaction may be a spur to switching.

Some readers may find it puzzling that feelings like satisfaction have such a weak relationship with retention but there are some good reasons why this should be so. One reason is that, usually, the measure of satisfaction employed is not *relative*. People retain a supplier because of the *superiority* of that supplier over others and using a relative satisfaction measure is more sensitive to this relative difference between alternatives. A second reason for the weak association between satisfaction and retention can be found in the reasons for defection. In services, defection often occurs as a consequence of specific failures, price changes or the emergence of superior competition, as found by Keaveney (1995); such reasons are unlikely to be anticipated by an earlier measure of satisfaction. The same could be true of some goods. A third reason why satisfaction fails to predict defection well is that the defection may be involuntary, as was found by East, Lomax and Narain (2001). People who move house will change their main supermarket if their old one is now inaccessible; this does not mean that it was unsatisfactory.

What does all this mean? Those who propose combination measures of loyalty need to show that this approach is useful and that the segments in Dick and Basu's typology behave in different ways. In particular, they need to show that the top-left loyalty segment shows more retention, share loyalty and recommendation than other segments, at least in some categories. If they cannot do this, the case for such combination measures fails. Meanwhile, those who are interested in the prediction of retention and recommendation need to treat these behaviours separately because they do not appear to have much common causation.

SECTION 4: REASONS FOR DEFECTION

Retention is often based on inertia. Behaviourally, consumers remain loyal by continuing to do what they have done before. In some cases, the inertia can be quite thoughtless as people continue with savings accounts and utility suppliers, even when alternative suppliers offer much better value. In the case of consumer durables, where an act of repurchase is required for retention, there may be more thought but, even here, the process may be fairly automatic. A study by Lapersonne, Laurent and Le Goff (1995) on car purchase showed that 17 per cent of the respondents considered only the brand of their current car.

We have mentioned how existing customers can attract new ones through positive word of mouth. It turns out that defection is also contagious. Using data on one million customers of a cellular phone company, Nitzan and Libai (2011) show that exposure to a defecting neighbour in their close social network increases a person's chances of defection by 80 per cent. Consumers with more social connections are more affected. But heavy users and customers with a longer tenure are less affected by their neighbours' defections.

When people defect, they often have reasons. The reasons for defecting from service providers were studied by Keaveney (1995).

Table 2.3   Reasons for switching from a service (adapted from Keaveney, 1995)

	All reasons (%)	When only one reason given (%)	Mean (%)
Core service failures	25	25	25
Failed service encounters	19	20	20
Response to failed service	10	0	5
Pricing	17	20	18
Competition	6	7	6
Ethical problems	4	4	4
Inconvenience	12	10	11
Involuntary switching	4	7	5
Other	5	7	6

Keaveney used her postgraduate students as investigators. They gathered evidence from people outside the university, asking them to focus on their most recent service defection, report what the service was and describe what happened. The narratives of what happened were reviewed by judges, who produced a typology of eight reasons for defection plus an 'other' category. Then the frequency of the different reasons was assessed from the narratives. Some people had more than one reason for defection and, in Table 2.3, we show the percentages for all the reasons cited and the percentages when one reason was given. There is not much difference between these two sets of percentages and we treat the average as typical of what Keaveney found (column 4).

The method used by Keaveney, called Critical Incident Technique (CIT), is suitable for establishing the typology of reasons for defection but rather less appropriate for measuring the frequency of the different reasons since some memories are more easily recalled because of *retrieval bias*. This was described by Taylor (1982: 192), who states that 'colorful, dynamic, or other distinctive stimuli disproportionately engage attention and, accordingly, disproportionately affect judgments'. Events are more changing and distinctive than conditions and are thus more easily retrieved. In Keaveney's list of reasons, the first three (core service failures, failed service encounters and responses to failed service) are clearly events (50 per cent), whereas inconvenience and involuntary switching (16 per cent) are likely to relate to persisting conditions. Keaveney asserts that managers can make changes that prevent events, and can thus stop defection; and she argues that her data support action to retain customers. But if Keaveney's method raises the proportion of events reported at the expense of conditions, a strategy of customer acquisition may be more profitable.

East, Grandcolas, Dall'Olmo Riley and Lomax (2012) used a different method of measurement. They put Keaveney's reasons into one item of a questionnaire and asked survey respondents to state which of these reasons was the most important in their decision to defect. This method should have reduced retrieval bias because all the possible reasons were prompted. Keaveney aggregated the data on all services mentioned by respondents

Table 2.4 Condensed table of reasons for defection compared with Keaveney's results (percentages by row) (from East et al., 2012)

	N	Service failure events	Pricing	Competition	Ethical problems	Conditions	Other
Located services	523	12	12	23	1	47	6
Non-located services	369	27	35	20	0	8	9
All services	892	18	22	22	1	31	7
Keaveney	211	50	18	6	4	16	6

but East et al. report findings for specific services. They chose some services that were delivered in a particular location (e.g. a favourite restaurant) and some services where delivery was independent of location (e.g. mobile phone airtime). They reasoned that conditions would be much more important as a reason for defection when service delivery was located because the inaccessibility of some locations could cause inconvenience and involuntary switching. East et al. combined data on the three types of service failure event and the two types of condition and their aggregate results are shown in Table 2.4, together with Keaveney's frequencies for comparison.

Table 2.4 shows that East et al. found a much lower proportion of service failure events compared with Keaveney (18 per cent instead of 50 per cent) and a higher proportion of conditions (31 per cent versus 16 per cent). The conditions came mainly from the located services, as expected. This evidence suggests that it is difficult to retain customers in located services and, here, it may be better to go for a strategy of customer acquisition.

SUMMARY

Several behaviours indicate customer loyalty. These are share-of-category requirement (SCR) in repertoire markets, and retention and recommendation in all markets. Feelings also indicate loyalty. The main feelings are attitude, satisfaction, commitment and trust.

Early work investigated SCR in grocery purchase and showed that consumers frequently divided their purchasing across several brands in a category. Divided loyalty patterns persist over long periods and reflect consumer habits.

With the rise in relationship marketing, attention turned to the retention of customers, particularly with regard to services. Reichheld (1996b) argued that there was substantial profit to be gained if customers could be retained for longer periods; however, many of his assertions have been undermined by subsequent research. Loyalty programmes are nevertheless very common. They can be optimized by thinking carefully about the reward frequency and status perceptions when there are different tiers of loyalty.

Marketing scientists have generally used behaviour measures such as share and retention while others have argued that loyalty should be seen as a composite of attitude and behaviour and should be tested by segment comparisons. The best-known composite model is by Dick and Basu (1994); however, although differences in behaviour have been demonstrated between the population segments defined by this model, there is little evidence that these segments differ in respect of retention and recommendation.

Defection from services has been studied by Keaveney (1995), who developed a typology of eight reasons for defection. Keaveney found that many reasons for defection related to events that managers could control and thus thought that much defection could be prevented. However, recent work suggests that much defection may not be controllable, which turns attention to customer acquisition rather than customer retention.

Additional Resources

The papers by Reichheld and his colleagues are clearly written and are more concise than his book. Keaveney's (1995) paper is much cited and easy to follow. Reinartz and Kumar (2002) provide a critical review in this area.

Notes

1 We do not describe the average SCR per brand as *brand loyalty* because there is no consistent usage here.
2 User-generated content online has given more voice and initiative to the consumer. See Chapter 12.
3 Tesco estimate the share of each customer's grocery purchases that they get (they call it *share of stomach*).

3 Brand Knowledge, Brand Equity and Brand Extension

LEARNING OBJECTIVES

When you have completed this chapter, you should be able to:

1 Understand ideas about the mental representation of concepts.
2 Understand what is meant by brand image, brand awareness, brand strength and brand equity.
3 Explain the potential gains and losses from brand extensions.
4 Understand how brand shares alter when new brands enter a market.

OVERVIEW

Brands are represented in the minds of customers as ideas, associations, feelings and purchase dispositions. Managers search for ways of exploiting these mental representations of brands by introducing line extensions (new variants in a brand's category) and category extensions (products with the same brand name in different categories). These extensions are not without risk. If the extension fails to capture new sales or avoid losses, then marketing effort will have been wasted. In addition, if the new introduction reduces allegiance to the brand, all the sales associated with the brand could suffer. We start by considering how consumers store and process brand knowledge in a network of related concepts. Then, we consider the way in which this processing gives brands strength and value, and the way in which brand names are recalled and recognized. Building on this, we consider the idea of brand equity, that brands are capital that can be exploited by their owner. Finally, we examine research on brand extension and the way in which new entrants to a market take sales from existing players.

SECTION 1: THE MENTAL REPRESENTATION OF BRANDS

In this chapter, we are first concerned with the way in which concepts such as companies, brands, services and categories are represented in memory along with all the other concepts that we have. Psychologists have described this cognitive world using mental representations theory, which is reviewed by Smith and Queller (2001). The fundamental idea is that memory is an *associative network* of interlinked nodes in which each node is a concept. The meaning of a concept is therefore given by the interrelationships it has with other concepts. Applied to brands, the interrelationships define how the brand is perceived and what developments of the brand are most likely to be commercially successful. These interrelationships are established in people through direct experience, from information received from other persons and from the mass media. In mental representations theory:

- Perception activates nodes that correspond to the perceived object.
- Thinking occurs when these activated nodes spread activation to other linked nodes.
- Links between nodes are strengthened slowly over time by such activation.
- The concepts relating to more frequently activated nodes are more easily retrieved from memory.
- Nodes are valenced (positive or negative), thus forming the basis of attitude.
- Long-term memory is the single, large associative structure covering all concepts whereas short-term memory is a currently activated subset.
- Simultaneous activations may occur (parallel processing), but much of this processing is unconscious.

To illustrate this thinking we have set out one possible mental representation map for iPhone in Figure 3.1. The mental node for iPhone could be linked to a wide range of concepts and only some are shown. These include product features such as reliability, ease of use and cost as well as a wider range of ideas. iPhones may be associated with Apple stores, with their novel store layout and merchandising. Another connection is to the Apple Corporation and its founder, Steve Jobs, who is credited with a string of original product developments. Other links might be to the vast range of apps that can be downloaded, such as the one that allows the user to pop bubblewrap (virtually). Brands are often associated with their competitors; in this case we have shown Nokia and BlackBerry. iPhone and other smart phones are thought to have played a large part in the mobilization of dissent in the Arab world in 2011, as indicated in the figure.

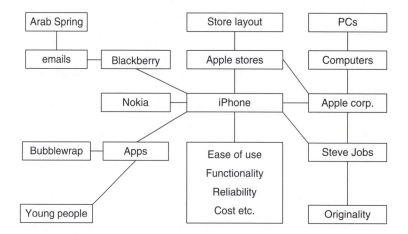

Figure 3.1   Concepts that might be associated with iPhone

We should be wary of drawing too close a parallel between mental representations and the evidence from brain research, but there is clearly some correspondence between the neurons in the brain which are connected to other neurons by synapses, and the nodes connected by links in mental representations theory. Brain research shows that consciousness is associated with the activation of hundreds of thousands of neurons and that each neuron has as many as two thousand synapses connecting it to other neurons (Greenfield, 1997). This suggests that mental-representations maps indicate only a very small part of the content and linkages involved when people think.

Brand Knowledge

The nodes and linkages in Figure 3.1 help us to describe two aspects of brand knowledge, *brand image* and *brand awareness*, which are discussed in the next two sections. Brand image is the set of ideas about the brand, as illustrated in Figure 3.1. Brand awareness is how these ideas are brought to mind, which depends on the nature of the linkages.

Brand Image

Gardner and Levy (1955) believed that brands have a social and psychological meaning as well as a physical nature and that these feelings and ideas about brands direct consumer choice; this thinking is also conveyed by terms such as 'the symbols by which we buy', 'brand personality' and 'brand meaning'. These ideas are created in consumers' minds by their experience with the brand, by word of mouth and through mass communications. To the extent that consumers have similar customer experiences and similar exposure to word of mouth and mass communication, we expect them to have similar brand images for products such as iPhone.

Applying the theory of mental representations, brand image is given by the concepts associated with the brand. These associations differ in respect of valence (positive or negative), number, uniqueness and linkage strength, as shown in Figure 3.2. Thus, we can break down brand image into a valence concept, brand attitude, and a cognitive concept, brand strength.

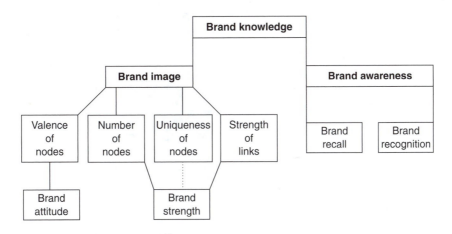

Figure 3.2   Main forms of brand knowledge

Brand attitude is given by the positive and negative feelings about brand features. Attributes like unreliability and cost are typically negative, while ideas such as ease of use and wide functionality are usually positive. In addition to this attribute basis for brand attitude, there is likely to be a 'mere exposure' effect whereby links become stronger on repeated exposure (usually usage but also exposure to advertising and word of mouth). This is explained further in Chapter 8.

Brand strength is important because it relates to the ease of retrieving the brand name from memory, together with the range of associations and the resistance to change in thought and feeling. If the number of links affects strength, we might expect brands in the choice set (the brands considered for purchase) to have an above average number of links. Supporting this, Romaniuk (2003) has shown that brands with more image attributes are more likely to be considered for choice, and Romaniuk and Gaillard (2007) have shown

---

Box 3.1 | Consumer confusion and look-alike brands

The term 'consumer confusion' is used in a variety of ways. In courts of law, it relates to passing off, when one manufacturer makes a product that is very similar to that of another manufacturer. In these circumstances, consumers may make mistakes and buy the wrong brand. This has been a concern in marketing but there is often little confusion on the part of the consumer. For example, a person buying Perigan's gin will normally know that they are not buying Gordon's gin, despite some similarities of bottle shape, colour and label design. But Gordon's gin has built up a buying propensity that is associated with the uniqueness of its pack, and some element of this buying propensity may attach to look-alike competitors, even when consumers are well aware of the differences between brands. This means that Perigan's gin is using brand strength that it did not create. However, it is not clear that their product damages Gordon's gin – it could even strengthen this brand because it draws attention to the Gordon's design. Also, if a brand is sold at a distinctly different price from another in the same category, there will be limited direct competition.

Gordon's and Perigan's gin. Both spirits are in squared bottles, use yellow and orange on the labels and have similarities of label design.

that the biggest brands have more attributes. Romaniuk and Sharp (2003) also found that respondents stated that they were less likely to defect from brands with a greater number of positive attributes. Thus, more associations and more positive linkage help to anchor brand use so that it is difficult to change consumers' choice sets.

If brand strength is affected by the uniqueness of nodes, retrieval of the brand name from memory should be greater when nodes are uncommon and differentiated from others in the brand image. However, the evidence does not support this effect of uniqueness. Romaniuk and Gaillard (2007) did not find that consumers thought that the brand they bought had more unique attributes than brands they did not buy, and they also found that large and smaller brands had similar numbers of unique characteristics. Thus, although we have included uniqueness in Figure 3.2, it is likely that this feature is overemphasized in brand theory. Customers need to be able to differentiate brands but this can be accomplished through quite trivial differences (see Box 3.1).

The variation in brand strength will relate to the extent to which categories are promoted, their importance in everyday life and the awareness consumers' have of them (their salience) in the environment. Box 3.2 illustrates two brands with rather different strengths.

Box 3.2	Brand strength

A weak brand

Some years ago, one of the DIY store groups in the UK found that the extra sales raised by its advertising were much the same as the extra sales they received when their competitor advertised. It seemed that the public made little differentiation between DIY stores; advertising probably reminded them of work that they had intended to do and they got any necessary supplies from the most convenient store. Thus, the advertising of any one store group had the effect of promoting the DIY retail category as a whole, rather than the named store group. In situations like this, where brand awareness is weak, store groups may use sales promotions and advertise these. In this way, consumers only gain advantage when they patronize the store group offering the promotion.

A strong brand

In Britain, the case of Hellman's mayonnaise illustrates the way in which strong brand awareness can pay off (Channon, 1985). In 1981, Hellman's was priced well above other brands of mayonnaise and was open to fierce competition from these other brands, particularly retailer brands. The advertising used the term 'Hellman's' rather than 'mayonnaise' to reinforce the brand name. The campaign was successful in making Hellman's the effective name of the category and the brand still has a large share of the market. Becoming synonymous with the category has always been an attractive possibility for a leading brand. In the UK, 'Hoovering' (from the one-time market leader, Hoover) means vacuum cleaning and is one of the best known examples of this effect.

Brand strength is associated with the size of the brand and Ehrenberg (1993) suggested that, because of this, there is no need for the concept of brand strength – size or market share would serve instead. However, most people see market share as the outcome of the wide associations and ease of recall of a strong brand. Furthermore, there may be occasions when brands lose market share because of competitor innovation but retain their associations, at least for a while. Thus, we do not see brand strength and market share as equivalent.

A number of techniques are used for measuring the components of brand image. Driesener and Romaniuk (2006) review three commonly used methods: brands can be rated, ranked or all those with a characteristic can be named – the 'pick-any' method. These techniques can be used for evaluative criteria such as good value, or for more descriptive criteria such as French-made or organic.

Brand Awareness

Brand awareness concerns the way in which ideas are brought to mind. There are two mechanisms, *recall* and *recognition* (Bettman, 1979). When people recall something, they use the links between concepts in their mental representation to get to the idea that is recalled. For example, they might be told of an app and then think of iPhone. Recognition involves a direct match between an external stimulus and a mental representation; this occurs when a person sees an object or an image of it, for example, an iPhone, and knows what it is. When the stimulus is partial or the mental representation poorly defined, the recognition will be harder to achieve. Human beings have very great powers of recognition, e.g. the ability to recognize people from their face, voice and other cues. Recognition is a specific-to-general process; for example, the iPhone is recognized as a smart phone.

Recall is usually a general-to-specific process; for example, the thought of a smart phone might bring the idea of an iPhone to mind. Often, the cue is the category or a need for the category. Clearly, a number of alternative brands can be recalled and it is the business of marketers to make their brand come to mind more easily than other brands so that it is more often chosen or at least considered.

The strength of brand recall may be measured as a top-of-mind effect. Top of mind means the first brand retrieved in response to a category stimulus; for example, FedEx might be recalled when a courier service is needed. Ease of recognition may be measured as speed of response when a brand stimulus is presented. Accuracy of recognition might be estimated by asking people to report whether a particular brand is present when a picture of several brands is exposed briefly.

Brands are thought about and chosen in a variety of contexts and these contexts affect whether recall or recognition is used to retrieve a brand from memory. For example, a person might want to repair a broken jug and recall that Loctite will do the job. Alternatively, the person might be in a DIY store and see Loctite on the shelf, recognize it, and then recall that this product is needed to repair the jug. Brands with a physical form are generally suitable for recognition because the brand 'makes itself known' to the consumer in the store. Services are often harder to represent in the environment and here the need for the category often occurs first, and then the brand is recalled in response. Rossiter and Bellman (2005) use the distinction between recall and recognition as a cornerstone of their approach to designing effective advertising and choosing suitable media. Visual media such as television are good for the recognition of physical brands because they can display the product, but radio is good for strengthening the link from category to brand and this medium therefore aids recall.

The distinction between recall and recognition would have less relevance if advertising and brand experience facilitated recall and recognition equally. However, the linkages in the mental representation have direction and a person who has a *brand → category* recognition may not have the same degree of *category → brand* recall, even though the same nodes are linked. The measurement of brand awareness should test these links separately.

SECTION 2: BRAND EQUITY AND BRAND EXTENSION

Brand Equity

Biel (1991) describes brand equity as the value of a brand beyond the physical assets associated with its manufacture or provision and says that it can be thought of as the additional cash flow obtained by associating the brand with the underlying product. Because brand knowledge usually changes slowly, a brand that is currently profitable is likely to continue to be so (barring unforeseen disasters such as serious PR gaffs by company employees that devalue the brand).

We should therefore conserve and exploit brands in the same way that we do with other assets. Some marketers have taken a *financial* approach and have tried to value the additional profit potential offered by a brand. Indeed some companies now estimate the value of their brands on their balance sheets – and certainly brand equity is of crucial concern in company mergers and take-overs. A second *customer-based* research approach has focused on consumer responses to the brand as measured by image, awareness, quality, loyalty and specific market advantages (e.g. Aaker, 1991).[1] These are the precursors to financial benefit; without these consumer responses to the brand, there would be no extra revenue stream or scope for brand extension. In consumer behaviour, we are primarily interested in this second approach and Figure 3.3 shows brand equity as the outcome of brand attitude, brand strength and context. Context covers such matters as market size and category differences such as prominence of the category in everyday life.

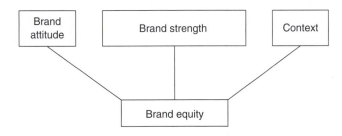

Figure 3.3   Determinants of brand equity

Because of the difficulty of measuring these different components of brand equity, and uncertainties about how they should be aggregated, customer judgements of quality are often used as a proxy for brand equity. For example, using brands of high and low quality, Krishnan (1996) compared the number of associations, valence, uniqueness and how the associations were formed (whether by experience or indirectly through communication). Krishnan's results were generally in the direction expected but there is a problem about using quality as a measure of brand equity; few people doubt the quality of Porsche but most people lack the means to buy such cars, which reduces Porsche's brand equity (hence the introduction of context in Figure 3.3). Kamakura and Russell (1991) and Keller (1993) have proposed an alternative measurement of brand equity. Instead of trying to measure aspects of brand knowledge, these researchers suggest that brand equity can be measured by comparing consumer responses to changes in the product specification, price, promotion and distribution of a named brand with the corresponding responses for an unnamed or unfamiliar product. The differences indicate the benefit conferred by the branding.

Exercise 3.1　　The scope for brand extension

1　Put in order of brand quality the following brand names: Samsung, Toshiba, Sony, Bush.
2　What does this suggest about the profit potential of the four brands?
3　What, in particular, do you associate with Sony?

In western countries, Sony usually tops the list and Samsung does less well (but not in South Korea where it is a national premium brand). Sony's ascendancy probably reflects product quality, innovation and advertising over many years. However, Sony is particularly focused on electronic goods and the assurance offered by the brand name might be much weaker when applied to a field outside electronics such as kitchen utensils. This introduces the idea that the extension should fit the parent brand strengths.

New Brand or Brand Extension?

Brand equity will affect the success of line, category and geographical extensions. A line extension is a variant within the category of a parent brand (e.g. a new pack size). One form of line extension, known as a vertical extension, introduces new lines at different price points (e.g. a premium version and a basic version). A category extension occurs when a brand name used in one category is applied in another category (e.g. when Stella Artois, known for lager, introduced a cider). Some extensions are more of a leap (e.g. when Amazon moved from being solely a retailer to being a manufacturer, when it introduced the Kindle for reading electronic books).

A geographical extension occurs when a brand that is marketed in some countries is introduced to other countries (where it is often well known already – perhaps from films or other popular media) (e.g. the introduction of US car brands such as Chrysler to Europe).

Can Stella succeed in the cider category?

Stella cider

In addition to extensions, companies with a strong brand may gain by taking over other companies and extending their name to the acquired company's products. For example, a well-established hotel brand, like Marriott, may be able to make more profit out of another hotel company's physical assets because of the strength of the Marriott name. Similarly, co-branding combinations can work well, e.g. Intel and Dell. Alternatively, a firm with a strong brand will come to an arrangement with a manufacturer with much weaker brand presence; for example Caterpillar boots are made by Wolverine World Wide under licence.

How to use the brand and sub-brand are difficult decisions for car manufacturers (see Box 3.3).

Box 3.3	The model name dilemma

The launch of a new car raises branding problems. Should the old model (or sub-brand) name be abandoned or kept? Some equity attaches to a model name which is lost when the name is dropped. On the other hand, it is important to show the novelty of the new model, and a break with the past helps this. Some companies, such as Volkswagen, have a policy of retaining model names such as Golf and Passat, whereas other manufacturers, such as Peugeot, usually drop the model name (but when faced with the continuing popularity of the 205, they retained this name for a while).

Nesting a new model name with the old one is not normally used in the car industry but it had to be done in Australia when Daihatsu found that their rather bizarre model name, Charade, was better known than the parent brand, Daihatsu. When the time came to end the Daihatsu Charade, they introduced the new model as the Daihatsu Charade Centro in order to benefit from the positive brand image that the Charade had gained amongst consumers (*Sydney Morning Herald*, 7 July 1995).

Line extensions are very common. In the USA, Aaker (1991) estimated that about 90 per cent of new products in the packaged goods industry were line extensions, though there was some cutback in line extension when the Efficient Consumer Response movement got underway and reduced wasteful marketing activity (Buzzell, Quelch and Salmon, 1991; Kahn and McAlister, 1997). More recently, *Les Échos* (2004) reported that new launches divided into 18 per cent new brands, 17 per cent category extensions and 65 per cent line extensions. Generally, the description of a product as a line extension is appropriate when the variant can compete with its parent. For example, those who buy fun-size Mars bars will usually do so instead of buying the normal size Mars bar. Sometimes, a line extension will raise additional brand sales but often it is defensive and designed to counter competition and prevent sales erosion when new variants are introduced by competitors. Normally, category extensions do not compete with sales of the parent brand. For example, Porsche sunglasses do not compete with the sale of Porsche cars and Caterpillar boots will not compete with the sale of the company's earth-moving equipment. Exceptions to this rule occur in food and drink categories; for example, it is possible that instead of buying a Mars bar, a customer may buy a Mars ice-cream or Mars mini roll.

Although there may be substantial value attaching to a brand name, it is not easy to decide whether to introduce a product as a new brand or to extend an existing brand name. Sometimes, there will be an incompatibility between categories that makes it unrealistic to extend a name. Procter & Gamble might see problems in extending the Pampers brand (disposable diapers) to baby food though they might be able to use the name on baby clothing. The Toyota brand was deemed unsuitable for the launch of a new luxury car because of its mass-market positioning. As a result, Toyota developed Lexus. By contrast, high-quality brands such as BMW and Mercedes have chosen to offer smaller cars and utility vehicles under the parent brand name. This underscores a general observation that high-quality brands are more extendable than lower-quality brands.

If a new name is used, managers should check that it is (1) different from other brand names, (2) easy to remember, (3) translates well (the Vauxhall Nova was unsuitable in Spain because it implied that the car would not go), (4) available (many brand names are registered but unused by other manufacturers) and, most importantly, (5) extendable itself, since extensions of a new brand can make further profits and help to justify creating the new brand name. One reason for the loss of interest in descriptive names such as 'I Can't Believe It's Not Butter' is that such names offer limited scope for extension.

New brand names are expensive. McWilliam (1993) found that cost saving was the most frequent reason cited by marketing practitioners for using an extension. Smith and Park (1992) studied the effect of extensions on market share and advertising efficiency and concluded that extensions capture greater market share and can be advertised more efficiently than new brands. Doyle (1989) also found that extensions needed less advertising and noted that they are more readily accepted by distributors as well as by customers. Tauber (1988) found that an existing name helps a brand to gain shelf space in stores.

Smith and Park (1992) did not find that the efficiency of a new extension was reduced by the number of extensions already made. Similarly, Dacin and Smith (1993) found that consumer confidence in a new extension was unaffected by the number of existing extensions, provided that the new entrant was compatible with its predecessors. Dawar and Anderson (1993) found that new lines were more acceptable if they were introduced in an order that made them coherent with the products that had already been introduced.

However, failure with a brand extension may damage the parent brand. This may occur because the extension so enlarges the associations of the brand name that it loses impact and all products under that name suffer in consequence (Tauber, 1981). There may also be a negative effect on the brand in downward vertical extension. Heath, DelVecchio and McCarthy (2011) examined the effect on the parent brand of vertical line extension up and down the quality range. They found that lower-quality extensions tended to reduce the parent brand's rating a little and higher-quality brands tended to improve the rating quite substantially so that the effect was asymmetric. Dall'Olmo Riley, Pina and Bravo (forthcoming) found that the scale of the negative effect depended on the product and that prestige brands were more sensitive than luxury brands. However, they found that the effect was reduced when the downward extension had a much lower price.

Aaker and Keller (1990) found that potentially negative associations could be neutralized by focusing on the attributes of the new brand rather than the strengths of the parent brand. In a subsequent study, Keller and Aaker (1992) examined how consumers saw the extensions to a brand when there were, and were not, prior extensions. They found that, if the prior extensions were regarded as successes, they improved the evaluation of a new extension; if the prior extensions were unsuccessful, they diminished the evaluation of a new extension. This suggests that brand owners should be wary of extensions after a failure.

Consumer Acceptance of a Category Extension

Aaker and Keller (1990) took six well-known brand names and examined how consumers reacted to 20 hypothetical category extensions. For example, they suggested the idea of Crest toothpaste extending into chewing gum and also Vidal Sassoon offering perfume. They found that three factors were related to the attitude of consumers to the potential extension. One of these was the *fit* between the categories of the parent and offspring. A second was the quality of the parent brand. The third factor was whether the extension was seen as difficult to make by the owner of the parent brand. These relationships are shown in Figure 3.4.

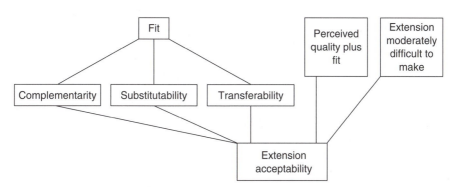

Figure 3.4   Factors contributing to extension success (adapted from Aaker and Keller, 1990)

Fit was positively associated with acceptability. It was measured as complementarity, substitutability and transferability. Complementarity concerns the matching of the new product with the parent expertise, thus skiing goggles would be a complementary product for a maker of skis. Substitutability applies when the new product could be used instead of the parent product; for example, snow boards would substitute for skis. Transferability relates to manufacture rather than usage; whether or not the producer of the parent product is believed to have the capacity to produce the offspring product. For example, a firm that made skis would not necessarily be seen as the best organization to manufacture snow-making equipment but would be acceptable for ice skates. This account of fit is neat but it may be inadequate when faced with brands like Chanel which embrace a wide variety of product types (e.g. fragrances, jewellery, clothing, skin care products). Although Chanel products share a quality image, they differ in other respects.

The second factor, the perceived quality of the parent brand, was positively associated with the acceptability of the extension according to Aaker and Keller, but only when there was a good fit. The third factor, the degree of difficulty perceived about making the extension, was positively associated when the difficulty was moderate: extensions that were very easy to make and very difficult to make were less acceptable. This may be explained in a number of ways. Aaker and Keller suggest that consumers might think that an easily made extension was overpriced. An alternative explanation relates to the cognitive effort involved. An easily made extension may take less effort to comprehend and may therefore not disturb a person's mental representation. When people have to do cognitive work on an idea, they may connect it with existing concepts, thus raising awareness of the extension. However, if the cognitive work required is too complicated, the extension may be rejected. Thus, an extension requiring moderate cognitive effort may be most acceptable. Related to this explanation, Hartman, Price and Duncan (1990) suggest that people will try to make sense of an extension but, if it differs too much from the parent product, they may dismiss the idea of the new product. Supporting Hartman et al., Meyers-Levy and Tybout (1989) showed that one unusual characteristic increased cognitive processing but too many unusual characteristics reduced it. In sum, the very obvious may be ignored and the inexplicable may be rejected.

Sunde and Brodie (1993) failed to replicate Aaker and Keller's (1990) findings. Following this, Bottomley and Holden (2001) reviewed the evidence on the acceptability of brand extension. They used data from the original Aaker and Keller (1990) study and from seven replications. They found that the original contentions of Aaker and Keller were broadly supported: fit makes an extension more acceptable and the quality of the parent brands increases acceptability provided that there is some fit. However, we should note that Aaker and Keller's method is quite weak; it rests on the judgement of respondents about how they will behave in hypothetical circumstances and this judgement can be mistaken.

Batra, Lenk and Wedel (2010) suggest that the success of an extension depends on the atypicality of the parent brand as well as the fit of the extension. By *atypicality* they mean having abstract (rather than concrete) associations since these can link to a wider range of categories. They suggest that a beer brand such as Corona, which has 'lifestyle' associations, is atypical compared to Heineken which is sold more on its performance as a beer. Batra et al. proposed a personality measuring procedure covering the brand and the category that permits assessment of atypicality. Their initial results are promising but this work still rests on the perceptions of consumers rather than their purchasing, which is the ultimate test. The circumstances governing the success of an extension are also covered by Keller and Lehmann (2006) in a wide-ranging review of the field.

Effective Marketing

Völckner and Sattler (2006) investigated ten factors that might predict extension success and found that fit was the most important; however, they found that marketing support and retailer acceptance were also needed. This suggests that marketing effectiveness may play a large part in brand extension success. Some poorly fitting extensions have worked because the appropriate marketing structures were available. Marks and Spencer, originally known for clothing, successfully diversified into food because they had an effective system of sourcing and distribution; Bic, known for disposable ballpoints and lighters, succeeded with a sailboard extension. Neither of these extensions were obvious fits. McWilliam (1993) points out that marketers are very reluctant to see a failure as the result of poor marketing, but this is often the reason. The potential of a category extension is affected by market size, product quality, market growth, economies of scale, distribution structures and profit margin, all of which should influence the marketing strategy. From this standpoint, some incongruous extensions may succeed because they are well marketed.

So, can we predict extension success?

It is clearly important that we understand how brands are accepted or rejected and therefore what scope there is for extracting more profit from a brand. However, the potential of a brand is difficult to measure. First, it seems likely that the unconscious cognitive activity involved in brand choice is large and, because it is unconscious, it is difficult to represent and measure this activity. Another problem is that brand choice is contextual. It occurs under a variety of circumstances and these different circumstances will relate to different parts of a consumer's mental representation map. This problem is aggravated when we take account of the way mental representations differ between people. The theory of mental representations may serve as a description of why certain effects are found, but it has limited value as a predictive model.

We are also rather sceptical about the methods used to determine the acceptability of potential extensions such as that by Aaker and Keller (1990). We do not dispute the findings of such work, now checked by Bottomley and Holden (2001). What we dispute is the generalizability of these findings to everyday life. Under research conditions, people will report on perceived quality and fit but, in the field, marketing activity and consumer adaptability may overcome lack of fit. In addition, until the work of Sattler et al. (2010), research in this area has focused on the acceptability of the extension without taking account of price and therefore profitability.

Despite these problems, there are some areas of promise. It is clear that brands do have value in the sense that people associate more benefits with some well-known brands and may pay more for a branded product than a functionally equivalent anonymous product. Tests based on such comparisons are likely to indicate brand strength and extension potential.

SECTION 3: SALES LOSSES BY THE PARENT OF A LINE EXTENSION

Sometimes a new entrant enlarges a market so that all the brands gain. One example was when Pampers entered the disposable diapers market in South Africa (Broadbent, 2000). Their campaign helped the category to become established as an alternative to cloth diapers and this helped Pampers' competitors to sell more volume. But this is unusual. Normally, markets have fairly static aggregate sales over the medium term so that the sales gained by a new brand are another brand's loss. When this applies, it is important to know how a new entrant takes sales from the existing players since this helps to decide a manager's strategy. This sales effect is often large when a line extension is launched, because existing lines can easily be substituted by the new line: the new line *cannibalizes* the existing lines. Sometimes, cannibalization is enforced by retailers who refuse to give manufacturers additional shelf space for a new line and stipulate that some other line in their portfolio must be abandoned in order to provide space. 'Line in, line out' is the terse name for this retailer practice. When extra space is given and the new line can compete with the previously established brands, there are two sales patterns that can occur:

- Existing brands may lose sales to the new entrant in proportion to their market share. This is the basic effect that may be expected when there are no special affinities between brands.
- An extra loss of sales occurs among brands that are perceived to be similar to the new entrant. With a line extension, the main similarity is likely to be the common brand name, with the result that the parent loses more sales than would be expected from market share alone. Extra losses may also be incurred when there are similarities of formulation, packaging, pricing, positioning, targeting, distribution and physical proximity to other brands in the store.[2]

Some data on the British detergent market illustrate the way in which consumers shift support from existing brands to a new brand. Table 3.1 shows how, 20 weeks after launch, the first liquid detergent on the British market, Wisk, was taking customers from other brands (right-hand column). Wisk was a new brand and took share from other brands roughly in relation to their market share (the correlation is 0.85), though Surf, with its value-for-money positioning, seemed to resist loss better. Because the sales loss is proportional to existing share, big brands lose more volume than small brands.

This effect was further investigated in a study by Lomax et al. (1996). Using new data, this work confirmed that Wisk took share in relation to the market share of the other brands. A second study by Lomax et al. showed the cannibalization effect of the same

Table 3.1 Brand market shares and percentage of Wisk gain 20 weeks after Wisk launch (AGB Data, 1992)

Brand	Midland market share before Wisk launch	Contribution to Wisk sales after launch
Persil	28	27
Ariel	17	22
Surf	16	8
Bold	14	12
Daz	9	11
Other brands	16	15
No previous purchase	–	5

brand name when a concentrated version of a German detergent took disproportionately more sales from its parent than from other brands. In a third study, Lomax et al. examined the gains of the Ariel liquid detergent that followed Wisk onto the British market. Here there was a parent powder brand and it was anticipated that this would be cannibalized by the new liquid formulation, but this did not occur. Instead, Ariel liquid gained sales at the expense of the whole powder section. Though unexpected, this finding is consistent with a notion of *cannibalization barriers* introduced by Buday (1989). Consumers apparently saw the new product in relation to its formulation rather than its branding. In the language of mental representations, there may be limited linkage between versions of the brand across formulations. This seems to be an advantage but there is a danger that, when this occurs, the new entrant will gain less benefit from the common brand name. A fourth study examined the sales of Persil Liquid, which was launched after Ariel Liquid; again the impact on the parent powder was not disproportionate.

This work shows that cannibalization is not inevitable. More generally, it seems likely that it is reduced by pricing, targeting and positioning the brand so that it is more similar to competitor brands and less similar to the manufacturer's existing brands.

SUMMARY

Memory can be represented as a network of interlinked nodes. Thinking involves the activation of parts of this network. The whole network represents long-term memory. Short-term memory is the currently activated section of the network. Within this system, brand knowledge has two aspects: brand image – the range of brand associations – and brand awareness, which is the retrieval of the brand via the associations using recall or recognition.

Brand equity is the value added to the basic product by branding. It is thought that brand equity is greater when the attitude to the brand is more positive, when the range of associations is large and strongly linked, when awareness is high and where the brand is prominent, well marketed and has large market share. In practice, there is no coherent way of measuring and aggregating all these factors so either perceived quality is used as a proxy for brand equity or it is measured by showing the difference in the value created when branded and unbranded products are promoted.

Marketers want to know whether a category extension will succeed. This has been approached by examining consumer judgements about different extension propositions. Acceptance is greater when the proposed extension *fits* the parent because it complements or substitutes for the parent product and when the parent is seen as suited to producing the offspring product. Acceptance of a fitting product is increased when the parent is seen to be high quality. However, this approach has been criticized for ignoring marketing expertise in the launch of an extension. Some fitting extensions have failed and some non-fitting ones succeeded and it is likely that success or failure owes a great deal to effective marketing.

When line extensions are launched, they often take a large proportion of their sales from the parent. Sometimes, this is accepted as part of the evolution of the product, but it is attractive to get extra sales from a line extension. There has therefore been interest in how a new entrant to a market draws sales from existing players. Sometimes, the sales losses of the parent are modest because consumers use formulation, price or another factor to distinguish the new line from the parent.

Additional Resources

Read Keller and Lehmann (2006) to understand one approach to brand equity and the scope for predicting successful extensions. For a more comprehensive treatment read Dall'Olmo Riley's (2010) introduction to the four-volume book of papers titled *Brand Management*.

Notes

1 A well-known method of valuing brands in this way is by the Interbrand Group. Seven factors are considered: leadership, stability, market stability, internationalization, trend, support and protection. Simon and Sullivan (1993) describe a method that compares branded and unbranded cash flows. Others have used the stock market to indicate the value of brands by subtracting the value of fixed assets from the market valuation.
2 These affinity effects are also seen when consumers buy more than one brand in a category. When they do this, their selection of brands may be linked by a common characteristic such as brand name or product formulation. This is discussed in Chapter 4.

4 Stationary Markets

LEARNING OBJECTIVES

When you have completed this chapter, you should be able to:

1 Describe the typical patterns of purchase found in mature, stationary markets.
2 Explain the role of stationary market models in evaluating brand performance.
3 Discuss the importance to sales of both light and heavy buyers.
4 Explain how market regularities set limits to marketing objectives.

OVERVIEW

Research on market patterns is done by analysis of the data provided by market research companies. In particular, academic researchers use the findings of consumer panel studies, described in Chapter 2, which are conducted by companies such as IRI, Taylor Nelson Sofres (now in WPP's Kantar group), GfK and Nielsen. Consumer panels record the purchases of many hundreds or thousands of individual households for several years. From such records we can see that most mature consumer markets are approximately stationary (i.e. brand sales change little from year to year).

In order to judge how a consumer brand is performing in a stationary market, we need to know the patterns of purchase that are commonly found in such markets. Then we can see whether a brand is behaving in a normal manner, or whether there are exceptional aspects to its sales. Marketing scientists have established elegant mathematical models that are very effective at mimicking the patterns found in stationary markets that are revealed by panel data. These models have been so successful that they now provide us with sales norms that can be used to assess the performance of a brand. When brand performance differs from the stationary market prediction, we can investigate why this is so. This work applies primarily to consumer goods and services and to frequently purchased repertoire markets (where consumers often buy more than one brand in the category).

SECTION 1: MODELLING MATURE MARKETS

The Stability of Mature Markets

In this chapter, we are mainly concerned with established consumer markets rather than markets for new goods or services or business markets. Established, or mature, markets cover the majority of our purchases. An important feature of these markets is that they usually do not change much (in terms of the market shares of the major brands) and are therefore described as *near-stationary*. Changes do sometimes occur in mature markets: whole sub-markets may decline, e.g. the 1980s saw a decline in the consumption of bitter beer and a corresponding rise in lager drinking in the UK. Normally, such changes occur quite slowly over a period of years. Only exceptionally do we see rapid changes that become permanent for specific brands or for the whole category. Such changes may occur when adverse publicity about a product damages its reputation, or when an advertising campaign is particularly successful (e.g. Stella Artois gained substantial share in the British lager market in the mid-1980s following a very successful advertising campaign). Markets may also change over short periods because of sales promotions but, usually, these gains are not maintained when the promotion finishes (Ehrenberg and England, 1990; Ehrenberg, Hammond and Goodhardt, 1994a). Because promotions run for short periods, the gains they produce have little effect when averaged over several months and, often, promotional gains are counter-balanced by losses when competitors run promotions. As a result, the market looks quite stable over a period of several months or a year.

One reason for the relative stability of markets has been explained in Chapters 1 and 2. Individuals form habits of purchase that limit change. In Chapter 2, we noted that a typical brand loses about 15 per cent of its customers over a year, and that these customer losses are usually offset by customer gains.

The Value of Mathematical Models

If a market does not change, brand performance measures, such as repeat purchase, the relative number of heavy and light buyers and the pattern of cross-brand buying in a category, will be much the same each time they are measured for a period of the same length. An effective mathematical model will let us predict these brand performance measures from other simple brand statistics. If a model is routinely effective, it acquires diagnostic value. When the observed brand performance does not fit predictions from the model, we need to find out why this is so and we may have to adjust our marketing support for the brand. The model used to predict the purchase patterns for a single brand is the negative binomial distribution (known as the NBD), while a more complex model used for predicting purchasing and cross-buying for competing brands is the Dirichlet (pronounced: *Dir-eesh-lay*).

Early research on brand modelling was conducted by Ehrenberg (e.g. papers in 1959, 1969) and then brought together in *Repeat Buying: Theory and Applications* (Ehrenberg, 1988, first published 1972). This book attacked conventional beliefs in marketing and caused a reappraisal of some of the traditional ideas about brand loyalty, brand positioning, the effects of advertising and the way in which sales grow. It was followed by work in the USA investigating the mathematical properties of stationary market models. Morrison and Schmittlein (1981, 1988), for example, gave detailed attention to the precision of models and to the modifications that might improve this precision.

Mathematical models can also be applied to other forms of stable repetitive behaviour. Goodhardt, Ehrenberg and Collins (1975, updated 1987) used such a model to study television audiences. Another application has been to store choice, with store groups being treated as brands (Kau and Ehrenberg, 1984; Wright, Sharp and Sharp, 1998). It is also possible to model other category divisions such as a pack-size (Singh, 2008). Models can be used to predict the performance of brand aggregations (e.g. all private label brands in a category, or a combination of many small brands in an 'other brands' grouping).

Stationary market research does not explain *why* some people buy more than others and one brand rather than another. Some critics argue that the lack of attention to such motivational issues limits the application of these models, particularly when the marketer is trying to induce change. What do you put in advertisements if consumer motivations are unknown? Do those who buy more have different reasons from those who buy less? Why do people avoid some brands? When markets do expand or contract, these changes may reflect changes in motivation, income or other household circumstances. But theorists such as Ehrenberg do not claim to cover all the problems that arise in marketing and specifically exclude motivation. What they do describe is the quantitative form of stable markets; if a market is stationary, the numerical predictions from the model are usually very close to the observations derived from panel data. If the market is not stationary, the difference between the observed facts and the model prediction is often instructive and may help us to understand the relative performance of different brands.

Definitions

Before we examine the patterns of purchase found in mature markets, the reader should be clear about the meaning of a number of terms. First, we usually work with *purchase occasions* rather than sales. On a purchase occasion, a buyer buys one or more units of a brand. In most markets, consumers buy one unit at a time so that purchase occasions are approximately equal to sales. Other important definitions are:

- The *penetration*, *b*, which is the proportion of all potential buyers (in the population we are studying) who buy a brand at least once in a period. (Think: *b* for b̲uyers.)
- The *purchase frequency*, *w*, which is the average number of purchases made by those who purchase *at least once* in a period. (Think: *w* for purchase w̲eight.)
- The *mean population purchase rate*, *m*, the number of purchase occasions in the period made by an average member of the population. (Think: *m* for m̲ean.) When *b* is expressed as a percentage, *m* will be the sales per hundred of the population.

These variables are linked by the *sales equation*:

$$m = bw$$

Thus when the penetration of Persil over three months is 0.25 and the purchase frequency is 4, m = 0.25 × 4 or 1. (In words: when a quarter of the population buy Persil, on average four times, then the average purchase occasion rate in the whole population is one.)

When people buy more than one unit per purchase occasion, we multiply by a correcting factor to get the sales rate. For example, if people buy, on average, 1.2 units of Persil per purchase occasion then the mean population *sales rate* m_s, will be given by:

$$m_s = 0.25 \times 4 \times 1.2 = 1.2.$$

Exercise 4.1   Applying the sales equation

1   In a stationary market, the penetration of Senso toothpaste is 0.07 over 24 weeks. Over 24 weeks, there are 21 purchases of Senso per hundred people in the population. What is the purchase frequency?
2   How many purchase occasions per 100 consumers will there be in 48 weeks?
3   If the purchase frequency for the 48-week period is 4.6, what are the mean sales and penetration?

Answers:

1   0.21/0.07 = 3.
2   In a stationary market, you double the purchase occasions if you double the period: 42 per 100.
3   $m = bw$; therefore 0.42 = b × 4.6. So b = 0.42/4.6 = 0.09, or 9 per cent.

SECTION 2: SINGLE BRAND PURCHASE PATTERNS

The Impact of Recent Purchase

How does recent purchase experience affect the next purchase? In particular, is there a bias towards purchasing the same brand as last time? Consider two people who have both bought Persil and Ariel an equal number of times over the last six months, as below:

Philip: Ariel, Ariel, Persil, Persil
Elizabeth: Persil, Ariel, Persil, Ariel

Both Philip and Elizabeth have bought Persil twice. Who is most likely to buy Persil at their next purchase? If people learn more from their recent experience, Philip is more likely to buy Persil next time. This is a *first-order* explanation because it relates to the last purchase. A *zero-order* explanation takes no account of the order of prior purchases and here there would be no difference between Philip and Elizabeth in terms of their likelihood of purchasing Persil. When the explanation is zero-order we can predict the likelihood of a future brand purchase using only the ratio of past brand purchases.

Since people do occasionally switch brands, their most recent purchase should be a slightly better guide to their next purchase than earlier purchases. Kuehn (1962) found some evidence to support a first-order effect; however, a study by Bass et al. (1984) showed that the majority of purchases in most markets are zero-order. All studies have their weaknesses and Kahn, Morrison and Wright (1986) argued that, because *household* panel data were used by Bass et al., the first-order behaviour of *individuals* might have been obscured. However, on balance, it seems likely that a zero-order pattern of purchase is more common in stable markets and that habit, rather than learning, provides the best way of thinking about repetitive purchase.

Do Consumers Buy at Regular Intervals?

We have habits about *what* we buy, but are we also habitual about *when* we buy? Purchase time habits would show up in panel data as an individual tendency to buy a category once a week or once a month. Habits of this sort would mean that a purchaser's probability of buying rises sharply at intervals. This pattern is also found for some frequent purchases, such as newspapers or cigarettes. It also applies to shopping trips (Dunn, Reader and Wrigley, 1983). Kahn and Schmittlein (1989) report that households tend to be loyal to a particular day for grocery shopping, and East et al. (1994) found that the majority of supermarket users were also loyal to particular times of the day (Chapter 11).

Despite the routine timing of many shopping trips, brands are usually bought at irregular intervals. There are several reasons for this. First, we should note that most brands are bought quite infrequently. For example, a typical US household buys a specific coffee brand about three times a year and the category about nine times a year. This gives an average inter-purchase interval between purchases of any brand of instant coffee of five to six weeks. Actual intervals are quite varied because household consumption may fluctuate and shoppers may stockpile or run out. The prediction of when a specific brand will be rebought is even more irregular because other brands in a category may be bought instead. So, although there is a long-term average frequency of brand buying, brand purchase occurs at irregular times. Mathematicians describe this random pattern as a *Poisson* distribution.

However, people rarely buy a brand again immediately after purchasing it. Because of this 'dead time' after purchase, the Poisson distribution does not fit well for short periods (such as a week or less). Over the longer periods covered in panel research, the fit of the Poisson assumption is close and provides a basis for the mathematical models described later.

How Does Purchase Frequency Vary?

People differ widely in how much they buy of the category and of specific brands. The range of purchase frequencies in a sample of buyers has a form that is described by the *Gamma* distribution, like the one illustrated in Figure 4.1. This is a histogram of purchases of a frequently bought category in which the largest number of buyers usually occurs at the lowest purchase frequency.

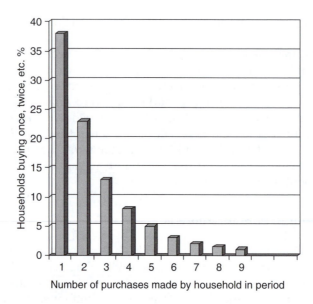

Figure 4.1   Gamma distribution of purchase for a brand showing that there are many light buyers and few heavy buyers

Few people buy heavily but those who do so are responsible for a large proportion of a brand's sales. Table 4.1 illustrates this with the purchases of Kellogg's Corn Flakes in the USA. In Table 4.1, you see that a sample of 100 households have bought 210 purchases of Kellogg's Corn Flakes, 2.1 per household, in three months. This average is based on the 55 per cent who bought once, 22 per cent who bought twice, 8 per cent who bought three times and so forth (a typical Gamma distribution). When we work out the sales from these sub-groups we get the NBD distribution, outlined in Section 1. This is the bottom row of Table 4.1 and it shows how important the few heavy buyers are for sales. Those who bought six or more times – 5 per cent of all purchasers – were responsible for 20 per cent of sales.

In general, a substantial proportion of purchases are made by relatively few heavy buyers; one rule of thumb, the *heavy-half* principle, is that the lighter-buying 50 per cent are responsible for about 20 per cent of all purchases while the heavier-buying 50 per cent

Table 4.1   Three-month sales of Kellogg's Corn Flakes in the USA (adapted from Ehrenberg and Goodhardt, 1979)

Penetration (%)	Purchase frequency	*Out of 100 purchasers, the number buying:*						
20	*2.1*	*Once*	*Twice*	*3 times*	*4 times*	*5 times*	*6+ times*	*Total*
		55	22	8	5	5	5	100
		Number of purchases:						
		55	44	24	20	25	42	210

are responsible for the other 80 per cent. When this rule applies, we find that the heaviest 20 per cent are responsible for about 50 per cent of sales. If you inspect Table 4.1 you will see that the 55 per cent buying once are responsible for 26 per cent of purchases and the heaviest 23 per cent (buying three or more times) are responsible for 53 per cent of purchases, so the data in Table 4.1 fit the heavy-half rule quite well. Other ratio rules are more extreme. The best known is the 80:20 rule, that 80 per cent of purchases are made by the heaviest buying 20 per cent of customers. The precise ratio depends partly on the category. For example, if we investigated those with savings accounts, we might find that very few heavy savers were responsible for a large part of the total savings in a savings institution. The ratio is less extreme when there is a natural ceiling on purchase within the time period being studied, e.g. people rarely buy more than one newspaper a day.

Ratios also depend on the period of time used to collect data. Because they buy frequently, most heavy buyers will be sampled in any short purchase period. Light buyers may not get round to buying in a short period but, as the period lengthens, more of them are captured. Therefore, if purchase data for instant coffee are collected over a period of years instead of months, a greater proportion of light buyers are recorded and the ratio moves from approximately heavy-half to approximately 80:20. Ratio rules were first highlighted by Pareto, an Italian economist, and they are reviewed by Schmittlein, Cooper and Morrison (1993).

The heavy-half principle shows that heavy buyers are an attractive segment in many markets and marketers may therefore try to focus their efforts on them. For example, promotions may give progressively more attractive benefits to those who buy more and the frequent-flyer schemes that airlines run are designed to benefit the heavier users. Sometimes, it is possible to target the heavy buyers by using a particular distribution system. For example, a wine warehouse, which sells wine by the case, may secure a larger proportion of heavy wine buyers than a supermarket. Also, it may be useful to focus research on heavy buyers since they are responsible for so much of the profit (e.g. Hammond and Ehrenberg, 1995). In B2B marketing, *key account management* has become a recognized speciality (the key accounts are the few big ones).

Ratio rules can apply to any phenomenon and Box 4.1 provides an interesting example. Another application has been to the imprisonment of offenders. If most crimes are committed by a relatively small group of offenders, crime will go down if these offenders are imprisoned for longer.

Box 4.1	Weight of consumption among feline consumers (Churcher and Lawton, 1987)

An interesting demonstration of how consumption varies was provided by a study of what the cat brought home to households in a Bedfordshire village. Over 70 domestic cats were studied over a year and their tendency to kill and bring home sparrows, frogs, rabbits, mice and so on was studied. One cat was responsible for 10 per cent of the total kill while, at the other end of the distribution, several cats brought back nothing in a whole year.

The ratio of light to heavy buyers depends on the break point chosen but we can compare the top 20 per cent of customers that is typically responsible for 50 per cent of sales with the bottom 80 per cent of customers that is responsible for the other 50 per cent. On this basis, light buyers are four times as numerous as heavy buyers. Because of their numbers, light buyers *in aggregate* may offer more scope for sales gain than the heavy buyers. However, when purchasers of a brand are considered *individually,* it is clear that more attention should be given to the few heavy buyers. This is partly because they could buy more and partly because their loss could be very damaging. Mass communications such as advertising are effective at reaching the large number of light buyers but, when marketing to customers needs substantial resources, it is better to concentrate on the heavy buyers.

It is easy to be confused by stationary market evidence. Although relatively few heavy buyers are responsible for a substantial proportion of sales, this does not mean that heavy buyers are responsible for most of the gain or loss when sales change. First, as noted, this depends on the proportion of buyers that are treated as 'heavy'. If this is only the heaviest 20 per cent, any change in buying patterns may be more obvious amongst the more numerous light buyers. Second, we find that light buyers tend to change their purchasing *proportionately* more than heavy buyers. As a result, light (and new) buyers are responsible for a large part of any gain in sales when a brand improves its market share. But when the new pattern of sales has stabilized, we are likely to still find that 20 per cent of buyers are again responsible for 50 per cent of sales as a number of light buyers will have been converted to heavy buyers. This analysis means that marketers must not ignore the light buyers since their purchasing is more changeable and, from their ranks, some new heavy buyers may emerge. Further, as discussed in Chapter 5, heavy buyers show some regression to the mean; that is, they do not necessarily stay as heavy buyers.[1] This evidence that sales gains come mostly from new and light buyers may surprise those who are wedded to relationship marketing with its emphasis on retaining customers. A popular book, *How Brands Grow* by Sharp (2010) has highlighted the fact that brands grow mostly by acquiring new buyers. This text draws on research by Riebe et al. (forthcoming) on pharmaceuticals and banking which shows that brands grow mainly because of customer acquisition and brands decline mainly because they fail to acquire new customers.

How Does the Type of Product Affect Purchase?

Brands in product categories that differ substantially (e.g. food products and household cleaners) may show similar patterns of customer purchase. For example, if two brands in quite different categories have the same purchase frequency and penetration, they will have much the same sole brand loyalty and repeat purchase rates. Effectively, the purchase characteristics of a brand are captured by purchase frequency and penetration, and a variety of other brand performance statistics can be predicted from these measures. This means that the specific brand or category need not be known in order to predict these brand performance measures, provided that we know the purchase frequency and penetration of the brand.

Repeat Purchase

If we compare any two adjacent sales periods, e.g. two quarters, we find that many of the buyers of a brand in quarter 1 (Q1) return in Q2, particularly the heavier buyers. But some do not return and these 'lapsed' buyers are replaced by an approximately equal number of 'new' buyers. These 'new' buyers are mostly light buyers of the brand, like those that they replace, and although they did not buy in Q1, they have usually bought the brand before and are not really new. At Q3 about the same proportion of Q2 buyers drop out and are replaced by others, including some of those who lapsed after Q1. This intermittent pattern of purchase does not show loss of loyalty but instead reflects the fact that many people buy a brand so infrequently that they often miss quarters. The change of buyers at each quarter is explained mainly as a probability effect, though a small part of the effect is due to more permanent acquisition of, and defection from, the brand.

This analysis helps us to understand that repeat purchase rates depend mainly on purchase frequency. A household that buys four times in one quarter is more likely to re-buy in the next quarter than one that bought only once, since the latter household may not need to buy again so soon. Because heavier buyers are more likely to repeat, we find that the purchase frequency of repeat purchasers is higher than the rate for the whole sample (by about 20 per cent). In addition, new purchasers tend to be light buyers and, whatever the category, their purchase rate usually does not rise much above 1.5 for any period.

Table 4.2 Repeat purchase for given purchase frequencies and penetrations

	Baseline case	Tenfold increase in penetration	Tenfold increase in purchase frequency
Penetration as %	2	2	20
Purchase frequency	2	20	2
Repeat purchase as %	57	85	60

Although repeat-purchase rates depend mainly on purchase frequency, penetration does have a small effect, illustrated in Table 4.2. Compare the baseline column with the next and you see that a tenfold increase in purchase frequency has a substantial effect on repeat purchase, raising it from 57 per cent to 85 per cent; compare the baseline column with the last and you see that repeat purchase moves only three points when the penetration increases tenfold. Note that it is the repeat purchase *rate* that is slightly affected by penetration. The *number* of repeat purchasers is directly affected by penetration; that is, as larger brands have more purchasers, they also have commensurately more repeat purchasers, even if the repeat purchase rate is little different.

Repeat purchase is an important diagnostic measure. If the purchase frequency for a reporting period indicates a repeat purchase rate of 50 per cent under stationary market conditions, then consistent deviations from this figure indicate that the market does not have the normal stationary characteristics. One application of this thinking was reported by Ehrenberg (1988: 97–98). A brand launched 18 months before was being heavily advertised but, despite this, sales were constant. Two explanations were possible:

- The advertising was ineffective and the brand was creating normal repeat purchase.
- The advertising was effective, consumers were trying the brand, but they were not repeat purchasing so the brand was not gaining sales.

To distinguish these two we derive the normal repeat-purchase rate for a stationary market and see whether this is what is found in the panel data. Evidence that repeat purchase is normal favours the first explanation and means that the advertising should be changed or stopped. Evidence that the repeat purchase is below the normal level supports the second explanation. In this case, the evidence suggested that the brand was weak, and that sales would collapse when the pool of potential trialists was exhausted, so the brand should be dropped before more advertising money was wasted. This case is presented in Exercise 4.4 below.

NBD (Negative Binomial Distribution) Theory

Negative binomial distribution (NBD) theory is a mathematical model that enables the prediction of repeat purchase and other brand performance measures from data on the penetration and purchase frequency of the brand for any given reporting period. NBD theory is based on the assumptions that the purchasing of a brand is stationary, that individual purchases follow a Poisson distribution, and that the long-run average purchase rates of individuals follow a Gamma distribution. These assumptions are set out by Ehrenberg (1988: ch4).[2]

Box 4.2	Does the NBD give the best prediction?

Marketing scientists have tried to improve on the predictions derived from the NBD by adjustment of the mathematics. One suggestion is that NBD theory might be modified to allow for the temporary loss of buying interest following a purchase. But any gain would be marginal since the theory is already very close to panel evidence. Usually, the random variation in consumer panel data is rather larger than any difference between the predictions of competing mathematical models. In a comparison of theories, Schmittlein, Bemmaor and Morrison (1985) concluded that the NBD model was hard to beat. A further paper by Morrison and Schmittlein (1988) identified three ways in which real behaviour tended to depart from NBD assumptions but noted that these effects tended to cancel each other out so that the NBD remained a good predictive model.

NBD Program

When purchase frequency and penetration are known, the NBD program (available from the Sage website) estimates a range of brand performance statistics. This computer program requires data on the penetration, purchase frequency and data collection period and computes repeat purchase and new purchase rates for different periods. The Gamma distribution of persons buying once, twice, etc. is worked out for each period and the proportion of sales attributable to different rates of purchase is calculated (the negative binomial distribution). These figures are tabled on the screen and the user then has options to change the rounding and to express data as proportions, percentages or actual numbers. A copy of the screened figures can be recorded as a file for printing.

Table 4.3 shows the output for Kellogg's Corn Flakes using the figures shown in Table 4.1 (a three-month penetration of 20 per cent and a purchase frequency of 2.1). Because the program does not have a three-month column, the figures were assigned to the 12-weeks period (highlighted). If you look down this column you see the input penetration and purchase frequency, then the predicted repeat purchase rate of about 62 per cent. Below this is the purchase frequency of repeat buyers, which is always found to be about 20 per cent higher than the purchase frequency of the whole group, and the purchase frequency of new buyers (usually not much greater than 1.5). The program estimates the number of buyers buying once, twice, etc. and then calculates the sale proportions contributed by these segments. In Table 4.4, the empirical data from Table 4.1 are compared with the theoretical predictions. If you inspect Table 4.4 you will see that the agreement is close.

Table 4.3 Output from NBD program (figures rounded to 2 decimal places)

	1 day	1 wk	4 wks	12 wks	24 wks	48 wks	1 yr
Penetration (b)	0.00	0.03	0.10	0.20	0.28	0.36	0.36
Purchase frequency (w)	1.02	1.11	1.40	2.10	3.04	4.73	5.01
Repeat purchase (%)	2.97	16.82	40.99	61.65	71.61	78.88	79.60
Purchase frequency of repeat buyers	1.03	1.18	1.63	2.55	3.67	5.60	5.91
Purchase frequency of new buyers	1.01	1.09	1.24	1.38	1.45	1.49	1.49
Proportion –							
not buying	1.00	0.97	0.90	0.80	0.72	0.64	0.64
buying once	0.00	0.03	0.07	0.11	0.11	0.11	0.11
twice	0.00	0.00	0.02	0.04	0.06	0.06	0.06
3 times	0.00	0.00	0.01	0.02	0.03	0.04	0.04
4 times	0.00	0.00	0.00	0.01	0.02	0.03	0.03
5 times	0.00	0.00	0.00	0.01	0.01	0.02	0.02
6 +	0.00	0.00	0.00	0.01	0.04	0.10	0.10
Proportion of sales due to those buying –							
once	0.97	0.82	0.52	0.25	0.14	0.07	0.06
twice	0.03	0.15	0.26	0.21	0.13	0.07	0.07
3 times	0.00	0.03	0.12	0.15	0.12	0.07	0.07
4 times	0.00	0.00	0.05	0.11	0.10	0.07	0.06
5 times	0.00	0.00	0.02	0.08	0.09	0.06	0.06
6 +	0.00	0.00	0.02	0.19	0.43	0.66	0.69

The output of the NBD program also allows us to see how penetration and purchase frequency change when periods of different duration are used. Table 4.5 shows how the penetration and purchase frequency rise as the period of time is successively doubled (Table 4.5 is obtained by assigning figures to incorrect time periods in program NBD, e.g. the 12-week figures are assigned to 48 weeks so that the tabled 12- and 24-week figures are then actually 3 and 6 weeks). Mean sales are given by the product of penetration and purchase frequency; in a stationary market, these must keep step with the time period, as recorded in the bottom row. Table 4.5 shows that each doubling in the period produces about the same absolute penetration increase. When the penetration is low, changes in sales are mainly related to changes in penetration. When penetration is high and approaching a ceiling, the sales changes appear as changes in purchase frequency.

Table 4.4   Quarterly sales of Corn Flakes in the USA (observed (O) and theoretical (T) values)

Out of 100 purchases, the number buying:

Once		Twice		3 times		4 times		5 times		6+ times	
O	T	O	T	O	T	O	T	O	T	O	T
55	53	22	22	8	11	5	6	5	4	5	6

Giving sales of:

55	53	44	44	24	33	20	24	25	20	42	36

Table 4.5   Change in purchase data over time (theoretical)

	3 wks	6 wks	12 wks	24 wks	48 wks	96 wks	192 wks
Penetration (b)	0.08	0.13	0.20	0.28	0.36	0.44	0.51
Purchase frequency (w)	1.3	1.6	2.1	3.0	4.7	7.8	13.5
Mean sales (bw)	0.1	0.2	0.4	0.9	1.7	3.4	6.9

Program NBD is easy to use and is needed to answer questions in Exercises 4.2 to 4.4. It has one technical limitation: when the penetration is high and the purchase frequency is very low, the mathematical procedure for estimating the parameter k breaks down and the user must then extrapolate from results obtained with lower penetration figures.

Exercise 4.2	Using the NBD program: how the period affects the data

1   Assume that 0.05 of the population buys an average of 1.5 Snickers in each 4-week period. Use program NBD to establish the penetration, b, and the purchase frequency, w, and mean sales, m (= bw), for the given periods and fill in the table below. (If you enter the 4-week data as 1-week data all results will be for four times the tabled period.)

Weeks:	6	12	24	48	96	192
b:						
w:						
bw:						

2   Can you compute the proportion of the population who buy *no* Snickers in four years?
3   Notice that the purchase rate for new buyers is relatively constant for longer periods. See whether it remains so for different b and w input data.

Exercise 4.3   Collecting panel data for comparison with NBD predictions

NBD predictions can be tested against panel data gathered by the class. You – and others – could keep a diary and record when you engage in a consumer activity such as phoning your friends or drinking beer. Table 4.6 records data from 224 students for one day together with the distribution that is predicted from the NBD model. You can see that the fit is close.

Table 4.6   Number of students making 1, 2, 3, etc. telephone calls in a day

Number calling:	Once	Twice	3 times	4 times	5 times	6+ times
Observed:	75	30	8	0	0	1
Predicted:	75	28	8	2	0	0
$b = 0.51$; $w = 1.46$						

Exercise 4.4   Marketing analyses

1   Brand R was launched 18 months ago. With continuing advertising support it has maintained a penetration of 4 per cent and a purchase frequency of 1.4 per quarter, but is scarcely viable. Panel research shows a repeat purchase rate of 21 per cent. Should you stop the advertising? Withdraw the brand? Maintain both? To answer this you need to calculate, using the NBD program, the theoretical repeat purchase and see whether it agrees with the observed figure. If the actual repeat purchase is below the stationary market norm, the brand is failing. Also, see the earlier section on repeat purchase.
2   The consumption of soup rises in the winter and falls in the summer. Find out whether all those who buy soup reduce consumption in the summer or whether there are two groups: those who buy it all the year with much the same frequency, and those who buy it only in the winter. Panel data show that those who buy soup in the

summer show a penetration of 32 per cent and a purchase frequency of 5 over 12 weeks. When these people are followed into the higher consumption winter period, panel data show that their quarterly repeat purchase is 79 per cent. What do you conclude? You need to calculate, using program NBD, whether this repeat purchase is the norm for a stationary market for the given particular levels of penetration and purchase frequency. If it is, then you have two separate groups: the all-year stationary buyers and seasonal buyers who only enter the market in the winter. For more information, see Wellan and Ehrenberg (1990).

SECTION 3: PATTERNS OF PURCHASE IN THE WHOLE CATEGORY

We now address the following questions:

- How do penetrations and purchase frequencies vary in a product category?
- What changes do we see in penetration and purchase frequency when market share changes?
- Can we predict the buying frequency and penetration of a new brand if it achieves a given market share?
- When people buy more than one brand, how is their purchase distributed between the different brands?
- Does the evidence of cross-purchase support the idea of niche positioning?
- Is television watching like brand purchasing?
- How is multi-brand purchase modelled mathematically?

Purchase Frequencies and Penetrations in a Product Field

The double jeopardy 'rule'

Table 4.7 presents data on the UK shampoo market, ordered by average sales. You can see that bigger brands (shown by market share) have greater penetrations and slightly greater purchase frequencies. This is typical of what is found in most packaged goods markets. It means that changes in brand sales will be seen mainly as changes in penetration. The low variation in purchase frequency is not so surprising. Why should one brand of shampoo be used more often than another by the people who like it?

The relationship between penetration and purchase frequency in a product field fits the pattern known as *double jeopardy* (Ehrenberg, Goodhardt and Barwise, 1990). Double jeopardy (DJ) was described by the sociologist McPhee (1963: 133–140), who credits the original idea to the broadcaster Jack Landis. McPhee noted how less-popular radio presenters suffer in two ways – fewer people have heard of them and, among those who have heard of them, they are less appreciated. Applied to brands, DJ implies the pattern seen in

Table 4.7 Market share, penetration and purchase frequency in the UK shampoo market (Taylor, Nelson, Sofres, 2005)

Shampoo brand	Market share %	Annual penetration	Purchase frequency
Head & Shoulders	11	13	2.3
Pantene	9	11	2.3
Herbal Essences	5	8	1.8
L'Oréal Elvive	5	8	1.9
Dove	5	9	1.6
Sunsilk	5	8	1.7
Vosene	2	3	1.7
Average			1.9

Table 4.7, that less popular brands are not only bought by fewer people (lower penetration) but are also bought less often (lower frequency) by those who do buy them. Ehrenberg, Goodhardt and Barwise show that DJ is a ubiquitous phenomenon, occurring not only in the purchasing of groceries, but also in such fields as the viewing of TV programmes and the purchase of consumer durables, industrial goods and newspapers.

Although DJ is easily seen, the explanation for the effect is less clear. McPhee's explanation took account of differential awareness. People who are aware of less-popular presenters are usually also aware of more-popular presenters and thus are more likely to 'split their vote' compared with those who have only heard of the more-popular broadcasters. But the DJ effect is seen in categories, such as supermarkets, where consumers are likely to be fully aware of all the major brands in a market.

We see DJ as a statistical effect. Consider a board with 100 slots that can receive counters. If you throw counters on to the board, the early ones will each tend to get a slot on their own and each time that you do this, they raise the percentage of slots with a counter (the 'penetration'). As more counters are thrown on to the board, they will increasingly land on slots where there are already counters and this will raise the average number of counters in occupied slots (the 'frequency'). Figure 4.2 shows the theoretical relationship that applies; further analysis of the theoretical double jeopardy line can be found in Habel and Rungie (2005).

Notice that the relationship is approximately linear for much of the penetration range. The statistical relationship between penetration and frequency will be disrupted in a number of ways in real markets. In particular, there may be feedback effects so that, once consumers have bought a brand, they may be more, or less, willing to buy the brand again. A second empirical effect is that some consumers will never buy in some categories. For example, those who do not own a cat rarely (if ever) buy cat food. This 'out-of-the-market' effect will vary across categories and buying segments and it means that predicted penetrations will underestimate observed penetrations, which are based only on those who are in the market.

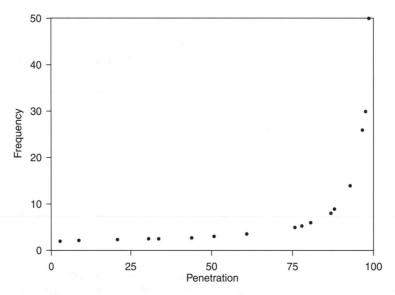

Figure 4.2   Theoretical relationship between penetration and frequency

What Else Changes When Sales Change?

Table 4.7 is useful in showing the way in which penetration and purchase frequency may be expected to change. Major changes over short periods of time are rare, but, looking at Table 4.7, if Vosene were to raise its share of sales to that of L'Oreal Elvive, it is very unlikely that it could do so by getting its existing buyers to buy two-and-a-half times as much of the brand as they currently do. The closeness of purchase frequencies across brands means that sales have to grow mainly by increasing their penetration. Sometimes a gain in frequency may be possible by persuading consumers to find new uses for a product, e.g. by eating cereals at tea-time, but this is a new use of the *category* which is likely to raise the purchase frequencies of all brands.

Some evidence on what changes when a brand gains sales comes from advertising cases. In 1982, advertising substantially increased the purchasing of Curly Wurly, a chocolate-coated toffee liked by children in the UK. Sales then remained approximately constant for the rest of the year (Channon, 1985: 168). From the published data, it appears that among children of 7–11, the two-monthly penetration increased by 60 per cent while the purchase frequency increased by a mere 6 per cent. Among adult purchasers the main gain was also in penetration. Thus, sales gains came mainly because the advertising attracted new buyers, in line with the DJ pattern. Other evidence comes from the sales of Hellman's mayonnaise (Box 4.3).

The relative constancy of purchase frequency is also important to those who are hoping to break into a market with a new brand. With enough advertising money and a sound product, marketers may occasionally achieve a high market share. If they succeed with the new brand, the DJ pattern will define how much of that success will come from penetration and how

---

Box 4.3 | **Attempts to raise purchase frequency**

There are some situations where increased consumption of a brand might be expected to come from more frequent use by existing buyers rather than by increased penetration. One such situation arose in the case of Hellman's mayonnaise when it was new to the British market. The manufacturers found that the British used Hellman's mayonnaise on little else but salads, a habit they had probably learned from earlier experience with salad cream, which looks rather like mayonnaise. The advertising for Hellman's was therefore designed to expand the number of situations in which the product could be used.

The case report (Channon, 1985) shows that, following the advertising, 40 per cent of users were trying the product in the new ways suggested in the campaign. However, the sales increase that was noted was still largely due to a gain in penetration in line with the double jeopardy rule.

---

much from purchase frequency. Supporting this, Wellan and Ehrenberg (1988) found that, after rapidly establishing leadership in the UK market, a new soap called Shield registered a purchase frequency appropriate to its new position, i.e. slightly more than its competitors.

For the reporting periods used in market research, most sales changes affect penetration but Treasure (1975) pointed out that when sales are aggregated over longer periods, changes in purchase level appear to be based more on changes in purchase frequency and less on penetration. This difference arises because of the way in which light buyers are counted over short and long periods. Over short periods, an infrequent buyer tends to be a non-buyer in the reference period and is therefore registered as a penetration gain when he or she buys in a later period. Over longer periods, the infrequent buyer is more likely to purchase in the reference period and therefore any gain in purchase in later periods will be recorded as a purchase frequency gain. There is a danger of too rigid an interpretation of the double jeopardy pattern; the important matter here is that it is light buyers that produce most of the change in brand purchase.

Patterns of Multi-brand Purchase

As we saw in Chapter 2, most buyers buy more than one brand in the category. In many grocery markets, the average share-of-category requirement (SCR) is around 30 per cent; this means that for every three purchases of a given brand, the average buyer makes seven purchases of other brands. Ehrenberg (1988) remarks that 'your buyers are the buyers of other brands who occasionally buy you'.

Is there a pattern to this multi-brand buying? There are two possibilities. One is that certain brands are mutually substitutable. If most buyers see brands X and Y as almost the same, we would expect a higher than average purchase rate for Y among purchasers of X and vice versa. Such cross-purchasing of brands would create purchase sub-sets or *market partitioning*. Ehrenberg and Goodhardt (1979) demonstrate that this effect does occasionally occur, e.g. in children's cereals where those who buy one sweetened cereal are more likely to buy another sweetened cereal rather than an unsweetened brand. An alternative pattern is that the purchase of one brand is unrelated to the purchase of other brands, and purchase rates simply reflect the penetrations of the other brands. We find both effects in grocery markets. The basic pattern is that other-brand purchasing is directly proportional to the penetrations of the other brands. Ehrenberg (1988) calls this the *duplication of purchase law*. Superimposed on this pattern are some cases of market partitioning.

Some people expect more market partitioning because they see some brands as close alternatives. But, although many of us will have our own personally preferred groupings of brands, there may be little agreement between individuals. For example, in the toothpaste market, during the course of a year one person may buy Colgate and Aquafresh, another person Aquafresh and Macleans, a third Macleans and a retailer's private label. When these diverse combinations are put together, the different individual cross-preferences will average out so that, usually, there is not much evidence of market partitioning at an aggregate level. When partitioning does occur, it can usually be connected with distinct product features such as price, product form (e.g. flavour, pack type) or a common brand name, rather than with the less tangible claims of the brand that may be identified in advertising. Collins (1971) has reviewed this issue.

Table 4.8 shows how buyers of one brand of toothpaste also bought other brands. The brands are arranged in market share order by column and row. The bottom row shows the average cross-purchase (or purchase duplication, the mean percentage of people buying a 'column' brand in addition to their 'row' brand). Table 4.8 shows some partitioning. There is a higher level of cross-purchase between Colgate GRF and Colgate gel than is implied by average cross-purchase. Compare the 32 per cent for Colgate gel bought by Colgate GRF buyers with 24 per cent average duplication, and compare the 53 per cent for GRF bought by Colgate gel buyers with 35 per cent average cross-purchase. This effect is common where two products with the same brand name compete in the same field; it provides a basis for line extension since some of the tendency to buy a brand seems to pass to the new line (see Chapter 3).

Table 4.8   Cross-purchase in the British toothpaste market (AGB Data, 1992)

Buyers of:		Who also bought:					
	Market share %	Colgate GRF %	Aquafresh %	Crest %	Macleans Fresh %	Mentadent %	Colgate gel %
Colgate GRF	18	–	19	18	20	12	32
Aquafresh	9	30	–	26	28	14	23
Crest	8	32	28	–	23	17	24
Macleans Fresh	8	31	27	20	–	12	21
Mentadent	7	28	21	22	18	–	20
Colgate gel	7	53	24	23	23	15	–
Av. cross-purchase (all brands)		35	24	22	23	14	24

Cross-purchase and Positioning

Positioning is heavily emphasized in marketing. It is the set of beliefs about the brand that the manufacturer and advertising agency seek to establish in the minds of potential purchasers: in other words, it is an *intended brand image*. One implication of the cross-purchase evidence is that new brands do not need to have some unique formulation or brand image to succeed, a finding which has worried those who attach strong importance to brand positioning. If cross-purchase between brands depends largely upon penetrations with exceptions relating only to price, formulation or brand name, we must conclude that positioning, with its implication that each brand occupies a distinct niche in the minds of consumers, is poorly supported. When advertising does succeed, it may be because it has been effective at producing high brand awareness and not because the brand is seen as subtly different from other brands in its category. Indeed, many successful brands may do well because they are perceived as typical of other brands in the category, rather than as different from those brands. Thus, manufacturers often focus on the strategy which Ehrenberg (1988) called 'me-too', i.e. copying the formulation and appearance of existing successful brands and thereby trading on established purchase habits. This is a strategy much used by retailers when they offer private label brands.

Positioning assumptions are well established in marketing. It is hard to abandon the idea that a brand has a unique selling proposition (USP), which is appreciated by consumers. This approach leads to the common idea of a niche brand, one that is appreciated by some consumer segments but not by others, even though they could buy it. This sometimes happens in fashion (see Box 4.4). Of course, advertisers do need to show that their offering fits consumer expectations but these expectations may relate more to the whole category or to variants. (As we saw in Chapter 1, there are more differences between the variants of a brand than between brands.)

The **Tesco** pack has much the same shape and design as the more established Head & Shoulders brand of Procter & Gamble

---

Box 4.4	Niche brands

Niche brands are those that are bought by one section of the population but not by other sections that could afford to buy them (in this sense, expensive brands like Porsche are not niche brands). To identify niche brands it is necessary to compare the consumers who buy different brands to see whether they differ in terms of demography or beliefs (e.g. age or politics). One study compared the demographic profiles of brand buyers in different grocery categories (Hammond, Ehrenberg and Goodhardt, 1996). This work showed very little difference between the buyers of different brands except in the case of cereals where certain brands were bought only when there were children in the household. Given this evidence, the realistic assumption is that there is normally little difference between the buyers of any two brands in a packaged goods category. This is not so surprising when

we remember that the buyers of one brand are often the buyers of another brand.

But niches can occur. One interesting case arose when the fashion designer Burberry launched a wide range of lower-price brand extensions which were taken up by 'chavs'. In the UK, chavs is a term for those perceived as 'uneducated and uncultured people' (Wikipedia). Their endorsement of Burberry was unwelcome for the fashion house because it could lead other potential buyers to avoid the brand. The chief executive, Rose Marie Bravo conceded that the adoption of Burberry by chavs may have been responsible for the half-year results (the *Daily Telegraph* (2005), 'Burberry boss is happy with the chav cheques' http://www.telegraph.co.uk/news/uknews/1480169/Burberry-boss-is-happy-with-the-chav-cheques.html).

The close association between other-brand purchase rates and penetration does not hold when brands lack a common distribution structure since the availability of brands obviously affects choice. Thus, local variation in distribution will produce local variation in other-brand purchases. This can occur with beer brands since many are regional and are not available in parts of the country. Uncles and Ehrenberg (1990) have shown this effect with stores; they found that, in the USA, the cross-purchase between two chains (Safeway and Lucky) was higher than predicted because these chains tended to have stores in the same areas.

Watching Television

Television viewing has been shown to have similarities to brand purchase (Goodhardt, Ehrenberg and Collins, 1987). When the programme is a serial, viewing the next episode is like repeat purchase and we can ask how much programme loyalty exists, as measured by repeat viewing. The evidence shows that there is loyalty, particularly for serials with very high ratings. In the UK, about 55 per cent of those watching a serial will repeat-view in the following week but this figure is derived from several different loyalties. Some people watch more than others (i.e. they are loyal to the medium) and this raises their chance of being a viewer of the next episode; some people are channel loyal so that serials on favourite channels have a better repeat-viewing chance; and some people watch more at particular times of the day so that time loyalty may enhance repeat viewing. These three loyalties ensure that people who have been watching a serial are quite likely to be tuned to the same channel at the same time of the week *after the serial has ended*. The difference between this end-of-serial viewing and the repeat viewing when the serial is running indicates the true loyalty to the programme. Such partitioning of loyalty can be applied to other categories, e.g. to the way in which loyalty to a car is divided between brand and model.

Goodhardt, Ehrenberg and Collins (1987) also found some programme partitioning, e.g. those who watch one sports programme are more likely to watch other sports programmes, but they also note that people watch a wide variety of programmes so that cross-viewing has limited partitioning. More recently, Lees and Wright (2012) found similar effects for radio audiences, with some limited partitioning between the 'talk' and 'music' formats.

Terrestrial TV is a *broadcast*, not a *narrowcast*, medium and this makes it difficult to target specific social groups accurately using the main television channels. However, television transmission by cable and satellite has increased the degree of partitioned viewing. Those interested in particular genres, such as sport or children's programmes, are able to access more of these channels, leading to increased duplication of viewing between these genre-specific channels. Collins, Beal and Barwise (2003) offer evidence on this point.

The Dirichlet Model

The Dirichlet is a mathematical model that predicts brand performance statistics for *all* the brands in a product field. It was described in work by Chatfield and Goodhardt (1975) and developed by Bass, Jeuland and Wright (1976). It was presented in a comprehensive form by Goodhardt, Ehrenberg and Chatfield (1984). The assumptions are similar to those for the single-brand NBD model but, in addition, it is assumed that the market has no partitioning. The model does not apply if there is appreciable evidence of brand clustering on any other basis than penetration.

Programs running Dirichlet analyses can give predictions of penetration, purchase frequency, sole buyers, sole-buyer purchase frequency, proportions of buyers at different frequencies and the repeat-purchase rates of those buying with different frequencies. Table 4.9 shows the real data for the US instant coffee market together with the Dirichlet norms. The fit is fairly close with the exception of Maxim and Brim which may be a sampling error effect since these are small brands.

The Value of Models in Marketing

Ehrenberg, Uncles and Goodhardt (2004) point out that mathematical models provide norms against which real markets can be assessed. One management application of such norms is to set out the realistic options that are open to those who want to improve the

Table 4.9   Observed and predicted annual penetrations and purchase frequencies in the US instant coffee market (Hallberg/MRCA, 1996)

	Market share	Penetration		Purchase frequency (w)	
		Observed	Dirichlet	Observed	Dirichlet
Folgers	24	11	12	3.2	3.1
Maxwell House	22	10	11	3.1	3.1
Taster's Choice	17	9	9	2.8	3.0
Nescafé	11	6	6	2.7	2.9
Sanka	9	5	5	3.0	2.8
High Point	1	1	1	2.6	2.6
Maxim	1	.3	.8	4.5	2.6
Brim	.3	.2	.2	2.1	2.6
Other brands	16	8	8	3.0	3.0

share of their brand or who want to launch a new brand on the market. Table 4.9 shows that the penetration and purchase frequency of a brand is anchored on its market share; brand share changes will relate mainly to changes in penetration rather than purchase frequency. Models also provide norms for cross-purchase in an unpartitioned market and show the long-run propensity to buy a repertoire of brands. When markets are partitioned, e.g. powdered and liquid detergent, we can see the extent to which this partitioning affects cross-purchase. In some cases the market analysis, coupled with Dirichlet norms, may help to show how much of a market is accessible to competition. For example, if a new environmentally friendly detergent is being contemplated, is the competition all detergents, or all detergents that make environmental claims, or some combination thereof?

A further value of this work lies in management education. An understanding of stationary markets helps managers to read their own brand statistics and to understand the ways in which change may, or may not, be brought about. When change does occur and the market stabilizes again, the new brand performance statistics will fit the Dirichlet norms.

One criticism of stationary market research is that it has generally been confirmatory in approach, showing the fit between data and models, rather than testing for exceptions. Exceptions need to be zealously pursued because it is information on such exceptions that may help us to see how to 'buck the market'.

SUMMARY

Over reporting periods of three months to a year the sales of most established consumer brands are approximately stationary: short-term fluctuations due to promotions are averaged out and longer-term trends are too slow-acting to have much effect. The steady state of such markets arises because most buyers in a category maintain their propensities to buy the same group of brands for long periods of time.

The penetration, purchase frequency and market share of a brand are key statistics. These measures encode most of the buying propensities of consumers so that there is no need to know anything more about the brand in order to predict other brand performance statistics. This makes mathematical modelling possible.

Brands have few heavy buyers but these are responsible for a large part of the sales; the heaviest 20 per cent of buyers typically account for about 50 per cent of the purchases. However, because there are many light buyers and some new buyers, a change in their purchasing can have a substantial effect on sales. Over shorter periods (3–12 months), sales changes are mostly seen as a change in penetration, as occasional buyers return to the category, with only a small change in purchase frequency in line with the rule of double jeopardy.

The NBD and Dirichlet models rest on assumptions that purchase incidence is Poisson, purchase rates in a population of buyers are Gamma, and that (in the case of the Dirichlet) there is no market partitioning. The predictions from such models usually fit the data derived from panel research. When the fit is poor, the model provides benchmark norms for interpreting the unusual brand performance.

Analysis of cross-purchase suggests that there is limited market partitioning. The absence of substitution patterns between specific brands indicates that the different brands in a category are seen by consumers in much the same way. In these circumstances, a positioning strategy based on brand differences may have little relevance.

Additional Resources

A clearly written but technical account of the NBD can be found in Morrison and Schmittlein (1988), while the phenomenon of double jeopardy is well explained by Ehrenberg, Goodhardt and Barwise (1990). For a useful review of the Dirichlet and its applications see Ehrenberg, Uncles and Goodhardt (2004). An exercise designed to bring home the features of stationary markets is available in Ehrenberg, Uncles and Carrie (1994b). A book designed for practitioners brings home the implications of research on stationary markets; this is *How Brands Grow* by Byron Sharp, Oxford: Oxford University Press (2010).

Notes

1 Firms sometimes conduct Pareto analyses and delete the worst-performing brands or discourage the customers who buy the least. It is important to consider whether such brands and customers could change. For example, a customer at a DIY store could buy little for several years but become a heavy buyer after moving house.

2 Within these assumptions it is possible to derive an expression for the probability of making r purchases in a period, p_r. For those interested in the technicalities: $p_r = [1-m/(m+k)]^{-k}$ where k is a parameter that is estimated from the purchase frequency and penetration. Expressions of the form $(1+x)^n$ are called binomial; the equation for p_r is a negative binomial because the exponent is negative. The calculation of the NBD requires the solution of the equation $1-b = (1+m/k)^{-k}$ to obtain the parameter k; this is done by the NBD program.

5 Market Dynamics

LEARNING OBJECTIVES

When you have completed this chapter, you should be able to:

1 Sketch a 52-week sales curve showing seasonality and sales promotions.
2 Explain what will happen if there is an imbalance between customer defection and customer acquisition.
3 Explain why the effects of marketing actions may take some time to become obvious.
4 Explain the social basis of diffusion theory.
5 Describe/sketch the technology substitution model, the Bass model and the typical trial growth curves for frequently bought products.

OVERVIEW

Chapter 4 described the regular patterns of purchase found in mature, stationary markets. But what if a market is not stable? Sales and market share do sometimes change and new products sometimes gather sales and become established. In this chapter, we explore aspects of this change.

In the first section, we discuss sales fluctuations in mature markets due to seasonality and sales promotions. These short-term changes can be large, making it harder to spot long-term trends. The second section describes the dynamic patterns in loyalty underlying stable markets. We document these, show how they lead to dynamic equilibrium and discuss the effects of disturbing this equilibrium. In doing so, we extend some of the material from Chapter 4. In the third section, we consider the launch of major innovations. These may create new markets or lead to the complete substitution of an old way of doing things. We draw on the theory of innovation diffusion, as described by Everett Rogers, introduce the technology substitution model and give an overview of Frank Bass's model of new product adoption. Finally, we consider frequently bought categories, such as grocery products. These categories exhibit recurrent minor product innovation, but arguably with a different social dynamic from that found in the work of Rogers and Bass. We document the growth of first purchases for these minor innovations, and discuss the development of loyalty to such new products.

SECTION 1: CHANGES IN AGGREGATE SALES

Variations in Demand – Seasonality and Sales Promotions

Most of the sales fluctuations seen in mature markets are transient, and do not affect underlying demand for a brand or category. Businesses typically experience large swings in demand that simply relate to the time of the year, holidays, sales promotions and other events. More butter and soup are sold in winter. There is little demand for Easter Eggs at Christmas. Americans buy barbecue sauce in summer, with demand skyrocketing for the 4th of July, assisted by heavy sales promotion. Similar patterns can occur in durables and business-to-business markets. The weather, holidays and tax refunds all nudge consumers towards buying certain products at particular times. Even sales targets and discounting policies can lead to seasonality in demand (see Box 5.1).

Box 5.1	Discounts create irregular sales

Early in his career, one of the authors worked for a large American computer company where the need to meet sales quotas led to a crescendo of effort at the end of the year. If sales were slow, management would authorize company-wide promotions in the final quarter, in the hope that they could still achieve their targets. Some IT customers responded to this by adjusting their capital purchase cycle. When pressed about low sales mid-way through the year, sales staff would tell management that their customers 'liked to buy at the end of the year, when the discounts are offered'.

It is important to be familiar with such temporary variations in demand. Figure 5.1 provides an example. The graph covers two and a half years of weekly data, and is representative of sales of widely used table condiments in a major western economy. The x-axis shows intervals of 13 weeks, or a quarter, which is a common management reporting period. The base of the y-axis is zero, so differences in the height of the graph are directly proportional to percentage differences in demand.

This figure shows spikes that increase sales by as much as 150 per cent above the baseline level. They tend to be about four quarters apart. In other words, the spikes occur at the same time (or season) every year. Why are these sales spikes so large? Because sales promotions are often timed to match holidays or seasonal upswings in demand, giving a large combined effect. As mentioned in Chapter 4, despite the magnitude of these changes there is usually little long-term increase in average yearly sales or in customer loyalty. This is because most of the extra sales come from a brand's existing users (Ehrenberg, Hammond and Goodhardt, 1994a; Gupta, Van Heerde and Wittink, 2003).

Many managers are surprised when they first see such period-to-period sales variations, so it is important to be aware of them. The size of these variations can cause

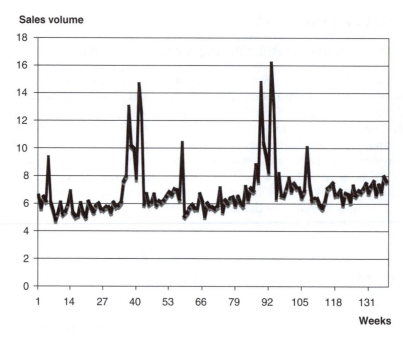

Figure 5.1   Category volume for a grocery product
Source: Simulated data based on known patterns

supply problems and managers should take steps to avoid stock-outs during periods of heavy demand, such as sales promotions.

Measuring Long-Term Sales Performance

These transient changes in demand make it difficult to identify underlying trends in sales. Figure 5.1, for example, shows an upward trend over time, although this is hard to pick out at first glance. One reason why market share is a popular measure of performance is that it controls for some of these fluctuations. Seasonality and holidays should affect all competitors equally, so market share is a more stable measure of performance than raw sales data. In addition, many companies measure market share using statistical techniques that reduce the period-to-period variation in the data and enable a clearer picture of trends in sales to emerge.

Some companies may apply seasonal decomposition to remove seasonality effects, or exponential smoothing to reduce the impact of random variations. Advanced econometric techniques, such as ARIMA (autoregressive integrated moving average), may combine both methods, include estimates of trend lines and use dummy variables for holiday effects. By using statistical models to identify the seasonal, promotional and holiday effects, the underlying trend is more clearly revealed.

SECTION 2: DYNAMIC EFFECTS AND BRAND LOYALTY

The Changes Underlying a Stable Market

Section 1 outlined the fluctuations in total sales that occur in stationary markets. In this section we examine fluctuations in individual consumer purchases. Even in a stationary market individual buying will fluctuate. Some of the commonly observed patterns include regression to the mean for heavy buyers, long-term erosion of loyalty, and churn (turnover in the customer base) as customers cease buying and are replaced.

We know from Chapter 4 that the NBD model describes the normal patterns of light buying, heavy buying and repeat purchase. We can expand on this, using a technique called conditional trend analysis (CTA). Conditional trend analysis was developed by Goodhardt and Ehrenberg (1967) to extend the NBD to different classes of buyers, so that repeat purchase can be predicted for light versus heavy buyers, or indeed for any group of buyers who made a specified number of purchases in the first period analyzed. Managers should be interested in this, because of the sales importance of heavy buyers, the desire to increase the purchase rate of light buyers, and the need to convert some proportion of zero buyers into regular customers. In particular, managers are often concerned that a loss of loyalty from heavy buyers presages a decline in brand sales and share. CTA reveals the level of repeat purchase that should usually be expected for each group of buyers – heavy buyers, light buyers, and even the purchase rate to be expected from people who were zero buyers in the previous period.

Consider a brand that is bought by 15 per cent of category purchasers, on average 1.6 times in a 13-week period, a fairly typical pattern. The NBD analysis in Chapter 4 tells us that the expected repeat purchase rate in the next 13-week period is about 50 per cent (i.e. half of the people who bought the brand in the first period will buy again in the second). But the NBD does not tell us how repeat purchase is distributed between light and heavy buyers. To compare actual repeat purchase with the norms for heavy buyers, we need to undertake CTA. Table 5.1 reports some results from both normal NBD analysis and CTA, broken down by the number of purchases made in the first period.

First, look at the set of buyers who made a single purchase in period 1. They are important, as they make up 65 per cent of all buyers. Given that they bought once in period 1, a manager may expect them to continue buying at the same rate. It may be a surprise to find that this set of buyers makes just 0.6 purchases (on average) in the second period. Likewise, the set of buyers who bought twice in the first period drops to 1.2 purchases in the second period and the heaviest buyers have gone from an average 4.8 purchases down to 2.7.

It would be easy to interpret this as an erosion of loyalty, and to conclude that you need to find the source of the problem and recruit replacement customers. That would be a mistake, though not an uncommon one. It is what Andrew Ehrenberg calls the 'Leaky Bucket Theory' (most recently, in Ehrenberg, Uncles and Goodhardt, 2004), the idea that customers are steadily leaking away, requiring replacement by freshly recruited buyers.

In fact, the values in Table 5.1 are theoretical norms, rather than observed values. They are exactly what we would expect in a normal, mature, stationary market. Period 1 shows familiar NBD patterns; most buyers make only one purchase, and 35 per cent of buyers

Table 5.1 Purchase and repeat purchase over consecutive 13-week periods

Number of purchases	Initial purchases – period 1		Repeat purchases – period 2	
			Average purchases per	
	% of buyers	% of sales	Period-1 buyer	% repeat buying
1	65	41	0.6	40
2	21	26	1.2	61
3	8	15	1.7	74
4+ (av. 4.8)	6	18	2.7	87

account for 59 per cent of sales. In period 2, we simply see how the NBD plays out over time. We see how the 50 per cent repeat-purchase rate is distributed across heavier and lighter buyers, and that the average number of purchases for each group declines in period 2. Instead of thinking of this as undesirable, we should recognize it as the typical pattern of purchasing over time. Heavier buyers show higher repeat rates simply because they are heavier and more regular buyers to start with. Despite this, their purchases decline in the second period, exhibiting the familiar statistical phenomenon of regression to the mean.

Total sales remain stable because those who do not repeat purchase in period 2 are balanced by an influx of other regular buyers. These are households who did not purchase in period 1, but are nonetheless established buyers of the brand. Similarly, a reduction in purchase frequency by some buyers will be matched by an increase in purchase frequency by others. Rather than a 'leaky bucket' in need of constant replenishment, this is the normal pattern of buying in repertoire markets.

Some companies do monitor erosion of loyalty by examining repeat-purchase rates for heavy buyers. This is sometimes called buyer flow analysis and data for this is available from consumer panel companies. If you want to undertake buyer flow analysis, be sure to use the NBD and CTA for a benchmark. You will find that much apparent erosion is simply the normal pattern of occasional purchasing.

Erosion of Loyalty in Repertoire Markets

The previous section demonstrates that much apparent erosion in loyalty is simply due to customer purchase rates fluctuating from period to period. That is not to say that there is no true erosion of repeat-purchase loyalty. There is, but it is smaller than implied by a simple buyer flow analysis. True erosion is revealed by examining the decline in repeat-purchase rates for the whole customer base. For example, East and Hammond (1996) examined repeat-purchase rates for supermarket products and found that they declined from around 55 per cent to 47 per cent over a year. This is 8 percentage points, and 8/55 is 15 per cent of buyers. Similar observations can be found in Zufryden (1996). In a study of four brands in two segments, he observed year-to-year retention of first-brand loyalty ranging from 79 per cent to 86 per cent. Thus, erosion ranged from 14 per cent to 21 per cent. These values are a little higher than those of East and Hammond (1996), perhaps because a loss of first-brand loyalty does not necessarily represent a complete switch. It may simply be a downgrade to a lower position in a customer's repertoire, such as moving from favourite to second-favourite brand.

So, there is erosion but it occurs slowly. The leaky bucket theory is not wrong, but the holes are quite small.

Defection and Churn in Subscription Markets

Leakage is often more obvious in subscription markets, where consumers have only one supplier, such as insurance, banking, utilities and mobile phone airtime. These markets may be based on an annually renewable contract, as in the case of insurance, or they may be a 'tenure' contract in which the subscription continues until terminated, as with banking or utilities. Some markets, such as hairdressing or the family doctor, are thought to show the same kind of persistent subscription-like behaviour, even when choice is not constrained by a contract (Sharp, Wright and Goodhardt, 2002).

In subscription markets, a loss of loyalty often represents a complete loss of revenue from the customer concerned. Thus, the rate of defection (or retention) is a key performance metric and a leading indicator of a brand's fortunes. Sometimes, a loss of loyalty may represent a downgrade rather than a complete defection, but may nonetheless be treated as if it were a full defection. Banking is a prime example of this. Customers often have relationships with more than one financial institution, and these relationships tend to be long-lasting and valuable. Banks are interested in whether they are a customer's main bank, with the largest share of wallet, and therefore the best opportunities for cross-selling. So main bank defection rates are treated in a similar way to other types of defection.

Annual defection rates in subscription markets typically range from 4 per cent to 20 per cent of a brand's customer base. Lees, Garland and Wright (2007) report a figure of 3.6 per cent for a main bank. Gupta, Lehmann and Stuart (2004) found figures of 5 per cent for online stock trading and 15 per cent for a credit card company. Wright and Riebe (2010) calculated, but did not report, category switching rates in both consumer- and business-to-business markets. However, these were 4.1 per cent for the main bank and 20 per cent for annual industrial pipe contracts. Reichheld (1996b) claimed that defection varied quite widely but averaged about 15 per cent across a range of services.

Turnover in the customer base, often called churn, is not always due to defection to or from another supplier. First-time market entry and market exit both play a part. People may enter some markets as they reach independence or form new households, and leave them as they cease to support a family. There may also be churn due to upgrades or downgrades in the product used or because of competitive pricing.[1]

In some fields, change is linked strongly to life-stage. Consider banking. Over a lifetime an individual may move from a child's savings account, to an overdraft, to a mortgage, to an on-call cash management account. People may move house or be affected by a major life event such as their first job, marriage, birth of a child and so forth. This can affect the types of product and service they require and thus their loyalty to previously purchased brands. Some car models are suitable for young people, others for executives and others for families. Similarly, there are regional banks in many countries that cannot offer a full range of services in large cities. A young family that moves from a regional centre to a large city may be forced to change their bank.

Some evidence on the reasons for switching banks comes from Lees, Garland and Wright (2007). They found that, in New Zealand, a change of main bank was due to better offers 32 per cent of the time, product or service failures 31 per cent of the time, reasons beyond the bank's control (such as moving house) 22 per cent of the time and a combination of these reasons 15 per cent of the time. Bogomolova and Romaniuk (2009) examined brand defection for a business-to-business financial service, and found that 60 per cent of defection was for reasons that managers could not control. Chapter 2 carried evidence of defection in other categories.

Consequently, as with buyer flow in repertoire markets, there is a certain level of inevitable turnover in the customer base. When interpreting defection figures, theoretical norms should be used to determine how much defection is normal, and how much is unusual. Wright and Riebe (2010) provide a method of calculating such norms for subscription markets.

Change from Market Imbalance

If erosion, or switching, from a brand is exactly matched by customer acquisition, a dynamic equilibrium will exist in which market share for that brand remains constant. An imbalance between the two will lead to a change. For example, reducing a brand's defection rate while maintaining the rate of customer acquisition will lead to an increase in market share. Conversely, if the defection rate increases while acquisition remains stable, market share will decrease. Defection reduction has been recognized as a possible source of growth for some time (Reichheld and Sasser, 1990). More recently, Reichheld (2003) pursued the idea of growth coming from dynamic forces through his 'Net Promoter Score', which takes account of the propensity to give positive word of mouth (see Chapter 12). Recent work has also integrated defection rates into an understanding of customer lifetime value (Gupta, Lehmann and Stuart, 2004) and compared the relative returns of customer acquisition and defection reduction efforts (Reinartz, Thomas and Kumar, 2005) to support an optimal allocation of the marketing budget.

However, work in this area tends to overlook the fact that defection reduction is *bounded*. That is, if a brand has 6 per cent defection, it can only reduce it by this amount, or less. No matter how superior the product or service, some loss of customers will occur due to market exit, changes in customer requirements, or other matters beyond the control of managers.

Further, recent work has compared unusual defection and unusual acquisition as sources of dynamic changes in market share (Riebe et al., forthcoming). The evidence leads to the conclusion that acquisition rates are much more important than defection rates in explaining changes in market share for both growing and declining brands.

| Exercise 5.1 | Defection reduction and share growth |

Question: Imagine you have a brand with a 3 per cent market share and an annual defection rate of 10 per cent. How long will it take to increase your market share from 3 per cent to 10 per cent, simply by halving your defection rate?

Answer: Assuming your market share has been in a dynamic balance and that all customers buy at the same rate, your 10 per cent annual defection rate will have been matched by a 10 per cent annual customer acquisition rate. If your defection rate halves to 5 per cent while your customer acquisition rate remains constant, you will grow by 5 per cent of your customer base per annum. That is, your market share after T years can be found by a simple compounding formula, as follows:

$$3\% \times (1 + .05) \wedge T$$

We suggest you conduct a simple spreadsheet analysis to find the answer. We did this and found that market share will rise above the 10 per cent threshold in the *24th year*. However, defection reduction can be an expensive exercise so there is a risk that market share growth will not be matched by profit growth.

Comment: This example is somewhat similar to that of MNBA, outlined in Reichheld and Sasser (1990). Reichheld and Sasser were more concerned with customer lifetime value than with growth. However, we hope our example makes it clear that brand growth requires a broader explanation than just defection reduction, especially when brands have a relatively low market share.

Ask yourself the question: what else could lead to brand growth?

Observing Market Change

One consequence of occasional buying and relatively low levels of erosion is that marketing actions can take a long time to bear fruit. Exposure to advertising, for example, cannot affect brand choice until the next purchase occasion. Similarly, defection-reduction programmes seek to plug a leak that may be fairly small to start with, while attempts to acquire customers will be limited by the number entering the market or looking to make a change. So it may take some time for marketing initiatives to play out in changes to sales. An exception is sales promotion, which tends to have a large effect during the period of the promotion, leading to the spikes in sales seen in Figure 5.1.

Similarly, market problems, such as a drop in perceived quality, may not be immediately noticeable. It may be some time before affected customers are ready to purchase the category again, or to renew a contract and have the opportunity to make a different choice. By that time, quite a weight of dissatisfaction may have accumulated so that many switch. This makes it important to use brand performance metrics such as satisfaction or perceived quality as well as average purchase frequency and, repeat purchase, as these more-qualitative data may indicate potential problems, allowing a manager to respond before the problems gather too much momentum.

SECTION 3: THE DYNAMICS OF NEW PRODUCT ADOPTION

So far we have examined change in mature markets. What about the more fundamental changes that result from the launch of new products? Whether they satisfy a previously unmet demand, or replace a previous technology, new products can result in more rapid and enduring change than is seen in mature markets.

How are such innovations adopted by a population of consumers? While there is a large literature on this topic, we will restrict ourselves to examining three approaches of particular importance to marketers. These are Rogers' innovation diffusion curve, Fisher and Pry's technology substitution model and the Bass model.

Rogers' Approach to Innovation Diffusion

Most marketers have some awareness of work on the diffusion of innovations. The most well-known author in this area is Everett Rogers (1962, 2003), whose book on the subject is a widely cited classic. Rogers brought together studies from many disciplines, but gave emphasis to sociology. He followed influential work by Gabriel Tarde (1903), who noted that cumulative adoption followed an S-shaped curve and saw adoption or rejection as a critical decision; George Simmel (1908), who introduced the idea of a social network; and Ryan and Gross (1943), who undertook a landmark study into adoption of hybrid corn. Later work incorporated Granovetter's finding (1973) that the spread of an innovation through a social system was helped if people were loosely bonded to many different groups.

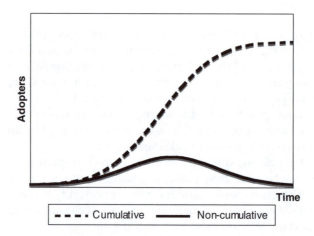

Figure 5.2   A normal adoption curve

In Rogers' work, these ideas are more fully developed and integrated, with diffusion defined as 'the process in which an innovation is communicated through certain channels over time among the members of a social system' (Rogers, 2003: 5). Rogers believed that adoption follows a normal distribution curve, with time as the x-axis and number of adopters as the y-axis. Figure 5.2 shows this normal curve. There are two versions: the standard normal curve of (non-cumulative) adoptions in each period and the S-shaped curve of total (cumulative) adoption. Historical examples of new products that become widely established include black and white televisions, computer chips, air conditioning units, facsimile machines and first-generation mobile telephones. Modern examples might include high-definition colour televisions, solar water heating, media recording devices and smart phones.

Characteristics of an Innovation

Innovations do not always follow this curve. They may fail. Or they may diffuse so slowly that the left tail, or lead-time, of the adoption curve extends for many years before rapid growth kicks in. Rogers cites as examples the Royal Navy's reluctance to use citrus juice as an anti-scurvy agent, resistance to the use of boiled water in Peru and the failure to displace the QWERTY keyboard on which this book has been rather inefficiently typed. He became interested in the characteristics affecting the innovation adoption rate and posited that it depended on:

- The *relative advantage* that an innovation has over previous methods of meeting the same need. Some innovations, such as text messaging and social networking tools, also have strong network effects, so that relative advantage increases with the number of adopters.
- *Compatibility*, or the consistency of an innovation with the existing experiences, needs and values of the adopting population. Cultural and religious incompatibilities may be particular risks for the adoption of innovations.
- *Complexity*, or how easy an innovation is to use and describe to others and whether it requires specialized expertise or substantial learning.
- *Trialability*, enabling experience to be gained with the innovation before purchase or full adoption.
- *Observability*, increasing both awareness and social influence, as we are influenced by seeing others use new products and tend to follow the consumption habits of the communities we live in.

There is also the perceived risk of an innovation. The higher the price, the less the confidence in after-sales service, or the harsher the returns policy the more reluctant people will be to adopt. Rogers' adoption characteristics also have an indirect impact on perceived risk, as this will be reduced by trialability or observability and increased by problems of compatibility or complexity.

Adopter Categories and Innovativeness

Perhaps the most famous part of Rogers' work is the division of the normal curve into adopter categories. People in the first 2.5 per cent of the normal curve in Figure 5.2 are labelled the innovators and the next 13.5 per cent the early adopters. Then we have the early majority (34 per cent), late majority (34 per cent) and laggards (16 per cent). These adopter categories are reproduced in most consumer behaviour textbooks, together with comments about their typical characteristics.

This approach has come in for some serious criticism. Bass (1969) famously described Rogers' approach as 'largely literary'. Wright and Charlett (1995) pointed out that Rogers' adopter categories were a *post hoc* tautological classification system, of no value for forecasting. This is because Rogers' categorization depends on the standard deviation from the mean time to adopt. Innovators are all those up to two standard deviations before the mean time to adopt; early adopters are between 2 and 1 standard deviations from the mean time to adopt and so on. Yet neither the mean nor the standard deviation can be calculated until the diffusion of the innovation is complete, at which point the adopter categories have little managerial value.

A counter-argument is that innovativeness is a normally distributed trait, associated with other consumer characteristics in a predictable manner, allowing innovators and early adopters to be identified and targeted. Rogers claimed that there were 26 character- istics that varied between adopter categories, including socio-economic variables, person- ality values and communication behaviour. However, empirical findings do not always support this claim. Taylor (1977) found that a striking characteristic of 'innovators' in grocery products was that they were simply heavy buyers of the category, a finding that was recently confirmed for pharmaceuticals (Stern and Wright, 2007). This hardly sug- gests an enduring personality trait. A more popular modern view is that innovativeness varies by product category (e.g. Crawford and Di Benedetto, 2006: 372).

The long lead-time that can occur before an innovation takes off is sometimes explained by the characteristics of the most innovative people. Rogers notes that innovators are often 'deviants', somewhat apart from the rest of the social system: they might be metaphorical hermits in the wood, dwelling apart from the community, or perhaps the archetypical computer geek. While such people may be innovative, they may have little social influence, so their behaviour has little effect on the broader community. Diffusion will only take off when more influential people, well connected within the social system, adopt the innovation. In a tribal village, this might be the chief or the chief's wife. In western social networks, it may be opinion leaders or celebrities, or people who offer marketplace advice to many others, such as Feick and Price's (1987) 'market mavens' (if they can be found; see Chapter 11). Rogers places such people in the early adopter category.

While these ideas offer insights into ways of speeding up adoption within particular social systems, they are not necessary to explain the S-shaped curve that we see in practice. A long lead-time can be explained through the cumulative effects of social forces, as we shall see later. Nonetheless, Rogers' work is very useful. The concept of an idea spreading through a social system via specific communication channels underlies much subsequent work on innovation diffusion. The insight that adoption follows a normal curve has been borne out in many product categories.

Fisher and Pry's Technology Substitution Model

Rogers' adopter categorization exploits the properties of the S-shaped normal distribution curve, but is not helpful for forecasting. Marketers need to make forecasts to assist launch decisions on new products, set targets against which performance can be assessed, and allocate marketing expenditure.

Fisher and Pry (1971) showed how to use an S-shaped curve to forecast the replacement of an inferior technology with a better one that meets the same need. This process is called technology substitution. They dealt with the problem of an indeterminate lead-time by assuming the substitute technology must achieve several per cent market share before complete substitution could be guaranteed to occur. They then treated substitution as a logistic function of time.[2] This has the practical effect of transforming the S-shaped cumulative adoption curve into a straight line. Extrapolation through regression then yields a forecast. They validated this model over 17 diverse data sets and found surprisingly accurate results.

Figure 5.3 is an example of the raw pattern of technology substitution, using some previously published data on diesel and steam locomotives in the USA. These data are expressed in relative percentages of the total number of locomotives. You will see that the growth curve for diesel locomotives is similar to the cumulative normal adoption curve shown in Figure 5.2.

Although quite old now, Fisher and Pry's (1971) model is likely to continue to be of great importance as we undergo accelerating technological substitution in areas such as tele-communications, computing and home electronics. This model has the useful feature of forecasting the dynamic decline of the old technology as well as the growth of the new one. This is potentially very helpful to companies in fields such as telecommunications, where there are substantial but declining revenue streams from products such as fixed-line telephone connections.

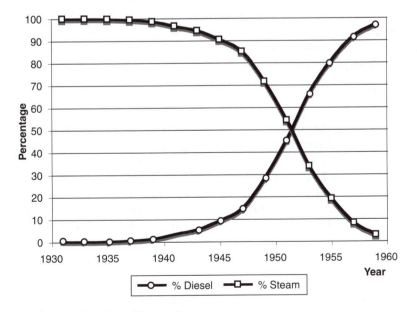

Figure 5.3 Cumulative substitution of locomotives

Source: Interstate Commerce Commission, Statistics of Railroads 1925–1960, as cited in Moore and Pessemier (1993: 79)

By way of example, consider the following forecast (Box 5.2). This applies the Fisher and Pry model to publicly available information on dial-up and broadband Internet connections in Australia. We describe the workings so you can see how easily the model is applied. Note that the date had to be adjusted to an equal interval scale to allow the statistical analysis to take place. Figure 5.4 graphs the example in Box 5.2, in this case in fractions rather than percentages.

Box 5.2 | The growth of broadband

We applied the Fisher and Pry model to forecasting the decline of Australian dial-up Internet access and, conversely, the growth of broadband in that country. Using Nielsen net ratings figures published at http://www.dcita.gov.au, we converted the proportions of Internet users that had dial-up and broadband access to a log odds ratio (LOR) and ran an OLS regression. The OLS regression predicted that LOR = 3.214 −0.068 × adjusted date. (We had to use an adjusted date to ensure an equal interval scale, as the time between reports varied.) We put future dates into this equation to predict changes in LOR and then converted these changed LORs back to predicted proportions of dial-up and broadband connections. Figure 5.4 shows our forecasts. Forecasts like this give useful long-range expectations about the size of the customer base and the support infrastructure needed from capital equipment to call-centre staff. They are also useful to help forecast market potential for Internet services relying on a broadband connection, such as Internet TV.

Postscript: The forecasts were based on data up until June 2006, at which stage 71 per cent of Internet users had broadband. This was forecast to grow to 95 per cent by the end of 2008. In 2009 a press release from Nielsen online revealed that the actual figure for broadband penetration in 2008 was 97 per cent.

The technology substitution model gives impressive forecasting ability, but it does not offer much explanation. It is also constrained by the simplicity of the assumptions. In their original article, Fisher and Pry (1971) applied their model to the substitution of margarine for butter, water-based for oil-based paints and artificial for natural fibres. We now know that those substitutions are partial – there is a limit on their potential that is less than the total usage of yellow fats, paint and clothes fibre respectively. Sometimes, silk is still preferred to nylon.

It would be ideal to have a model of innovation diffusion that offered the forecasting ability of Fisher and Pry, the explanation of Rogers and a variable ceiling on the number of adopters. As it happens, there is such a model in marketing – the Bass model.

The Bass Model

Frank Bass's approach to diffusion of innovation (1969) is one of the most well-known models in marketing. Bass drew on epidemiological theory – the theory of the spread of

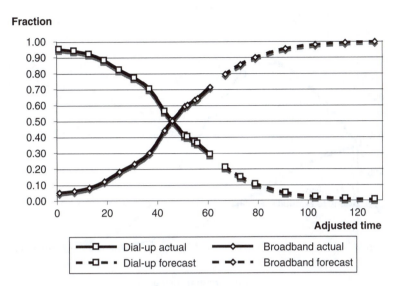

Figure 5.4   Cumulative substitution of Internet access

diseases – to examine the spread of an innovation throughout a connected social system. Bass modelled the effect of both innovative and imitative forces in promoting adoption up to a saturation point. He saw innovative forces as those external to the social system, such as advertising and personal selling. Innovation therefore acts throughout the diffusion process rather than being limited to the first 2.5 per cent of adopters. Conversely, imitative forces reflect social influence, which is internal to the social system. Therefore imitative forces are exerted by previous adopters as they model and recommend the innovation to others. For example, you might buy an iPad simply because you see an advertisement (innovation), but your purchase becomes more likely the more you see people using one, the more your friends and family own them, and the more they tell you about it or show you how it works (word of mouth). Unlike earlier researchers, Bass found a way to quantify these social influence variables within a mathematical model. An early success of the Bass model is illustrated in Box 5.3.

Box 5.3	A strong test of the bass model

The Bass model is lauded for having passed the key scientific test – prediction. Bass used his model to predict the peak of the colour television adoption curve in the USA. He was roundly criticized at the time by industry figures for his 'pessimistic' forecasts. However, when actual sales figures became available, he was proved right. Ignoring his forecasts led the consumer electronics industry to build too much production capacity, at considerable cost.

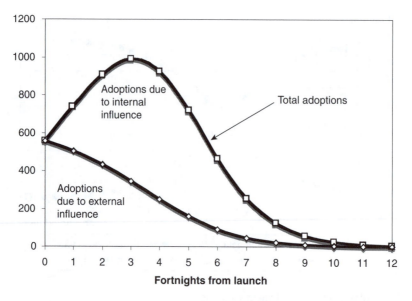

Figure 5.5   Adoption of an interactive telephone enrolment system (non-cumulative)

Source: Model parameters from Wright, Upritchard and Lewis (1997)

Parameters, Shape and Equations

Bass's model is elegant. It requires only three parameters: innovation (p), imitation (q) and the eventual number of adopters, known as market potential (m). The dependent variable is either cumulative or non-cumulative adoption by time period – $Y(T)$ or $y(t)$ respectively. Importantly, sales data can be equated with adoption data if the purchase is a high-value durable or service that is bought once and does not need replacement for some time.

In the first period (usually a year), the probability of adoption, given that no adoption has yet taken place, is simply p, and the predicted number of adopters is $p \times m$. However, as more of the population adopt, social influence (q) increases and the probability of adoption becomes $p + q \times [Y(T)/m]$. This basic equation can be expressed in a variety of forms, both algebraic and probabilistic and for either cumulative or non-cumulative adoption.

The mix between internal and external influence can be seen in the Bass curve in Figure 5.5, estimated on data for first-time use of a telephone enrolment system at Massey University in New Zealand. The parameters of this curve are $p = 0.10$, $q = 0.47$ and $m = 5,788$. This p value is quite high for Bass modelling, so the adoption curve starts at a point well above zero, peaks early and is over quickly. This shows the extra flexibility of the Bass model compared to a simple normal distribution curve.

Validation, Replication and the Extension of the Bass Model

Box 5.3 notes a famous case of forecasting success for the Bass model but Bass may have been lucky on this occasion. More cases are needed to assess the model. In a review of early replications, Wright, Upritchard and Lewis (1997) noted that a poor fit was sometimes found for the model outside North American and European settings. They also found that the predictive ability of the model was limited by variations in the early data. As early sales (or adoptions) are quite few, fluctuations are proportionately larger and so have a larger effect on long-term forecasting accuracy. Putsis and Srinivasan (2000) subsequently found that Bass model forecasts generally do not stabilize until the peak of the adoption process had passed. Also, the assumption of constant social influence may be an over-simplification. As we shall see in Chapter 12, word-of-mouth production may vary with the period a person has owned a product.

Notwithstanding this, there has been a wealth of successful research on the Bass model, including applications to other historical data sets, methodological improvements and many useful extensions, such as allowing population size to vary or modelling the successive generations of new technologies. Bass models have accurately described innovations in areas as diverse as consumer durables, consumer electronics, education, agriculture services, telecommunications and even United Nations membership. In these areas, only one purchase is normally made; thus sales (or membership) data give a direct measure of diffusion, up to the point where replacement purchases commence.

Using the Bass Model to Predict

To predict the sales of an innovation using the Bass model, we need to know the values of p, q and m. The usual way to estimate these is through non-linear regression against sales data for the first few periods. However, this requires several years of such data and some degree of statistical skill. Furthermore, as noted earlier, the results tend to be unstable until the data include the peak of the adoption process.

It would be much more helpful to apply the model before the launch of a new product. Then it could be used for initial sales forecasting, launch decisions, capacity planning and marketing budgeting. Two traditional approaches to doing this are to forecast by analogy or to use management judgement.

To forecast by analogy, known values of p and q from other innovations are used. Sultan, Farley and Lehmann (1990) report the results of a meta-analysis of these parameters, and tables of them have been published elsewhere (e.g. Lilien and Rangaswamy, 2002). However, Rogers' theory tells us that the characteristics of the innovation and the characteristics of the social system are the key drivers of adoption, so it is questionable whether p and q values are generalizable unless they are from a similar innovation in a very similar social system. For the m parameter, the value cannot be derived by analogy, but may be estimated through market research.

The techniques for applying managerial judgement are not made very clear in the literature and should generally be seen as a last resort. Managers may not understand the social basis or typical values of the Bass model parameters p and q. Managers will therefore have little basis to apply their judgement. Also, Armstrong (1985) has evaluated evidence on the performance of subjective estimates – managerial judgement – in forecasting. He found that they do not perform well compared to forecasts from objective methods and that integrating objective information with managerial judgement typically provided substantial improvements over managerial judgement alone (Armstrong, 1985: 387–420). So it is doubtful whether management judgement will show much accuracy unless the judge already has substantial experience with the Bass model and takes steps to combine this judgement with other, objective, information.

Lessons for Market Dynamics from the Bass Model

What lessons does the Bass model offer us in understanding market dynamics? First, consider the domain of the model. It concerns new products, not brands. It is typically applied to high-value products or services that have long inter-purchase times. These may be completely new or substantial technological improvements (although it can be applied to other behaviours if true adoption data is available, as in Figure 5.5). Bass modelling has shown that sales curves following the introduction of such products and services will be roughly normal or S-shaped.

Second, the exact shape of the curve will depend on social factors relating to the social system involved. Understanding the relative importance of these external and internal influences will give richer insights for marketing planning and more accurate forecasts of product sales growth.

Third, a long lead-in time can be explained simply by the values of the parameters. It will occur if the innovation parameter, p, is relatively low. Rapid acceleration of adoption will then occur if the innovation parameter, q, is relatively high.

Therefore, knowledge of the Bass model gives a good understanding of market dynamics following the introduction of a new product, at least for durables or high-involvement services. However, the Bass model has little to say about frequently bought products or new brands in established markets. We address this in the final section of this chapter.

Exercise 5.2   The flexibility of the Bass curve

The following graphs show how changes to the parameters affect the shape of the Bass curve. Examine each one of the four examples and then consider the questions that follow.

1 For each curve, identify a social system and innovation it could be describing. (Hint: think about the level of innovation and the extent of word-of-mouth recommendation.)
2 Consider Rogers' innovation characteristics. How might they affect the shape of the cumulative adoption curve?
3 Which do you think are the most and least common shapes? Justify your answer.

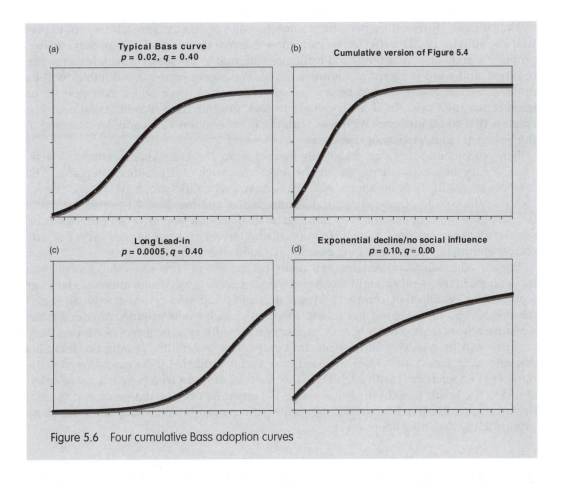

Figure 5.6   Four cumulative Bass adoption curves

SECTION 4: THE SALES DYNAMICS OF FREQUENTLY BOUGHT CATEGORIES

Low-Innovation Products

Section 3 described what we know about sales changes that occur when new categories are introduced, or when technological substitution causes a wave of change in an existing durable category. Yet most new products are much more mundane, and involve incremental 'me-too' products in familiar, frequently bought, low-value and low-involvement categories. We cannot expect that the same dynamic processes will necessarily apply in such different circumstances. Rather, new products in these frequently bought, low-involvement categories rely on familiarity and existing memory structures, as discussed in Chapter 3, and most sales come from repeat purchases rather than from the initial adoption decision. Occasionally, there may be a major innovation, such as the first olive oil spread or low-fat calcium-enriched milk. However, even these are typically presented as new brands launched into a familiar category (yellow fats and milk, respectively).

Nonetheless, diffusion theory offers some useful insights. In general, we can expect trial and adoption will be affected by influences external to the social system (advertising, promotion and personal selling) and influences internal to the social system (observation of others and word-of-mouth recommendation). We expect high-value durables will be more visible, and will tend to be a topic of conversation, because of their novelty or because the high price level leads people to seek pre-purchase recommendations. The result is that social influence increases with the number of previous adopters, leading to the S-shaped cumulative adoption curve.

Now, consider a low-value, frequently bought item. The low value means lower risk. Also, it may be one of many dozens of regularly purchased product categories. The category is less likely to be a topic of conversation – who talks much about toilet paper, bleach, milk, baking powder, flour, light bulbs, butter and the like? Of course there will be exceptions – a cooking club may talk a great deal about a new type of flour. However, such exceptions represent a small fraction of the buyers and we are not aware of any corresponding light bulb-changing or milk-drinking clubs.

Rogers' adoption characteristics can easily be applied to such low-value incremental innovations in frequently bought categories. We suggest that such innovations are familiar (compatible), simple (not complex), cheap (trialable) and widely present on the shelf (observable). So there are few barriers to adoption of such a new product, provided it has a relative advantage. Conversely, such products are less likely to be topics of conversation, so there will be relatively little social influence.[3] The probability of adoption remains constant over time rather than increasing as social influence increases; however, the number of adopters falls with each period as the pool of those who have not yet adopted shrinks. The result is a curve whose shape is known as exponential or an exponential decline. Figure 5.6(d) in Exercise 5.2 shows the pattern of cumulative adoption for such an exponentially declining adoption curve.

Exercise 5.3   Sketch an exponential decline curve

It's easy to see for yourself how an exponential decline curve works. Imagine that a population of 100 people has an adoption rate of 10 per cent. In the first period, 10 will adopt; in the second period, 9 (10 per cent of the remaining 90 who had not yet adopted); in the third period 8.1 are expected to adopt (10 per cent of the remaining 81) and so on.

1   In Excel, calculate the number of adopters for each of the first 20 periods. Assume a population of 100 and an adoption rate of 10 per cent. (Hint: you might find it helpful to have columns for those yet to adopt, adopters in the period, and total adopters to date.)
2   Graph both the cumulative and non-cumulative adoption curves.
3   Repeat the exercises for adoption rates of 30 per cent and 5 per cent.

Empirical Patterns in First Purchases

The shape of adoption curves for frequently purchased products has been studied empirically. Wright and Stern (2006) examined 12 national product launches and 19 controlled test market product launches for a variety of frequently bought categories. Figure 5.7 sketches some of their findings. It is noteworthy that the individual product launches showed similar patterns, despite varying degrees of innovativeness in the product or brand being launched. Similar curves are presented in Du and Kamakura (2011).

These curves are not obviously S-shaped and so show little evidence of an increasing word-of-mouth effect (although see note 3). They show an exponentially declining pattern of growth in first purchases. There is a slight bend in the curve for national launches, although this may be due to distribution growth. Yet, even with this, the curve still generally follows the declining exponential pattern. Nonetheless, it is worth remembering that while changes to distribution are beyond the scope of this chapter, they are nonetheless a primary cause of permanent sales change. Availability is a necessary precursor to purchase.

After the First Purchase

For durable products, adoption and sales are measured by the simple act of a purchase. However, the picture is not so clear for frequently bought items such as groceries. Exponential models of cumulative first purchase do not assume that the first purchase is an adoption, or tell us what the long-term purchase frequency will be. We might instead expect buyers of these new products to make one or two trial purchases before choosing either to drop the new product or to include it in their repertoire. This is the traditional view in most consumer behaviour texts and is consistent with Rogers' theories on innovation diffusion, with exposure being followed by evaluation and then an adoption or rejection decision.

This traditional view turns out to be surprisingly controversial. Light buyers may only buy the category two or three times a year, so trial will continue for some time and it is hard to say when a light buyer will have completed their evaluation, or even whether such a question is meaningful. If somebody makes a low-involvement purchase of a brand once or twice a year, it is not clear that this involves much cognition or post-purchase evaluation, as is expected by traditional theory.

Evidence on this point is provided by Ehrenberg and Goodhardt (2001), who found that the long-term average purchase rates for a new brand are achieved very quickly. In a study of 22 grocery product launches, they compared average purchase frequencies for new brands with those of the existing brands. In the first quarter, the new brands had an average purchase frequency of 1.4 – a little lower than established brands, which averaged 1.9. In subsequent quarters, the new brands showed purchase frequency of 1.8, 1.9 and 2.0, virtually identical with the established brands. Wright and Sharp (2001) found similar results for an Australian grocery product launch. These findings are inconsistent with the traditional idea of a trial purchase followed by an adoption or rejection decision.

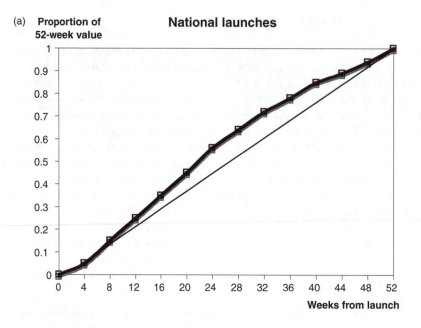

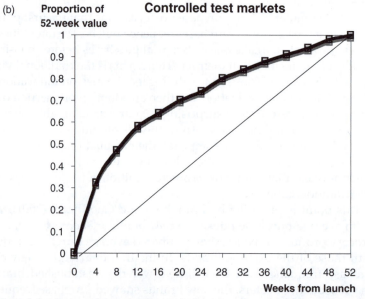

Figure 5.7　Cumulative first purchases for 52 weeks from launch

Source: Values reported in Wright and Stern (2006), partly derived from data downloaded from www.brucehardie.com

How could such near-instant loyalty come about? One explanation is that new brands in low-involvement categories are immediately included in the consumer's repertoire. The trial curve may then just reflect distribution growth, the occasional nature of category purchases and the shuffling of purchases around the consumer's repertoire.

This explanation remains somewhat unsatisfying. Intuition tells us that consumers sometimes simply do not like a new product. They may buy it once, and then decide it tastes awful, or does not work for their household. The reliance of the near-instant loyalty hypothesis on *average* purchase rates, rather than *repeat* purchase rates, excludes this effect altogether.

Repeat-purchase rate is therefore a more direct measure of loyalty, and has greater face validity. Yet there is surprisingly little evidence on patterns in repeat-purchase rates for new products. One difficulty is that early buyers are more likely to be heavy buyers; Taylor (1977) demonstrated this, Fourt and Woodlock (1960) made a similar assertion and Stern and Wright (2007) have confirmed it. These heavy buyers may complete trial purchases and evaluations quickly. Therefore, initial repeat-purchase figures may be misleading, as they combine heavy buyers, whose repeat-purchase rate has settled down, with lighter buyers who may still be making evaluative purchases. So the overall repeat-purchase figure will keep changing until light buyers have finished making evaluative purchases.

Eskin (1973) sought an early indication of final repeat-purchase rates by separating out heavy buyers and examining their repeat-purchase rates. Yet we know from Chapter 4 that the top 20 per cent of buyers only account for 50 to 60 per cent of sales, and CTA leads us to expect that heavy buyers will have different repeat-purchase rates from light buyers, and that these purchase rates will regress to the mean in subsequent periods. So Eskin's approach, which has been highly influential, seems incomplete.

Fader, Hardie and Huang (2004) took a different approach. They adapted a standard trial-repeat model to allow consumers' purchase rates to be revised after experiencing the new product. The result was an extremely accurate forecasting performance for the single brand that they examined. This suggests that their assumption, that purchase rates are revised *slightly* following experience, is a reasonable one, although replication across other data sets would give more confidence in their conclusions.

Some indirect support is provided by Singh et al. (2012), in a study of sales growth for 47 brand extensions in the United Kingdom. They found that, in the third quarter after launch, those with a positive sales trend had an average repeat purchase rate of 32 per cent while those with a negative sales trend had an average repeat purchase rate of 22 per cent. This difference is consistent with a post-experience revision of purchase probabilities suggested by Fader et al. (2004). Such work is needed on the evolution of repeat-purchase rates, for both successful and unsuccessful new packaged goods. As a practical matter, it would be helpful to have empirical studies that identify the typical evolution of repeat-purchase rates across a wide range of conditions. This would enable managers to benchmark the repeat-purchase performance of their new brands against an existing knowledge base.

SUMMARY

Markets undergo sales change for many reasons. First, time of year, holidays, sales promotions and other events have a temporary effect. Second, a dynamic equilibrium underlies stable markets, with buyers churning between brands or migrating between heavy and light buying. Disturbances to this equilibrium may result in changes to market share. However, changes often occur slowly due to the low rate of erosion or switching and the long inter-purchase times of occasional buyers.

Third, the launch of new products is a major source of more rapid and enduring change. Sociology helps us to understand the underlying forces, while models such as the technology substitution model and the Bass model provide tools for analysing and forecasting new product adoption. Fourth, social forces may be different for low-value, frequently bought items. We can capture the first purchase process in these markets with exponential models (which assume little social influence). For repeat purchase, the analysis is a little more complicated, due to early trial by heavy buyers, the large number of light buyers and the unclear role of evaluative purchases. One approach is to assume near-instant loyalty. Another is to use statistical models that allow purchase rates to be revised after experience with the new product. Recent evidence shows that differences in repeat purchase rates for succeeding and failing brand extensions can be detected in the third quarter after launch.

In studying or managing markets, you need to know what fluctuations can be expected, even in stable markets, and also how genuine change will play out over time. From this chapter, we hope you have developed a good understanding of the mechanisms that underlie changes in sales figures.

Additional Resources

The classic text on the diffusion of innovations, Rogers (2003), gives a good review of the diffusion literature and offers many interesting examples, although it has little on alternative models. For an appreciation of the technological substitution model, go straight to Fisher and Pry (1971), which remains readable and interesting and has a number of case studies. An overview of the Bass modelling literature can be obtained by reading Bass (1995), Mahajan, Muller and Bass (1990) and Sultan, Farley and Lehmann (1990). Finally, if you wish to know more about new product development, there are many excellent textbooks in the area, such as Crawford and Di Benedetto (2006).

Notes

1 The term *churn* is widely used in industry but, if the defection and recruitment rates are different for a brand, what is the churn? We prefer to use 'churn' to describe the average replacement rate in a category. Average defection and acquisition will be the same across the category if it is stationary.
2 A logistic function is a function of logits, or log-odds ratios. Odds ratios are simply the ratio of possible outcomes. If a football team is expected to win 80 per cent of the time, the odds of victory are 8:2 (or 4:1), and the natural logarithm of this is $\ln(4)$, which is 1.39. The logit is widely used in some other types of market modelling, such as the multinomial logit choice model.
3 An alternative view has recently been put forward by Du and Kamakura (2011), who argue that weak contagion effects can be observed in new consumer packaged goods, provided the modelling of such effects properly controls for potential sources of bias.

6 Consumer Group Differences

LEARNING OBJECTIVES

When you complete this chapter you should be able to:

1 Identify consumer differences that are relevant and those that are less useful to marketers.
2 Categorize cultures along the dimensions proposed by Hofstede.
3 Give examples of how these dimensions have been used in consumer research.
4 Understand the criticisms of Hofstede's approach.
5 Describe how values can be used to understand fundamental consumer motivations.
6 Explain how gender and age are related to consumption.

OVERVIEW

Marketers need to take account of group differences when they design and promote products, since what may appeal to one group may be of no interest to another. Group differences may reflect local conditions or history and may be related to ways of viewing the self and others in society. Some differences, such as individualism versus collectivism, can be seen as orientations shaping consumer consciousness; these have interested social scientists who seek to characterize pervasive features of whole societies. Other differences relate to divisions within society and we focus on age and gender since there are new developments here.

We start by asking what differences are relevant in consumer research and note that many personality differences are hard to use because it is difficult to target people with a particular disposition unless this is associated with physical segregation or differential consumption of media. Deep-seated cultural differences are approached via Hofstede's (1980, 2001) five dimensions and Rokeach's (1973) value system. We look at the use of these ideas in consumer research and show that it may be quite difficult to derive predictions from them. We also note that there may be simple social differences in consumption that are best revealed by market research rather than academic study.

Contrasted with consumer group differences is the idea of convergence – that a process of globalization is ongoing and that societies, at least in market practice, are becoming similar. We explore this idea and look in particular at China, comparing it with the west. On age, we focus particularly on the older members of society. The proportion of over-65s is growing rapidly and represents a considerable burden on more productive, younger groups. Though many are poor, much wealth is held by the older generation and recent work has focused on the relatively conservative decision-making of older consumers. On gender differences, there is evidence that women make more interpersonal bonds than men, which affects their loyalty patterns.

In this book, we do not cover segmentation by brand. This is because there is a body of robust evidence showing that there is generally little difference between the customers of any two brands in a category. Brands do not usually differ enough to appeal to different sub-groups in the population. Uncles et al. (2011) summarized the empirical evidence on comparisons of user profiles of directly competing brands. Through a series of replication studies and extensions, these authors reconfirmed that user profiles of directly competing brands seldom differ. The study used data spanning 25 years, across 50+ categories and 60 data sets, and confirmed lack of user segments for brands in emerging markets, private labels, variants and composite segments. Similar findings are reported in other studies. For example, in a study on Japanese buyers' purchase intentions, Singh et al. (2012) showed demographic similarity across the users of top Japanese grocery brands. Similar findings were also reported by Uncles and Lee (2006) amongst Australian customers and in the UK by Singh, Ehrenberg and Goodhardt (2008).

SECTION 1: RELEVANT DIFFERENCES FOR CONSUMER RESEARCH

Segmentation, a fundamental notion in marketing, means grouping consumers into discrete segments according to their similarities or differences. The segments may differ in needs, consumption habits, responsiveness to marketing actions, etc. Although it is useful to diagnose differences between consumers concerning a specific product or issue with dedicated market research, understanding the fundamental drivers that account for differences across a broad range of behaviour has more potential.

Socio-demographic characteristics were the first fundamental drivers examined in marketing. Some characteristics like social class and profession have lost appeal to marketers over time because the significance of the social norms attached to them has faded. Other characteristics have remained important but have taken on a different meaning. Gender and age for instance still account for important consumption differences, but in new ways, partly because of the changed economic conditions. We address research linking these two factors to loyalty in Chapter 2.

Personality traits are obviously an important determinant of consumption behaviour. For instance, Venkatraman and Price (1990) show that a consumer's openness to innovation correlates with his or her impulsivity and inclination towards social risk taking. This type of finding is not easy for marketers to apply because, if managers want to target consumers with certain personality traits, they not only have to identify them, but also they need to find ways to communicate with a specific segment without too much spillover to other segments.

Identification ideally requires a personality survey, difficult to apply in practice, unless indirect indicators are available (like the types of activities a consumer engages in). However, a person's dispositions and behaviours are not only affected by his or her personality make-up, but also by the norms and beliefs of the cultural environment (Triandis, 1989). Culture shapes people's personal perceptions, dispositions and behaviours. More concretely, the cultural environment stimulates individual dispositions that fit that environment and restrains those dispositions that are not a good fit (Triandis, 1989). Hofstede (2001) talks about 'mental programs' developed in early childhood in the family and reinforced later on in schools and other organizations. Most research in this area studies the influence of national culture and reviewing this work is the main topic of this chapter. This nationally defined cultural environment is much easier to identify for marketers and there is substantial research that examines its influence on consumption behaviour.

SECTION 2: NATIONAL CULTURAL DIFFERENCES

Hofstede's Five Dimensions

Analyses of cultural differences among people have often been influenced by the seminal work *Culture's Consequences* by Hofstede (1980, 2001). Hofstede reports an analysis of more than 116,000 questionnaires filled out by IBM employees from 50 subsidiaries around the world. This research on the influence of national culture has become a classic for both academics and practitioners. In an era of increasing globalization, Hofstede's work drew attention to the importance of cultural differences on attitudes to work in an international organization.

In his analyses, Hofstede aimed to capture cultural differences between nations in four dimensions: power distance, uncertainty avoidance, individualism–collectivism, and masculinity-femininity. For instance, the first dimension – power distance – was based on three items, of which the central one was 'How frequently, in your experience, does the following problem occur: Employees expressing disagreement with their managers'. An additional dimension, long- versus short-term orientation, was added in a new book, a decade later. Some of these dimensions had been around in the social science literature for some time but Hofstede provided quantitative data on the differences in responses across nations (see Table 6.1).

Table 6.1 Hofstede's five dimensions categorizing national cultures

Name of dimension	Description of dimension
Power distance	The degree of acceptability, by the less powerful members of an organization, of the inequality of the distribution of power
Uncertainty avoidance	Intolerance of the unpredictable, ambiguous or uncertain
Individualism versus collectivism	The degree to which individuals are supposed to look after themselves or remain integrated into groups (usually around the family)
Masculinity–femininity	Economic and other achievements. Taking care of other people
Long- versus short-term orientation	The degree to which people accept delayed gratification or their material, social and emotional needs

Exercise 6.1   Where would you place these countries?

Hofstede presents the aggregate scores for individuals from each country in two-dimensional maps. For this exercise, focus on individualism versus collectivism, and weak and strong uncertainty avoidance, and assign two countries to each of the quadrants of Hofstede's map below (eight countries in total). In alphabetical order these countries are: Canada, France, Great Britain, Hong Kong, Italy, Mexico, Singapore and South Korea. (Answers in endnote 1.)

	Weak uncertainty avoidance	Strong uncertainty avoidance
Collectivistic		
Individualistic		

A CRITICAL ANALYSIS

Hofstede produced a monumental study that was, and is, referenced by virtually all those dealing with cultural differences. His work clearly has implications for individuals working in another culture than their own and for companies operating across different cultures. His findings have also often formed the basis for consumer research on cultural differences, as we will see later on in this chapter.

Although Hofstede's work was very influential, it also met with criticism. A fundamental concern was that he carried out an eclectic analysis of data, based on theoretical reasoning and correlation analysis. In other words, although his framework is based on hard data, he uses some creativity in the analysis. McSweeney (2002) summarized this verdict in the title of his article 'A Triumph of Faith – A Failure of Analysis'. He also attacks the assumption that one can extrapolate the results of IBM employees to an entire nation. IBM employees may not be representative for their nation. McSweeney thinks they may even be atypical. Moreover, the number of relevant questions in the IBM questionnaire was limited, and they may not be adequate to test Hofstede's propositions fully. The questionnaire was not designed to identify national cultures, and purposely designed questionnaires by other researchers have produced different results (see below). A third critique is that what Hofstede uncovered in the workplace may be situationally specific and not transferable to other situations (e.g. home, retail behaviour, recreational consumption). Fourth, again on the method side, McSweeney objects to the way in which Hofstede sought to validate his results by an analysis of historical and contemporary events, and he claims that these illustrative stories ignore counter-evidence. The 2001 edition of the book also presents cross-validation with other studies and claims that the findings are consistent with those from 140 other studies. A further criticism comes from Ailon (2008), who argues that, rather than capturing and mapping differences in societal values, Hofstede's work actually constructs reality and is therefore a product of a specific cultural milieu and knowledge-producing tradition. It therefore reaffirms a scheme in which western values are always the idealized reference point. Hofstede anticipated this criticism; he realized that his personal value system might influence the results and therefore outlined in the book his personal position on various questionnaire items. Revealing this potential bias does of course not eliminate it.

There is a danger of stereotyping. *On average*, one population may differ from another but plenty of people in the two populations could still share the same values and react in the same way to innovations. Work continues in this area; one recent paper by deMooij and Hofstede (2010) reviews the work and applies it to work on global branding and advertising strategy.

THE UNIVERSAL CONTENT AND STRUCTURE OF VALUES

It was Hofstede's intention to analyze the values held by his respondents. Rokeach (1973: 159–160), the key reference on this topic, defines values as enduring beliefs 'that a specific mode of conduct or end-state of existence is personally and socially preferable to alternative modes of conduct or end-states of existence'. These values are fairly general and Rokeach suggests they are activated in a large variety of situations. As already implied in this definition, Rokeach distinguishes between terminal values, referring to desirable end-states that a person would like to achieve during his or her lifetime, and instrumental values that are modes of behaviour to achieve the terminal values. When taking the Rokeach Value Survey (see Table 6.2), respondents have to order lists of values according to the importance each has as a guiding principle in their lives. Using this instrument, those in different cultures and sub-cultures can be compared.

Exercise 6.2	The Rokeach Value Survey

Take the Rokeach Value Survey (Table 6.2). Arrange the 18 terminal values, followed by the 18 instrumental values, into an order of importance to YOU, as guiding principles in YOUR life (Rokeach, 1973: 27). To what extent does your ranking relate to your consumption behaviour? How do you explain divergences?

It is interesting that the work on cultural values discussed here was done by psychologists. Until the 1980s, culture was still thought of as 'out there' rather than an individual disposition (Triandis, 2004). Most psychologists therefore held the view that cultural differences were a topic for anthropologists to work on. A major turning point came with

Table 6.2 The Rokeach Value Survey

Terminal values		Instrumental values	
1.	True friendship	1.	Cheerfulness
2.	Mature love	2.	Ambition
3.	Self-respect	3.	Love
4.	Happiness	4.	Cleanliness
5.	Inner harmony	5.	Self-control
6.	Equality	6.	Capability
7.	Freedom	7.	Courage
8.	Pleasure	8.	Politeness
9.	Social recognition	9.	Honesty
10.	Wisdom	10.	Imagination
11.	Salvation	11.	Independence
12.	Family security	12.	Intellect
13.	National security	13.	Broad-mindedness
14.	A sense of accomplishment	14.	Logic
15.	A world of beauty	15.	Obedience
16.	A world at peace	16.	Helpfulness
17.	A comfortable life	17.	Responsibility
18.	An exciting life	18.	Forgiveness

the publication of a review by Markus and Kitayama (1991) that showed major cultural differences in cognition, emotion and motivation.

The programmatic work of Schwartz and Bilsky (1987, 1990) provides a comprehensive academic reference on cross-cultural research into values. They developed a theory of a universal psychological structure of human values and tested it with an analysis of data from the Rokeach Value Survey. Their theory received empirical support from 97 studies in 44 countries with 25,000 respondents. The analysis is an interpretation into groupings and mapping of all the values as shown in Figure 6.1. It turns out that the groupings are stable across samples and they correspond to ten value types. The value types also always have the same neighbours. In fact, the five value types that primarily serve individual interests (power, achievement, hedonism, stimulation, self-direction) form a contiguous region opposite to another contiguous region formed by the three value types that serve primarily collective interests (benevolence, tradition, conformity). Universalism and security serve both types of interests and are located on the boundaries between these regions. The relationship among value types can also be summarized in terms of four higher-order value types that form the bipolar dimensions of Figure 6.1:

- Openness to change (following your own intellectual and emotional interests) versus conservation (preserving the status quo and the certainty it provides).
- Self-enhancement (advancing personal interests, even at the expense of others) versus self-transcendence (promotion of the welfare of others and nature).

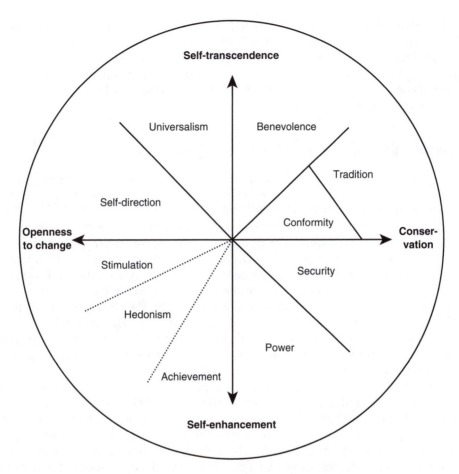

Figure 6.1   Relations among motivational types of values (Schwartz, 1992)

Note: the dotted lines around the hedonism wedge signal that this value is linked both to openness to change and to self-enhancement

Different societies share different values and value types, but not all combinations are possible. The simultaneous pursuit of some value types is possible while other combinations are incompatible.

SECTION 3: CULTURAL DIFFERENCES IN CONSUMER RESEARCH

The research in cultural psychology discussed in the previous section influenced consumer research and marketing in two ways. First, it helped us to segment markets and to understand their differences so that they could be targeted with different strategies and marketing plans. Second, it helped researchers to test their theories on how opposite mindsets such as individualistic versus collectivistic affect consumer behaviour. Cultural psychology indicated that nations have different cultural mindsets and that consumer researchers needed to take this into account when developing and advertising products, especially those designed for export to other national markets. Below we give two examples of these influences.

Cross-National Comparisons of Consumer Psychology

Steenkamp and Geyskens (2006) examine how country characteristics influence the perceived value that consumers derive from visiting websites, using data from almost 9,000 consumers in 23 countries. In general the experience of visiting a website has a utilitarian (acquiring useful information) component and an emotional component (the authors focus on pleasure and arousal). According to the authors, consumer evaluations of websites (in this case for consumer packaged goods) are driven by perceived privacy and security, customization to the individual's needs, and congruity with the local culture. The central proposition of this research is that the perceived value of the experience and the website characteristics mentioned above are influenced by the characteristics of the consumer's country. The authors examine the influence of individualism/collectivism and propose that when national-cultural individualism is higher, the effect on perceived value of the emotional experience, of the perceived privacy and security protection, and of the customization, are higher.

Consumer differences in innovativeness are explained by individual-level and national-cultural values by Steenkamp, Ter Hofstede and Wedel (1999). They use the Schwartz Value Survey to measure individuals' values (Schwartz and Sagiv, 1995) and categorized the 11 European countries of the sample in terms of individualism, uncertainty avoidance and masculinity by using an update of Hofstede's earlier work. Using Schwartz's bipolar value dimensions they hypothesize that a consumer's tendency to seek out new products and brands is impacted negatively by conservation and positively by self-enhancement (see Figure 6.1). In terms of Hofstede's cultural dimensions, individualism would be expected to have a positive effect and uncertainty avoidance a negative effect. Masculinity stands for assertiveness (versus nurturance) and should have a positive effect on innovativeness. In this large-scale consumer survey all hypothesized effects were supported but the finding for self-enhancement was not statistically significant.

Cultural Differences as Contrasts in Consumer Research

Aaker and Williams (1998) examine the effectiveness of emotional appeals in advertising. More specifically, they compare ego-focused (e.g. pride) and other-focused (e.g. empathy) advertising appeals. The contrast between individualist and collectivistic cultures in this work represents the effect of self-perception (referred to as self-construal) that is either independent (a focus on qualities of uniqueness) or interdependent (the self as inseparable from others and from the social context). According to the authors, these cultural differences lead to differences in the accessibility of certain types of emotions: ego-focused emotions should be more accessible in individualistic cultures and other-focused emotions in collectivistic cultures. This in turn should have a positive influence on the ability to process the respective emotions when they are presented in persuasive messages. As a test of their hypotheses, they presented a print ad for a fictitious new beer with one of the two following appeals (Aaker and Williams, 1998: 245):

- 'Acing the last exam. Winning the big race. Receiving deserved recognition. Ohio Flag Beer. Celebrating life's accomplishments.'
- 'Reminiscing with old friends. Enjoying time together with family during the holidays. Relaxing near the fire with best friends. Ohio Flag Beer. Celebrating the relationships that matter most.'

They compared the effect of each appeal on two samples: Chinese students (born and raised in China), as members of a collectivistic culture, and North American students, as members of an individualistic culture. The results showed a pattern opposite to the expectations: Chinese students showed more positive attitudes towards the advertisement and brand when exposed to the ego-focused emotions, as compared to the other-focused emotions, while for American students the scores were reversed. As explanation, the authors propose the novelty of the appeal as the driving factor. For members of a collectivistic culture, ego-focused appeals are more unusual and therefore trigger more attention. Similarly, the North American students may have found the collectivist messages unusual and were therefore more responsive to them. This idea was tested in a new study with ads for colour film that showed either (individual) happiness or peacefulness. The results confirmed that the novel thoughts provoked by an unusual appeal drove the subsequent attitudes to the advertisement and to the brand.

Members of collectivist cultures are generally considered to be caring and understanding. Does this also mean that they are easier to satisfy as consumers and that they are more tolerant of service failures? A recent review of the literature on cross-cultural services seems to indicate so (Zhang, Beatty and Walsh, 2008). But Chan, Wan and Sin (2009) addressed a different facet of collectivism: the need for attention and care. They proposed that, in some situations, consumers from more collectivistic cultures may be less tolerant of failure than those from individualistic cultures. The criterion is whether the service failure is social (e.g., status and esteem) or non-social (e.g. money and time). They developed a scenario for each and exposed it to American or Chinese students (a between-subjects design where each student sees one scenario). The students had to imagine going to a restaurant where either the waiter does not smile, messes up the order and does not apologize or the restaurant ran out of the food they selected and does not have the second choice available. The Asians were indeed more dissatisfied with a social failure than the westerners and less dissatisfied with a non-social failure. This research also examines the factors that drive this effect. The Asians' belief in fate explains their higher tolerance of non-social failure. Their concern for face (i.e. a positive image of self that is affirmed by interaction with others) makes them more sensitive to failures in a social context.

Box 6.1	Back-translation and other problems

A particular challenge for cross-cultural research, be it academic or commercial, is the translation of the measurement instrument. When questionnaire items are translated into another language, there may be no exact way of rendering the same meaning. This problem has been addressed by back-translating the translation into the original language to see whether the original and the back-translation have the same meaning. Brislin (1970) claimed that a functionally equivalent translation can be demonstrated when responses to the original and target versions are compared and found to be near-identical. However, it is pointed out that some bad translations that merely substitute terms (as in a machine translation) are easy to back translate, but may be poor in conveying the same meaning.

It seems reasonable to argue that meaning differences that are introduced in translation may be a basis for apparent cross-cultural differences. Such concerns are alleviated when studies using different methods and measures converge on the same outcome – if they do. Note that this problem is not necessarily removed by conducting all studies in English since this restricts sampling to those familiar with English, and even in such sub-groups, there may be differences of usage.

Other problems in comparing across cultures include differential response rates, differing responses to incentives and variation in the tendency to please interviewers.

MARKET-RELEVANT FACTS

Broad cultural differences between nations are of great interest but sometimes quite specific facts about difference in practice and thinking are important. For example, when Levi 501s were relaunched in Europe by BBH and McCann, they argued that jeans were perceived differently in the USA and Europe and, because of this, the existing US advertising was inappropriate for Europe (see Box 6.2).

There are other cases where cultural differences have particular forms that marketers should know about. For example, it is common practice on the Indian Subcontinent to stay with relatives. Indians and Bangladeshis have been heard to complain about the discomfort that occurs when relatives squeeze up to make room for a visitor. Sometimes the visitor would prefer to stay in a hotel but this would cause offence. Hotel firms in the west that seek to expand in other countries need to know about such practices.

Globalization

Up until now we have stressed the cultural differences among consumers living in different regions of the world. However, with the globalization of markets, these differences may be diminishing and the debate of globalization versus localization has concerned

---

Box 6.2 | A small difference in perception

When Bartle Bogle Hegarty and the McCann agencies handled the relaunch of *Levi 501* jeans in Europe in 1985 they refused to use the US advertising (Feldwick, 1990). Their analysis was that, in the USA, jeans were workaday clothes and increasingly old-fashioned but, in Europe, wearing jeans could still be a fashion statement. Moreover, 501s had genuine provenance and were worn by a small number of opinion leaders. Thus the agencies sought to re-establish the slightly baggy 501s as 'the right look' for young people, the definitive classic jean. To do this, they needed different advertising.

A set of commercials was developed of which the most famous was 'launderette' featuring Nick Kamen sitting in the *launderette* in his boxer shorts as he waited for his 501s to wash; the music backing was Marvin Gaye's 'I Heard It Through the Grapevine'. It is still to be found on YouTube if you search using 'Levi' and 'launderette'. These ads multiplied Levi's sales twenty-fold in the next three years at a higher price and it was claimed that even the sale of boxer shorts increased.

The point of this example is that the successful strategy related to a difference in perception about jeans – hardly a matter of cultural difference but immensely important to the success of the advertising. Such differences of perception are more a matter of market research than cross-cultural investigation but they cannot be ignored by marketers.

---

international marketing practitioners in the past few decades. Advocates of globalization stress convergence of consumer attitudes and behaviours across geographical boundaries and try to identify and reach consumer segments across boundaries with common products and marketing programmes. In this context, three Dutch researchers segmented European consumers from 11 different countries using a means-ends chain survey (Ter Hofstede, Steenkamp and Wedel, 1999). A means–ends chain examines how consumers connect to a product by asking questions about the link between attributes (e.g. organically produced, low fat) and benefits (e.g. spending less money, good taste) and that between benefits and values (e.g. self-respect, warm relationships). They identified four cross-national segments that then were linked to descriptive data on socio-demographics, product consumption and media usage, and information on personality and attitudes.

Marketing in China

China, as well as being the home of a large part of the world's population, shows a spectacular rate of GDP growth. In 2010 it was 10.4 per cent (World Bank) and eased to an annual rate of 8.1 per cent by the first quarter of 2012. Meanwhile, western markets recorded low or negative growth.[2] Because of its importance, we have compared China with western markets. How different is China? Although Chinese consumers buy different foodstuffs from the west, many other aspects of purchase are very similar and the Chinese are purchasing a large number of luxury brands from the west, from perfume to whisky. Uncles (2010) believes that the main theme is convergence – 'Significant aspects of the Chinese retail landscape now conform to what might be described as an international norm and, superficially at least, consumer attitudes and behaviours appear to be more alike.' Uncles (2010) notes that 'retail formats, institutions, infrastructures, and management practices are becoming similar to those seen in international markets'. In grocery retailing, hypermarkets and supermarkets are rapidly growing and took 62 per cent of grocery sales in 2008, a figure not far behind that of many Western countries. By comparison, traditional retailing such as wet markets are stationary. Uncles notes that much of the modern retail expansion is driven by international companies such as Carrefour and Tesco who often work in partnership with Chinese companies. This speeds the transfer of western business practice.

Chinese consumers accept the new pattern of retailing. One reason for this is environmental determinism. In Chapter 1 we noted that behaviour is moulded by the conditions under which people live; the environment defines what actions are possible and rewards and punishes behaviour according to how it fits the environmental conditions. It is hardly surprising that attitudes and values develop that broadly endorse a retail system that meets consumer needs and it would be naïve to assume that values always come first and systems are developed to be consistent with them. This control by the environment is enhanced when urban renewal projects replace the traditional market with a western format. Uncles notes that more traditional retailing practices persist in China but points out that there are corresponding traditional forms in the west.

Uncles, Wang and Kwok (2010b) studied brand performance metrics to see whether patterns familiar in the west are also found in China. They found the double jeopardy effect with toothpaste and soy sauce in two different cities, Shanghai and Xi'an, which was consistent over five years. They also showed that multi-brand loyalty was the norm, just as it is in Europe, Australasia or the USA. In two other studies, Uncles and Kwok (2008, 2009) examined patterns of category purchase by store. Again, the Dirichlet patterns were found, so what people buy may differ but how they buy fits patterns of behaviour found in the west.

In another study, Thøgersen and Zhou (2012) investigated the take-up of organic food. They found that Schwartz's universalism value lay behind the adoption of organic food in China, as in the west. Furthermore, buying organic food was strongly linked to beliefs about health, taste and care for the environment in both the west and China. Thus, this research suggests that globalization has proceeded fast in China and that, in many respects, there is convergence in the consumption patterns of China and the west.

SECTION 4: AGE AND GENDER DIFFERENCES IN CONSUMPTION

Age

The present scale of population ageing is 'unprecedented, pervasive, enduring and has profound implications for many facets of human life' (United Nations, 2002). The post-retirement proportion of the population is rising and many members of this group are becoming richer. Euromonitor (2011) reports that the percentage of the world's inhabitants over 65 has moved from 5.9 in 1980 to 8.0 in 2011 and that, in western Europe, the percentage is 16.5. In Japan, it is 23 per cent. Moreover, the current over-65s are closely followed by an even larger group of those born between 1946 and 1964 (the 'baby-boomers') who are now beginning to retire; these people also vary widely in their spending, social commitments and lifestyle and are, collectively, the wealthiest group of older people in history (Euromonitor, 2006). Marketers and policy-makers must take account of these changes and understand them because they will change economic priorities. Central to this understanding is how older consumers buy (Uncles and Lee, 2006).

Market research has focused on the goods and services that are typically bought by consumer segments. However, to explain preferences among older consumers, it is necessary to study how the *process* of decision-making varies with age. So far, this aspect of decision-making has focused mainly on variation in cognitive and affective processes as people age (Cole et al., 2008; Drolet, Schwarz and Yoon, 2010; Lambert-Pandraud and Laurent, 2010; Lambert-Pandraud, Laurent and Lapersonne, 2005).

Lambert-Pandraud et al. (2005) examined the impact of age on loyalty. They analyzed the answers of 30,000 respondents to a survey of recent new-car buyers who had replaced a previous car. The survey covered the purchase process of both the recently acquired and the previous car. Because a car purchase is one of the most involving consumer purchases, one would expect consumers to engage in at least some information search and comparison. In fact, 21 per cent of consumers between the ages of 60 and 74 considered only one brand, and among consumers 75 or over, 27 per cent were in this group. Many respondents purchased the same make of car and, as age rose, so did the repeat-purchase rate, shown in Figure 6.2. The effect of age remained strong in a multivariate model that includes contextual variables and other socio-demographics. Older car-purchasers showed other characteristics. They considered fewer car models when they considered more than one, they dealt with fewer dealers and, when they did change the make of their car, they were likely to buy a familiar national brand. They were also more prone to defer purchase, a matter that should interest marketers (and governments when economies are stagnating).

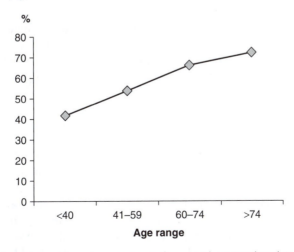

Figure 6.2   The repeat purchase of cars by age group (from Lambert-Pandraud, Laurent and Lapersonne, 2005)

Taking all these facts together, we can see that the decision-making of the older consumer can be described as *conservative*.

The conservatism of older buyers could relate to *cognitive decline*, which increases the cognitive effort in decision-making and pushes the older person towards decision heuristics such as choice repetition or purchase deferral (Lambert-Pandraud et al., 2005; Phillips and Sternthal, 1977). However, there is evidence that it is the speed rather than the ability to process information that is measured in tests of cognitive process (Cole and Houston, 1987; Roedder-John and Cole, 1986). This suggests that older people may have the capacity to decide effectively but make less use of this capacity because of their slower processing speed.

A second explanation is *socio-emotional selectivity*: that older persons tend to have more activation of emotional centres leading to a focus on affective information as age advances. This leads to more attention to established emotional contacts and less to gaining new information, which results in older consumers having fewer social interactions and concentrating on the people they know well (Castensen, Isaakowitz and Charles, 1999). This could explain the smaller choice set of car brands/dealers among older people found by Lambert-Pandraud et al. (2005).

A third mechanism producing conservative behaviour is *change aversion* (Wallach and Kogan, 1961). Change aversion leads to purchase deferral and draws decision-makers toward more familiar options where risks may be lower. However, such change aversion may relate to a justifiable cynicism about brand differences that grows with experience and therefore age. *Risk aversion* was studied by Simcock, Sudbury and Wright (2006). They found that older buyers of cars were more likely to express risk-related concerns.

These three explanations for age-related conservatism suggest a fairly inexorable process of change as people age that is difficult to influence. However, it is possible that this work has focused too much on individual processes and not enough on the social element in consumer decision-making. We know that many decisions occur because advice from others draws attention to new alternatives and pushes the individual to think through the possibilities. To explore this, 16 accumulated studies on word of mouth (WOM) conducted at Kingston University were reviewed to see whether there were any age-related differences in volume of word of mouth received. These studies covered bank accounts, cameras, computers, holidays, credit cards, and two studies each of mobile phones, mobile phone airtime, coffee shops, restaurants and supermarkets. The results were startling and are shown in Figure 6.3.

From Figure 6.3 we can see that word of mouth about brands received by respondents falls sharply with age. On average, respondents aged 65 and over receive 1.5 instances of WOM compared with 3.9 by those aged 25. Men tend to report receiving more WOM than women except in the 65+ segment. A number of explanations could fit these findings. The older respondents might recall fewer instances of advice because of cognitive decline but, against this, the effect is fairly continuous and seems to start before the age when cognitive decline is believed to start. Also, retirement, the death of friends and the departure of children from the household – leading to reduced social contact – are consistent with the decline in advice observed. The same research also examined the period of time that respondents had owned their current brand in seven categories and this period jumped to

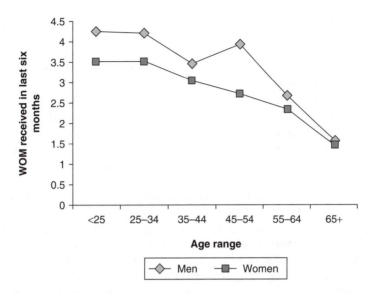

Figure 6.3 Average sum of received positive and negative word of mouth about brands by age and sex (2600 respondents from 16 studies)

nearly twice the level for the post-65-year-olds. Using regression analysis the researchers examined whether word of mouth received was related to the length of time that the current brand had been owned (which was seen as evidence of purchase deferral). It was found that the volume of positive advice did have a significant effect, reducing purchase deferral, so we can say that those respondents who received a greater volume of positive advice were more likely to state that they had changed their brand of bank account, mobile phone, credit card, etc.

This evidence therefore suggests another explanation for conservative behaviour by the older consumer: that, compared to younger consumers, they have lower levels of social influence. If this is so, the older consumer may be induced to consume more if marketers can influence those who give advice, such as children, or if the deficit in advice can be covered by increased advertising designed for this age group. There is clearly more to find out about age differences. We have not discussed how the importance of different categories changes as people get older; older people may process decisions like younger people when the decision is more important to them, for example when it concerns finance or medical decisions.

Gender

It is a common stereotype that men show lower levels of sexual loyalty than women. How about consumer loyalty? Melnyk, van Osselaer and Bijmolt (2009) make the distinction between loyalty towards people and towards companies. They present a series of studies indicating that female customers are more loyal to individuals, whereas male customers are more loyal to groups and firms. They cite work (Cross and Madson, 1997) that shows that in western cultures, women, more than men, want to connect to other people and maintain existing relationships. Thus women focus on interdependence. One view is that men see themselves as independent and focus on uniqueness and individuality but Melnyk et al. also discuss the idea that both women and men are interdependent, but in different ways. In their account, women attach more importance to close relationships with specific individuals while men focus on relationships with larger and more abstract groupings of people. Thus, men are interdependent too but their interdependence is with groups rather than individuals.

Applying this thinking, Melnyk and her co-authors propose that women may be more loyal to individual employees while men are more loyal to companies/brands. In a scenario study, the authors present participants with a situation where instead of going to the closest bakery for a birthday cake, there is the option of going to a bakery owned and run by somebody they went to high school with. In an alternative condition, the word *somebody* is replaced by a group of people. In subsequent studies they asked participants directly whether they were more loyal to individual service providers or to companies in different categories for their actual consumption behaviour. Across these studies they show that women do not always exhibit more consumer loyalty than men. But their loyalty does indeed extend to individual employees, while men show more loyalty towards companies. They also found evidence that these types of loyalty are driven by the quest for relational versus collective interdependence, for women and men respectively.

The difference in loyalty between men and women found by Melnyk et al. could be underpinned by genetic difference or adjustment to social norms. The generalizability of the findings will depend on which explanation applies; if the difference relates to role differences that are widely found in western economies, we might find different patterns of loyalty in other societies where the role relationships are different. This would mean that the loyalty difference is more cross-cultural than inherent in genetics. From the findings of Melnyk et al., we might expect women to talk more about categories where interpersonal relationships were common. Some unpublished work at Kingston University indicates the product fields that women talk about to others more than men. Men talk more about mobile phones, airtime suppliers for mobile phones, computers, credit cards and bank accounts while women talk more about holiday destinations, luxury brands, supermarkets, restaurants and coffee shops. These differences fit gender roles. Women may give more advice about supermarkets because they do so much more food shopping than men (Chang-Hyeon, Arentze and Timmermans, 2006), but women use phones more than men according to Nielsen (2011b) in evidence from the USA and, despite this, men appear to talk more about mobiles. Perhaps devices like phones, being impersonal, attract more interest from men. Whatever the bases for these differences, they are of importance to marketers and ad agencies making decisions about the targeting and content of communications.

SUMMARY

The cultural environment in which an individual is raised and lives obviously shapes his or her perceptions, dispositions and behaviour. National cultural differences have been studied extensively, largely under the influence of the seminal work of Hofstede. Hofstede categorizes countries on the level of power distance that is accepted by their members, their tolerance for uncertainty, the degree to which economic achievement versus caring for other people is valued, the degree to which the delay of gratification is accepted, and the degree to which individuals are supposed to look after themselves or remain integrated in groups. This last dimension, referred to as individualism versus collectivism, has been much used in consumer research. An excellent mapping of all relevant cultural differences is provided by Schwartz and Bilsky (1990); based on the Rokeach Value Survey, they identify ten value types.

As examples of how consumer researchers have used these classifications of cultures, we described how the perceived value of visiting websites and consumer innovativeness are influenced by differences in individualism-collectivism. We also examined differences between American and Chinese consumers in their sensitivity to ego-focused and other-focused appeals in advertising and in their tolerance to service failures.

National differences between consumers continue to influence marketing communications and service format but at the same time we observe convergence. We illustrated this with an international segmentation study and a study of consumption behaviour in China.

Understanding consumer group differences is useful for market segmentation. Behavioural differences between individuals and groups are often easy to observe but understanding the fundamental drivers of this behaviour has broader application potential. We examined the reasons for increased brand loyalty of older consumers. We also compared loyalty of men and women and found that men are more loyal towards companies while women more so towards individual employees.

Further reading on cross-cultural studies

This chapter examined the most relevant consumer differences that also received research attention. For the reader specifically interested in cross-cultural issues from a marketing practitioner's point of view, we recommend the following handbooks:

de Mooij, M. (2011) *Consumer Behavior and Culture: Consequences for Global Marketing and Advertising*, 2nd edition, London: Sage Publications Ltd.

de Mooij, M. (2010) *Global Marketing and Advertising: Understanding Cultural Paradoxes*, 3rd edition, London: Sage Publications.

Usunier, J.C. and Lee J. (2011) *Marketing Across Cultures*, 5th edition, Prentice Hall.

Notes

1 Answer to Exercise 6.1:

	Weak uncertainty avoidance	Strong uncertainty avoidance
Collectivistic	Hong Kong Singapore	Mexico South Korea
Individualistic	Canada Great Britain	France Italy

2 Some of the spectacular growth in consumption in China is attributable to the one-child policy in the country. Demographers have drawn attention to the resources that have to be spent on servicing an increasing population. If the population increases by 2 per cent each year, so must the schools, firms and other social institutions if the new generation is to have the same opportunities as before. This is called the demographic investment and it holds back development. The problem is made worse by the fact that a growing population contains a larger proportion of children who do not assist the economy and who need the attention of adults, thus further restricting economic activity. China has avoided the demographic investment. The one-child policy has the eventual consequence that the ratio of old to young shifts and a large older population has to be supported by a smaller workforce. However, by then, China may have established the economy at a higher level so that everyone can benefit. In India, population growth has continued at a rate of 1.6 per cent per year (Rosenberg, 2011) and this helps to explain why India's economy is not expanding as rapidly as that of China.

Part 3
Explaining Decision-Making

7 Predicting and Explaining Behaviour

LEARNING OBJECTIVES

When you have completed this chapter, you should be able to:

1 Define attitude, belief and intention, and explain how these concepts are measured.
2 Understand the expected-value theory of attitude applied to products.
3 Report on the research linking attitude and intention to behaviour.
4 Describe the theory of planned behaviour, its applications, strengths and weaknesses.
5 Understand the problems of predicting behaviour.

OVERVIEW

The cognitive approach to consumer behaviour relates consumers' attitudes, beliefs and intentions to their behaviour. Among the theories used, the theory of planned behaviour has been most successful, although a number of problems with this theory remain. We first examine the nature and measurement of attitudes, beliefs and intentions and their relationship with behaviour, and then we explain how the theory of planned behaviour can be used to predict and explain behaviour. This has a clear relevance to marketing: we need to predict purchase and to understand why people prefer one brand to another if we are to create products in the right quantity and of the right quality.

SECTION 1: DEFINITIONS AND MEASUREMENTS

Attitudes are what we feel about a concept, which may be a brand, category, person, theory or anything else we think about and attach feelings to. An important class of concepts are *actions*, particularly commercially relevant behaviour such as buying, renting, using and betting. We focus on attitudes to such actions because these attitudes help us to predict the consumer behaviour that concerns marketers. Thus, it is the attitude to *playing* the National Lottery or *buying* a smart phone that most interests us. The attitude to the object (the National Lottery or the smart phone itself) is less directly related to the action.

A person's attitude may be inferred from his or her actions or measured using a systematic questioning procedure. According to the mental representations model, introduced in Chapter 3, a concept is a node linked to other nodes. The linkages to other nodes can be seen as beliefs about the central concept. When the concept is an action, the beliefs often concern the outcomes of the action. If I play the National Lottery, there are outcomes such as dreaming of untold wealth, being excited by the draw and, usually, being disappointed by the result. Such beliefs have an outcome likelihood (or belief strength) and an evaluation which can be measured by the scales below:

If I play the National Lottery I will be excited by the draw

unlikely	1	2	3	4	5	6	7	likely
	extremely	*quite*	*slightly*	*neither*	*slightly*	*quite*	*extremely*	

Being excited by the draw is:

bad	−3	−2	−1	0	1	2	3	good
	extremely	*quite*	*slightly*	*neither*	*slightly*	*quite*	*extremely*	

The first scale measures the likelihood of the outcome, the second measures the value of the outcome if it occurs. These seven-point measures, called semantic differential scales, were first used in research by Osgood, Suci and Tannenbaum (1957). We usually denote the likelihood measure as b (for belief) and the evaluation measure as e. The full outcome measure is the product of b and e, which we call the *expected value* of the outcome. An expected value can be negative as well as positive because the evaluation can be negative.

The Expected-Value Theory of Attitude

Most of the alternatives from which we choose are *multi-attribute*. To assess the value of going to Wales for a holiday, I have to take account of weather, cost, travelling effort, food, opportunities for recreation, etc. Using the method above, we can measure an expected value for each outcome, and my overall (or global) attitude to going to Wales for a holiday is given by the sum of the expected values. So, if A is the global attitude:

$$A = b_1e_1 + b_2e_2 + b_3e_3 + \ldots$$

or $A = \sum b_i e_i$

Rosenberg (1956) pioneered this approach in attitude theory and Fishbein (1963) tested the relationship by separately measuring the global attitude, A, and the sum value, $\sum b_i e_i$. If the theory is correct and A is related to $\sum b_i e_i$, then subjects with high scores on one measure will have high scores on the other. Thus, by correlating respondents' scores on the two measures, we can find out how much A is related to $\sum b_i e_i$. Fishbein found a correlation between the sum score and the global measure of 0.80, which gave strong support to the idea that global attitudes are based on the sum of the expected values of the attributes. Fishbein's expected-value treatment of attitude has been confirmed in a large number of subsequent studies though the correlations are generally lower than 0.8 (typically, in the range 0.4 to 0.6).

Fishbein's treatment of attitude assumes a process of compensation: for example, that the unspoilt beaches can offset wet weather in Wales. At best, compensation is likely to be partial. Just taking account of the main outcome of one alternative requires some thought and when several outcomes are involved the assessment is obviously more complicated. As noted in Chapter 1, extended thought before choice is a rarity but we probably consider more attributes when important decisions are taken. People choosing between several options usually take the one with the largest expected value. Edwards (1954) described this as the subjective expected utility (SEU) model of decision. This way of thinking about decisions treats any product as a bundle of expected gains and losses.

Modal Salient Beliefs

Fishbein's theory of attitude is about what *individuals* think and feel, but it has to be tested on *groups* of people and each member of the group may have a somewhat different basis for their attitude. To take account of this, some studies have asked each person separately about the attributes that he or she thought were important, e.g. Budd (1986) on cigarette use and Elliott and Jobber (1990) on company use of market research. This technique increases the observed association between global and sum measures but is laborious. Fortunately, on many issues there is substantial agreement between people on the factors that are important, and the same questionnaire can be used on all respondents with only a modest loss of precision.

To establish the commonly held beliefs about a concept it is necessary to perform an *elicitation*, which is described in Exercise 7.1. This is a series of questions about the positive and negative associations of the concept which are put to members of the target group. The beliefs that come easily to mind are recorded and those that occur frequently in a group, called *modal salient beliefs*, are used for the questionnaire. In an elicitation, the questioning should be low pressure. Fishbein and Ajzen (1975) ('Ajzen' is pronounced 'Eye-zen') argue that beliefs which have to be dredged up from the recesses of the mind are unlikely to have much effect on behaviour. Exercise 7.1 covers not only the gains and losses of a prospective action, but also factors discussed later in the chapter – the influence of other people and the personal and environmental factors that make the action easier or more difficult to perform.

Exercise 7.1   Eliciting salient beliefs

1   **Define the action clearly**. For example, 'buying Snickers', 'getting a new computer', 'giving blood when the blood transfusion service comes to the campus'.
2   **Define clearly the target group**. For example, you might be particularly interested in children buying Snickers, or women computer buyers.
3   **Elicit salient beliefs**. In a sample of people from the target group, ask each person questions about the advantages and disadvantages of the defined action. After each response prompt with: 'anything else?' but do not press hard for ideas. Record the responses for each person. A typical encounter might be:

Q.   Can you tell me what you think are the advantages of getting a new computer?
A.   You get a lot for your money now.
Q.   Anything else?
A.   Probably more reliable.
Q.   Anything else?
A.   Not really.
Q.   Can you tell me what are the disadvantages of getting a new computer?
A.   It will have to be set up with the right programs.
Q.   Anything else?
A.   I'll have to get used to new versions of Word and PowerPoint.
Q.   Is there anything else that you can think of about getting a new computer?
A.   No.

4   **The negative action**. Certain actions may have different salient beliefs associated with *not* doing the action. For example, 'not having children' and 'not taking drugs' may be seen as actions with their own rationale and are not just the opposites to having children and taking drugs. For such negative actions, it is wise to also elicit salient beliefs about the negative action.
5   **Salient referents**. Ask each respondent in the sample whether there are people or groups who think that the respondent should do the defined action. Repeat with 'should not'. Ask if there are other people or organizations that come to mind when they think of the action. Use the prompt 'anyone else?' but do not press for responses. (Recent work has often included measures of what salient referents think the respondent *will* do as well as *should* do.)
6   **Control factors**. Ask each respondent about conditions that make the action easier or harder to perform. Again, prompt with 'anything else?'
7   **Refine the list of beliefs**. Combine similar beliefs. Compile a list of modal salient beliefs using the ones most frequently mentioned. The decision to include a belief depends on the frequency with which it is mentioned and the time and money available to support the research. When the questionnaire is intended to be used *both before and after* exposure to advertising or the product, it is important to include beliefs that may *become* salient as a result of this exposure.
8   You can use the computer program NEWACT (available from Sage) to create a questionnaire according to the methods of planned behaviour theory.

After similar responses have been grouped together, the list of modal salient beliefs is usually quite short. Complex issues, such as getting married or using oral contraceptives, may have about ten salient beliefs relating to attitude; simpler issues, such as buying specific chocolate bars, will have fewer.

Do Attitudes Predict Action?

Our interest in attitudes is partly based on the belief that they predict behaviour. Following Allport (1935), an attitude is usually seen as 'a preparation or readiness for response' and thus should be a predictor of behaviour, except when freedom of action is restricted. However, when Wicker (1969: 65) reviewed 47 studies on attitudes and behaviours, he concluded that: 'It is considerably more likely that attitudes will be unrelated or only slightly related to overt behaviors than that attitudes will be closely related to actions.'

Schuman and Johnson (1976) suggested that other unreported variables affected behaviour in addition to attitude. This was supported in work by Fishbein and Ajzen (1975), Ajzen and Fishbein (1980) and Ajzen (1985, 1991). These researchers showed that, in addition to attitude, behaviour is controlled by beliefs about the wishes of people and groups important to the respondent and by beliefs about the way personal ability and the environment can promote or restrict behaviour.

In addition to the 'other variables' explanation for the poor prediction of behaviour, Ajzen and Fishbein (1977) pointed out that researchers frequently measured the wrong attitude. The correct attitude for predicting behaviour is the attitude to that specific behaviour. Fishbein and Ajzen (1975: 360) concluded that 'many of the studies that have been viewed as testing the relation between attitude and behaviour are actually of little relevance to that question'. Thus, if you want to predict quitting smoking, it is the attitude to quitting smoking not the attitude to cigarettes, or even smoking in general, that should be measured. This lack of compatibility between the attitude and behaviour measures is neatly demonstrated by an unpublished study conducted on 270 women by Jaccard, King and Pomazal (reported by Ajzen and Fishbein, 1977). In this work, three attitudes relating to birth control were measured and correlated with the use of birth control. As the attitude comes closer to the specification of the behaviour, the correlation rises (see Table 7.1). This effect is readily explicable if we think of the motivations of different women. For example, a woman who wanted to become pregnant would neither use the pill nor be positive in her attitude to using it (giving a high correlation between her behaviour and her attitude), but she might still be positive about the pill and birth control in general (giving a low correlation with her non-usage of the pill). Similar results were obtained in another study of the correlations between attitudes to 'religion', 'church', 'attending church this Sunday' and actual church attendance this Sunday.

Another example of using the wrong attitude takes the form of trying to predict what people *will* do from measures of *past* satisfaction. As we saw in Chapter 2, satisfaction can be a poor predictor of future behaviour because people can be positive about their past experience with a product without necessarily wanting to use it in the future. Needs change and sometimes products change so that what was satisfactory in the past may not be expected to be satisfactory in the future. A somewhat better prediction of retention would be obtained by using the attitude to 'buying the product again'.

Table 7.1 Correlations are greater when measures of attitude and behaviour are more compatible (Ajzen and Fishbein, 1977)

Attitude to:	Correlation with use of the birth control pill
Birth control	0.16
The birth control pill	0.34
Using the birth control pill	0.65

Specifying Measures

From this work it is clear that the more compatible the measures of attitude and behaviour, the more they will correlate. Compatibility is specified by target, action, context and time (think TACT). In the case of oral contraceptive use, the target is the oral contraceptive, the action is using it and the context/time is implicit in its use. In other cases, the context and time could be more important. For example, shopping in my local supermarket on a Saturday morning might be avoided because the local store is so busy at that time. In addition to the TACT variables, it is important to ensure that respondents are talking about their own attitudes and behaviour rather than some general idea. Ajzen and Fishbein (1977) applied these compatibility criteria in a meta-analysis of 142 attitude–behaviour associations. They sorted the studies into those with low, partial and high compatibility between the measures and sub-divided the last group because some measures were not clearly specified. Table 7.2 shows their findings. It is clear that low compatibility between attitude and behaviour explains why many previous studies showed a weak connection between attitude and behaviour.

Another measurement challenge occurs when attitudes embrace a *set* of behaviours rather than one specific behaviour (Ajzen and Fishbein, 1977). For example, a measure of a person's attitude to the environment might give a rather low prediction of their bottle recycling behaviour because specific factors may affect the decision to recycle bottles. If a multiple-act measure of environmental behaviour is constructed that also includes use of recycled paper, use of low-energy bulbs, installing insulation, recycling of metals and newsprint, donations to environmental groups, refusal to buy tropical hardwoods,

Table 7.2 Analysis of attitude–behaviour studies (adapted from Ajzen and Fishbein, 1977)

Compatibility	Significance of attitude–behaviour relationship		
	Nil	Low	High
Low	26	1	0
Partial	20	47	4
High–questionable measures	0	9	9
High–appropriate measures	0	0	26

boycotting the products of environmentally suspect firms, criticizing women in fur coats, etc., we would expect this measure to have a stronger correlation with the attitude to the environment. This is because the specific factors affecting single actions tend to cancel each other out in the combined measure leaving the common theme of helping the environment. Consistent with this, Weigel and Newman (1976) found that the attitude to environmental preservation correlated better with a multiple-act measure of environmentally concerned behaviour than with single measures.

In consumer research, the compatibility principle means that attitudes to the *purchase*, *hiring* and so on of the product must be measured if it is these actions that we want to predict. This simple lesson about using compatible measures has not been well learned. Usually attitudes to the brand are studied rather than attitudes to purchasing the brand. Often there is substantial overlap between these measures but, as Ajzen and Fishbein show (1980: ch. 13), this is not always so. Many of the early studies reviewed by Wicker (1969) in this field used incompatible measures, thus explaining the low association that he found between attitude and behaviour. The notion of compatibility has much improved attitude research.

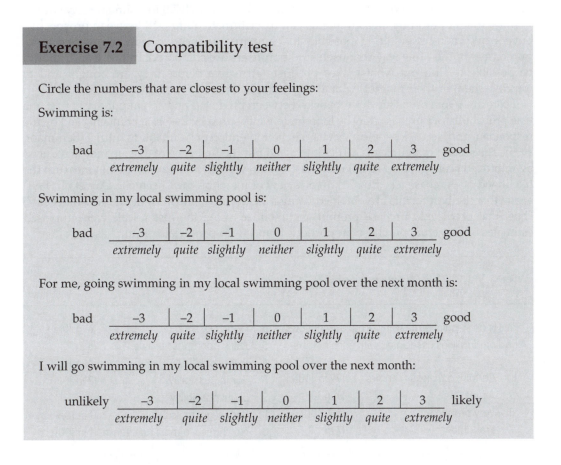

Exercise 7.2   Compatibility test

Circle the numbers that are closest to your feelings:

Swimming is:

	bad	−3	−2	−1	0	1	2	3	good
		extremely	quite	slightly	neither	slightly	quite	extremely	

Swimming in my local swimming pool is:

	bad	−3	−2	−1	0	1	2	3	good
		extremely	quite	slightly	neither	slightly	quite	extremely	

For me, going swimming in my local swimming pool over the next month is:

	bad	−3	−2	−1	0	1	2	3	good
		extremely	quite	slightly	neither	slightly	quite	extremely	

I will go swimming in my local swimming pool over the next month:

	unlikely	−3	−2	−1	0	1	2	3	likely
		extremely	quite	slightly	neither	slightly	quite	extremely	

In Exercise 7.2, we are not able to measure behaviour so a measure of intention, the last scale, is used as a proxy. The scores of students in a class can be entered on a data file and the correlations between the last intention measure and each of the other measures calculated. You should find that the more compatible a concept is with the intention measure, the higher the correlation between the measures.

Purchase Intentions

Intentions may predict behaviour but do not tell us why the behaviour is undertaken; for this, reasons are required. However, sometimes in marketing, prediction of behaviour may be all that is needed.

Purchase behaviour may be predicted either from stated intention or from a person's estimate of their purchase probability. Measures of intention have been well tested in the field of consumer durable purchase. In early research in this area, Pickering and Isherwood (1974) found that 61 per cent of those who said they were '100 per cent likely to purchase' actually did so; this compares with the 5 per cent of respondents who made a purchase even though they had expressed no intention to purchase the durable in the next 12 months. These findings were close to those obtained by Gabor and Granger (1972) in a similar early study.

Since intention-to-buy measurements can discriminate quite well between prospective buyers and non-buyers it is possible to compare prospective purchasers and non-purchasers in the same way that users and non-users are compared. In this way, it should be possible to find out what makes products attractive before they are bought and to improve them or their marketing at an early stage.

There are two reasons for discrepancies between predicted and actual purchase: first, the true probability of purchase may be inaccurately measured by the scale point checked by the respondent and, second, people may change their intention or be unable to fulfil it (Bemmaor, 1995). The second inaccuracy is difficult to avoid but the first type of discrepancy is reduced by improved scaling. Juster (1966) used an 11-point, verbally referenced scale to measure the likelihood of purchase (see Box 7.1). In a review of intention measurement, Day et al. (1991) argue that the best results are obtained using a Juster scale, and Wright and MacRae (2007) show that predicted purchase proportions obtained using the Juster scale were unbiased estimates of the actual purchase proportions found from panel data or purchase recall.

Box 7.1 | The Juster scale

This is an 11-point scale with verbal descriptions and probabilities associated with each number:

			6	Good possibility	(6 in 10)
			5	Fairly good possibility	(5 in 10)
			4	Fair possibility	(4 in 10)
10	Certain, practically certain	(99 in 100)	3	Some possibility	(3 in 10)
9	Almost sure	(9 in 10)	2	Slight possibility	(2 in 10)
8	Very probable	(8 in 10)	1	Very slight possibility	(1 in 10)
7	Probable	(7 in 10)	0	No chance, almost no chance	(1 in 100)

Intention measures are used in the planned behaviour research reported next. In planned behaviour research, the seven-point semantic differential scale has usually been used (rather than the eleven-point scale described above), either as a direct measure of intention or as a self-prediction by the respondent that he or she will perform some behaviour. Often, there is little difference between the two measures but self-prediction seems likely to be more accurate because it may take more account of conditions that may prevent action. For example, people may intend to give up cigarettes but be more realistic if asked to estimate the likelihood that they actually will give up. However, Sheppard, Hartwick and Warshaw (1988) reviewed a large number of attitude–behaviour studies and found only marginal superiority for self-prediction over true intention measures.

Normally, with durable goods like cars, a large majority of people express no intention of buying in the next year so that even a small percentage of this group who do buy provides a large fraction of the total number of buyers. Pickering and Isherwood (1974) found that 55 per cent of all buyers came from the group expressing no intention to buy. Theil and Kosobud (1968) in the USA, and Gabor and Granger (1972) in Britain, found that 70 and 65 per cent of purchasers respectively were in the group stating a zero purchase probability.

The extent to which people fulfil their intentions was reviewed by McQuarrie (1988), who assembled data from 13 studies. McQuarrie found that those who intended to purchase did so, on average, 42 per cent of the time whereas those not intending to purchase did not purchase 88 per cent of the time; this asymmetry is probably related to the fact that it is easier not to do something than to do it (see Box 7.2).

Box 7.2	Reasons for inaction

Why don't people do what they intend? East (1993) found that only two-thirds of those intending to apply for shares in British government privatizations actually did so. When the other third were asked why they hadn't followed through on their intention, they were equally divided between changing their mind (e.g. because the investment looked less advantageous) and inertia (e.g. forgetting, too much trouble). Pickering (1975) investigated failure to follow through an intention to buy consumer durables. In this case, respondents had usually changed their mind due to unforeseen circumstances, such as lack of money, or because their current durable was lasting better than expected.

Discrepancies between attitude and behaviour may also increase with the period that elapses between attitude measurement and behaviour measurement. The longer the period, the more opportunity people have to change their minds in response to new information or changed circumstances. For example, the attitude to voting for a political party may be affected by unfolding political events, and a measure of voting attitude taken close to an election should naturally be expected to have more predictive value than one taken a year before. However, although this effect of time lapse seems common sense,

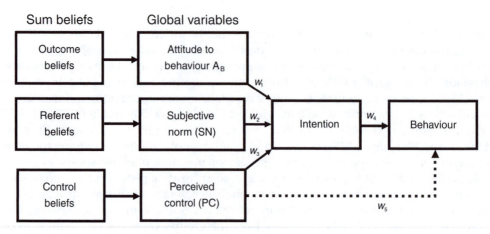

Figure 7.1 The theory of planned behaviour (TPB)

a study by Randall and Wolff (1994) found no evidence that the length of the interval was related to the correlation between intention and behaviour.

One study has raised some concern about the prediction of behaviour from intention. Chandon, Morwitz and Reinartz (2005) found that correlations in surveys between intention and subsequent behaviour are artificially increased by the process of asking about the respondent's intentions. It appears that the research process affects the respondents so that, after questioning, they are more likely to do what they said they were going to do.

SECTION 2: THE THEORY OF PLANNED BEHAVIOUR

Attitudes, intentions and behaviour have been combined in a comprehensive model of consumer choice called the theory of planned behaviour. Figure 7.1 illustrates this theory and Figure 7.2 shows it applied to playing the UK National Lottery.

The theory of planned behaviour (TPB) was developed over a long period, starting with Fishbein's (1963) expected-value theory of attitude. This theory was extended in a number of studies to predict intention and behaviour (e.g. Ajzen and Fishbein, 1969; Ajzen, 1971; Ajzen and Fishbein, 1972). In addition to attitude (A_B), the authors included subjective norm (SN) as a determinant of intention. SN measures the person's beliefs about what other people think they should do. This extended model was renamed the theory of reasoned action by Ajzen and Fishbein (1980) in a book in which they applied the theory to practical concerns such as health, consumer behaviour and voting. In 1985, Ajzen introduced the theory of planned behaviour by adding perceived control (PC) as a determinant of intention. PC measures a person's beliefs about the opportunities for an action which are based on the environment and their own abilities. The relative strengths of A_B, SN and PC in determining an action are given by the weights w_1, w_2 and w_3. Since

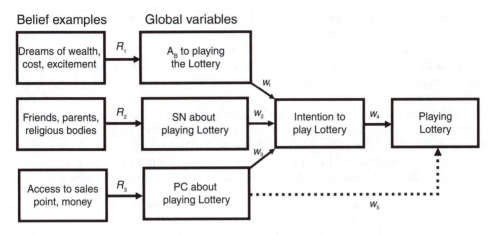

Belief examples

Global variables

Figure 7.2   The theory of planned behaviour applied to playing the National Lottery

these weights vary from category to category, they are established empirically, using regression analysis or structural equation modelling.

As can be seen from Figure 7.1, the three global variables determine intention, which then determines behaviour. The weight w_4 reflects the fact that circumstances may stop people from realizing their intentions, or that their intentions could change. Finally, the model includes a second direct effect of perceived control on behaviour, with weight w_5. This covers behaviours such as giving up smoking and eating less where lack of personal control can undermine intention. This might apply to compulsive gamblers who find the National Lottery difficult to resist.

This theory also covers altruistic behaviour, which can be driven by the subjective norm, and it takes account of a person's self-assessed abilities and opportunities. As such, it is an advance on simple subjective expected utility (SEU) models that do not allow for such influences. The subjective norm is an internalized influence, exerting its effect through the agent's memories and values. The social agents that are recalled need not be present, or even exist, for them to have an effect. In recent work, a measure called the descriptive norm has been added. This is what others expect that the respondent *will* do (as opposed to *should* do). For example, Forward (2009) found that adding a descriptive norm variable to the model improved prediction of driving violations. Similarly, White et al. (2009) found that the addition of descriptive norm improved the prediction of recycling behaviour. Among the many behaviours to which the TPB has been applied are: taking exercise, attaining college grades, condom use, health self-examinations, escaping addiction, blood donation, mothers' diet management of their babies, food choice, recycling, buying environmentally friendly products, Internet use, reducing risky driving, accident avoidance, seeking funding, buying gifts, applying for shares in initial public offerings, and complaining. It is suitable for any behaviour where there are reasons for action but it is more appropriate for explaining category use than brand use if there are few differences in beliefs and attitudes between brands.

When behaviour has yet to occur, or is difficult to measure, studies predict intention rather than behaviour, so it is important to know how strong the link (w_4) is between intention and behaviour. Conner et al. (2007) measured intention and actual behaviour with regard to breaking speed limits using an extended model of planned behaviour. The model predicted 82 per cent of intention but only 17 per cent of actual behaviour was predicted. A review of 185 studies by Armitage and Conner (2001) found that, on average, 39 per cent of intention was predicted and 21 per cent of objectively measured behaviour. However, these figures may have been inflated by the effect of prior questioning, as indicated earlier (Chandon, Morwitz and Reinartz, 2005). In marketing, we are concerned with behaviour, since this is where money is made, and evidence that there is usually only a relatively modest link between intention and behaviour is a matter of concern.

Using the Theory of Planned Behaviour to Explain Action

The TPB can be used in three ways to explain actions.

Level 1: Behaviour

The immediate precursors of behaviour in the TPB are intention and perceived control, so one form of explanation concerns the relative impact of these two factors. This has been examined by Madden, Ellen and Ajzen (1992) who found that usually perceived behavioural control is the weaker factor and may have no direct impact on behaviour.

Level 2: Intention

Next, we need to know the relative importance of A_B, SN and PC in predicting intention. This varies from application to application. For example, Jaccard and Davidson (1972) found that, among college women, the use of the contraceptive pill was associated more with A_B than with SN; this probably reflected the importance of avoiding pregnancy for this group at that time. Davidson and Jaccard (1975) found that among married women with children, the intention to use the contraceptive pill was more determined by SN.

Level 3: Specific Factor Explanations

The third type of explanation relates specific outcome, referent and control beliefs to intention or behaviour. In the theory, specific beliefs relate to intention through the appropriate global variable but it is not always clear which global variable a factor belongs to when a research study is being conducted. For example, embarrassment about complaining might be seen as an outcome or as a control factor. East (2000) found that embarrassment acted primarily as a control factor, obstructing complaining, rather than as an emotional cost if a complaint was made. At a practical level, this issue can be resolved by correlating beliefs directly with intention.

Sometimes, the obvious reason for an activity is not its prime motivation. Membership of sports clubs may be driven by the need to meet people, for example. East (1993) found that application for shares in state privatizations was driven more by access to finance,

Box 7.3	An application to giving up cigarettes

In 1978, the UK Joint Committee on Research into Smoking recommended that a new study should be undertaken on attitudes towards smoking. One stimulus for this work was a 1977 report on attitudes and smoking behaviour prepared by Fishbein for the US Federal Trade Commission. This recommended a shift of focus from 'attitudes to smoking' to 'attitudes to giving up cigarettes'. The new study was conducted by the Office of Population Censuses and Surveys by Marsh and Matheson. The findings were published by the government in 1983 but the main features appear in a paper by Sutton, Marsh and Matheson (1990). The research measured A_B and confidence in being able to stop smoking, which was a form of PC measurement, but did not measure SN. This work provided one of the most substantial tests ever given to a theory in social psychology.

The researchers predicted behaviour on the basis of the difference between the expected values of stopping and continuing to smoke. It is this difference that shows the personal gain or loss of taking one option rather than the other. The research showed that the majority of smokers accepted that smoking caused lung cancer (73 per cent) and heart disease (59 per cent), but the study showed that most of these people believed either that they did not smoke enough to do any damage or that any damage was already done and was irreversible. For such people, cessation held little promise of reduced risk. The only smokers who saw a benefit from stopping were the minority who believed both that they had an enhanced risk and that cessation would diminish this risk. The researchers predicted that these people would make more attempts to stop and this was confirmed when smokers were followed up six months later. This evidence therefore supports a causal process from attitude to action.

This research showed where to place emphasis in health education in order to get people to try to quit smoking; for example, by explaining that the risk from cigarettes is related to the number smoked, that there is no threshold at which health hazards begin and that there are health benefits for nearly all people who stop smoking. The study also showed that eventual success in quitting was strongly dependent on confidence and that health education should therefore emphasize 'how to stop' methods which would build this confidence.

a PC factor, than by the expected financial outcomes, an A_B factor. This suggests that business people should not become too focused on the good value of their product or service since many of the people who might buy it may be constrained by finance or other control factors.

Level 3 explanations help us to choose intervention strategies. For example, if a firm wants to encourage customers to let it know about service failures, the key factors affecting complaining must be addressed. If many people lack confidence about complaining, it is best to provide a clear procedure, explain that it is supported by the company, and draw attention to this procedure on receipts and on the company website.

Exercise 7.3   Research using planned behaviour theory

1   Choose an action that is individually performed and voluntary, e.g. watching a popular TV programme, carrying an organ donor card, installing solar water heating, going to the dentist regularly or playing the National Lottery. Make sure that the action is appropriately specified in terms of target, action, context and time.
2   Choose the target group.
3   From a sample of the target group elicit the salient outcome, referent and control beliefs about the action, using Exercise 7.1. Ideally, about 20 people should be used. Reduce the salient beliefs by merging similar ones and dropping those that are rare.
4   Use the NEWACT program to create a planned behaviour questionnaire. The program asks for:

  • the title of the questionnaire
  • the intention
  • the outcome beliefs
  • the referent beliefs
  • the control beliefs.

The program sets up the different scales for each item and the form of the items from input. Mistakes and poor grammar in the questionnaire need to be eliminated by word processing. Often the phraseology for control items is clumsy and needs adjustment. Some items are added automatically but these may be deleted if not required. The questionnaire will usually cover two sides of paper when printed in two-column landscape format. The questionnaire looks better if scale referents such as 'extremely', 'quite' and 'slightly' are italicized. The scaling is designed for a proportional font such as Times Roman.

5   Gather data from 50+ respondents.
6   Analyze the data.

Use the COMPUTE function in SPSS to:

a) Create products between outcome probability and outcome evaluation (and the corresponding products for the referent and control beliefs, but see later comment, Multiplying Ordinal Measures).
b) Produce three sum measures by aggregating products for the outcome, referent and control items.
c) Aggregate measures for each of the global variables and intention when more than one scale is used. (A reliability test may be appropriate here to check that each scale is measuring the same variable.)

Next:

d) Test the correlations between sum and global measures.
e) Perform a structural equation analysis or regression analysis to test the theory and establish the relative weights of A_B, SN and PC in the prediction of intention. (If you use regression, ordinal regression is appropriate.)

7 Examine your analysis and answer the following questions:

- Is intention most related to A_B, SN or PC?
- Do the sum measures correlate with the corresponding global measure better than with the other two global measures?
- Which belief factors correlate most with intention?
- Which belief factors might be used to improve the product's design or positioning, if any?
- What are the shortcomings of this study and analysis?

Applying Evidence from Planned Behaviour Research

When the findings from planned behaviour research are used to influence others, the influence attempt may not succeed for a number of reasons. First, correlations do not mean that there is a causal relationship. Second, beliefs may be strongly anchored and resist change, or may not change because of a ceiling effect (no room for change). Third, the attempt at influence may be interpreted in an unexpected way that does not bring about the intended change. Fishbein and Ajzen (1981) stated that studies of the existing basis for action give only an indication of where to place emphasis in an influence attempt; tests are needed to clarify this. Even so, planned behaviour research can suggest what may be important in decisions on product development, positioning and advertising themes.

SECTION 3: PROBLEMS WITH THE THEORY OF PLANNED BEHAVIOUR

Multiplying Ordinal Measures

In planned behaviour research, scales may be unipolar (1 to 7) or bipolar (−3 to +3). Bagozzi (1984) and others have explained that the scale measurement used in planned behaviour research is ordinal, but it is treated as ratio-scale when a two numbers from scales, such as outcome likelihood and evaluation, are multiplied to form a product. This introduces error and alters correlations with other variables. This alteration can be substantial when a switch is made between bipolar to unipolar scales. In this situation, Ajzen (1991) recommends *optimal scaling*, i.e. adding a constant to each scale to produce the highest correlation between the sum and global variables. This procedure gives some benefit to random effects and there is no specific justification for taking the scaling that gives the best correlation. An alternative method is to use the four combinations of 1 to 7 and −3 to +3 to see whether the results vary much. If similar results are obtained, whatever the scaling, there is more assurance about the results. The NEWACT program numbers all the scales 1 to 7 but the scales can be recoded in the analysis.

The Principle of Sufficiency

The TPB is based on beliefs. Therefore, any change in global variables, intention or behaviour must come about through the acquisition of new beliefs or the modification of existing beliefs. In other words, belief changes are a *sufficient* explanation for subsequent changes in global variables and intention. Ajzen and Fishbein (1980) accept that variables *external* to the theory, such as past experience, personality, age, sex and other social classifications, will be associated with behaviour but they argue that this occurs only because these variables are related to relevant beliefs and hence to A_B, SN or PC. They state:

> Although we do not deny that 'external' variables of this kind may sometimes be related to behaviour, from our point of view they can affect behaviour only indirectly. That is, external variables will be related to behaviour only if they are related to one or more of the variables specified by our theory. (Ajzen and Fishbein, 1980: 82)

Thus, beliefs and the other components of the TPB should mediate the effect of external variables as shown in Figure 7.3. This argument has been tested in a number of studies by including external variables in the regression analysis to see whether these significantly improve the prediction of intention compared with the global variables alone. Often, demographic variables have little effect; for example, Marsh and Matheson (1983) found no direct effects of age or sex on intention in their study on smoking cessation and Loken (1983) found no direct effect of external variables on television watching.

However, it is usually found that past experience has a direct effect on intention and behaviour (Bagozzi and Kimmel, 1995). In the Marsh and Matheson (1983) study, the previous experience of attempting to stop smoking had a direct effect on intention and a small direct effect on attempts to stop smoking. Similar direct effects of past behaviour on both intention and subsequent behaviour have been found by Bentler and Speckart (1979, 1981), Fredricks and Dossett (1983) and Bagozzi (1981). One possible explanation is that people are partly controlled by their environment as a result of habits set up by experience but that this control is not fully captured by the global measures (Bentler and Speckart, 1979; Fredricks and Dossett, 1983; Triandis, 1977). This may be because habits are sometimes controlled by stimuli that are not consciously recalled.

The Development of A_B, SN and PC

As experience increases, people become more informed and the belief basis for future action is changed. This is a situation that is particularly relevant to consumer behaviour. Consumers are naïve when they enter markets that are new to them and, as they repeat purchase, they become more experienced. When the experience is positive, intention will be enhanced in a positive feedback loop; if the experience is negative, intentions will be reduced and further trial curtailed. Thus, under the voluntary conditions that attach to most consumer behaviour, we would expect to find that those who are highly experienced have stronger intentions. Applying the TPB, there should be changes in A_B, SN and PC as intention develops, as illustrated in Figure 7.3. This can occur because the beliefs underlying the global variables become more numerous and more strongly linked to the behaviour. If experience makes the belief basis of planned behaviour more complicated, we may ask whether it has the same effect on A_B, SN and PC. East (1992) suggested that the progression from novice to expert consumer involves a movement from actions based mainly on SN to

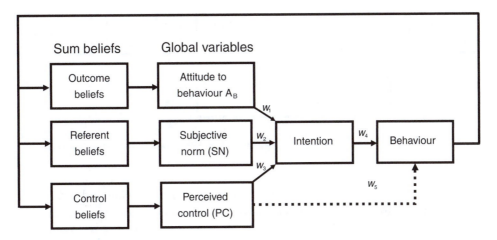

Figure 7.3   Feedback from experience should affect beliefs

actions based more on A_B and PC. This proposal is founded on the idea that, in the absence of detailed knowledge, people have to make decisions on the basis of naïve ideas, and that 'what others think I should do' is better known, or more easily guessed, than the benefits and opportunities related to an unfamiliar prospect. East identified three minor studies that supported the idea that SN gave way to A_B and PC as people became more experienced. However, as further studies accumulated, no clear-cut pattern emerged and the work was not published. This issue has yet to be resolved. The studies that did not support the theory were mainly financial decisions, such as the purchase of endowments and pensions, and these may not have permitted much development of knowledge from experience.

Despite the lack of support for the theory, the issue of how experience affects the different beliefs underlying global variables is important and deserves further study. In many TPB studies, SN is a relatively weak determinant of behaviour and there has been some tendency to downgrade it (e.g. Sheppard, Hartwick and Warshaw, 1988). Armitage and Connor (2001) found that part of the weakness could be attributed to poor measurement. It seems quite likely that the contribution of SN in the determination of intention depends on the experience of respondents.

Deliberate and Spontaneous Action

Fazio (1990) divides the explanation of behaviour into two fields. Where decision-making is deliberate, Fazio supports the TPB, but when the decision is spontaneous, he proposes a different model in which attitude comes first. This second model is shown in Figure 7.4.

In Fazio's (1986) account, attitudes are automatically activated by observation of the attitude object. The attitude then guides perception and the individual becomes aware of aspects of his or her environment related to the attitude. The definition of the event then occurs as these perceptions are associated with a normative understanding of the situation and, out of this definition of the event, behaviour may follow. The main point here is that

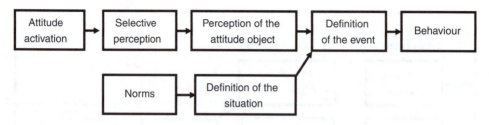

Figure 7.4   Fazio's (1986) theory of the attitude–behaviour process

the environment is driving cognitive processes in an automatic way and attitude rather than belief is the foundation of the internal process.

Fazio argues that attitude activation occurs only when the object and its evaluation have been well established in memory, usually through direct behavioural experience. Thus spontaneous production of behaviour is restricted to familiar contexts, leaving planned behaviour to explain the more unusual situations. However, this rather cosy division of the field has been disrupted by evidence from Bargh et al. (1992) that a wide range of objects can elicit attitude-driven effects. This casts doubt on the separation between the automatic and deliberate control of behaviour. It seems possible that these two types of explanation may often work together. Fazio (1990) showed that responses in measurements of deliberate behaviour are affected if people are asked to focus on emotion-evoking objects before measurement. Baldwin and Holmes (1987) found that systematically different measurements were obtained when different social referents were visualized before response. These findings reflect the effect of automatic processes even when people are making considered responses.

Adjustments and Alternatives to the Theory of Planned Behaviour

A number of researchers have suggested modifications of the theory. Bagozzi and Kimmel (1995) and Bagozzi (1992) suggest distinctions between intention, desire and self-prediction, and Armitage and Conner (2001) find some support for these distinctions. There have also been proposals to include a moral norm to cover the respondent's personal normative control, but this has been found to have an additional predictive function only for some actions.

Ajzen and Driver (1992) distinguish between the short-term and expressive consequences of action and the longer-term and more cognitive consequences of action. Often, a short-term pain has to be balanced against a long-term gain. On this basis, A_B should be seen as having two components.

In its present form, the theory includes only one type of subjective norm – what respondents think that others think that they *should* do. As noted earlier, what others actually do (descriptive norm) exerts an additional influence on behaviour (Deutsch and Gerard, 1955). When descriptive norms are included, predictions are usually better supported (Rivis and Sheeran, 2003). Other developments are possible; Armitage and Conner (2001) separate measures for the control element in the theory into the control that a person has by virtue of his or her abilities and the control that is made possible by the environment. However, all these adjustments raise the complexity of the theory and make it harder to use.

In the consumer behaviour context, the technology acceptance model (TAM) has been offered as an alternative method of predicting the intention to use new systems (Davis, 1989). This theory bases behavioural intention on two factors: perceived usefulness and perceived ease of use. This model has the advantage of simplicity and avoids elicitation but it applies to some situations only and may not give as much explanation as a belief-based model. In TAM, usefulness has some correspondence with A_B, and ease of use with PC, and while the theory originally did not include SN, Venkatesh and Davis (2000) have modified the TAM model to incorporate SN.

Reviewing Planned Behaviour Theory

The development of the theory of planned behaviour has been a success story. Social psychologists have emerged from the dark days of 1969 when Wicker claimed that there was little or no connection between attitude and behaviour. We now have a predictive and explanative model which works effectively though there remains a nagging doubt about the scale of behaviour prediction.

However, there is a concern about the methods that have been used to test the theory. If the theory is causal, it should be possible to instigate change by supplying information and then to follow how the effects of that change 'cascade' through the components of the theory. This requires research designs in which comparisons are made between experimental conditions that induce changes of belief. The fact that there is little published evidence of this sort may indicate that little has been done in this area or that the results of such research have not been conclusive.

Finally, there is a need to apply the theory more effectively in marketing. It may be used to study the activities of marketers – why they opt for or against particular practices (e.g. Elliott, Jobber and Sharp, 1995) – and it applies to a host of consumer practices. The theory is of limited use in explaining the preference for one brand over another, unless the brands are markedly different (e.g. one restaurant versus another, or one holiday destination rather than another). The main strength of planned behaviour research is at the category level. It can explain why categories are liked and, therefore, it can assist managers to position brands, target more responsive population segments and select themes for advertising.

SUMMARY

Attitudes are an evaluative response to a concept. The concept is a cluster of attribute beliefs about a particular topic, and each belief has values attaching to it. Thus the attitude to the concept should relate to the aggregate value of the attribute beliefs. Generally, this view of attitude has been upheld by research and it fits the idea that the purchase of a product can be seen as the acquisition of a bundle of expected costs and rewards.

In many studies the correlation between attitude and behaviour measures is found to be weak. There are two reasons for such weak relationships. The first is that 'other variables' may swamp the association between attitude and behaviour. The second reason is that the measures of attitude and behaviour may not be compatible, i.e. these measures may not refer to the same action, target, context and time. A mismatch here means that the wrong attitude is being used to predict behaviour.

The closest prediction of behaviour is provided by measures of intention – those who state that they will buy a product are, unsurprisingly, found to be much more likely to buy it than those who state that they will not buy it.

The theory of planned behaviour (Ajzen, 1985, 1991) formalizes this link between beliefs, attitudes, intentions and behaviour. In this theory, there are three global variables – attitude to a behaviour, subjective norm and perceived control. These three variables have a combined effect on intention. Behaviour is predicted by intention and perceived control. The global variables rest on beliefs about the outcomes of behaviour, the referents who think that a person should or should not engage in the behaviour, and the ability and opportunity to engage in the behaviour. The theory of planned behaviour provides different levels of explanation which can be used in product positioning, development and advertising themes.

Additional Resources

Issues on the nature of attitudes and their relationship with behaviour are well discussed in chapter 4 of Eagly and Chaiken (1993) and by Eagly and Chaiken (2005). A review of the theory of planned behaviour is provided by Ajzen (2002) and by Armitage and Conner (2001). Ajzen's website is www.people.umass.edu/aizen/faq.html (note: 'aizen' is an alternative spelling).

8 Information Processing and Decision-Making

LEARNING OBJECTIVES

When you have completed this chapter, you should be able to:

1 Understand the way schemas and response competition are involved in thinking.
2 Explain what is meant by a heuristic mechanism and describe how these mechanisms may bias decision-making.
3 Describe how human beings respond to objective probability and value.
4 Understand the ideas of framing, mental accounting and editing.
5 Describe how this work can be used to influence others and improve consumer choice.

OVERVIEW

In the previous chapter, the theory of planned behaviour was described. Though it assists prediction, this theory does not really describe how people think. People do not assign likelihoods and evaluations, multiply them and sum the products to form their attitudes. Planned behaviour theory works *as if* people figure out their interests in this way, but no claim is made that they actually do so.

An alternative approach, described here, focuses on automatic mechanisms that guide information-seeking and choice. This approach seems to get closer to the thought processes (often unconscious) that govern behaviour. We deal first with the way structures called schemas can guide thought and recognition. Then we consider the situation where there is no clear schema available to interpret a stimulus, which leads to response competition and sustained attention as alternative schemas are tried. When such ambiguous stimuli are repeatedly exposed, they may be liked more as response competition is reduced. After this discussion of how people think, the majority of the chapter is devoted to findings relating to prospect theory. This work by Kahneman, Tversky and many of their colleagues has transformed thinking about the way human beings process information and make choices. Kahneman and Tversky show that human decision-making is modified by local conditions. Their methods have mainly involved simple choices, presented to participants, with a count of the preferences expressed. Using such methods, they have documented many instances where judgement is biased away from a rational model, and decision-making departs from economic assumptions.

SECTION 1: SCHEMAS AND ATTENTION

Schemas

According to Crocker, Fiske and Taylor (1984: 197), a schema is:

> an abstract or generic knowledge structure, stored in memory, that specifies the defining features and relevant attributes of some stimulus domain, and the interrelationships among those attributes. ... Schemas help us to structure, organize and interpret new information; they facilitate encoding, storage and retrieval of relevant information; they can affect the time it takes to process information. ... Schemas also serve interpretive or inferential functions. For example, they may fill in data that are missing or unavailable in a stimulus configuration.

The notion of the schema was implicit in the early work by Bartlett (1932) on remembering. Bartlett wrote of the 'effort after meaning' and showed how unusual structures that fell short of representing any object were interpreted by reference to more familiar ideas. One of Bartlett's stimuli was a diagram of an ambiguous object that was variously recognized as a battleaxe, turf cutter, anchor or key, although it was not quite like any of them. People used a schema for a more familiar object to make sense of the ambiguous object.

More frequently encountered stimuli are more easily retrieved. In addition, stimuli with particular characteristics are recognized or recalled more easily. 'Colorful, dynamic, or other distinctive stimuli disproportionately engage attention and, accordingly, disproportionately affect judgements' (Taylor, 1982: 192). This leads to the idea that thinking is based on cognitive accessibility. The more rapidly an idea can be brought to mind, the more likely it is to figure in cognition and subsequent processing. This *retrieval bias effect* has parallels with accessibility in the physical environment. For example, people buy more from those supermarkets that are nearby. Internet search engines use a related process when they take account of the frequency of past interest in the search outcomes. Retrieval bias is quite efficient because it ensures that the more likely candidates are considered first. However, concepts that occur infrequently or are hard to visualize for other reasons will tend to be left out of cognitive processing. In general, experience-based concepts are more easily retrieved than communication-based concepts, events are favoured over states, recent occurrences over long-past occurrences and the clearly defined concept over those that are obscure. Bartlett's example involves the simplest of schemas, those used to classify objects. More elaborate schemas include classifications of persons or groups, grammatical forms and social roles. In their most abstract form, schemas may cover relationships like logical validity, causality and symmetry.

When more than one schema fits a situation, people experience *response competition* as they struggle to give meaning to the stimulus (see Box 8.1). This leads to extended attention as people grapple with the problem.

Box 8.1	Response competition

Response competition is demonstrated by the Stroop test. In this test you are asked to call out the colour that is written the moment that it is displayed. In one condition, the word is RED written using a red colour; in the other condition, RED is written using a blue colour and, in this second case, respondents take longer to respond than in the first condition. In the second case, two competing responses are aroused – to say 'red' (reading the word) and to say 'blue' (noting the colour of the text) – and the competition delays the production of the correct response.

Managing Schemas

Since thought is guided by schemas, it follows that negotiation and other forms of influence may succeed by manipulating the selection of schemas that people use to interpret their experience. One standard ploy in negotiation is to try to anchor the discussion around a particular range of outcomes. Early in the discussion, a negotiator might say, 'The normal rate for this type of work is £1,000 a day'. This can constrain offers to those fairly close to the rate mentioned. Turning to advertising, schemas may be used to develop the product concept. For example, 'No FT, no comment' implies that those who read the *Financial Times* are likely to be better informed – it conjures up the notion of the business expert dispensing wisdom. Often public relations exercises can be seen as attempts to manipulate the schemas used in judgement. For example, firms may play up their green credentials by drawing attention to their energy-saving actions. Some interesting examples of schema management are shown in Box 8.2.

Do People Like Response Competition?

Jokes are often based on response competition. People may anticipate one outcome and have their expectations confounded at the punch line. But other forms of response competition may be disliked. Even jokes may be disliked when a person is under stress. The explanation for this variable reaction is that it depends upon the degree of arousal of the person involved. Boredom (low stimulation) and high stress (high stimulation) are both conditions of high

---

Box 8.2	New schemas for old

An activist group took on the tobacco companies in Australia in the 1980s. The group was called the Billboard Utilising Graffitists Against Unhealthy Promotions (BUGA UP) and they specialized in 'refacing' tobacco posters. When a cigarette company offered a car as a prize, their poster was given the caption 'From the people who put the 'car' in carcinogen'. The adjustments to the posters, and the speeches in court when members of the group were prosecuted, gave entertainment to many Australians, who much appreciated the sight of multinational tobacco companies being humbled in this way.

When a tobacco company sponsored work at the Sydney Opera House, well-dressed members of BUGA UP distributed leaflets expressing regret at this unsavoury association between tobacco and the arts. Another BUGA UP enterprise sabotaged a Marlboro 'Man of the Year' competition in Australia. BUGA UP proposed their own candidate – a man disabled by smoking, confined to a wheelchair, and smoking through the hole in his throat provided by a tracheotomy operation. The man himself was a willing accomplice and starred in a poster which was printed and sold in large numbers. The schema of the strong heroic figure that Marlboro had tried to cultivate was ridiculed. In its place were put the schemas of disease and disability which are more accurately related to smoking cigarettes. A further 'anti-promotion' counteracted the distribution of free cigarettes in shopping malls. To most people a gift is a kindness and the giver is regarded as well-meaning. To oppose such promotions, BUGA UP arranged for children to parade around the mall with banners saying 'DANGER – DRUG PUSHERS AT WORK'. This changed the perception of the tobacco companies' motives from kindness to self-interest. Tobacco companies have a squalid history of refusing to admit to the hazards of their products; they are licensed drug sellers and an important part of their public relations has been to counter such facts by sponsoring orchestras, sport and research. BUGA UP's achievement was to reassert the drug seller schema as the one by which the tobacco companies' actions could be judged.

---

arousal. People prefer an intermediate level of stimulation because, in this region, arousal is lower. Conceptual conflicts may be welcome when people are inactive or bored (e.g. when watching television) because the extra stimulation will reduce arousal; at other times, unusual stimuli may raise arousal (Berlyne, 1965; Berlyne and McDonnell, 1965) and, when this occurs, the stimuli may be disliked. This explains why Harrison (1968) and Saegert and Jellison (1970) found that the stimulating objects were often disliked.

Mere Exposure

Response competition has been used to explain an interesting phenomenon first reported by Zajonc (pronounced Zi-onse, 1968). Zajonc observed that repeated exposure to a new stimulus often made people like it more. This effect of *mere exposure* was so called because the change in the observer's evaluation occurs without the use of reinforcement (discussed in Chapter 1). Zajonc observed this effect in both laboratory and field experiments, using nonsense words, obscure characters and photographs of unknown faces as the unfamiliar stimuli. For example, in Zajonc and Rajecki's (1969) field experiment, nonsense words such as NANSOMA were printed like advertisements in campus newspapers. Later, the researchers got large numbers of students to rate the words on evaluative scales and there was clear evidence that the frequency of exposure correlated positively with the evaluative rating. Zajonc's explanation for this was that the nonsense words created response competition in the minds of readers and that this was reduced as people developed a familiarity with the nonsense word after repeated exposure. If the response competition created by nonsense words is generally disagreeable, a reduction in competition (e.g. through familiarity with the nonsense word) should produce a more positive evaluation. Harrison (1968) measured response competition as the time delay before any response to the stimulus and found that the delay was reduced as the number of exposures increased. Lee (1994) offered another ingenious explanation which is based on the availability heuristic discussed later in this chapter: repeated exposure speeds up recognition; the stimuli that we recognize more easily tend to be those that we like; this association guides judgement and leads us to give the stimuli higher evaluations.

However, not all stimuli become more liked on repeated exposure. This suggests that prospective brand names (which are often like nonsense words) should be pre-tested to see whether they are well liked after they have become familiar.

The Response to Thought and Feeling Stimuli

We tend to think that recognition is a necessary precursor to any evaluation of a stimulus. If you do not know what the concept is, how can you have any affective response to it? Strangely, it seems that we can have an evaluative response without recognition. Zajonc (1980) showed that thought and feeling are initially processed independently and Kunst-Wilson and Zajonc (1980) found that evaluative responses occurred slightly ahead of recognition. Zajonc points to the survival value attaching to a fast response to dangerous stimuli: it is better to jump without thought than to recognize that it is a car that is hitting you!

In a further experiment, Marcel (1976) used an instrument called a tachistoscope to present stimuli at speeds and levels of illumination at which they were hard to recognize. The stimuli were either words or blank spaces, with equal likelihood. Words were either short or long and either 'good' or 'bad'. A good word might be 'food' while a bad word might be 'evil'. If the participants in the experiment thought they saw a word, they were asked to judge its length against comparison words and also to give an evaluative judgement, to say whether the word was good or bad. The duration of exposure was reduced until the subjects were guessing the presence of words at chance level and could not therefore have been recognizing anything. At this duration, Marcel found that word-length judgements (also cognitive) were at chance level too. However, at this point the subjects were still scoring at above chance on their evaluative judgements of words when these were present, indicating that the evaluative response was generated faster than the recognition response. Vanhuele (1994) reviews this work.

Fast recognition judgements of the sort studied by Zajonc are quite different from the choices typically faced by consumers, but these studies show how unconscious mechanisms can underlie consciously experienced thought and feeling.

Attention and Value

In decision-making, the observable action is often restricted to the overt choice. However, when the alternatives are physically present, it is possible to observe the direction of gaze and to infer from this which alternative a person is thinking about. Gerard (1967) used this method of investigation; he employed two projectors to show two alternatives (Impressionist paintings), while light reflecting off a mirror attached to the back of the participant's head showed which alternative was receiving attention. A multi-channel recorder logged the data. Gerard reported that the participants looked most at the alternative that they did *not* choose and suggested that they were trying to come to terms with not having this alternative.

To test Gerard's result, East (1973) conducted two experiments using a battery of slide viewers connected to a hidden time recorder (illustrated). As in the earlier study by Gerard (1967), the choice was made between French Impressionist paintings. The participants were led to believe that they would get a poster of the picture that they chose.

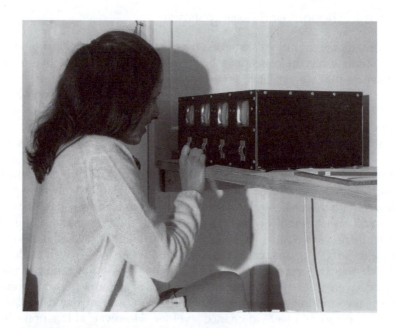

Using the slide viewer equipment (East, 1973)

Control of the viewing equipment was left entirely in the hands of the participant so that the time spent on the different alternatives was unconstrained.

East's first experiment presented subjects with two alternatives, while a second experiment presented three alternatives. Both experiments had two levels of choice difficulty: high, between alternatives that had previously been rated equally by the subject, and low, between alternatives that had been rated unequally.

The results showed that the subjects spent more time looking at the alternatives that they liked, so that the ratio of attention times was an approximate function of the ratio of the evaluations (see Table 8.1). East's result was the opposite of Gerard's reported findings and it is possible that, with Gerard's rather complicated method for recording attention, the records were inadvertently linked to the wrong alternative. A later study by Russo and Leclerc (1994) supports East's finding. Russo and Leclerc used video equipment in a simulation supermarket situation and measured the number of eye fixations on alternatives (rather than duration of time spent) at different phases in the decision sequence. They found that in the main phase of the decision the number of fixations clearly favoured the alternative later chosen. In another study, Pieters and Warlop (1999) also found more attention to the alternative that was eventually chosen.

Thus there is a simple mechanism that directs attention to the more valued alternative. This mechanism is unconscious; when asked about their potential behaviour, people do not know which alternative they would look at most. This evidence suggests that the more valued features of a person's environment generally get more attention compared with those of lesser value. We can see that this mechanism helps people to benefit from their environment. To avoid harm, it is possible that people attend more to unpleasant stimuli than neutral ones but we do not have data on this.

If evaluation guides attention, it means that second and third preferences will get proportionately less attention and their worthwhile attributes are less likely to be discovered. Only when investigation of the first preference leads to it being down-rated will more time will be allocated to lesser alternatives. This mechanism therefore carries a bias in favour of existing preferences but it is an efficient way of using time since it ensures that little time is wasted on low-rated prospects. Given this evidence, people may be encouraged

Table 8.1   Mean durations of attention to alternatives in choice experiments (East, 1973)

	Order of evaluation	Two alternatives: Time spent (seconds)	Three alternatives: Time spent (seconds)
High choice difficulty	1	46	25
	2	37	23
	3	–	21
Total time		83	69
Low choice difficulty	1	24	24
	2	18	16
	3	–	9
Total time		42	49

to buy an initially lower-rated brand if information about this brand is attached to a message on the initially preferred alternative since, in this arrangement, it is more likely to receive attention. This may be done by using comparative advertising, and there is evidence that small brands benefit from this procedure (Grewal et al., 1997).

SECTION 2: HEURISTICS

Exercise 8.1   Availability effects

In the UK, approximately 600,000 people die each year from all causes. How many people die prematurely each year from the following two causes? Enter the figures that you think apply:

Smoking:
Road accidents:

We now consider biases that may affect everyday decision-making. *If you want to find the river, go downhill!* This is a heuristic rule which often helps but may mislead when there is no river in the valley. The term 'heuristic' was used by Kahneman, Slovic and Tversky (1982) to cover inexact or rule-of-thumb processes which may be used consciously or unconsciously to assess the likelihood of an uncertain event. Kahneman et al. argue that people do not appear to follow the statistical theory of prediction when making such judgements. Instead, they rely on a limited number of heuristic processes which often yield reasonable judgements but sometimes lead to error. In particular, people seem to attach higher probability to ideas that are easily retrieved; this is called the *availability heuristic*. This arises because frequently experienced concepts become easier to retrieve; as a result higher probability and ease of retrieval become associated in heuristic thinking.

Markus and Zajonc (1985) provide an example of the way in which availability may quite unjustifiably support the prestige of the medical profession. People often get better without treatment but, when treatment has been given, there is a tendency to assume that this treatment was the cause of the recovery. The treatment is more cognitively available as a cause of recovery than ideas about the natural processes countering disease that occur unseen within the body. As a result, people may judge therapy to be more effective than it is.

The judgement of risk is notoriously erratic. Some of the reason for this may lie in the poor information about actual risks in the media but judgement may also be distorted by the action of heuristics. Lichtenstein et al. (1978) suggested that the risk of occurrences that are referred to often in the media becomes exaggerated because of the availability heuristic. Those who completed Exercise 8.1 are likely to have overestimated the risk of death from road accidents because these events are more salient in media reports. Smoking deaths are less well reported and are likely to be underestimated. The approximate annual numbers of deaths in the UK by cause are:

All causes	600,000
Smoking	100,000
Road accidents	2,000

Misjudgement of risk has also affected the use of oral contraceptives. Exaggerated fears of potentially harmful side-effects have caused women to abandon the pill, even when the identified risk was very small in absolute terms. In 1996, a 10 per cent increase in legal abortion in Britain was attributed to earlier announcements that a number of contraceptive pills should be phased out because of small associated risks.

People seem to have difficulty in taking account of background risk and may focus instead on large percentage increases. For example, women may be shocked to hear that those who are over 35 and who smoke and take the contraceptive pill have 18 times the risk of pulmonary embolism compared with those who do neither of these actions. The '18 times' fact seems to be more available and to dominate in judgement, but embolisms are very rare in the 35–45-year-old range so this is 18 times a very small number and other hazards present far more risk. A more responsible way of handling the data would be to report the personal increment in the risk for smokers of using the pill. For example, that a smoker who takes the pill has an extra risk of dying of one in a million. The effect of the information on embolism was to encourage women to abandon the pill. They would have done better to quit smoking since this causes smokers to lose, on average, about six years of life.

Exercise 8.2	Who was to blame? (Abridged from Tversky and Kahneman, 1980: 62)

Solve the following problem:

A cab was involved in a hit-and-run accident at night. Two cab companies, the Green and the Blue, operate in the city. You are given the following data:

- 85 per cent of the cabs in the city are Green and 15 per cent are Blue.
- A witness identified the cab as a Blue cab. The court tested his ability to identify cabs under appropriate visibility conditions. When presented with a sample of cabs (half of which were Blue and half of which were Green) the witness made correct identifications in 80 per cent of the cases.

Question: What is the probability that the cab involved in the accident was Blue rather than Green?

Decide on your answer before reading on.

The tendency to ignore base rates such as market share is the basis of the *representativeness heuristic*. Likelihood is judged by reference to visible similarities rather than background probabilities. For example, a person may be seen as a barrister because of features of dress and delivery of speech. In this case, the judgement draws on the stereotype of a barrister, but such a judgement takes no account of the low number of barristers in society which makes it unlikely that a person belongs to this group.

Exercise 8.2   (continued)

Tversky and Kahneman (1980) put this problem to several hundred participants; the median response was an 80 per cent likelihood that the cab was Blue. Thus participants tended to take note of the witness's skill in recognizing cabs and ignored the market shares of the two cab companies. Clearly, if there had been no Blue cabs, the witness could not have been right so the proportion of Blue cabs is relevant. The probability that the witness was right is the ratio of correct identification of cab colour as blue to total identification as blue (both correct and incorrect). The chance that the cab was Blue (0.15) and was recognized correctly (0.8) is 0.15×0.8 and the chance that the cab was Green (0.85) and was recognized wrongly as Blue (0.2) is 0.85×0.2. The required ratio of correct identification to total identifications is therefore:

$$\frac{(0.15 \times 0.8)}{(0.15 \times 0.8) + (0.85 \times 0.2)}$$
$$= 0.41$$

So there is 41 per cent chance the cab was Blue.

In Exercise 8.2, the bias towards the witness test and away from the market shares of the two cab companies probably relates to the fact that the witness test is an event. As previously reported, events are more available than continuing states such as market share. We seem to be tuned to change and direct our thinking to the more active aspects of a problem. In contrast, data dealing with an unchanging background do not attract as much attention. This mechanism serves a useful purpose by drawing attention to aspects of the environment that require response but it can cause mistakes in some cases. In particular, it means that consumer financial decisions may be related to more active features of the environment rather than their impact on wealth. Wealth is a state rather than an event and does not usually figure in individual judgements even though, normatively, it should.

People are also prone to give more weight to causal data, which is related to change. For example, respondents are more likely to agree with the proposition that *a girl has blue eyes if her mother has blue eyes* than *a mother has blue eyes if her daughter has blue eyes* though the two events are equally probable (Tversky and Kahneman, 1980). The mother-to-daughter inheritance is causal, unlike the daughter-to-mother relationship and it is this that influences respondents.

The focus on events rather than states and the different heuristic rules were described by Kahneman (2002) as intuitive thinking in his presentation following his award of the Nobel Prize for economics. Kahneman likens such thinking to the way perception seems to be governed by mechanisms over which we have little conscious control. What we perceive is a function of the context from which reference points are drawn. Small changes in problems can affect the reference points and change the judgement. There are criticisms of this work; see, for example, Gigerenzer (1991), who has raised questions about the interpretation of effects (response by Kahneman and Tversky, 1996).

Relevance to Marketing and Management

The greater cognitive availability of events and causal data has a relevance to marketing. For example, we may exaggerate the impact of market interventions, such as a brand extension. As we saw in Chapter 4, conditions such as market share control the likely outcome of such interventions, but these conditions may get less attention than they deserve because of their constancy.

In addition, retrieval bias will move decisions towards the option that is easiest to bring to mind. This may lead us away from the prevention of undesirable occurrences before they happen (proaction) so that we have to respond to undesirable occurrences after they have happened (reaction). The choice between proaction and reaction depends on costs. Sometimes, it is best to let things happen and then to focus resources on the problem – management by exception – but in other cases, for example avoiding accidents, prevention is usually best. Our point is that there is a bias against proactive intervention because successful prevention produces no visible outcome and this choice is therefore less cognitively available. In addition to supporting reactive solutions, retrieval bias will operate in favour of the visible, well-defined events and against those that are hard to bring to mind. This suggests that people may:

- give too much support to the status quo: what is happening is available, but what could happen is harder to bring to mind;
- make poor assessment of the opportunity cost, which is the alternative use of resources when a course of action is selected;
- find it easier to sell products that have a physical form that is easily seen.

SECTION 3: PROCESSING VALUE AND PROBABILITY

Objective value, expressed in money or other units, and objective probability, the likelihood of something occurring, are processed by human beings to produce subjective evaluations

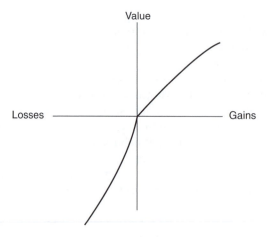

Figure 8.1   The value function (from Kahneman and Tversky, 2000)

(or utility) and subjective estimates of probability. These subjective representations do not exactly correspond with the objective forms and this affects decision-making.

Value

The relationship between objective value and utility has a long history going back to Bernoulli (1738), who described how the curve of utility against wealth flattens as wealth increases, and marginal utility therefore diminishes with each increment in wealth. Benoulli gave the example of a pauper who, finding a lottery ticket offering an equal chance of winning 20,000 ducats or getting nothing, might quite reasonably ensure a gain by exchanging his ticket for a guaranteed 9,000 ducats. The value function is curved, so that half the *utility* of 20,000 ducats is less than the utility of 9,000 ducats.

This curvature assists exchanges. To a person who has enough of a good, the marginal utility of additional supplies is low and this will encourage exchanges with others who possess different goods that the person needs. Both parties in such an exchange can gain in utility. However, Benoulli was mistaken to think that such exchanges were reckoned against total wealth. Normally, people assess gains or losses against a more salient criterion – and this is often the zero point. This relationship between gains and losses relative to zero, and utility, is shown by the curve in Figure 8.1. You can see that the curve is concave to the *x*-axis for both gains and losses and that the response to losses is larger than the response to gains. This relationship has been established by observing the preferences expressed by individuals about different choices. Comparisons between positive and negative choices have been particularly interesting (see Exercise 8.3).

Exercise 8.3   Positive and negative choices

1   Which do you prefer?

   A: £9,000 for certain, or
   B: £10,000 with a probability of 0.9; otherwise nothing.

2   Which do you prefer?

   C: Losing £9,000 for certain, or
   D: Losing £10,000 with a probability of 0.9; otherwise nothing.

In Exercise 8.3 people generally prefer A to B. The shape of the value–utility relationship for gains explains why people prefer £9,000 for certain rather than have 0.9 × £10,000. They also prefer D to C. The shape of the value function in the negative region means that losing £10,000 with a probability of 0.9 is less painful than losing £9,000 for certain and people prefer the smaller disutility. These outcomes mean that people are generally *risk averse on gains but risk prone on losses*. This pattern of preference reversal is regularly found and is called the *reflection effect*. However, in 1992, Tversky and Kahneman suggested that the data were more consistent with the idea that people are risk averse on gains and risk prone on losses when outcomes had medium or high probability; for low probability outcomes they suggest the reverse risk profile occurs. This modification arises because of the way people weight low probabilities, as we explain later.

Figure 8.1 shows another interesting effect. This is the steepness of the negative part of the value function in comparison to the positive part. This effect is captured by the aphorism *losses loom larger than gains* and, more formally, as *loss aversion*. Loss aversion is behind the *endowment effect* which is that people often demand much more to give up an object than they would be willing to pay to acquire it. The endowment effect has been demonstrated in a number of studies reviewed by Kahneman, Knetsch and Thaler (1991a). One simple example of the effect is the reluctance of people to engage in a 50:50 win/lose bet. On average, people will only wager a dollar on a coin toss if they can win more than two dollars. Generally, people will be reluctant to trade what they own, except at a high price. Not surprisingly, the endowment effect has been tested by critics; see for example Shogren et al. (1994).

As we stated, gains and losses relate to some reference point. In some cases it will be a prior cost. For example, a person may see the $20,000 cost of building work on a newly acquired house as an addition to the $1million price paid for the house. Viewed like this, the $20,000 seems a modest increment to the purchase price but, ten years later, when the purchase of the house had faded into the past, further building work costing $20,000 will be evaluated on its own and will be psychologically more painful. Thaler (1999) points out that the extent to which a cost is psychologically linked to a benefit can vary. When people pay a fixed cost for a service, irrespective of their amount of use, usage is decoupled from the payment since any extra use is free. Another decoupling occurs when a credit card is used. This postpones payment and also aggregates costs into one bill which reduces the total psychological cost compared with the sum of several smaller separate costs.

Probability

What are your answers to Exercise 8.4?

Exercise 8.4   The Allais paradox (Allais, 1953)

Allais asked one group of subjects to choose between the two options:

- A: $4,000 with a probability of 0.8; otherwise nothing.
- B: $3,000 for certain.

Which do you prefer?

Another group were asked to choose between:

- C: $4,000 with a probability of 0.2; otherwise nothing.
- D: $3,000 with a probability of 0.25; otherwise nothing.

Which do you prefer?

Faced with the choices in Exercise 8.4, Allais found that 80 per cent of respondents preferred option B to A but 65 per cent preferred option C to D. This seems paradoxical because the ratio of the probabilities is the same in each choice pair. One explanation for this pattern is that probability is weighted as it is converted to subjective probability. Figure 8.2 shows how the weighting of objective probability reduces the subjective impact of high probabilities and increases the impact of low probabilities. The x-axis is objective probability and the y-axis is the weighted outcome. Applied to the data in Exercise 8.4, the weighting reduces the appeal of A and increases the appeal of C.

No mathematical expression has been given for the probability weighting function; it is determined empirically. One partial explanation for the effect is that a rule of diminishing sensitivity with distance from a reference point applies. The probability function has two natural reference points, 0 and 1; the weights, or relative differences between subjective and objective probability, initially increase with distance from these anchors. However, as these relative differences are in opposite directions, they must come together again somewhere in the central area.

The weighting of small objective probabilities fits the evidence that people are positive about insurance and like to place long-odds bets. Above an objective probability of 0.40, the weighting depresses subjective probability so that risks are subjectively discounted; for example, a 50 per cent probability is nearer to 40 per cent, subjectively. At the extremes,

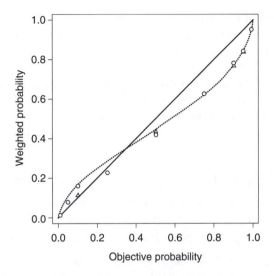

Figure 8.2   The probability function (from Kahneman and Tversky, 2000)

the weighting is unstable; a one in a thousand chance may be dismissed as no chance or taken seriously (bettors on national lotteries accept very long odds).

The sensitivity near the reference point (0, 1) is illustrated by Exercise 8.5.

Exercise 8.5   **Risk preferences**

Suppose that you have a 99 per cent chance of getting $1,000. How much would you pay to move that probability to certainty?

Suppose that you have a 50 per cent chance of getting $1,000. How much would you pay to move that probability to 51 per cent?

Suppose that you have 0 per cent chance of getting $1,000. How much would you pay to move that probability to 1 per cent?

Most people will pay more in the 0 per cent and 99 per cent conditions for a one per cent increment in probability but the long-run benefit of a one-per-cent gain in probability is the same at any point on the probability range.

Prospect Theory

Kahneman and Tversky (1979) and Tversky and Kahneman (1992) incorporate the subjective conversion of value and probability into a theory of choice called prospect theory, and they propose that the choice of an alternative (prospect) is established in two stages. In the first stage, the choices that are *framed* in a communication are restructured or *edited* by the receiver. Then, in the second stage, the receiver chooses the best option based on the values assessed in the first stage.

Framing refers to the manner in which the choice is presented to the decision-maker, and editing refers to the processes used by the decision-maker to rethink the choice. In framing, an alternative or prospect may be presented either as a loss or as a gain, as in Exercise 8.6.

Exercise 8.6	Life and death (Tversky and Kahneman, 1981: 453)

An unusual disease is expected to kill 600 people. Two interventions are proposed. Which intervention do you prefer on the basis of the following information?

- If programme A is adopted, 200 people will be saved.
- If programme B is adopted, there is $\frac{1}{3}$ probability that 600 people will be saved and $\frac{2}{3}$ probability that no people will be saved.

When you have decided, consider how you would react to these alternatives:

- If programme C is adopted, 400 people will die.
- If programme D is adopted, there is $\frac{1}{3}$ probability that no one will die and $\frac{2}{3}$ probability that 600 people will die.

The second pair of alternatives in Exercise 8.6 is the same as the first (A = C, B = D). Yet Tversky and Kahneman found that 72 per cent preferred programme A to B and 78 per cent preferred programme D to C. By framing the problem in terms of the gains (lives saved), it is possible to steer preference to the risk-averse option, A, rather than B. In the second-choice pair, the framing in terms of lives lost makes people risk prone, and steers them to option D. Using the appropriate frame is clearly a 'must' for anyone in the field of persuasive communication.

Thaler (1985) suggests some interesting implications of framing for those presenting gains and losses to others. Losses are best presented in aggregate, to minimize their impact, and gains are best presented singly to maximize their effect. It may also be better to offset some losses against gains because, separately, losses have more impact than gains. Framing effects seem to apply to the presentation of discounts. A saving of $10 on a $50 item may be presented as such or as a 20 per cent discount. When the percentage discount is small it may be best to present it as an absolute cost reduction.

In the editing phase of decision-making, complex choices may be simplified. Thus a person may see the price of a car not as $20,000, but as $2,000 less than he or she expected to pay; another edit by the prospective buyer may be to aggregate the cost of extra features with the basic price so that there is a single purchase price.

Box 8.3	Overpaid?

The way bond traders are paid may help them to get very high remuneration. Bond dealers typically work on commissions that are very low percentages. A commission of 0.1 per cent does not seem much. However, if it is based on a principal of $100 million, it is $100,000. In general, people assess costs in proportional terms and will take more trouble to save $5 off a $20 item than $5 off a $100 item.

In negotiation, our editing processes may lead us into a poor deal and we should beware of the way the other side frames choices. It is wise to focus on the total cost of a deal. Give way on small items but resist concessions on the larger ones. It could even be worthwhile to include small items in a proposal so that you can concede them later.

Thaler (1999) introduced the term *mental accounting*, which covers some of these editing functions. This uses the metaphor of accounting to explain the way in which people organize, evaluate and keep track of financial activities. As in accounting proper, people maintain separate accounts for different activities; for example they may accept the idea of flying business class to Australia at an extra cost of $6,000 but find it difficult to justify spending $6,000 to save two days' discomfort in another area of their life. Also people may close an account after a defined period; gamblers on the race track tend to think of gains or losses over a day and investors in the stock market may operate with a one-year horizon.

Box 8.4	The Nudge Unit

Thaler and Sunstein (2008) have written a popular book called *Nudge* in which they argue that national administration can be much more effective if it incorporates the known findings from mental accounting and other psychological research. They focus on activities such as paying taxes, investing in pensions and securing organ donation. These ideas have caught the interest of governments. In the UK, the Cabinet Office is advised by a 'Nudge Unit' which claims to have saved substantial sums of money by simple changes such as the redrafting of letters to tax payers.

SECTION 4: FINANCIAL APPLICATIONS OF PROSPECT THEORY

Prospect theory provides explanations for some puzzling behaviour. We now provide several examples of its explanatory power, drawing on a review by Camerer (2000).

Investment

One of the effects of loss aversion is that people tend to hang on to losers and sell winners in share markets. Investors may have some equilibrium concept in mind, believing that the swing of the pendulum will take a losing stock back towards its purchase price and that a rising stock could similarly fall. They may also be reluctant to sell a losing stock because this turns a potential loss into an actual loss, so that it is more painful. From a rational standpoint, the buying price is sunk cost and should not figure in the decision to sell shares, except for calculating capital gains tax. The selection of an alternative to sell should be based on prospective return, based on the current valuation of the share.

A bias in favour of selling winners and keeping losers has been demonstrated experimentally by Weber and Camerer (1998) and in real data by Odean (1998). Such behaviour appears to be a mistake since Odean estimated that investors lost an average of 3.4 per cent in the subsequent year compared with selling losers and keeping winners. However, this behaviour by investors may contribute to the effective operation of share markets. These markets are potentially unstable since a loss of confidence can precipitate selling, which may further aggravate the loss of confidence and lead to a collapse of the market. In practice, panic selling on a large scale is rare and markets show corrections but do not usually collapse. If the market has fallen, many investors will bide their time and refuse to sell. There seems to be evidence that market professionals are much more willing to realize a loss (see Box 8.4). They may operate with a momentum rather than an equilibrium concept of the market. Computerized share trading may lead to more market instability if it circumvents the effects of loss aversion.

Box 8.5	'Mutual-fund pros panicked in peso crisis while small investors stood their ground' (Headline in the *Wall Street Journal*, 13 January 1995)

Among share-trading professionals the folklore is to stay in a rising market and sell when it turns. Loss aversion suggests that small investors might find this difficult. In particular, once they see that the market has fallen, and that they have made a loss by reference to recent prices, they may resist selling because now they are risk prone. Also, by selling, they close the account so that the potential loss becomes a real loss. The headline above suggests that ordinary investors follow loss aversion but that the professionals have learned to reverse it.

The Equity Premium

Equities have traditionally provided a greater return on investments than fixed interest investments (bonds). Sometimes bonds give a return that is little better than inflation, while equities have given an average return in the USA of about 10 per cent over the period

1926–2003 and 9.6 per cent in the UK over the period 1900–2003 (Dimson, Marsh and Staunton, 2004). Traditionally, the equity premium has been explained as a compensation for the greater risk associated with equities but an alternative explanation has been offered by Benartzi and Thaler (1995). A feature of equity markets is that they rise and fall in market value much more than bond markets. Investors who look at their equity investment a month after purchase are about equally likely to see a gain or a loss compared with the purchase price but, after ten years, there is nearly always a gain. Since losses loom larger than gains (the ratio of the dis-attraction of losses to the attraction of gains is about 2.25), an investor with a short-term horizon will suffer more pain from the losses and may be put off from investing in equities. Benartzi and Thaler therefore explain the equity premium as the additional return required to compensate for the loss aversion effect. This explanation would be still more convincing if there were evidence that those investors with longer-term horizons held a greater proportion of their portfolios in equities rather than bonds.

Long-Shot Bias and the Value Premium

As noted, when the probabilities are low, the psychological weighting of probability makes long odds more attractive. This seems to operate in betting. In racetrack betting there is a tendency to back outsiders or long shots – horses with high odds that are unlikely to win. This may reflect the overweighting of small probabilities. Bookmakers tend to offset risk so that disproportionate betting on outsiders will tend to reduce the odds on these horses and raise the odds on favourites. The result is that, in the long run, long shots do worse than favourites. This effect becomes more pronounced over the course of the day as bettors lose money. Their mental accounting period is a day and, in order to end up 'in the money', they increasingly need to win on a long shot, so still more money goes on such horses. Under these circumstances, an each way bet on the favourite for the last race will make money, on average, even allowing for a 15 per cent tax on winnings (Ali, 1977). If you want to test this out yourselves, when visiting the racetrack it is best to place the bet on the Tote which compensates for weight of betting more effectively.

Long-shot bias, or something rather similar, may lie behind the persistent value premium effect in share investment. Value or income stocks typically give fairly high dividends and sell at prices that are rather lower than is justified by their fundamentals. Value stocks are contrasted with growth stocks that pay low dividends. With growth stocks, investors forgo current income and hope for more rapid growth. By analogy, the growth stock is rather like a long shot and some companies like Google and Apple emerge to give spectacular results. However, the fundamentals are just that and Dimson, Marsh and Staunton (2004) find that, in the long run, value stocks give a distinctly better performance and show a premium of about 3 per cent over growth stocks. This effect is transnational. In a comparison of 14 countries, only one country (Italy) showed a superior return from growth stocks.

Impact on Economics

Economics is founded on rational assumptions. These include an assumption that the accumulation of wealth drives individual behaviour and that alternatives should be assessed against this wealth criterion. However, it is apparent that individuals do not think about their wealth but instead about gains and losses relative to norms defined by the context. Furthermore, they operate with a number of accounts so that a gain in one is not necessarily offset (in their minds) by a loss in another. This pattern of behaviour violates the principle of fungibility, that money in one account is as good as money in another account. Also, it is possible to construct choices where preferences violate the principle of dominance. People may prefer A to B and B to C, but C to A.

Thus, people do not think according to the canons of economic logic, and traditional economics has been severely challenged by prospect theory. Previously, economists have argued that wealth will increase most rapidly if people act rationally and money is fungible. This is a normative theory. They claim that those who do not apply normative economic principles will lose out, so that self-interest or reinforcement will direct behaviour towards a rational pattern. Thus, actual economic behaviour will be driven towards the rational pattern. But if people do not act rationally, normative economics needs to take this into account. The most rational policy is to anticipate the irrationality of others and adapt to it. Therefore, a study of everyday decision-making is needed so that the rational person (or policy-maker) can exploit the systematic biases in the choices of others.

Problems with Prospect Theory

The possibility of using prospect theory to explain behaviour, choose profitably and negotiate successfully has seized the imagination of researchers but the potential may be reduced when the theory is more widely evaluated. Van der Plight and van Schie (1990) gathered evidence on risk aversion and risk proneness among European populations. Their work confirmed Kahneman and Tversky's findings, but the effects were less strong. In addition, Leclerc, Schmitt and Dubé (1995) find that people making decisions under risk were often risk averse about time loss when, according to prospect theory, they should be risk prone.

Many of the studies on prospect theory have used hypothetical and rather artificial examples. In these studies, the judgement of the majority has been used to decide response and it would be interesting to know more about those people who do not fit the model. However, there is plenty of field evidence which supports the theory though, often, only after *ad hoc* assumptions have been made about the mental accounting period and the separation of accounts.

The more fundamental problem with prospect theory is the lack of an underlying rationale that could relate the different phenomena that are reported. Why do losses loom larger than gains? Why do costs affect consumers less than other losses? Why is time different from money in terms of loss aversion? What we have in prospect theory is an accumulation of important findings but no fundamental explanation. One possibility is that the effects we see are related to the relative frequency of different types of occurrence. We have seen that frequency affects availability but it may have a wider relevance. If there are generally more positive than negative events, reference points will tend to be based on the positives. As a result, negative outcomes are more at variance with assumptions and are therefore more disturbing. This is the explanation offered by Fiske (1980) for the greater impact of negative information (considered in Chapter 11). However, more research is required before this provides a coherent explanation.

SUMMARY

This chapter is about the automatic mechanisms involved in recognizing, evaluating, judging, investigating and deciding. One process that seems to underlie a person's thought processes is the use of schemas – cognitive structures that are fitted to information to make sense of it. When the fit is poor, people may give more attention to the stimulus until a fit is achieved. Repeated exposure of a stimulus that is initially obscure often leads to increases in the evaluation of that stimulus.

The evaluative response to stimuli is often faster than the cognitive response and these evaluative responses, in the initial stages at least, seem to involve relatively independent processing. When we make choices, attention is related to the evaluation of alternatives.

When making judgements, people use simplifying processes called heuristics. They make more use of information that is more available – that is discrete, eventful, recent or established through personal experience – and they tend to neglect information dealing with persisting conditions. More available information is also given higher probability.

We convert objective value and probability into subjective forms. The effect of this is that people are risk averse on gains and risk prone on losses at medium and high probabilities. The value function is steeper in the negative region. This gives rise to loss aversion and makes people more reluctant to part with things that they own.

The way choices are presented (framed) and the information processing of receivers (editing) affect the way in which decisions are made. If the framing is manipulated, people can be pushed towards particular alternatives. People tend to think in terms of different accounts which may be closed after different periods. Thus, mental accounting, loss aversion and risk tolerance will affect the evaluation of prospects.

These processes produce effects that are contrary to axioms in economics but they help to explain a number of puzzles. These include the preference for selling winning rather than losing shares, reluctance to fully invest in shares as opposed to bonds, and a tendency to buy growth shares rather than income shares.

Additional Resources

In 2002, Kahneman was awarded the Nobel Prize for economics – no mean achievement for a psychologist. The lecture that he gave at the time is available at: http://nobelprize.org/nobel_prizes/economics/laureates/2002/kahneman-lecture.html.

Much of the work referenced here has come from two volumes edited by Kahneman, Slovic and Tversky (1982) and Kahneman and Tversky (2000). In particular, read Thaler (1999) 'Mental accounting matters' (reprinted in Kahneman and Tversky, 2000: 241–260). Kahneman (2012) has incorporated many of the findings from this research stream in his book *Thinking Fast and Thinking Slow*. This book brings out the practical implications for decision-making and national policy in a thoughtful and accessible way.

9 Consumer Satisfaction and Quality

LEARNING OBJECTIVES

When you have completed this chapter, you should be able to:

1 Describe theories of consumer satisfaction/dissatisfaction (CSD).
2 Measure customer satisfaction and service quality.
3 Know the evidence on the relationship between satisfaction and company profit.
4 Understand research on consumer complaining behaviour (CCB).
5 Report on research on how consumers respond to service delay.

OVERVIEW

In the USA, Hunt and Day set up the first conference on consumer satisfaction in 1976 and work in this field grew rapidly. In 1993, Perkins noted over 3,000 academic references relating to this area. In Europe, consumer satisfaction and dissatisfaction (CSD) has received rather less emphasis than in the USA and, starting with the work of Grönroos (1978), the focus has been more on the perception of quality, particularly with regard to services. Customer satisfaction often depends on the quality of goods and services and, therefore, CSD research is closely associated with quality research. The measurement of quality has been developed in the USA by Parasuraman and his colleagues but this work has been widely criticized. This chapter reviews the field, describes measurement of satisfaction and quality, examines theories of CSD, reports research linking satisfaction and company profit, and sets out evidence on complaining behaviour. This chapter relates to work on the effects of CSD on customer retention/defection described in Chapter 2.

SECTION 1: INTRODUCTION

It is not a surprise that customers are sometimes dissatisfied with products or services that they have purchased. However, quantifying this dissatisfaction and comparing levels of satisfaction reliably across different product categories or in different countries has not always been straightforward. Andreasen (1988) quoted a general figure of 15–25 per cent dissatisfaction across a range of goods and services in the USA; Stø and Glefjell (1990) found similar figures for a range of goods and services in Norway. Peterson and Wilson (1992), who reviewed this topic, found lower levels of dissatisfaction; for example, 83 per cent were satisfied, with the remainder divided between neutrality and dissatisfaction. This suggests that, roughly, there is one dissatisfied customer for every ten that are satisfied.

Much of the work on consumer satisfaction and dissatisfaction has focused on services. Maintaining the quality of a service is difficult because of the nature of services. A service is consumed as it is produced and any mistake by the provider becomes part of the service delivered. In contrast, mistakes in the production of goods can often be corrected before sale. Quality is usually raised by uniformity in goods but attempts to make services uniform can be counter-productive. Service providers need to adapt to the needs of the customer and what suits one person may not suit another; for this reason, service standardization can produce a rather formulaic interchange with customers, which may not meet their requirements. Getting services right is important because they constitute an increasingly large fraction of modern economies. In most OECD countries, services accounted for more than 70 per cent of GDP (OECD, 2000); the European Service Forum reported 71 per cent in 2007, indicating little change. Given the greater difficulty in delivering services, it is likely that these will cause more problems than goods and, in a study conducted by Technical Assistance Research Programs (TARP, 1979), unsatisfactory service quality was responsible for most of the complaints reported (see Table 9.1).

There are several reasons for an interest in satisfaction and quality. People like to deliver something that is appreciated but it also pays to deliver quality. Buzzell and Gale (1987) showed that when a firm's quality was high, profit margins were larger and firms could grow more easily. Reichheld (1996b) and others have argued that it costs less to retain existing customers than to gain new ones, and that quality helps to retain customers (Chapter 2). Brand extensions are likely to be more successful when the brand has higher perceived quality (Chapter 3). Thus, those who deliver a lower quality than their competitors may lose market share (see Box 9.1). Hirschman (1970) suggested that unsatisfactory delivery of goods and services led to two types of consumer response, which he described succinctly as *exit* and *voice*. Exit is switching to other products or suppliers. Voice has a number of forms: complaining to suppliers and seeking redress, negative word of mouth to other consumers and, occasionally, formal complaints through legal or trade authorities. In Chapter 2, we noted that dissatisfaction is related to defection. However,

Table 9.1 Reasons for complaint (TARP, 1979)

Problem	Households reporting a problem (%)
Unsatisfactory repair or service	36
Store did not have advertised product for sale	25
Unsatisfactory product quality	22
Long wait for delivery	10
Failure to receive delivery	10

although repurchase intentions are much reduced by dissatisfaction, Oliver (1980), Oliver and Swan (1989), Feinberg et al. (1990) and Fornell (1992) find that many consumers are reluctant to change. For example, Feinberg et al. (1990) found that, after an unsatisfactory warranty repair, repurchase intentions for different goods were still 47–84 per cent compared with more than 90 per cent repurchase intention when the repair was satisfactory. Often, it is not feasible to change a supplier; sometimes the product is satisfactory in other respects and there may be substantial switching costs.

Box 9.1	Quality in all things (abridged from *The Guardian*, 11 August 1993)

Heidi Fleiss, accused of running an expensive call-girl circuit for the elite of Hollywood, rebutted criticism from Madam Alex, the previous leader of the circuit, who claimed that she had stolen her clients. 'In this business', Heidi Fleiss is reputed to have said, 'no one steals clients. There is just better service.'

SECTION 2: THEORIES OF CONSUMER SATISFACTION

The Confirmation Model

Early thinking about satisfaction treated it as meeting consumer expectations. This is the *confirmation model* of consumer satisfaction which is illustrated in Figure 9.1. Oliver (1989) described the outcome as *contentment*; for example, we are contented when a refrigerator continues to keep food cold. This low arousal state is matched by low-arousal *discontent* when negative expectations are met. Such discontent applies to the routine use of inadequate services, such as congested roads, late buses and long queues at airport security, and to unsatisfactory products such as dripping taps, lumpy mattresses and toasters that eject the toast prematurely. In these situations, the discontent is subdued because of habituation. People get used to a problem and no longer notice it. As a result, it does not occur to them to do anything about it and any effect on behaviour is weak (shown as a dotted line in Figure 9.1). Consumer contentment and discontent may not be expressed but are revealed when people are questioned, or when other factors raise the salience of a product's performance; for example, others may comment on the dripping tap or an ad for beds may make people think of their own bedtime discomfort.

The toleration of product deficiencies is explained by adaptation theory (Helson, 1964). In this theory, perceptions are relative to some standard which itself is a function of all previously experienced outcomes. As long as positive and negative deviations from expectation are small, they will be accommodated and will have little effect on thinking and behaviour.

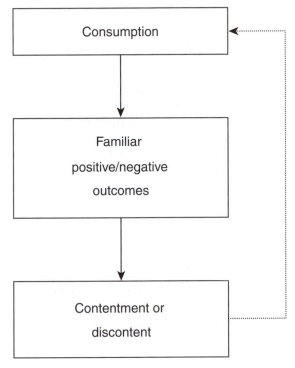

Figure 9.1 The confirmation model of consumer satisfaction: meeting expectations

Exercise 9.1   Recognizing dissatisfactions

Think of everyday products that you use, for example, refrigerators, shoes and clothing. Are these satisfactory? If you look at these products with a more critical eye, are there weaknesses that could be corrected? Does your refrigerator ice up or fail to drain condensation? Are your shoes too worn? Are you using clothes sizes (bras, collars, etc.) that are no longer appropriate? Such generally unrecognized problems often occur because what was once satisfactory has slowly become less so – too slowly to be noticed. What should advertisers do to draw your attention to the needs that you have not recognized yourself?

Some problems persist for a long time before a solution is found. Many of these solutions could have been invented earlier; what is often missing is the idea, rather than new technology. Consider the wheels on luggage which are now so common. These could have been produced years before they became common. Often, people may not have had the idea for the innovation because habituation stopped them from recognizing a problem. Can you think of products that we take for granted but which could be made better?

If consumers have little awareness of the shortcomings of everyday products, they will feel little pressure to change their behaviour and this can be a matter of concern. Our tendency to adjust to our environment may be to our disadvantage. When poor products are frequently experienced, any improvement would be frequently experienced too. Although people may not notice deficiencies in currently used goods and services, they may well notice and appreciate the change when the product is improved; thus, it is a pity if habituation leads to an absence of complaint or a lack of effort to find a better product. However, many of the discontents that we experience relate to public services (e.g. transport and parking constraints), and here, because of limited choice and influence, it may be difficult to achieve change. Research has moved away from the confirmation model but we can see this model relates to much consumer behaviour, particularly the toleration of delay, which is considered later.

The Disconfirmation Model

If our experience with goods and services is greatly different from what we expect, we are usually motivated to do something about it. Most research has focused on this high arousal condition where experience of goods or services disconfirms expectation, either by exceeding it and giving satisfaction, or by falling short of expectation and causing dissatisfaction (see Figure 9.2).

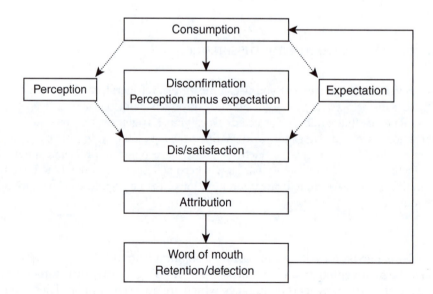

Figure 9.2   The disconfirmation model: exceeding or falling short of expectations

In the disconfirmation model the consumer is surprised by product features that are better or worse than expected.[1] The magnitude of surprise is related to the size of the discrepancy between expectation and experience. Two additional determinants are shown in Figure 9.2 – we show these with dotted lines because they are not part of the core disconfirmation model. The perception of the performance of the goods or services affects satisfaction directly; the better it is, the more we like it. Expectation also has a direct effect. There is variation in the emphasis placed on the different factors affecting satisfaction. Some researchers (e.g. Oliver, 1980, 1981; Swan and Trawick, 1981) have emphasized expectations, while others (e.g. Churchill and Surprenant, 1982; LaTour and Peat, 1979; Tse and Wilton, 1988) have given attention to perceptions. Several studies (e.g. Oliver, 1980; Swan and Trawick, 1980) found that satisfaction is influenced mainly by disconfirmation. At odds with these results, Churchill and Surprenant (1982) found that satisfaction with a video disc player was determined by perceived product performance, and any disconfirmation had no additional impact on satisfaction. It is quite likely that the relative importance of the different components of the model depends on the category.

The disconfirmation explanation of satisfaction has gradually evolved. Cardozo's (1965) laboratory work is often cited as the first empirical treatment of disconfirmed expectation and Howard and Sheth (1969: 145) were among the first to suggest that people use standards of assessment in judging products when they wrote that satisfaction was 'the buyer's cognitive state of being adequately or inadequately rewarded for the sacrifice he has undergone'. Oliver suggests that the emotion felt from disconfirmation of expectations decays into the attitude to the product:

> ... the summary psychological state resulting when the emotion surrounding disconfirmed expectations is coupled with the consumer's prior feelings about the consumption experience. Moreover, the surprise or excitement of this evaluation is thought to be of finite duration, so that satisfaction soon decays into (but nevertheless greatly affects) one's overall attitude toward purchasing products. (Oliver, 1981: 34)

Attribution

Disconfirmations may be interpreted in different ways by consumers. The model in Figure 9.2 therefore has an *attribution* stage where a causal explanation is developed in reaction to the product experience that generated the dis/satisfaction. This attribution will affect later behaviour by the consumer. When consumers explain a positive experience as a chance effect, they are unlikely to recommend the product but if a negative experience is attributed to neglect by the service provider, negative word of mouth and complaint to the provider may ensue. Burns and Perkins (1996) cover a wide range of possible responses in such situations. The attribution that consumers make may be affected by other conditions and, in particular, the *availability of explanations* and types of *causal inferences* have been studied. Exercise 9.2 relates to attribution.

Sometimes subtle cues can change the attribution that is made and therefore influence the satisfaction with a consumption experience. Pham, Goukens, Lehmann and Stuart

(2010) show that the presence of mirrors increases the likelihood that consumers attribute service outcomes to themselves, rather than to the service provider. As a result, unfavourable outcomes create less expressed dissatisfaction. The downside of the phenomenon is that favourable outcomes also lead to less expressed satisfaction. Self-awareness is the key driving factor here: cues that increase self-awareness (e.g. the small talk of a sales person centred on the customer) make self-attributions more likely. The effect is shown both in experimental scenarios in a lab setting and in real-life shopping situations. Interestingly, it also operates for the evaluation of past experiences. A limiting condition is that consumers have to bear some responsibility for the negative outcome (e.g. returning or exchanging previously purchased items).

| **Exercise 9.2** | Your experience |

The apparently fresh Brie is acrid, the new vacuum cleaner blocks or the waiter in an expensive restaurant is unhelpful; here the dissatisfactions arise because we expected a better experience. Conversely, we may be pleasantly surprised and satisfied when expectations are surpassed, e.g. when the roads are unusually clear, the fruit in supermarkets is ripe or the plane arrives early.

  Think back to the last time you were surprised by your experience as a consumer. Did the surprise make you satisfied, dissatisfied or neither? How would you explain what happened? Who was responsible?

Availability

According to the availability heuristic, vivid events are more easily brought to mind than routine occurrences and, in addition, these vivid events are judged more probable than they are in reality (see Chapter 8). Folkes (1988) gives an interesting example of how this can work. She asked people who were approaching the escalators to their apartment in a six-storey building how often the escalators broke down. The escalators only went to the fourth floor so that those who lived on the fifth and sixth floors always had to climb the stairs for the last part of their ascent. Those who always had to use the stairs for part of their journey estimated that the escalators broke down *less* often than the people who used the first four floors, for whom an escalator failure (leading to the unusual event of climbing the stairs) was more vivid. The distinctiveness of a product failure raises its vividness, and the availability heuristic raises the *perceived* likelihood that it will occur again (chapter 8). This, in turn, raises dissatisfaction. The supplier should, therefore, try to make failures less distinctive. For example, if customers are occupied in some way when service quality is reduced, they may form a less distinct memory of the poor performance.

Worse-than-expected outcomes have more impact than better-than-expected outcomes (DeSarbo et al., 1994). This difference could be explained as an example of losses looming larger than gains (Chapter 8).

Causal Inferences

Weiner (1980, 1990) has examined the explanations given for success and failure and has suggested three causal dimensions that are relevant to consumer response: *stability*, *locus of causality* and *controllability*. Stability occurs when the cause can be consistently attributed to a particular person or feature of the environment; locus of causality relates to whether the purchaser, the supplier or some other party is seen to be at fault; and controllability reflects the ability of an agent to intervene and change outcomes. An unstable negative event may not trigger negative attributions by consumers; for example, an out-of-stock item may be seen as exceptional (unstable) and unlikely to be repeated. It is, therefore, better for a seller if the cause of their failure is seen as unstable by the customer. By contrast, it is better to have stability in product success since this encourages continued usage. Folkes (1984) suggests that, when failure is perceived to be stable, a consumer will prefer to have a refund for a product failure since a replacement carries the same risk as the original; if the failure is seen as unstable, consumers will be more willing to accept a replacement. Stability may vary across customer segments. Bolton (1998) examined defection from the service supplier as a consequence of the failure of a mobile phone network. If the customer was long-term, the failure was offset against past good performance and seen as unstable, so the customer was disinclined to defect. Recent customers who lacked this experience were more likely to see the failure as stable, blame the supplier, and defect.

Weiner's other dimensions also affect consumer response after product failure. For example, with respect to locus of causality, customers may blame themselves when they purchase a poor product, and therefore expect no redress; but if they see the failure as the responsibility of the manufacturer or retailer, they may then expect a replacement or refund. If people feel that they have no control over their outcomes, they may feel anger towards those whom they think do have control, for example when public transport services are inadequate.

Exercise 9.3   Managing satisfaction

Understanding the implications of research findings on CSD can help us create better goods and services and to manage the process better when things go wrong. Create a scenario in which a major service failure is occurring and you are managing the service.

What are you going to say to customers? Consider the attributions they will make and the response they will want. What are the customer expectations and how can you manage these so that the failure is more acceptable? What compensation should you give, if any?

SECTION 3: MEASURING SATISFACTION AND SERVICE QUALITY

Satisfaction

Satisfaction with a product is experienced by a customer or ex-customer. In this respect, it is more restricted than the attitude to the product and assessments of quality, which may be given by anyone, customer or not. However, satisfaction with the product is an attitude; people are satisfied for reasons that can be measured, as reported in Chapter 7, and they will give an overall satisfaction like the global attitude described in the theory of planned behaviour. This overall satisfaction can be measured by a question such as:

Considering your main supermarket, would you say you are:

> Very satisfied [7]
> Quite satisfied [6]
> Slightly satisfied [5]
> Neither satisfied nor dissatisfied [4]
> Slightly dissatisfied [3]
> Quite dissatisfied [2]
> Very dissatisfied [1].

However, as we saw in Chapter 2, if we are trying to predict what people will do, a relative measure is better because it indicates the advantage of one product over another. Once relativity is admitted, we have a choice of comparators. In the American Customer Satisfaction Index (ACSI, www.theacsi.org), Fornell, Johnson and Anderson (1996) use three questions about recently purchased brands that relate to overall satisfaction, expectancy disconfirmation and perceived performance compared with ideal performance (see Box 9.2).

Box 9.2	The American Consumer Satisfaction Items

1 Please consider all your experiences to date with your main supermarket. Using a ten-point scale on which '1' means "very dissatisfied" and "10" means "very satisfied", how satisfied or dissatisfied are you with your supermarket overall?

Write in number (1 to 10) ....

2 To what extent has your main supermarket fallen short of your expectations or exceeded your expectations? Using a ten-point scale on which "1" now means "falls short of your expectations" and "10" means "exceeds your expectations", to what extent has your supermarket fallen short of or exceeded your expectations?

Write in number (1 to 10) ....

3 Forget your main supermarket for the moment. Now imagine an ideal supermarket. How well do you think your supermarket compares with that ideal supermarket? Please use a ten point scale on which "1" means "not very close to the ideal" and "10" means "very close to the ideal".

Write in number (1 to 10) ....

Here, the latter two items are relative to two different comparators. For practical purposes, the ACSI is the average of responses to the three items, though Fornell and his associates use different weights for specific predictions. When a firm markets several brands, a composite ACSI score for the firm can be derived from the scores for each brand. The ACSI items are part of a larger set of questions that cover complaints, loyalty, expectations, value and quality.

There has been less research emphasis on the components of satisfaction – the specific reasons why a product is liked or disliked. We can measure this using the methods of the theory of planned behaviour discussed in Chapter 7, treating satisfaction as a reaction to a bundle of costs and benefits. Westbrook (1980) tested this approach. He examined the way in which customers combined the dis/satisfactions relating to a store and found that a global measure of retail satisfaction correlated well with a simple addition of the satisfactions and dissatisfactions customers felt about different aspects of store service.

Quality

Whereas satisfaction measures focus on the global attitude, quality measures tend to give more attention to the reasons why a product is high quality. The field of service quality measurement has been dominated by an instrument called SERVQUAL, designed to assess any service using one standard set of questions. It was developed by Parasuraman, Zeithaml and Berry (1985, 1988). SERVQUAL measures customers' expectations of what firms should provide in the industry being studied and their perceptions of how a given service provider performs against these criteria. The 1988 version of the instrument contained 22 expectation questions covering such specific service facilities as up-to-date equipment, visually appealing premises and polite employees. In 1991, Parasuraman, Berry and Zeithaml modified the instrument slightly. They changed two items and altered the wordings of some others; the negative scoring on some items was removed and the wording of the expectation measures was changed so that respondents were asked what an 'excellent service would provide', rather than what 'firms in the industry should provide'. Box 9.3 shows the expectation items in the 1991 scale, applied to telephone companies. A second set of questions (not shown) would deal with the perceptions about a specific telephone company.

Parasuraman, Zeithaml and Berry (1988) showed that these 22 items could be allocated to five dimensions – tangibles, reliability, responsiveness, assurance (knowledge and courtesy of employees and their ability to inspire trust and confidence) and empathy (caring and individual attention to customers). However, the five-factor structure has not been well supported; Cronin and Taylor (1992) found only one general factor.

The idea that SERVQUAL will apply to a variety of services without much modification has also been contested. Carman (1990) found that some functions require additional measures for adequate explanation. Koelemeijer (1992) and Finn and Lamb (1991) found that the SERVQUAL instrument performed poorly in retail contexts. Dabholkar, Thorpe and Rentz (1996) developed a scale for retail quality measurement which customized the measure to the retail context. It is easy to argue that some of the items are inappropriate for certain services, e.g. religious services having modern-looking equipment or neat appearance in academic settings. Thus, customization of SERVQUAL seems to be required

Box 9.3	SERVQUAL expectation components and classification (from Parasuraman, Berry and Zeithaml, 1991: 446–447)

Tangibles

1 Excellent telephone companies will have modern-looking equipment.
2 The physical facilities at excellent telephone companies will be visually appealing.
3 Employees of excellent telephone companies will be neat-appearing. [Did they really say this? Or is it neat in appearance?]
4 Materials associated with the service (such as pamphlets or statements) will be visually appealing in an excellent telephone company.

Reliability

5 When excellent telephone companies promise to do something by a certain time, they will do so.
6 When customers have a problem, excellent telephone companies will show a sincere interest in solving it.
7 Excellent telephone companies will perform the service right first time.
8 Excellent telephone companies will provide their services at the time they promise to do so.
9 Excellent telephone companies will keep error-free records.

Responsiveness

10 Employees of excellent telephone companies will tell customers exactly when services will be performed.
11 Employees of excellent telephone companies give prompt service to customers.

12 Employees of excellent telephone companies will always be willing to help customers.
13 Employees of excellent telephone companies will never be too busy to respond to customer requests.

Assurance

14 The behaviour of employees of excellent telephone companies will instil confidence in customers.
15 Customers of excellent telephone companies will feel safe in their transactions.
16 Employees of excellent telephone companies will be consistently courteous with customers.
17 Employees of excellent telephone companies will have the knowledge to answer customer questions.

Empathy

18 Excellent telephone companies will give customers individual attention.
19 Excellent telephone companies will have operating hours convenient to all their customers.
20 Excellent telephone companies will have employees who give customers personal attention.
21 Excellent telephone companies will have the customers' best interests at heart.
22 The employees of excellent telephone companies will understand the specific needs of their customers.

for application to different services and, although Parasuraman, Zeithaml and Berry (1994) accepted this, the changes in questions may need to be substantial.

The computation of quality judgement from the questionnaire responses has also raised problems. SERVQUAL uses the difference scores between expectation and perception but expectations tend to be uniformly high and show little variance. Although the difference measures correlate reasonably well with an overall measure of quality (Babacus and Boller, 1992; Cronin and Taylor, 1992; Parasuraman, Berry and Zeithaml, 1991), the low variance in the expectation measures makes these irrelevant to the score so that perception-only scores are equally predictive. For this reason, Cronin and Taylor (1992) recommended that the measure be restricted to performance perceptions (which they call SERVPERF), giving a questionnaire of half the length. An alternative to this is to measure the gap between expectation and perceived performance with a single question that combines the two elements. Babacus and Boller (1992) suggested a way of phrasing this and Box 9.4 shows the binary form and the combined measure. In a review of SERVQUAL's history, Smith (1995) concludes that few of the original claims remain undisputed. The aim of generic measurement of service quality is attractive, but this goal may be unobtainable because of variation in the nature of services and because of a lack of agreement about concepts and measures.

Box 9.4	Alternative scales

1   SERVQUAL expectation and perception scales:

Firms in XYZ's field should have modern-looking equipment:

strongly disagree   1 | 2 | 3 | 4 | 5 | 6 | 7   strongly agree

Firm XYZ has modern-looking equipment:

strongly disagree   1 | 2 | 3 | 4 | 5 | 6 | 7   strongly agree

2   Combined item:

XYZ's modern-looking equipment:

greatly falls short of   1 | 2 | 3 | 4 | 5 | 6 | 7   greatly exceeds
my expectations   my expectations

SECTION 4: OUTCOMES OF SATISFACTION AND DISSATISFACTION

Does Increased Satisfaction Lead to Increased Profit?

If managers can increase product and service quality and hence customer satisfaction, a number of beneficial effects may follow for the supplier, as detailed in Figure 9.3. These

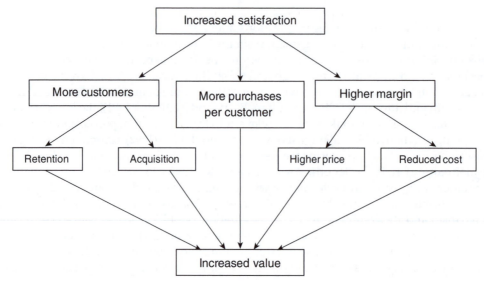

Figure 9.3   Routes to increased value

are more customers (either by retention or acquisition), additional purchases per customer and a higher profit margin, either through an increase in price or a reduction in costs per sale. There are, however, also additional costs associated with innovation and quality management. Thus, evidence is needed on whether an increase in satisfaction is normally associated with increased profit and, if so, how this comes about.

To investigate the consequences of increased satisfaction, the measure of satisfaction developed for the American Customer Satisfaction Index (ACSI) is often used. This is because the ACSI, and similar indexes in other countries, provide comprehensive measures across a range of industries, in the case of ACSI for more than 200 specific companies. In a review of studies using such measures, Zeithaml (2000) found a generally positive association between quality and profit and suggested that this was mediated by improved customer retention. Using the Swedish Customer Satisfaction Barometer, Anderson, Fornell and Lehmann (1994) were able to demonstrate small increments in return on investment over five years as a result of increases in satisfaction. These authors suggest that the connection between satisfaction and profit could be mediated by a range of effects. They cite greater retention, reduced price elasticity, lack of interest in competitor offerings, reduced costs for future transactions, reduced costs from failure, lower costs of customer acquisition, advertising and new product advantage through increased reputation of the firm, more customer recommendation, greater willingness to try products and stronger relationships with suppliers. These more specific explanations are largely covered by the aggregate effects shown in Figure 9.3.

Anderson, Fornell and Mazvancheryl (2004) have shown that increases in customer satisfaction are associated with increases in shareholder value, as measured by Tobin's q (see note 2). Anderson et al. argue that higher customer satisfaction may raise the bargaining power of a firm with its suppliers and other partners because these partners value relationships with companies who 'own' a valuable customer base. Increased bargaining power may assist margin and sales and may thus contribute to shareholder value. Gruca and Rego (2005) found satisfaction influenced shareholder value by both increasing cash flows and reducing their variability; this provides a financial account of the relationship, but tells us little about the underlying changes in consumer behaviour. Fornell et al. (2006) examined the growth obtained from investing in stock portfolios of high satisfaction companies. They found impressively high returns compared with standard investment indices and they argue that this extra gain was achieved without incurring greater risk. This study was conducted over 1997–2004 but, subsequently, Fornell, Mithas and Morgeson (2006) report that, up to October 2008, the investment portfolio had generated an average return of 15.1 per cent compound in the previous eight years while the S&P 500 index changed little. Aksoy et al. (2008) also find that changes in the satisfaction score predict stock value changes, but only when the economy is expanding. Anderson and Mansi (2009) make the connection between satisfaction and the corporate bond market. They show that firms with higher customer satisfaction ratings (as measured by ACSI) benefit from better credit ratings and lower debt costs and therefore obtain a financing advantage. Luo, Homburg and Wieseke (2010) also check the impact of satisfaction on financial markets and analyze the relationship between ACSI satisfaction scores, recommendations of financial analysts and company value, for about 100 firms over a 12-year period. Customer satisfaction is informative for the analysts because it predicts the growth and volatility of future cash flows. Luo et al. (2010) find that firms with higher levels of customer satisfaction receive more positive stock recommendations from analysts. The effect is higher in more competitive markets and also in situations of higher uncertainty in financial markets. They also show that satisfaction impacts financial returns, both directly and indirectly through the analysts' recommendations.

Although there is little *evidence* favouring any specific pathway from quality/satisfaction to increased value, there has been some tendency to emphasize the retention route (Anderson and Mittal, 2000; Zeithaml, 2000). This emphasis on retention may be misplaced, since a review of the connection between satisfaction and retention generally found weak associations (Chapter 2). In addition, Wangenheim and Bayón (2007) show that increased customer satisfaction does lead to new customer acquisition via increased word of mouth. We suspect that this is the main route to increased profit but definitive research is needed here. Word of mouth is considered further in Chapter 12.

Complaining

Factors Affecting Complaining Behaviour

People are often reluctant to complain when they are dissatisfied with goods or services. There is evidence that the degree of dissatisfaction has a modest relationship with the likelihood of complaint (Day, 1984; Malafi et al., 1993; Oliver, 1981, 1987; Singh and Howell, 1985). Oliver (1981) reports a correlation of about 0.4 between dissatisfaction and complaining. However, there is considerable inertia: Andreasen (1988) and Stø and Glefjell (1990) both found that 60 per cent of dissatisfied consumers did nothing, while Benterud and Stø (1993) found that 95 per cent of those dissatisfied with their TV shopping did not complain.

Day (1984) and Singh and Howell (1985) have noted that complaining is affected by how people explain product failure, their expectation of redress and the likely time-cost and effort involved. Research on complaining needs to take account of all the possible reasons that people might have for this behaviour. We can cover these reasons by using Ajzen's (1985, 1991) theory of planned behaviour, as discussed in Chapter 7. This deals with three types of influence.

1 **Expected outcomes**. Hirschman (1970) suggested that complaining by customers was related to the expected returns and costs. Positive outcomes may include replacement, apology and better goods or service in the future, while negative outcomes may include lost opportunities, wasted time and embarrassment. The perceived likelihood of success in obtaining redress has been found to be associated with complaining in a number of studies (Day and Landon, 1976; Granbois, Summers and Frazier, 1977; Richins, 1983, 1987; Singh, 1990). Richins (1985) also found evidence that the importance of the product affects the likelihood of complaining.

2 **Normative influences**. Consumers may also be influenced by what they believe others think they should do, even when these other people are not present. Normative influences on complaining have not been studied systematically, although Richins (1981) has noted instances where consumers felt that they *ought* to complain.

3 **Control factors**. These are knowledge, skills, time and other factors that can make complaining easier or harder. Examples are the ease of access to key personnel, an understanding of the workings of the organization causing dissatisfaction, and confidence about complaining. Control factors help us to distinguish between those who complain and those who do not. Two studies (Caplovitz, 1967; Warland, Herrmann and Willits, 1975) found that non-complainers seemed powerless and had less knowledge of the means of redress. Grønhaug (1977) found that there were more complaints to a Norwegian consumer protection agency from citizens who lived closer to it. Grønhaug and Zaltman (1981) also recognized the importance of resources such as time, money and confidence and this study is cited by Yi (1990) as important in showing differences between complainers and non-complainers. A matter of concern is that vulnerable consumers (the old, ill and disadvantaged) complain less than others (Andreasen and Manning, 1990) and this is likely to be related to the reduced control that such consumers have.

East (2000) used the theory of planned behaviour to investigate complaining in the UK. He found that complaining was focused mainly on getting a refund or replacement, standing up for one's rights, doing what friends expected and confidence about being able to complain. Such evidence helps us to see what factors may encourage complaining. For example, in order to increase confidence, suppliers should make it clear that they welcome complaints and should explain a clear procedure for handling them.

The Benefits of Receiving Complaints

Fornell and Wernerfelt (1987) argue that, within cost limits, it is profitable to gather and evaluate complaints from dissatisfied customers. Companies increasingly put toll-free telephone numbers and e-mail addresses on goods packaging for this purpose. One reason for the profitability of receiving complaints is that these supply information about product deficiencies, which can then be corrected. A second reason is to gather further sales when the complainer gets in touch. For example, the complainer may be advised that there is a newer version of software or an improved design of outdoor clothing and this information may lead to a further purchase. A third reason is that an effective response to the aggrieved customer by the company may reduce negative word of mouth to other potential customers, which could damage sales. Finally, if the complaint is well handled, the company may be able to stop defection or recover customers who have already left.

There is evidence that customers who are retained after a service failure may be more satisfied than they are without the failure. This is called the service recovery paradox (SRP). One explanation is that, if customers appreciate the efforts of the company to satisfy their concerns, they may recommend it more and be more inclined to repurchase. Examples of SRP were found by TARP (1979) and Gilly and Gelb (1982) but Solnick and Hemenway (1992) found that those who complained about health provision were over four times more likely to defect than those who did not. More patronage after complaint may occur because the complaint handling resolved the customer's dissatisfaction and exceeded expectation, but it is also possible that those who intend to remain with the supplier complain because they want to benefit from any changes resulting from their complaining.

Magnini et al. (2007) used role-play studies to investigate the SRP. They found that the effect occurred when the failure was not severe, the firm had not failed the customer before, the cause of the failure was seen as unstable and the customer believed that the company had little control over the failure. In a meta-analysis, De Matos et al. (2007) found a significant SRP effect for satisfaction but not for repurchase intention or word of mouth.

Response to Delay

Delay in the delivery of service is a perennial feature of retailing and other services. Indeed, it is an inherent liability of something that is produced and consumed during an interval of time. Consumers wait for counter service in post offices, for train tickets in booking offices and at the checkout in supermarkets; they also wait for public transport and get held up in traffic jams; they may have to wait to talk to someone on the telephone. For the individual, delay is frustrating and for the economy it is wasteful because people waiting in line are neither producing nor consuming. Bitner, Booms and Tetreault (1990) noted that delay was a major feature of incidents causing dissatisfaction. Pruyn and Smidts (1993) found that Dutch consumers waited, on average, over half an hour per day for various services and that supermarket checkout delay was the most irritating hold-up. In Britain, 70 per cent of respondents in a Consumers' Association report on supermarkets (*Which?*, February 1990) mentioned 'a lot of staffed checkouts' as desirable, placing it fourth in importance compared with other store features, and another report on post offices (*Which?*, September 1989) put cutting queuing time at the top of service improvements suggested by respondents, even though the research recorded an average wait of only 3.5 minutes.

Queuing for crêpes in Hampstead

It appears that dissatisfaction with waiting can affect the total service experience: the longer the wait, the lower the evaluation of the whole service (Feinberg, Widdows and Steidle, 1996; Katz, Larson and Larson, 1991; Taylor, 1994; Tom and Lucey, 1995). Organizations may not see delay in the same way as their customers. Feinberg and Smith (1989) found that the customer at the checkout thought the average delay was 5.6 minutes when the staff though it was 3.2; the actual time was 4.7 minutes.

It is likely that people are less bothered by delay when it is expected (Maister, 1985). Supporting this, an experiment on bank queues by Clemmer and Schneider (1989) showed that the more unexpected the delay, the more it was disliked. This suggests that we can identify two types of dissatisfaction with delay: a low involvement discontent when the delay is predicted and a high involvement disconfirmation effect when it is unanticipated. As delays get more common they also become more predictable and, paradoxically, consumers may put up with them more easily. This may be why Taylor (1994) did not find that common delays were associated with significantly more irritation.

People also tolerate a wait better if they know how long it is. The provision of delay information is standard for airlines, and London Transport provides display boards reporting the wait before the next train or bus arrives. This information seems to be much appreciated despite the fact that it does nothing to reduce the waiting time. A similar facility is queue position information for those waiting on the telephone for their turn to speak to a customer service representative.

Maister also notes that people are less irritated by delay if they are occupied in some way. One example here is the way in which Disneyland entertains its queues with costumed characters; another is the provision of mirrors in places where people have to wait, for example at lifts. Taylor (1995) used two groups in an experiment to test the effect of occupying people when they had to wait. Both groups were delayed by ten minutes but only one was allowed activities to offset the delay. In this study, the evaluation of the service was reduced by delay but the reduction in evaluation was less when people were occupied. In fact, some of those who were delayed did not even realize that they had been held up and most of these people were in the 'occupied' group. One explanation for this effect of keeping people occupied is that, with this distraction, they do not retrieve expectations about acceptable delay and therefore do not form an assessment of their experience. Taylor's work also suggested that, if the service provider was thought to have control, customers assessed the service more negatively. This is consistent with Weiner's (1980, 1990) suggestion that people become more irritated when they believe that the service provider has control of the situation.

Studies by Dubé-Rioux, Schmitt and Leclerc (1989) show that when delay occurs at the beginning or end of a process, in their example a restaurant meal, it was evaluated more negatively than mid-process delays. For example, it was better for waiters to take the order, and then impose the delay, than to wait before taking the order. However, it is not always clear when a service starts and finishes. For example, delays to air travel occur when going to the airport, at check-in, baggage check, passport control, the departure lounge, in the plane before take-off, before landing, at baggage reclaim and again at passport control and customs. People may think of this sequence as a number of services or just one, and the way they regard it may affect how they tolerate delay at different points.

A study of the service experiences of UK customers by East, Lomax and Willson (1991) showed that 31 per cent did not mind waiting at the checkout in supermarkets. In banks and post offices, this figure rose to 50 per cent and in building societies to 57 per cent. A cynic might see this as evidence of British stoicism, and Maister (1985) has noted dryly that, if the British see a queue, they join it. However, further evidence showed that most people (52 per cent in the UK and 63 per cent in the USA), either did not mind, or minded a little, when delayed at the checkout (East et al., 1992). The data could indicate that delay is tolerated better in the USA than in the UK. However, the dislike of delay was related to how long people expected to be delayed; the US respondents expected delays to be briefer and this probably explains their greater tolerance.

Dislike of queuing is also likely to be related to the reason for waiting and the amount of spare time that people have. Table 9.2 shows the evidence on post offices subdivided by age and whether the customer was paying or receiving money. Older people, who might be expected to have more spare time, were more tolerant of delay. People were also more tolerant when they were receiving a benefit rather than paying for something.

Table 9.2 Percentage who dislike waiting at the post office (East, Lomax and Willson, 1991)

Age	Those buying stamps, licences or paying bills (%)	Those receiving pensions, allowances or other benefits (%)
Under 65	61	49
65+	50	18

Perceived Responsibility for Delay

Of particular interest is the way people explain who is responsible when they have to wait for service. If customers see the service provider as responsible, they are likely to be more irritated by the delay and complain more (Weiner, 1980; Taylor, 1995). Folkes, Koletsky and Graham (1987) found that customers became angrier and expressed more resistance to repurchase when they felt that a delay was avoidable by management. Taylor (1994) also found that those who blamed management were angrier about the wait.

In the study by East, Lomax and Willson (1991), respondents were asked whom they held responsible when they were delayed at the checkout of a supermarket. Table 9.3 shows that more of the people who blamed management disliked waiting. The investigations of delay in post offices, building societies and banks gave very similar results. We see from the bracketed numbers in Table 9.3 that few people are self-blaming; they are much more likely to blame other customers than themselves. This is consistent with the actor–observer bias (Jones and Nisbett, 1972), that an actor tends to see others as choosing and therefore responsible for their behaviour while the actor sees the same behaviour in himself as caused by the situation (e.g. circumstances or other people).

Table 9.3   Those held responsible for delay in the supermarket (East, Lomax and Willson, 1991)

Response to delay	No one (99) (%)	Self (9) (%)	Other customers (96) (%)	Checkout staff (19) (%)	Management (208) (%)	Total (431) (%)
Don't mind	48	33	46	37	16	31
Dislike it	52	67	54	63	84	69

When serious delays occur, managers may receive much of the blame. Often the cause is accidental or brought about by other service providers on whom a firm had relied. This suggests that management needs to distinguish between the cause of the delay and responsibility for its consequences. Staff should clearly accept responsibility for remedying a problem, but it will help if, when appropriate, they can explain that they did not create the problem, since Taylor (1994) has shown that the service is liked less when blame is attributed to the service provider. For example, the cause of an aircraft take-off delay may be that a service company has failed to deliver airline food on time, a mechanical fault has been revealed by standard checks before take-off, bad weather has delayed the plane's arrival, or that airport congestion is worse than normal. In all these cases, timely announcements may help to deflect blame.

Queues can be organized as either multiple-line or as single-line. Sometimes it is possible to use a queuing ticket system, which allows people to conduct other business while they wait. The relative attraction of these three systems was tested by East, Lomax, Willson and Harris (1992) in their investigation of bank and building society use (see Table 9.4). The single-line queuing system is much preferred to queuing at each counter despite the fact that this introduces a slight delay as customers make their way to a vacant counter.

Box 9.5	Delay management

Research on the response to delay helps us to understand how to manage this service problem better. There are three approaches:

1 **Operations management**. Where feasible, managers should try to avoid delays by increasing service supply in line with demand. For example, supermarket managers can count shoppers entering the store and open checkouts in advance of the calculated demand; also they can try and use their fastest checkout operators at peak times.

2 **Influencing demand**. The second approach uses regulation and incentives to draw demand away from busy periods and towards quiet periods. A reservation system is used for many services and differential pricing may also shift demand, e.g. Monday is often a cheap day at the cinema in Britain. However, East, Lomax, Willson and Harris (1994) judged that the scope for promoting the off-peak periods in supermarkets was limited (see more on this in Chapter 11).

3 **Perception management**. The third approach is to try to ensure that the customer sees the delay in a way that does least damage. Tom and Lucey (1995) suggest putting literature at the checkout and advise that this is a good location for free samples. Maister (1985) also recommends diverting the queue but the form of the diversion should be chosen carefully; it is easy to irritate customers with mindless music on the telephone and irrelevant advertising on screens set up for the queue. Such arrangements imply that the delay is normal (stable) and management is interested in alleviating, rather than eliminating, the discomfort of waiting.

Table 9.4   If there were queues, would you rather have ...? (East, Lomax, Willson and Harris, 1992)

System	Banks (%)	Building societies (%)	Mean (%)
... separate queues at each counter	15	12	14
... a single queuing system	78	81	79
... queuing tickets	7	7	7

The advantages of single-line systems are twofold: delays are approximately equal and therefore fair and they are more predictable since excessive delays at one counter will not affect waiting time much when there are several counters in use. A single-line system seems particularly useful when the start of a service is imminent, for example, in train stations where there is a danger of missing the train. Work by Pruyn and Smidts (1993) indicates that, although people may prefer the single line, the queuing system is of less consequence than the duration of delay and the quality of the waiting environment.

Waiting as a Cue for Quality

Although our coverage of waiting has so far considered it as a negative experience, we should not forget that consumers can also be attracted to service providers with long waiting times. A long line outside a restaurant or nightclub can be perceived as the promise of a great experience. Consumers often rely on the behaviour of others for guidance, and other people waiting in line is an easily observable cue. In a series of four experiments, with either scenarios or actual waiting experiences, Giebelhausen, Robinson and Cronin (2011) show that a required wait can increase purchase intentions and experienced satisfaction. They also examine different moderators of this effect. It appears more pronounced when the product or service is difficult to evaluate because of a lack of familiarity or objective criteria and when quality, as opposed to convenience, is a decision criterion.

SUMMARY

Consumer satisfaction, dissatisfaction, quality perception and complaining behaviour are important because they relate to profit via word of mouth and repeat purchase. A particular emphasis in this field has been on the quality of services because these are more prone to failure than goods and constitute a large and growing proportion of modern economies.

Consumers are contented when products meet positive expectations and are discontented with goods and services that show expected weaknesses, but this fulfilment of expectations normally produces little arousal and, therefore, little 'exit' or 'voice' by the customer. Much research has focused on those occasions where product performance surprises the consumer (the disconfirmation model). Surprise is arousing and causes more behavioural response and, therefore, more potential impact on profit. There is some variation in the way researchers describe the detail of the disconfirmation model but there is agreement that the discrepancy between expectation and perception is the main focus; expectations and perceptions may have additional direct effects on dis/satisfaction. In addition, researchers now recognize an interpretative phase in which consumers' explanations of their experience may modify their responses to it.

There are a number of consequences of satisfaction, some of which were covered in Chapter 2. An important concern is the association between satisfaction and profit. Companies that increase satisfaction have been found to show subsequent increases in profit. This gain in profit does not appear to be fully anticipated in the share price so that buying shares in companies that show satisfaction gains appears to be a sensible investment strategy.

When customers are dissatisfied, they rarely complain. Companies can benefit from complaints being expressed and research has been conducted to explain the motivation to complain. Delay is a general liability of service provision that causes dissatisfaction. Unexpected delay (causing disconfirmation) is particularly disliked. When it occurs, delay is tolerated better if people understand why they are delayed and how long it will last. Also, if consumers can occupy their time they are less dissatisfied. It is better to start a service and then impose a delay than to begin or end with the delay. In some cases, delays can be a signal of success of the product and therefore a cue for quality.

Additional Resources

For reviews of SERVQUAL, see Smith (1995) and Buttle (1996). For evidence of the impact of satisfaction on shareholder value, see Anderson et al. (2004) and Gruca and Rego (2005).

Notes

1 Expectations are often reported as though they are held in mind prior to the experience and then compared with the delivered product, but the experience, pleasant or unpleasant, usually causes us to bring to mind what would be appropriate in the circumstances, which we then call our expectation.
2 A firm's q value is the ratio of its market value to the current replacement cost of its assets (Tobin, 1969). Thus it is higher for those firms that are perceived to be using their assets more effectively.

Part 4
Market Response

10 Consumer Response to Price and Sales Promotions

LEARNING OBJECTIVES

When you have completed this chapter, you should be able to:

1 Describe how consumers process price information.
2 Explain how marketers assess consumers' price sensitivity.
3 Evaluate the different tactics you observe in the marketplace to present prices and price changes.
4 Assess the effectiveness of promotions by distinguishing between possible sources of extra sales.
5 Compare the advantages and disadvantages of price discounting versus couponing.
6 Discuss the long-term effectiveness of promotions.
7 Assess the effectiveness of the customization of promotions for both Internet and 'bricks-and-mortar' stores.

OVERVIEW

Consumers verify the prices of products in order to make sure they buy at the right price and, for expensive items, stay within budget. Buying at the right price means getting good value for money, compared with alternative products and this may involve buying at the right moment and place. Benchmark prices may be externally available but often consumers have to rely on their memory of previously encountered prices to make comparisons. Price memory, unfortunately, appears to be rather unreliable.

Marketers have developed different methodologies to estimate how consumers react to price changes. Price increases, though often necessary and justified, are unpopular and are often considered unfair. Consumer researchers have examined the conditions under which perceptions of fairness or unfairness occur. Prices also influence the perceived quality and even the emotional experience of using the product.

Price decreases are usually sales promotions. Two decades of access to scanner data has given researchers the opportunity to develop sophisticated quantitative models to evaluate promotion effectiveness. Combining a price cut with additional promotional activities, such as in-store displays and advertising features, may have a synergistic effect. Promotions usually have large short-term effects on sales, but there is doubt about their long-term effectiveness and contribution to profit. Customization of promotions, to adapt them to the characteristics and purchase habits of individual consumers or consumer segments, seems to hold promise. However, initial results show that customization is not necessarily more profitable compared to mass promotions, especially in 'bricks-and-mortar' retailing.

SECTION 1: CONSUMER RESPONSE TO PRICE

Reference Prices

A price is rarely treated in isolation: prices become informative by relating them to other prices, a phenomenon studied under the heading of reference price. A price in combination with a reference price, whether accurate or not, allows a consumer to determine if it is better to buy here and now or to wait and buy elsewhere. When a product is cheaper than expected it is more likely to be purchased and vice versa.

The concept of reference price was introduced to marketing by Monroe (1973). It was inspired by Helson's (1964) adaptation-level theory that states that stimuli are judged with respect to internal norms. These internal norms represent the aggregate effect of past and present stimulation. There are two views on the origin of reference prices. According to the first view, consumers call on their memory of past prices they paid or encountered. They hold what is referred to as internal reference prices (IRP). The second view posits that reference prices are formed during the shopping occasion itself, based on prices observed, known in the literature as external reference prices (ERP).

Interestingly, most research on reference price does not ask consumers for their reference prices but instead infers them from choice models estimated on panel data (Winer, 1986). These models include as explanatory variables the elements of the marketing mix, including price, but also a reference price term. This term captures the difference between the current price of the product and some mathematical function of past prices (in the case of IRP) or currently observable other prices (in the case of ERP). The fact that this difference variable helps explain choice is taken as evidence that consumers make comparisons with reference prices. The wide availability of individual-level scanner data has permitted an extremely productive stream of research in this area (see the review in Mazumdar, Raj and Sinha, 2005).

Researchers have provided a broad range of reference price models. Hardie, Johnson and Fader (1993) compared a model with ERP and one with IRP and found that, at least for orange juice, the category they examined, ERP, was a better representation of reference price. Briesch et al. (1997), however, showed that IRP gave a better model fit in other categories. It is of course possible that the use of IRP or ERP varies across consumers and situations. Mazumdar and Papatla (2000) pursue this idea and show that there are indeed segments of consumers that differ in the extent to which they use IRP or ERP. They also show that IRP is more frequently used for more expensive product categories while ERP is more often used in categories with a longer interpurchase time and greater frequency of promotions.

Although most research examines ERP and IRP as defined above, a number of alternative definitions of reference price have been proposed. People may compare with the price they *usually* pay but they may also compare with the price they would *like* to pay, the price they *expect* to pay, given the expected evolution of prices, or the price they regard as *fair*. Winer (1988) even proposed eight different possible definitions of price reference.

Although most research treats reference prices as precise points, it may be that consumers actually have price zones in mind. Kalyanaram and Little (1994) estimate a 'latitude of acceptance' around the reference price. This is a zone in which the consumer is indifferent to deviations between the observed price and the reference price. As with most reference price models, they also find the asymmetric price effect predicted by prospect theory (see Chapter 8), with stronger negative responses to price increases than positive responses to price decreases.

Exercise 10.1 Your price knowledge

Keep the till receipt of one of your next trips to the supermarket. When you get home, unpack your products and, without looking at your receipt, write down the prices you paid. Indicate each time whether you think you remember the price accurately or whether you are just making an estimate. Also indicate how accurate you think you are (very accurate, rather accurate, not accurate). Score your responses according to whether they are exactly right, within 10 per cent or outside this range. Compare your results with others.

1 How easy or difficult was it to determine whether your knowledge is directly drawn from memory? In other words, how good is your introspective access to the cognitive processes you use to answer the questions?
2 Is there any evidence that frequently bought items are better remembered?
3 Do you have other hypotheses about why you remembered some prices better than other ones?
4 How can these hypotheses be tested in a study?
5 Are students likely to remember prices better than other consumers? If so, why?

Price Memory

If consumers use IRP to assess the attractiveness of an offer, it is interesting to verify how accurate their knowledge of prices is. Dickson and Sawyer (1990) found that less than half of US shoppers could give the correct price for the item that they had just put into their shopping trolley. They mention in their article that marketing executives and academics who attended presentations of this study were surprised by how imperfect shoppers' attention to, and retention of, price information was at the point of purchase. Nevertheless, the finding was corroborated by Le Boutillier, Le Boutillier and Neslin (1994) for coffee, but not for soda, where 71 per cent could recall the exact price they paid. In addition, using the same interviewing procedure, Wakefield and Inman (1993) report percentages of correct responses ranging from 52 to 78 per cent for four product categories.

These in-the-aisle price knowledge surveys have received two types of response. Some researchers consider that these survey results bring reference price findings into question, because price knowledge is much lower than most researchers intuitively expected (Kalyanaram and Winer, 1995). A second type of response concerns the interpretation of the results. The Dickson and Sawyer results are often interpreted as indications that price memory is poor. Vanhuele and Drèze (2002) point out that what may be measured in these in-the-aisle surveys is short-term memory, not long-term price memory.

Vanhuele and Drèze (2002) examined how price information is stored in long-term memory and, based on theories from numerical cognition, hypothesized that three types of coding are used: verbal (similar to recording your voice), visual (photographic) and magnitude coding (you remember that the price was somewhere between 35 and 40). They show that recall questions measure only part of price memory. Recognition memory is clearly better and some knowledge is also only present in an approximate form in memory. The Dickson and Sawyer results are therefore not necessarily in conflict with reference price research.

Overall, price knowledge surveys may suggest that the current price is of no consequence to many purchasers but this simplifies the issue too much. Although consumers may take prices on trust on many occasions, they may, at other times, check on how much they are paying and react against suppliers who are seen to overcharge. In addition, the price of a limited number of goods may be used as a key to the overall value for money offered by a store. Even if there is only a small segment of consumers who examine prices carefully most of the time, this segment of so-called price vigilantes (Wakefield and Inman, 1993) may be sufficiently important for retailers to keep prices low.

Although some price learning may be incidental and unconscious – and therefore less available to recall (Monroe and Lee, 1999; Vanhuele and Drèze, 2002) – other price learning may be intentional and conscious, especially for motivated price-sensitive consumers. What if we are motivated to learn prices? How good can we become at price recall? How well is our cognitive system adapted to memorizing prices? With a series of experiments Vanhuele, Laurent and Drèze (2006) examined how immediate memory for prices functions. Participants had to keep prices for two or three products in a given category (DVDs, cameras and candy) in memory for five seconds before feeding them back. Analyses of the responses confirmed that the three types of numerical coding discussed by Vanhuele and Drèze (2002) are used: verbal, visual and magnitude coding. Most intriguing is the effect of verbal coding. If people want to hold a price (or whatever other information) in short-term memory, they cycle it through a sub-system of working memory. Because the capacity of this sub-system is restricted to 1.5 to 2 seconds of length of speech, prices that take longer to pronounce are less well remembered. Also, consumers who speak slower have poorer immediate memory, because of this capacity restriction. And consumers who do not respect the official pronunciation of prices and use shortcuts instead (e.g. twelve ninety instead of one thousand two hundred and ninety) have a memory advantage. An implication of this finding, not examined in the article, is that, across regions, language differences handicap some consumers in their price memory. For the French, for instance, a price of 90 euros is 'quatre-vingt-dix euros', but French-speaking Belgians and Swiss know it in a shorter form as 'nonante euros'.

The Price–Quality Relationship

When comparing different goods, consumers may use price as an indicator of quality. In a review of over 40 studies, Rao and Monroe (1989) found robust but moderate evidence that consumers indeed use price as a proxy for product quality. When such inferences occur, they may actually be mistaken. An analysis of US studies by Tellis and Wernerfelt (1987) found a mean correlation between price and *objective* product quality of only 0.27. Zeithaml (1988) reviewed nearly 90 studies and only found mixed support for a relationship between price and *subjectively* assessed quality. It seems that the inference of quality from price is therefore rather weaker than has been supposed. One important reason is probably that quality perceptions obviously depend on a number of factors in addition to price, such as the appearance of the product, the reports of others, the brand and the store that sells the product. Consumers who believe that price and quality are related may persist in this belief because they selectively focus on cases that confirm their belief, i.e. they attend most to high-price/high-quality and low-price/low-quality products. Kardes et al. (2004) show, however, that belief-inconsistent information can be processed for price–quality inferences when consumers are motivated and have the opportunity to do so.

Combining this review with that on reference price, we see that price can influence acceptability either because of quality inferences or because of the comparison with reference prices that highlight the economic sacrifice. This gives us the model shown in Figure 10.1. Notice that, as price rises, the acceptability of the product is raised by the price–quality relationship but reduced by the comparison against reference prices. Normally we expect the reference price effect to be stronger since otherwise sales would rise with increase in price, which is not usually observed. In a series of experiments, Bornemann and Homburg (2011) showed that when consumers evaluate a product for consumption in the distant future, the price–quality relationship receives more weight, while for near future consumption, price is instead interpreted as a sacrifice. (For example, participants in the experiments had to imagine the launch of an electronic book reader that would be available in the university book store in two days or six months.)

In a variation on the price–quality inference theme, Shiv, Carmon and Ariely (2005) show that consumers who pay a discounted price for an existing energy drink that is thought to enhance mental acuity are, after consumption of the drink, able to solve fewer word-jumble puzzles than consumers who paid the regular price. An additional surprising finding is that the effect, which in the medical world would be called a placebo effect, is apparently unconscious. Plassmann et al. (2008) demonstrate that when we believe that a wine is more expensive, we experience more pleasure while drinking it. They presented

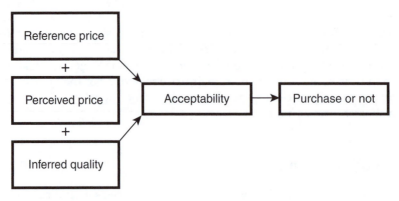

Figure 10.1 Price, acceptability and purchase

the same wines at different prices. A 90-dollar wine was in fact presented twice, once at its real price and once marked at 10 dollars. Similarly a 5-dollar wine was also presented at 45 dollars. Subjects in this study rated the pleasantness of each wine but the researchers also used fMRI scans to measure activity in the part of the brain that is involved in the experience of pleasantness and showed increased activity in that area for higher-priced wines. The fMRI scans indicate that the ratings cannot be dismissed as rationalizations and are the result of genuinely experienced pleasantness.

SECTION 2: ESTIMATING PRICE SENSITIVITY

The sensitivity of sales to changes in prices is usually quantified as price elasticity. Price elasticity is the ratio of sales change to price change, expressed in relative terms. Thus, if sales go up 20 per cent when the price is cut by 10 per cent (a negative change), the price elasticity would be –2. For some products, for instance prescription drugs, price changes produce very little change in demand. Price elasticity is close to zero and demand is called 'inelastic'. Conversely, the price elasticity for any supplier in a commodity market is highly 'elastic' and the absolute value of price elasticity is very high, indicating that sales will drop steeply if price is increased and will increase considerably when price is dropped. It is important to keep in mind that price elasticities are not the same at all price levels. A price elasticity estimation is therefore only valid for the region of prices used for its estimation. Price elasticities can, of course, also change with general economic conditions or changes in specific market factors (for instance, the development of new distribution channels such as the Internet).

In consumer markets three methods are used to estimate price sensitivity. For new products, customer surveys are often used. For new and established products, price experiments can be run. When historical information on the market is available, econometric modelling can be applied. Quantitative research in marketing has made enormous progress over the past 15 years in developing models to evaluate the impact of marketing actions in general and price in particular. In particular, the wide use of checkout scanners and other forms of information technology has permitted detailed recording of transaction data. The result has been an enormous increase in the ability of researchers to evaluate price effects.

Customer Surveys

There are two approaches to surveying consumers to assess their price sensitivity. In the direct-survey approach, consumers receive a product description, or are exposed to the product itself and then have to react to potential prices. This method, developed in the 1960s, is simple to apply and easily understood by respondents (Gabor and Granger, 1961, 1966; Wedel and Leeflang, 1998). There are a number of biases that typically lead consumers to overstate their willingness to pay, but corrections are possible. An important drawback is, however, that price is treated in isolation in these surveys while, in real-life choices, product characteristics have to be weighed against price.

Conjoint analysis (Green and Krieger, 2002) is a widely used customer survey method that presents consumers with simplified product descriptions and asks them for their preference among these products while considering all information conjointly. Price sensitivity and the sensitivity to changes in other attributes are then inferred using estimation methodology. Conjoint analysis is widely applied for new product designs in general, not just for price analysis. Running conjoint surveys by computer and on the Internet has now become standard practice. The method is rarely used in consumer research but has become a standard tool for commercial market researchers and a large number of applications have been published (see reviews in Green, Krieger and Wind, 2001; Wittink, Vriens, and Burhenne, 1994).

Price Experiments

The objective of an experiment is to control factors that influence the outcome of interest (usually sales) but which are not the object of the study. Sales are not only influenced by price changes but also by all the other marketing actions of the firm, those of its competitors and changes in the context. Running a price experiment in one store and comparing sales at the end of the experiment with sales before is therefore rarely conclusive; an observed change in sales can usually be attributed to other factors that have changed.

The art of running a good price experiment is in selecting a good comparison basis, usually called the control group, which cancels out the influence of other factors. Price experiments can be carried out in a simulated shopping environment, but large market research companies, such as Kantar, Nielsen and GfK in Europe, have test cities in different countries in which they run experiments with consumer goods on a regular basis. All the variables of the marketing mix can be controlled during these experiments (for an example see Fader, Hardie and Zeithammer, 2003). Price experiments can also be conducted on the Internet (see Box 10.1).

Ehrenberg and England (1990) investigated price elasticity using a field experimental method. Staff made fortnightly home visits to housewives and offered a limited selection of cereal, confectionery, soup, tea and biscuit brands for sale at prices that were a little below those in local supermarkets. After two visits, the prices of some brands were raised or lowered. The order of price changes was altered for different sub-groups so that any effects based on price sequence could be detected. The authors found that the response to price changes was immediate and was unaffected by the order of earlier changes, i.e. it was zero order. Price increases had slightly less percentage impact on sales than decreases. The mean elasticity obtained by Ehrenberg and England (weighted by brand size) was –2.6.

Box 10.1	Price experiments on the Internet

Technically, the Internet allows price experimenting on a constant basis. In practice, consumer reactions may complicate things (but see Exercise 10.2). In early September 2000, *Computerworld* reported that consumers logging on to Amazon at about the same time could be charged very different prices for the same DVD. For example, at 2.40 pm a search for the *Planet of the Apes* DVD on the Amazon site using a Netscape Web browser turned up a quoted price of $64.99 – 35 per cent off the original price of $99.98 but, several seconds later, a similar search performed with Microsoft Corp.'s Internet Explorer browser resulted in a price of $74.99 for the same product. A company spokesperson acknowledged that Amazon was running price experiments. 'Some customers will pay the same for a certain item as customers paid last week, some will pay more and some will pay less', she said. In a statement several weeks later, Amazon formally denied published rumours that the price differences in the test were based on customer demographic information and said that the price reductions, which were in the 20–40 per cent range, aimed at determining how much sales are affected by lower prices. Amazon also promised that, if they ever were to run such a test again, they would automatically refund customers who purchased at a price higher than the lowest test price for the same item.

Econometric Estimation

Econometric estimation of price elasticities has a long history and research has sought to combine the knowledge accumulated over decades of pricing research. A meta-analysis by Tellis (1988b) brought together 367 elasticities, drawn from 42 prior studies using a variety of estimation methods. Tellis showed that a number of market factors were related to elasticity and that the mean elasticity across all the studies was –1.8.

Bijmolt, van Heerde and Pieters (2005) presented a more recent meta-analysis, and across 1,851 price elasticities drawn from 81 studies, they found a substantially larger average of –2.6. They examined the evolution over time between 1961 and 2004 and found that the (absolute) sales elasticity became larger each year, at a rate of one percentage point per 25 years. They also compared different market and category characteristics and found that price elasticities have greater magnitude in the introduction and growth stages of the product life cycle compared with the maturity and decline stages. Consumers are more price sensitive for durables than for other products. Inflation also increases the magnitude of price elasticity. They found no effects of country, income, data source (firms, retail panels, household panels) and brand ownership (private labels versus manufacturer brands).

SECTION 3: PSYCHOLOGICAL REACTIONS TO PRICES AND PRICE CHANGES

Perceived (Un)fairness of Prices and Price Changes

Consumers can react to prices and price changes by purchasing now – and even stockpiling – if the current price is attractive, or by cancelling or postponing a planned purchase if the current price is unattractive. They may also develop perceptions of fairness or, more commonly, unfairness about the seller. These perceptions can lead to negative attitudes about a company or an entire industry (e.g. 'pharmaceutical prices should be controlled more strongly because of the excess profits of the industry'), boycotts and negative word of mouth.

What is considered as fair or unfair? Fairness is a judgement about the justness, reasonableness or acceptability of an outcome (the price) or the process to reach the outcome (often communicated by the seller as a reason for a change, or inferred by the consumer). It is a judgement that is induced by a comparison to another outcome, such as 'I paid more than another customer did' or 'I paid more than I usually do' (Xia, Monroe and Cox, 2004).

Kahneman, Knetsch and Thaler (1991a, 1991b) identified, in a series of surveys and experiments, the price conditions that consumers consider as fair or unfair. They developed the principle of dual entitlement as an explanation, arguing that fairness perceptions are determined by a belief that firms are entitled to a certain profit and customers are entitled to a certain price. Increasing prices to increase profits when there is heavy demand is considered unfair, but it is fair to protect profit from rising costs. The classic example is that a retailer is entitled to raise the price of snow shovels in reaction to an increased wholesale price, but not in response to extra demand brought about by a snowstorm.

Campbell (1999) expands on the dual entitlement principle and identifies two important factors that affect the perceived fairness of a price change: consumers' inferences about the firm's motive for a price change, and inferred profit, relative to the past. The core idea is that consumers make inferences about a marketer's motive or intention for a particular price increase. This idea is based on evidence from attribution research that people search for causal explanations for negative and unexpected events. When consumers infer that the firm has a negative motive (e.g. exploiting a sudden increase in demand), the increase is considered unfair. When the firm has a good reputation, consumers give it the benefit of the doubt. Even when the scenario suggests a negative motive, if the firm does not appear to make extra profit, consumers infer a more positive motive.

Exercise 10.2   Price discrimination

Yield management is a pricing practice in which prices are adapted over time to optimize profits and capacity usage. It is used in industries where capacity is fixed, such as the hotel and airline business. Marginal revenue at a low price may be worthwhile if the room or seat would otherwise be empty, but not if it forces a reduction of the overall price level. So, while tourists might get a concessionary rate on the weekend, because they book well in advance and have flexible travel times, this should not undermine the full price charged to business travellers. It is now commonly accepted that, on any given flight, passengers pay widely varied prices for their tickets as a result of the use of yield management pricing software.

Pick with a friend a couple of flying destinations that are served by a low-cost carrier (like Ryanair, EasyJet or Virgin Blue). Agree on a departure date and hour and check the prices of your flights a couple of times over the next week. Do prices change? By how much and in which direction? Why do they change? Under what conditions would you find it acceptable if your friend found a lower price than you for a given flight? What if you both logged on at the same time, and got a different price quote?

Bolton, Warlop and Alba (2003) examine, in ten different studies, how information about prices, profits and costs influences consumer perceptions of price fairness. They show that consumers underestimate inflationary trends, even when provided with explicit quantitative information, and therefore overestimate the profits that sellers are drawing from price increases. When comparing the price of the same product in different types of store (such as a department store versus a discount store), they tend to attribute price differences to different profit motives instead of to different cost levels. Some marketing strategies are considered unfair, even when they are not under the store's control. When they are given information about the cost structure of a firm, consumers tend to focus on the cost of goods sold and ignore other cost categories. In conclusion, unfavourable comparisons seem to dominate: consumers apparently have a tendency to believe that the selling price of a good (or service) is substantially higher than its fair price.

Framing of Price and Price Reductions

Sometimes prices can be presented in different ways in order to make them look more attractive, a practice that is referred to as 'framing'. Likewise, temporary price reductions can be presented in different formats, such as 'up to 50% off', '30–50% off' or 'buy two get one free'. Rationally speaking, consumers should be indifferent to different frames that result in the same cost. However, Chapter 8 showed how framing can affect people's judgements. The frequency of use of price framing suggests that it is an effective pricing tool.

To encourage subscriptions, magazines present their per-issue subscription price. Membership fees of clubs can be framed in terms of the amount per day (only $2.50 per day) instead of the actual total amount to pay ($912). Internet-based suppliers may separate packaging and delivery ($4.95) from the cost of the product ($24.95). Charitable donations explain the benefits you can bring to children in poverty 'for less than a dollar per day'. Gourville (1998) posits that consumers evaluate unfamiliar single-alternative transactions by comparing them to known transactions that involve similar expenses. Different frames therefore foster the retrieval of different comparison bases and influence the evaluation of the offer and compliance. The 'pennies-a-day' frame, as Gourville describes it, triggers comparisons to small ongoing expenses like buying a cup of coffee or a train ticket, which makes the transaction more acceptable.

The effect of the face value of foreign currencies can be considered as an extreme example of framing. Consumers confronted with prices in foreign currencies that have an exchange rate that is a multiple of their own currency tend to underspend because the price looks higher. The reverse happens when the exchange rate is a fraction of the consumers' currency (Raghubir and Srivastava, 2002). This effect occurs even though the exchange rate is provided.

The Effect of Price Endings

Prices often fall just below a round number, a practice referred to as odd pricing. A price of, for instance, $10 is converted to $9.99. According to some counts, between 30 and 65 per cent of all prices end in the digit 9 (Schindler and Kirby, 1997; Stiving and Winer, 1997). The clearest demonstration of the effect of 9-endings on sales comes from Anderson and Simester (2003), who varied prices on identical items in different clothing catalogues that were sent to tens of thousands of randomly selected customer samples. In the different experiments demand for the items with 9-ending prices increased by 7 to 35 per cent. The effect was stronger for new items.

There are two dominant explanations of the phenomenon. A first theory posits that consumers ignore the right-most digits or at least do not give them sufficient weight because of left-to-right processing. A price starting with a 2 therefore looks a lot smaller than a price starting with a 3, even if the complete price is 2.99. Thomas and Morwitz (2005) indeed show that the phenomenon only occurs when the leftmost digit drops by a unit (3 to 2.99) and not when it remains unchanged (3.60 to 3.59). According to a second theory, the 9-ending signals a good deal or a promotion. Schindler (2006) analyzed retail price advertisements and found that 99-ending prices are much more often used in advertisements that carry other low-price cues. He hypothesizes that consumers' repeated exposure to this form of advertising leads to an association between 99-ending prices and low prices. Manning and Sprott (2009) compared choice situations between two alternatives with round or 9-ending prices. A round price difference between (a) 2 and 3 dollar can be presented as (b) 2.00 and 2.99, (c) 1.99 and 2.99 and (d) 1.99 and 3.00. The lower-priced option attracted the highest choice share with frame (d), and the lowest share with frame (b). There was no difference between the two other options.

SECTION 4: CONSUMER RESPONSE TO SALES PROMOTIONS

The effectiveness of sales promotion started receiving attention in the 1980s when the use of promotions increased considerably with the arrival of scanner data. Before the introduction of checkout scanning, companies had to rely on store audit data, collected by auditors on a sample of stores, which were released on only a bimonthly basis. These data did not have the detail necessary to see the real effect of promotions that are usually run on a week-to-week basis. When weekly data became available and marketers realized the full size of the boost to sales, they started investing much more in promotions. Promotions usually have a clearly identifiable impact on sales. Graphs of sales over time show a sales spike after a promotion launch, a phenomenon that is much less apparent for advertising (unless, of course, the advertisement communicates a promotion). Despite enthusiasm for promotions, the consulting company Accenture found, in 2001, that 80–90 per cent of trade promotions do not generate a positive return on investment.

In reaction to the increased use of promotions, academics oriented their research attention to the analysis of promotional effectiveness, usually by using sophisticated quantitative modelling. In his 1995 review of the promotion literature, Chandon counted 200 academic studies published over the previous ten years, while for the period between 1965 and 1983 he only found 40.

Promotions can take many forms but promotional campaigns are usually short-lived (see Box 10.2). The distinction has to be made between promotions offered by retailers and manufacturers to consumers, and trade promotions offered by manufacturers to retailers. Examples of trade promotions are co-op advertising funds and display allowances. The retailer may or may not pass on cost savings to the consumer (called the 'pass-through').

Most research focuses on price promotions, feature advertising, display and couponing. In recent years the interest of promotions has been questioned. Advertising agencies tend to dislike them since they may take part of the ad budget, although this attitude has somewhat changed now that many advertising agencies have converted themselves into full-service agencies that handle all forms of communication, including promotions.

Box 10.2	Types of promotion

- **Direct price reduction** – also known as 'discounts' or, in the USA, as 'deals'.
- **Couponing** – refers to the distribution of certificates that can be redeemed for a discount when purchasing.
- **Rebates or cash back** – price refunds that can only be obtained after the purchase by mailing an application, for instance.
- **Display** – refers to in-store display.
- **Feature advertising** – refers to stand-alone circulars, also known as flyers, that consumers receive in their postbox. This is a form of cooperative advertising in which manufacturers pay retailers to feature their products.
- **Games and contests**.
- **Multibuy** – for example, three for the price of two.
- **Extra quantity** – for example, 10 per cent extra length on a chocolate bar.
- **Bonus offers** – buy product X and get product Y free.

Supplying companies also have mixed feelings about promotions because they have to carry the costs of administration, pack changes and the production and inventory costs associated with peaks and dips in demand. On top of this, a successful promotion may bring retaliation from competitors, which damages later profits. In aggregate, the effects of competing sales promotions may cancel out, leaving a cost that has to be added to the price of goods. Maybe all players (except the sales promotion agencies) would be better off if discounting in mature markets was limited (see Exercise 10.3).

Much of our evidence on sales promotions comes from the USA, where marketing practices are rather different from those applying in Europe. In the USA, we find:

- more lines are normally offered on deal
- discounts are usually larger
- promotion periods are usually a week – shorter than in Europe – and they are often driven by short-life coupons. In other countries coupons are less popular.

Exercise 10.3 Coupon war

In autumn 2002, Tesco and Sainsbury became involved in a coupon war in the UK. Sainsbury had issued coupons on its home delivery service, offering, for instance, discounts of £2 for every £20 of shopping. Tesco reacted by announcing that it would itself honour these coupons on its own service. In retaliation, Sainsbury printed thousands of coupons to send to customers in areas where it was not present, hoping that customers would redeem them with Tesco. Its objective was to decrease Tesco's margins. A Tesco spokesperson replied: 'It is usually our job to promote shopping with Tesco, but if our competition want to do that as well, that is fine with us ... The risk is that by encouraging consumers to get discounts with us, it actually makes them more loyal to the Tesco brand.'

Analyze the moves of the two players. Were there alternatives? Under what conditions is there an interest in this type of escalation and for whom? What would you do next if you were Sainsbury?

Sources of Extra Sales

Observing a promotional sales spike or bump does not necessarily mean the promotion was effective. Whether a sales promotion is beneficial, from a managerial perspective, depends on whether the additional sales can be attributed to brand switching (usually good news for the manufacturer, but the retailer's evaluation depends on the relative margins of the competing brands), category expansion effects (even better news, both for manufacturer and retailer) or purchase acceleration and stockpiling (usually mixed news because this can be considered as 'borrowing' sales from the future). Researchers therefore have built sophisticated econometric models to decompose the promotional bump into these three sources of sales.

Initial results were conflicting, with some researchers finding that most promotional sales volume comes from brand switchers (e.g. Gupta, 1988; Totten and Block, 1987) and others observing that category expansion is a more important source of additional sales (e.g. Chintagunta, 1993). One possible explanation of the contrasting findings is product category differences. When comparing category expansion, brand switching and purchase acceleration, Pauwels, Hanssens and Siddarth (2002) found a breakdown of 66/11/23 for a storable product (canned soup) and 58/39/3 for a perishable product (yoghurt). In the most recent analysis to date, van Heerde, Leeflang and Wittink (2004) found that each source contributes to about one-third of the sales bump on average; they used four products, two from an American and two from a Dutch data set.

As already mentioned, stockpiling is considered the least interesting contributor to promotional sales, because it is assumed that consumers would otherwise buy the brand later, at the regular price. However, Ailawadi et al. (2007) demonstrate that stockpiling can also have benefits in two forms – category consumption can increase because consumers have (more of) the product at home, and the extra inventory of the promoted brand may pre-empt the purchase of a competing brand. They observe that the first benefit is the most important and that, together, the two benefits offset the downside of stockpiling.

Price promotions are an important competitive tool for retailers. In a large-scale experiment over 16 weeks in 86 stores across 26 product categories, Hoch, Drèze and Purk (1994) compared an everyday low price (EDLP) strategy (more or less constant low prices) with a Hi-Lo strategy (higher prices but with frequent promotions). For the EDLP condition, they lowered prices by 10 per cent while they increased those for the Hi-Lo condition by 10 per cent. As a result, sales increased by 3 per cent in the EDLP condition while they decreased by 3 per cent in the Hi-Lo condition. There were, however, also large differences in profitability, but now in the opposite direction. EDLP reduced profits by 18 per cent and Hi-Lo increased them by 15 per cent. The authors explain that in general the results depend on how the customer base is divided among price-sensitive store switchers and store-loyal customers. The main interest of the EDLP strategy is that it attracts switchers from other stores. If many consumers are loyal, this will not work well and the profit level will fall because everyone will pay a lower price. In the Hi-Lo strategy, loyal customers purchase their product basket both when the products are on deal and when the price is at the normal level. On average they therefore generate more profit than in the EDLP strategy. Store switchers, on the other hand, will buy more when prices are lower. Overall, the Hi-Lo strategy is therefore a good price discriminator, while the drawback of EDLP is that it offers low prices to everyone, irrespective of price sensitivity.

The Combined Effect of Discount, Display and Ad Features

Research reports by practitioners and consulting agencies claim that the best promotion campaigns are built on synergies between price deals, feature advertising and display. For instance, IRI (1989) have circulated an analysis of these effects based on their 1988 data on sales in 2,400 grocery stores in 66 markets in the USA. The data are normalized on a price

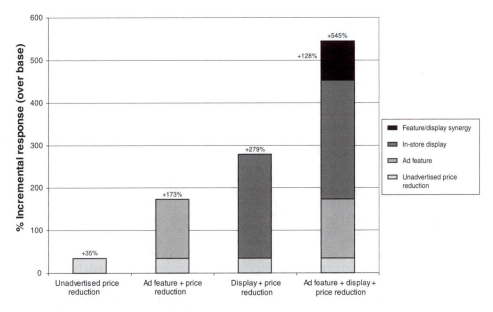

Figure 10.2 The combined effects of discount, display and ad feature

cut of 15 per cent. The main findings are shown in Figure 10.2. The price cut on its own increases sales by 35 per cent (an elasticity of –2.3). When the discount is coupled with an ad feature the effect is 173 per cent, i.e. 138 per cent more than the price cut on its own. When the price cut is paired with an in-store display the sales gain is 279 per cent, 244 per cent more than the sales gain alone. Of particular interest is what happens when price cut, ad feature and display are combined. The sales effects could simply add together, thus:

35% + 138% + 244% = 417%

Figure 10.2 shows instead that there is a gain of 128 per cent above the 417 per cent, which suggests that the three components of promotion act synergistically.

Later academic research, however, reported mixed findings. Gupta (1988) observed negative interactions of display and feature with price cuts, which he attributes to a possible overlap or substitutability among these promotional instruments. Lemon and Nowlis (2002) found, across different brands, a mix of small positive and negative inter-actions of display and price cut and a negative interaction of feature and price cut. In an experimental setting, East, Eftichiadou and Williamson (2003) found no synergistic effect for a double, as opposed to a single, display. Zhang (2006) provided an explanation of these mixed patterns. She observes first that promotion markers can serve as a proxy for a price cut, as shown by Inman, McAlister and Hoyer (1990); a promotion signal is in this case taken as a cue for a price cut that influences choice even in the absence of a real reduction in price. Second, another stream of research has shown that in-store displays and feature ads can influence the formation of consideration sets (e.g. Allenby and Ginter, 1995). Zhang builds a model of brand choice that incorporates both processes: consumers use promotion markers either as price cut proxies, or for consideration set formation, or for both. If display and feature have mainly a price cut proxy effect, then negative interactions are observed in choice models. In contrast, if they help get a product into the consideration set, then they create a positive interaction. Differences across past studies can therefore be explained by the mechanism that dominates the choice process.

Carryover Effects

What happens after the sales promotion has finished? This depends partly on the mix of category expansion, brand switching and purchase acceleration or stockpiling, but also on the extent to which these effects persist after the promotion. Consider the possibilities (which are illustrated in Figure 10.3):

- Some consumers may buy and consume a discounted brand more with no effect on later consumption.
- Some buyers may switch brands or maintain a raised consumption after trying a brand on promotion.
- Some regular consumers may accelerate purchase and stockpile a brand on a deal; as a result they may buy less later. This requires more planning than is usually found among consumers of frequently purchased goods.

The availability of scanner data has made research on the carryover effect more feasible and the *overall* picture shows little carryover effect. The most comprehensive study in this area is by Ehrenberg, Hammond and Goodhardt (1994a) using panel data from Britain, Germany, America and Japan on 25 established grocery products. The researchers identified 175 sales peaks of 25 per cent or more for different brands in these product fields

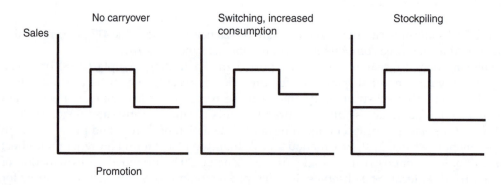

Figure 10.3   Post-promotion sales

and compared sales levels before and after these promotional episodes. The procedure excluded cases where the sales pattern was irregular either before or after the peak.

The overall outcome of this study was a sales increase of 1 per cent which is effectively no effect. A check was made by measuring the repeat buying rates for the 8-week period after the peak; the average was 43 per cent, almost the same as the 44 per cent inferred from NBD theory (see Chapter 4) which showed that buying was stationary in the post-promotion period. Differences between countries were small and there was no evidence that categories showed a consistent movement when data were available on the same category from more than one country.

In sum, these studies show little evidence of carryover effect. A lack of carryover effect is quite difficult to explain. How is it that a spike of extra sales, often several times the normal level, does not disturb the base-level sales? One explanation offered by Ehrenberg et al. is that deals touch only a minority of the brand's customer base; many regular buyers would not see a promotion and their behaviour could not be affected. A second explanation offered by Ehrenberg et al. is that the extra purchasers attracted by the deal were nearly always people who had bought the brand in the past (see Table 10.1); thus a promotion does not introduce *new* buyers to the brand. Those who respond to promotions are past and current buyers who are already familiar with the brand characteristics.

A thoughtful paper by Neslin and Stone (1996) compared seven different explanations for the lack of post-promotion effect. They suggest that many people are insensitive to the stock of purchases already made so that household inventory has little effect on purchase decisions. But the enlarged inventory will eventually slow purchasing and produces a generally lower sales level rather than a post-promotion dip. So, the effect of discount sales is to reduce base-level sales; without promotions the base rate would rise.

Table 10.1   Percentage of those buying on promotion who had bought the brand before (adapted from Ehrenberg, Hammond and Goodhardt, 1994a)

Product	Bought promoted brand in previous:			
	6 months (%)	1 year (%)	2 years (%)	$2\frac{1}{2}$ years (%)
Ground coffee (Germany)	78	83	91	95
Detergent (USA)	76	76	88	93
Yogurt (USA)	71	78	90	91
Ketchup (USA)	52	68	88	91
Detergent (Germany)	61	90	98	na
Soup (USA)	75	90	91	na
Carbonated drinks (Germany)	70	79	90	na
Instant coffee (USA)	70	80	90	na
Crackers (USA)	55	65	78	na
Average	68	79	89	93

Long-Term Effects of Promotions

There has been concern that there may be a long-term negative effect of promotions that is not revealed in the shorter-term studies that test for carryover effect. Broadbent (1989) and Ogilvy (1987) are among those who have suggested that the heavy use of sales promotions will degrade brand equity.

There are four bases for concern about promotional activity. The first comes from reference price research. Promotional prices may become integrated in the reference price and consumers therefore start perceiving the normal, non-promoted price as high (Kalwani and Yim, 1990). A second basis for concern comes from attribution theory, suggesting that consumers make causal attributions of promotional events; they wonder why the brand is promoted. Lichtenstein and Bearden (1989), for instance, concluded that consumers' reactions are more positive when they think that a promotion aims to attract customers, as opposed to when they think the promotion's objective is to get rid of unwanted goods. Third, customers may see the lower price as evidence of poorer quality. Finally, frequent promotions may condition consumers to only buy on deal. Bolton (1989) and Raju (1992), for instance, observed that the sales spikes are smaller when promotions are more frequent.

In a review of research up to 1995 on the possible negative effect of promotions, Blattberg, Briesch and Fox (1995) conclude that, given the mixed evidence, the 'jury is still out'. However, more recent studies, based on time-series analysis, converge on an absence of positive and a possibility of negative long-term effects. Dekimpe, Hanssens and Silva-Risso (1999) find positive effects for only one brand out of 13 in an analysis of four categories. Nijs et al. (2001) examine the possibility of category expansion but find this type of effect in only 36 of 560 product categories. Pauwels, Hanssens and Siddarth (2002) find no permanent effects of promotions for purchase incidence or purchase quantity. In only one of the 29 cases do they find permanent effects on brand choice.

Couponing

Couponing is vastly popular in the USA. For packaged goods a total volume of almost 300 billion coupons were printed in 2005. For groceries specifically, the total face value of coupons issued that year added up to $190 billion, of which $3 billion were effectively redeemed (Hartnett, 2006). Research has mainly focused on whether and, if so, how coupons create incremental sales. Coupons can increase category consumption (Ailawadi and Neslin, 1998), encourage brand switching (Neslin, 1990), trigger trial (Neslin and Clarke, 1987), and also reward brand loyalty. Neslin (2002: 49) reports several studies that show that brand-loyal consumers are more likely than others to redeem coupons.

Coupons can be considered as an instrument for price discrimination. Instead of giving a discount to all buyers, coupons reserve the discount for consumers who make the effort to obtain the saving. Coupons have to be found, stored, organized and redeemed before expiry for the correct product. The 'cost' associated with this effort, including the opportunity cost of time, is higher for some individuals than for others. Narasimhan (1984) develops this argument in more detail and his analyses conclude that users of coupons are more price-sensitive than non-users of coupons.

American consumers are attached to coupons (see Box 10.3). An explanation for consumers' attachment to coupons is that highly coupon-prone consumers are not only drawn to reduced prices but also are seeking psychological benefits. For instance, they get a sense of achievement by purchasing products on deal and view themselves as smart shoppers, an idea Garretson and Burton (2003) confirmed in a store exit survey.

Box 10.3	Life without coupons?

Procter & Gamble launched in January 1996 an 18-month 'no-coupon' test in upstate New York, a region where 90 per cent of shoppers used coupons. Procter & Gamble believed that across-the-board lower prices offered more efficient savings than coupons. In a survey by the trade journal *Supermarket Business*, 80 per cent of manufacturers and 69 per cent of retailers and wholesalers considered that Procter & Gamble was on the right track and some manufacturers followed its lead (Partch, 1996). However, consumers reacted fiercely with public hearings, petition drives and boycotts. Some put up 'Save Our Coupons' signs on their front lawns. A county official claimed that the elimination of coupons by the 'big guys' was intended to hurt the 'average Joe'. The *Wall Street Journal* observed that 'coupons, to many people, are practically an inalienable right' (Narisetti, 1997: 1). Procter & Gamble stopped the test after 14 months.

Heilman, Nakamoto and Rao (2002) examine responses to in-store instant coupons such as electronic shelf coupons and peel-off coupons on product packages. They show that these 'surprise' coupons increase market basket sales for two reasons – unplanned purchases are made as the result of the psychological income effect in reaction to the unexpected financial gain, and the coupons raise the consumers' mood.

In conclusion, coupons – and promotions in general – are not just forms of price reduction. As Chandon, Wansink and Laurent (2000) show, promotions give consumers hedonic benefits (opportunities for value expression, entertainment and exploration) in addition to utilitarian benefits (savings, the possibility to upgrade to higher product quality and improved shopping convenience).

Customized Promotions

To increase the effectiveness of promotions, marketers have recently explored the use of customization, both in online and offline ('bricks-and-mortar') stores. In an offline environment, coupons are usually printed at the checkout register or sent by mail. They can be redeemed on the next purchase trip. In an online setting, the store interface can be customized for each visit and promotions therefore can be offered for the current shopping occasion. Zhang and Wedel (2009) compare the effect of the degree of customization in these two settings, using a model of purchase incidence, product choice and quantity. The depth and frequency of discounts can be customized at a segment level or at the level of the individual customer. The authors also compare two types of promotions: 'loyalty promotions', aimed at customers who bought the now promoted product at the previous purchase occasion, and 'competitive promotions' for customers who bought a different brand previously. The data come from a large supermarket chain that also sells its products through an internet store. After the estimation of the model parameters they determine the profit maximizing promotional strategy in 300 different scenarios. The authors find that loyalty promotions are more profitable in online stores than in offline stores, while the reverse holds for competitive promotions. This result is driven by the fact that customers of online stores are in general more loyal than those of regular stores. Inducing switching is therefore easier in an offline environment. Surprisingly, individual-level customization is only slightly more profitable than segment-based customization or no customization at all. The effects of customization are particularly small for offline stores. The main problem here is the very low redemption rates of targeted coupons. In an online environment, customization has more potential, but only for promotion-sensitive product categories.

Exercise 10.4 Optimal discounts

Plus is a canned soft drink selling at $1 for a four-pack. The margin is 50 cents and the elasticity is –4.

1   Assuming no additional fixed costs or competitor retaliation, would a discount of 12.5 per cent make money?
2   What is the optimal discount? The profit is given by the number sold multiplied by the margin, i.e. profit = $(100 + 4d)(50 - d)$ where d is the discount as a percentage. If you multiply this out, differentiate, equate the differential to zero (the slope is zero at highest point), you can calculate the optimum discount.
3   Is the promotion still profitable if sales over the period of the promotion are 1 million and fixed costs for the promotion are $40,000, ignoring competitor response?
4   If competitor retaliation reduces subsequent profits by $20,000, is the promotion still worthwhile?

Answers:

1   For every 100 sales at normal price there will be $100 + 4 \times 12.5$ sales at the 12.5 per cent discount, i.e. 150 sales, and the profit will be $0.375 \times 150 = \$56.25$ instead of $0.5 \times 100 = \$50$. Therefore the discount is more profitable than the usual price, assuming no other costs.
2   Multiplying out, profit = $5000 + 100d - 4d^2$. Differentiating, slope = $100 - 8d$. Therefore, equating slope to zero, $d = 12.5$ per cent. In words, the optimal discount is 12.5 per cent.
3   On a million sales the profit is $0.375 \times 1,000,000 = \$375,000$ and without the discount the profit on the reduced sales would be $333,333. The profit advantage is $41,667, reduced to $1,667 after taking account of fixed costs.
4   If competitor retaliation costs a further $20,000 the exercise would be loss making.

SUMMARY

Consumers compare observed prices to reference prices in order to determine their interest in buying a particular product at a particular time and place. Reference prices can be externally available or recalled from memory. Price memory is, unfortunately, not reliable for many people. One reason is that prices are not encoded correctly because of their verbal length.

When comparing different products, consumers do not necessarily prefer the product with the lowest price because many associate low price with low quality. In reality, however, price is not a good predictor of quality, but that is not how consumers perceive it.

Market researchers apply different methodologies to assess consumers' price sensitivity. For hypothetical new products they often use conjoint analysis and direct questioning. To examine reactions to large changes in existing prices or to alternative prices for new products, price experiments are used. When historical data are available, econometric estimation of price elasticity is possible.

Consumers react to price changes by adapting their purchase behaviour, but they may also express their agreement or disagreement in ways that affect a company's image and, possibly, its brand equity. There is a clear tendency to interpret price increases as unfair. If companies do not give explanations for price increases that show that increasing profit is not the motive, consumers often infer that profit is the motive. Interestingly, the way a price (or discount) is presented can influence the perception of expensiveness.

Promotions can clearly boost sales temporarily, but long-term positive effects seem to be absent. Even the obvious short-term effects have to be interpreted with caution, because promotions ultimately risk becoming a costly zero-sum game among competitors. Everything depends on the source of the additional sales. If promotions increase switching and bring new customers to the market, they can be profitable. If they just offer the product at a lower price to brand-loyal customers, they may be counter-productive. Customizing promotions could target them more efficiently but recent research indicates that customization is only profitable in certain conditions.

Additional Resources

An excellent overview of pricing research is given in Gijsbrechts (1993). This overview not only shows what the main findings are but also explains how they were obtained. It is not restricted to pricing and also covers some promotion issues. Schindler has published a lot of research on odd pricing and 9-endings. Schindler (2006) is a nice example of how simple observations of the marketplace can be very insightful. This chapter referred several times to meta-analyses. A good recent example of this type of analysis can be found in DelVecchio, Henard and Freling (2006).

11   The Retail Context

LEARNING OBJECTIVES

When you have completed this chapter, you should be able to:

1   Understand the main ideas about gravity models.
2   Discuss the reasons why people use different types of retail store and how they use them at different times.
3   Report on the factors related to loyal, heavy and compulsive shoppers.
4   Discuss the evidence on store atmospheric effects and explain these effects.

OVERVIEW

First, we consider how store location affects shopper choice according to aggregate models. Then, at the individual level, we examine the reasons that individual shoppers give for their choice of supermarket and consider the way in which store use varies over time. We focus on three types of customer: loyal, heavy and compulsive shoppers. We also briefly review loyalty schemes. In conclusion, we assess the ways in which the store environment can influence spending, particularly research on atmospherics, and the impact on shoppers of music, smell, colour and crowding in the store.

SECTION 1: SHOPPER CHOICE

Gravity Models

The number of people who buy from a particular store depends upon nearby population densities, transport access, the store type and the presence of competing retail locations. Gravity models are used to analyze retail data and show how shops, stores, shopping centres and cities draw customers from the surrounding environment.

The early research in this area focused on the attraction exerted on a shopper by two cities at varying distances. Reilly (1929) argued that trade was attracted in direct proportion to the population of each city and inverse proportion to the square of the distance from the city. The similarity with Newton's explanation for the movement of planets under gravity led to theories of this sort being called *gravity models*. Reilly's model implies that there will be a *breaking point* between two cities where customers are equally attracted to each city. The model was tested on 30 pairs of cities and found to be quite accurate. However, it does not allow for the strong appeal of particular stores. However, distance is only an approximate indicator of the travel effort and cost which really control customer demand; Reilly's model is less applicable when good transport facilities make distant locations easily accessible. In addition, neighbourhoods vary in their preferences and spending power so that population size is only a crude indicator of expenditure per head.

As store location models became more sophisticated, Huff (1962, 1981) modelled the pulling power of a retail centre within a city. In this model the attraction of a centre, A_1, is a function of its selling area (S), divided by a power λ (lambda) of the travel time (T):

$$A_1 = S/T^\lambda$$

The probability of a consumer using a shopping area is a function of A_1 divided by the sum of the attractions of all the available shopping centres, i.e.

$$p = A_1/\Sigma(A_1 \ldots A_n)$$

Wee and Pearce (1985) found that Huff's model was well supported and that the exponent, λ, was approximately two, as Reilly hypothesized. Huff's approach includes all the possible shopping centres, although in practice a consumer might rule many of these out. Wee and Pearce modified Huff's model and used only the shopping centres that the shopper considered. With this adjustment, predictions were better but even the improved model gave an R^2 of only 0.25, showing that much of location preference remained unexplained. This is hardly surprising since a gravity model cannot take account of the detail of a particular shopping environment or of the exact way in which information is processed. For example, Foxall and Hackett (1992) found that stores that were located at path junctions were better remembered. One use of gravity models is to calculate the impact on sales in existing stores when a new store is opened in a particular location. Using Wee and Pearce's (1985) approach, it is possible to estimate the loss of trade.

Because shoppers are attracted to retail centres, store growth also happens at these centres. *Central place theory* (Christaller, 1933; Losch, 1939) uses the importance of a centre and the economic distance as basic concepts to explain how centres develop and how retail units tend to cluster together, with each taking advantage of the custom generated by the others. Businesses in the same field can benefit from proximity since together they increase the total custom. We can find examples of this effect in most cities; one example is the concentration of restaurants in particular locations (see Box 11.1).

Box 11.1	Retail clusters

Some quite small locations can become specialists in a particular field. In and around the ancient Shropshire town of Ludlow there are seven restaurants with entries in the *Michelin Guide*. People can take a long weekend in Ludlow and eat excellent cuisine. As a result, Ludlow may draw gourmets from great distances. A similar effect is found in Ireland, at Kinsale, which again is a hub for award-winning restaurants.

Store Preferences

Gravity models and central place theory provide explanations of retail attractiveness at an aggregate level. At an individual level, we can ask about the shoppers' preferences for store types and assemble the reasons given for using stores. We can also investigate when the stores are used, and how frequently. Complete Exercise 11.1 below on your personal use of supermarkets.

Exercise 11.1   Supermarket use

Which supermarket do you use most? What is the reason for this? Do you have a regular day and time of day for doing your shopping? Many people do have regular times – why do you think this is so? Would you say that you were loyal to your main supermarket? What does this mean?

Try to answer these questions now. In the sections below, we provide answers from data gathered over twenty years.

Reasons for Using Supermarkets

In the 1990s, surveys of supermarket use were conducted in the UK at Kingston University in concert with colleagues in the USA and New Zealand. These surveys sought the reasons why respondents used their main supermarket (the one where they spent most). Table 11.1 shows the principal reasons across different years and continents. One message from Table 11.1 is that the reasons for shopping at supermarkets do not vary that much between different advanced economies. The two most important criteria were location and good value; these account for an average of 55 per cent of the main reasons given for patronizing a specific supermarket. There was more interest in good value in the USA and New Zealand, compared with the UK. When the figures are compared for 1992 and 1994, we find that, in the USA, good value dominates in 1992, probably because of a recession at that time. Recession hit the UK rather later and we see an increase in the importance of good value there in 1994. Then, as the economy became more settled from 1994 to 1998, the

Table 11.1   Reasons for patronizing main supermarkets

Reason	1992		1994		1998		Mean (%)
	UK (%)	USA (%)	UK (%)	USA (%)	UK (%)	New Zealand (%)	
Location (easy to get to)	32	25	29	33	31	24	29
Good value/lowest price/sales promos	14	34	24	29	20	35	26
Good quality	15	15	14	11	14	5	12
Wide choice	18	13	13	12	10	7	12
Other (familiarity with store, parking, etc.)	21	13	20	15	25	29	21

Sources: Consumer Research Unit, Kingston University, UK; Debra Perkins, Florida Memorial University, USA; Phil Gendall, Massey University, New Zealand

importance of good value eased slightly. This evidence shows that supermarket choice criteria can change in response to economic conditions; retailers are alert to such changes and adjust their offerings and communications accordingly. Thus, with the onset of the global economic crisis in 2008, there has been an increased emphasis on price. This can be seen in Figure 11.1 in data provided by Nielsen for the UK. Focus is on the main store shopping which is mostly done in supermarkets.

We see that in the severe economic conditions of 2011, getting good value is important for the main shopping trip since 'value for money' together with 'low prices' and 'in-store promotion' account for 82 choices out of 200. Convenient location gets only 27 out of 200 for the main store while range and quality criteria combined get 63 out of 200. We should be wary about direct comparison between Table 11.1 and Figure 11.1 because of the

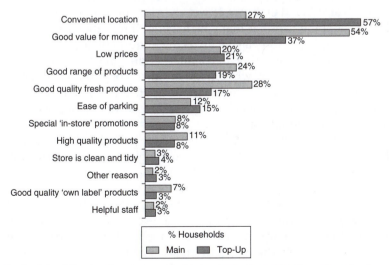

Figure 11.1   Which of the following factors are most important when choosing where to do your shopping? (Check two reasons) (UK data supplied by Nielsen for 2011)

different methods used for gathering data but if we compare top-line findings, it appears that, compared with the 1990s, in 2011 low prices are considerably more important, location less so and quality/range much the same.

In the past location has been the main advantage for convenience stores but, since supermarket groups have invaded the convenience field with their small store formats, the independent convenience stores have little protection from the competition of the big supermarket groups. What then is the future for the small independent grocer? In the UK, the big four, Tesco, Asda, Sainsbury and Morrison accounted for 75 per cent of all grocery sales in 2010, according to the Kantar Worldpanel reported in *The Guardian* (2011). However, there do seem to be some hazards for the big groups. As often happens when firms get larger, there has been a groundswell of resistance to some aspects of modern store management. There has been worry about the power exerted by retailers over suppliers and about their ability to outspend local authorities that oppose new store developments. There have been complaints about the air freighting of vegetables from Africa to Europe because of carbon emissions and demands for more local sourcing. Despite this last criticism, small stores have failed to capitalize on the demand for local sourcing which has been met by farmers' markets in many countries.

Shopping Trip Patterns

The previous section outlined the reasons shoppers give for their choice of store. However, it is important to understand not just why and where people shop but also how often and when. While consumers go shopping for a great variety of goods, researchers have mostly studied grocery shopping (partly because of the wealth of detailed data available from consumer panels). Households tend to have a routine of supermarket shopping that often includes one weekly main trip and one or more top-up trips. In the USA, McKay (1973), Frisbie (1980) and Kahn and Schmittlein (1989) found this pattern. In Britain, Dunn, Reader and Wrigley (1983) also found evidence of weekly trips supplemented by secondary trips.

The timing of shopping trips has many managerial implications, ranging from staffing and stock management to store layout, parking requirements, likely effectiveness of in-store promotions and the best time to conduct product demonstrations. The store may be little used over much of the day while, at other times, congestion and delay may reduce the quality of service delivered. Off-peak periods are useful for staff relaxation, cleaning, restocking, training and maintenance, as Sasser (1976) notes, but smoothing demand remains a desirable managerial objective.

Store use varies over the year; it rises before holiday periods and can be affected by bad weather. The weekend is a holiday too and shopping tends to be heavier on Thursday, Friday and Saturday, as shown in Figure 11.2. East et al. (1994) investigated whether fully employed customers used supermarkets at different times from other shoppers; Figure 11.2 shows the way 1,012 shoppers in 1992 were divided over the week and Figure 11.3 shows the distribution of these shoppers over the day, by employment status. These figures show that those who are employed full-time tend to shop later in the week and later in the day and it is likely that this pattern still persists. We can infer from these two distributions that those shopping late on a Friday or on Saturday are very likely to be employed full-time. This separation of the employment segments could be useful to store

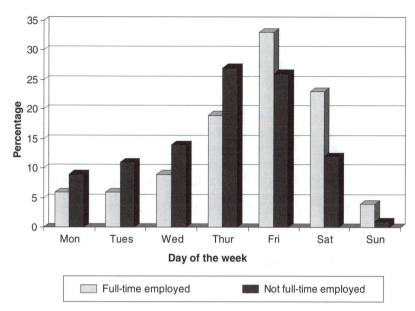

Figure 11.2   Percentage of shoppers on each day by employment status (East et al., 1994)

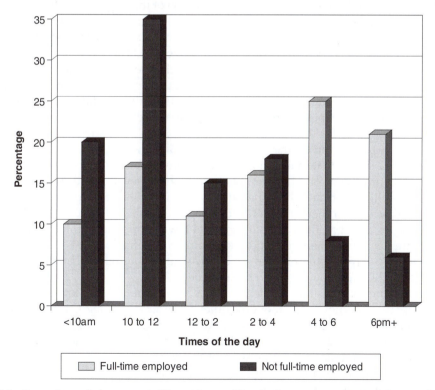

Figure 11.3   Percentage of shoppers at different times of the day by employment status (East et al., 1994)

owners; if these groups prefer different goods, both displays and in-store promotions could be switched to take account of these preferences.

Focusing on those who are not in full-time employment, who make up much of the customer base, Figure 11.3 shows that there are two main periods of high demand over the day. The first is in the morning, peaking at 10–11am, and the second, in the early evening. It is difficult to provide a clear figure showing the combined effect of day and hour preferences but our analysis shows that, as the week progresses, the morning peak is distributed in much the same way each day. The evening peak only occurs Wednesday to Friday. Saturday shopping is concentrated in the morning.

This evidence indicates that it could be profitable to alter prices and promotions over the day. Some supermarket groups use electronic price display, which can be used for time-of-day price changes. However, shoppers may resent short-term price changes, so this strategy would need careful evaluation before being implemented.

The Flexibility of Shopping Times

Store efficiency would be increased if demand was smoother over the day and over the week. East et al. (1994) investigated the flexibility of the times of use of stores and, in particular, whether shoppers deliberately avoided busy times. This was tested in supermarkets in two ways. The first method compared the times of shopping of the 48 per cent who disliked being held up at the checkout with the 52 per cent who minded this less. There was no significant difference in the times when these groups used supermarkets, which suggests that those who disliked delay took no particular action to avoid congestion. The second method compared those who claimed to avoid busy times with the rest of the shoppers. The 'avoiders' used quiet times only slightly more; the researchers judged that, at most, 6 per cent of all shoppers changed times to avoid congestion. This shows little flexibility in shopping times and East et al. (1994), seeking an explanation for this, found that over 60 per cent of consumers had routine days and times for their main grocery shopping, which suggests that habits limit flexibility. The reasons given for these routines are shown in Table 11.2.

This evidence shows that many shopping trips are related to factors over which shoppers have little or no control. They cannot choose when they are paid or when they have to collect their children from school. Because of this, their shopping times are fairly rigid; shoppers *could* shop at other times, and they reported this in the survey, but they have good reasons for their practices and stores would have to offer substantial inducements at off-peak times to change their customers' shopping trip behaviour. It is also clear that the reasons shoppers have for their habits are relatively unchanging so that any inducements that a store might offer would have to be sustained.

East et al. found that customers knew the *days* when demand was low in supermarkets but had more limited knowledge about the quiet times *during the day*. Customers might use off-peak hours somewhat more if these were advertised. Overall, these findings suggested limited scope for redistributing demand in supermarkets. Demand peaks are also a headache for online retailers who may attempt to manage this by manipulating the fee for home-delivery, essentially offering discounts on delivery charges during quiet times and premiums for deliveries at weekends.

Table 11.2   What was your main reason for shopping on …? (East et al., 1994)

On a specific day	%	At a specific time of day	%
Near weekend	28	Fitted in with other shopping	25
Day not working	16	Store less busy	25
Store less busy	13	Left work then	15
Ran out of food, needed item	13	Car/lift/help available	13
Wages/pension day	12	Ran out of food, needed item	6
Car/lift/help available	12	On route to/from work	5
Food fresher/better stocked	5	On route to/from school	4
Open late	2	Easier parking	4
		Happened to pass store	3
		To meet people	1

Exercise 11.2   Analysis of store data

On the website associated with this book (www.sagepub.co.uk/east) you will find UK98, which is the data in SPSS format from a survey conducted in the UK. Findings from this survey were used for this chapter. The questionnaire for the survey is supplied as SU6. Use SPSS to compare stores (question 3) in respect of comparative checkout delay, how much the store is recommended and the relative share of requirements (questions 13, 16 and 21). Use **Compare means**, **means**, to get the means per store.

For all stores, what factors are associated with the rating of the store? To do this, select potential predictors and run an ordinal regression to predict the answers to question 17. Is rating related to recommendation and share of requirement? Use a Spearman correlation to test for this.

How strong are these findings? What alternative explanations are there for the associations you find?

SECTION 2: CUSTOMER TYPOLOGIES

Textbooks sometimes contain classifications of customer types. These may be hypothetical or derived empirically from data. For example, one might hypothesize that shoppers divide into 'prospecting' and 'reluctant' shoppers. The 'prospectors' are generally positive about shopping and see the retail environment as a hunting ground for new ideas, fashions and bargains; these people play a game with retailers in which they feel they have won when they get good value for money. The 'reluctants' have little interest in shopping and see it as a necessary means for achieving other goals. Using this classification, we might be able to predict other behaviour. For example, we might expect more window shopping by prospectors.

Perhaps the most sophisticated classification of shoppers is made by the Dunnhumby agency in their analysis of Tesco's loyalty data. Dunnhumby uses a selection of frequently bought products to classify customers on 30 criteria. For example, a large size of oven-ready chips will indicate positively for budget consciousness and negatively for health consciousness or gourmet propensity. Those who purchase organic produce indicate another type of concern and those who buy Tesco's own label disproportionately may be classified as Tesco loyalists. These behaviour-based classifications are used to ensure that coupons go to those who will appreciate them, and new products are promoted to customers who are likely to buy them.

In this section, we consider three types of store customer: store-loyal, heavy, and those whose shopping behaviour seems out of control – compulsive customers. The first two are important for profit; the last indicates a social problem that may concern us.

Store-Loyal Customers

Like brand loyalty (Chapter 2), store loyalty can be defined in a number of ways. The attitude to, or satisfaction with, the store provides one measure of loyalty. As behaviour, loyalty can be measured by *share-of-category requirement* (SCR), which is the proportion of spending in a specific store or group. Interest tends to focus on the SCR to the primary store, called *first-store loyalty*. Another behavioural measure is *retention* of the store in the shopper's store portfolio; high retention loyalty occurs when customers patronize the store for a long time. Despite the assumption that different loyalty measures have some common basis (discussed in Chapter 2), these measures may show little association. East et al. (2005a) found that the SCR for the primary store and attitude to the store showed only weak correlations of 0.13 and 0.15 in UK and New Zealand studies.

Store loyalty can be investigated using the market regularities described in Chapter 4. We may use models like the Dirichlet to show the relationship at an aggregate level between SCR requirement and factors such as penetration, purchase frequency and market share (Kau and Ehrenberg, 1984; Uncles and Ehrenberg, 1990; Uncles and Hammond, 1995; Wright, Sharp and Sharp, 1998). We may also search for economic, demographic, behavioural or attitudinal factors that predict SCR or retention at an individual level. Such variables include age, the frequency of store use, the accessibility of the store, brand loyalty, shopping on a particular day, the amount spent in the retail category, income, attitude to the store and free time. Retailers will also be interested in whether the customers of different store groups show differences in average loyalty (Box 11.2).

Box 11.2	Average supermarket loyalty

Average levels of loyalty to different stores depend on the retail category, market concentration, average store size and the period of time taken for measurement. For supermarkets in the UK, AGB (1992) reported that over an 8-week period approximately 75 per cent of expenditure took place in the primary supermarket. Also in the UK, Mason (1991) reported that the SCR for the primary store was 72 per cent over one month, 65 per cent over 12 weeks and 60 per cent over 24 weeks. Loyalties to the store group are slightly higher than the loyalty to the individual store. In keeping with the double jeopardy rule (Chapter 4) bigger stores and larger store groups tend to have higher SCRs.

Box 11.3	Purchase and loyalty on the Internet

In Chapter 1, we drew attention to the rapid growth of Internet purchase. In the early days of Internet use, it was argued that this channel was particularly suited to 'bit-based' products such as music, booking travel, share purchase, banking, gambling and pornography. These fields have certainly prospered but the Internet is now frequently used to purchase a range of physical products. Some of these are familiar, such as groceries, books, CDs and clothing, while others benefit from the ability to search the Web for unusual products. For example, if you want to find a specialized product that might not be sold in your neighbourhood such as an orthopaedic back support or home fire-escape ladder these are easily located online and delivered to your door. Thus, some use of the Internet is driven by the convenience of this method of purchase. The ability to deliver relevant information is a powerful incentive in other cases, e.g. for the purchase of stocks and shares, and this could raise loyalty.

From the standpoint of the supplier, the Internet may save costs, particularly for bit-based products that can be distributed 'down the wire'. The customer can also save because price comparison is easy on the Internet. Nielsen (*Online Shopping*, 2011a) found that 30 per cent agreed strongly and 37 per cent slightly that you could save money on groceries by buying on the Internet. However, there are drawbacks and the Nielsen study showed that the inability to select for oneself when buying groceries on the Internet was the most common problem reported about Internet grocery purchase. Internet grocery shopping is well established in the UK and has been growing at 20 per cent a year but still only accounts for five per cent of all grocery shopping and ranks twentieth in everyday usage of the Internet (Nielsen, *Online Shopping*, 2011a).

Grocery buying has been studied to see whether brand loyalty is stronger when purchase is made on the Internet. Degeratu, Rangaswamy and Wu (2001) found that brand names played a stronger role in choice and that fewer brand switches were made in the online environment. But Degeratu et al. studied relatively early adopters of online shopping and also compared those who shopped online with those who shopped offline and any differences may be due to the different abilities and interests of the two groups rather than to the channel used. Arce and Cebollada (2006) improved the analysis by comparing the online and offline grocery purchasing of the same people. They confirmed that there was less brand switching online. One explanation for this is that, on the Web, buyers may work from a list of past purchases and take less advantage of the discount opportunities available. As a result, they stick to the same brands and have high loyalty.

Heavy Shoppers

Some shoppers are obviously more important than others; in particular, heavy buyers and loyal buyers should be a focus of management attention. According to the 'heavy half' principle (Chapter 4), the heaviest 50 per cent of buyers will make about 80 per cent of all purchases. Retailers want to identify these heavy buyers and aim to target promotions to these shoppers in order to recruit and retain them.

It might be thought that those who spend more would use more shops and therefore have lower first-store loyalty but Dunn and Wrigley (1984) and Mason (1991) found that first-store loyalty did not change with increasing total expenditure in supermarkets. Knox and Denison (2000) found a small positive association ($r = 0.24$) between store loyalty and total spending for supermarkets but a negative relationship for other types of retail outlet. If bigger spenders in supermarkets are more loyal, it follows that they are doubly attractive to the retailer who gets their main custom. Not only do they spend more but a larger proportion of this spending goes to their favourite store. Stores with loyalty data may be able to identify heavy buyers directly from their spending and direct promotions to them. (Note that loyalty data only show purchases at the single store chain but spending in other stores may be inferred from the goods bought in the single chain.)

Unpublished data gathered at Kingston University on heavy supermarket shoppers suggests that, more than other segments, heavy shoppers tend to have larger incomes and households, be under age 45, prefer large out-of-town stores, shop later in the day, less often, and have a regular day for shopping.

Compulsive Shoppers

In the USA, 15 million people are estimated to exhibit the deviant pattern of compulsive purchase; they buy clothes, shoes and other goods which they do not need and sometimes never use (Arthur, 1992). Scherhorn, Reisch and Raab (1990) have reported on compulsive shopping in Germany and Elliott (1993, 1994) has researched this phenomenon in the UK. Faber and O'Guinn (1988) saw this type of shopping as part of a wider range of compulsive behaviour, which they describe as: 'A response to an uncontrollable drive or desire to obtain, use, or experience a feeling, substance, or activity that leads an individual to repetitively engage in behaviour that will ultimately cause harm to the individual and/or others.' Compulsive purchase has been reviewed more recently by Black (2007) who reports that nearly six per cent of the US population fit this classification and that this compulsive pattern is associated with other compulsive behaviour.

Compulsive shopping is clearly a serious problem, which often causes financial and psychological distress to the shoppers themselves and to their families. One reason for compulsive shopping could be the more attractive shopping environment of the present day but, to explain why some people suffer from this compulsion more than others, we need to focus on the behaviour and background of the compulsive shopper. D'Astous (1990) argues that this type of behaviour is the extreme end of a continuum and that many people have strong urges to buy that they can barely hold in check.

Compulsive shoppers tend to be owners of credit cards (D'Astous, 1990); 92 per cent are women, and they tend to be younger and to have lower self-esteem (Faber and O'Guinn, 1992). Research in this area is by survey and it is difficult to assign cause and effect; compulsive shoppers may have low self-esteem because of their behaviour but it seems more likely that it is a cause, rather than an effect.

Compulsive shoppers appear to get some emotional release, or temporary 'mood repair', out of the process of buying. Elliott, Eccles and Gournay (1996) interviewed 50 compulsive shoppers and probed their thinking and motivation. The respondents accepted that their behaviour was abnormal and potentially very damaging but they could not easily control it. In this respect it functioned rather like a drug and Elliott et al. emphasize this by describing the behaviour as addictive. Elliott et al. also found that this type of shopping was often related to unsatisfactory relationships with partners. Women whose partners worked excessively, ignored them, or were controlling, were more likely to be compulsive shoppers. In many cases, their behaviour was a form of revenge or was deliberately designed to rile their partner. In other cases, their treatment by their partner may have lowered their self-esteem and made compulsive shopping more likely.

Dittmar, Beattie and Friese (1995) suggested that the way in which products are bought reflects the way in which people see themselves. These researchers suggested that the sexes might differ in this respect. They found that men tend to buy instrumental and lei-sure items impulsively, reflecting their independence and activity, while women tend to buy symbolic and self-expressive goods concerned with appearance and the emotional aspects of self. The researchers suggested that similar patterns might be found in compul-sive shoppers. Dittmar (2005) stresses that materialistic values are one key to compulsive shopping. Those with low self-esteem can only get mood repair from shopping if posses-sions have importance to them (see Figure 11.4).

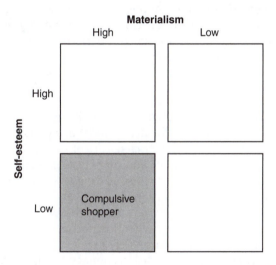

Figure 11.4   Compulsive shopping as a product of high materialism and low self-esteem

Theories of Store Loyalty

There may be no overarching explanations for giving most of one's shopping spend (high SCR) to one store, or for remaining loyal to a specific store for many years (high retention). These effects may be the result of a large number of weak influences that have little in common. However, it is reasonable to look for one or two mobilizing influences that are responsible for much of the effect and here there have been two competing theories about the nature of store loyalty. We report these theories and suggest a third possibility.

Resource Constraint

The first theory of store loyalty was suggested by Charlton (1973), who drew on earlier work by Enis and Paul (1970). In this theory, store loyalty is the outcome of limited resources: those who lack money, time and transport, or whose environment lacks choice (Tate, 1961), are forced to use one store much of the time and are therefore obliged to be loyal. Carman (1970) offered a variation of this model, suggesting that some people had little interest in shopping and therefore did not use the choice that they had. Such people had commitments outside the home, full-time work, little home entertaining and a lack of interest in deals, advertising and shopping. As a result, they were loyal to both brands and stores because they did not seek alternatives. However, East, Harris, Willson and Lomax (1995b) found that shoppers with different loyalty levels gave similar ratings for the pleasantness of supermarket shopping, which does not support Carman's lifestyle theory.

Carman (1970), and Enis and Paul (1970), found that those with low incomes were more loyal, so resource constraint probably did affect loyalty at the time when the research was conducted but it is unlikely that this still applies. Shoppers now have more choice because they have wider access to stores through car ownership or by shopping online, and, specifically, they can buy groceries for longer periods because of almost universal availability of home refrigerators and freezers.

Discretionary Loyalty

Dunn and Wrigley (1984) argued that Charlton's negative concept of store loyalty needed review. They suggested that some store loyalty arose from a pattern of one-stop shopping, often in large supermarkets. We call this *discretionary* store loyalty. Discretionary loyalty could be an adaptation to being time poor and money rich. People can spend less if they use several stores and cherry pick the bargains (leading to low loyalty) but this takes time and effort. Those with less time and more money may choose to buy most of what they need from one outlet because this is easier; as a result, they will show high loyalty. Mason (1991) found that store loyalty was higher when the housewife worked and was under 45 years of age (when family commitments are likely to take a lot of time). Flavián, Martínez and Polo (2001) found general support for discretionary loyalty in Spain. However, East et al. (2000) found that neither free time nor income was significantly related to SCR in a regression analysis covering many factors and this leaves some doubt about the basis of discretionary loyalty.

Loyalty as Habit

An alternative way of thinking about loyalty is that it is a habit. The habit may be set by the conditions under which a person lives; for example, those with routine work patterns are free at specific times and may fit shopping at a particular store into one of these times;

after a while, this arrangement will become routine. Another basis for habit is personal disposition; some people may find routines more attractive than other people. Either way, we would expect to find that those with high store loyalty tend to have other similar habits, such as brand loyalty and a regular day for shopping. Evidence from East et al. (2000) gave support to this explanation.

The Effects of Loyalty Schemes

Loyalty schemes take a variety of forms. All schemes have some form of customer incentive. Many schemes, such as supermarket loyalty programmes, give cash or product incentives. Some schemes raise service levels for a more valuable part of the customer base, for example the provision of executive lounges for frequent air travellers. A loyalty scheme has two potential effects. First, the incentives may raise customer acquisition, share of wallet and retention by directly influencing customers. Second, when data on the purchases of different card holders are collected, the store owner may use those data to target shopper segments more accurately and produce further gains in customer acquisition, spending and retention.

Incentives are very expensive. They take about one per cent of turnover; thus, if the store group makes 5 per cent on turnover, the incentives reduce margin by 20 per cent and sales must be increased to compensate for this. Furthermore, competitors can run loyalty schemes which may cancel out any gains. In an effort to reduce the effect of competitor response, some schemes, such as Air Miles and Fly Buys, only allow one retailer in each sector. If Shell gives Air Miles, BP, Esso and others are excluded. However, competitors can still run alternative schemes.

A loyalty scheme provides a database covering most customers together with information about their purchases. Retailers can use this information to ensure that promotions (often by vouchers) are well targeted. Tesco, with its analysis agency Dunnhumby, is recognized as a world leader in this field. Tesco is interested in the types of purchase made – and not made – by a card holder. If the customer buys no meat, vouchers for meat are never sent, to avoid offending vegetarians, but if the customer does not buy toothpaste at Tesco, vouchers might be used in an effort to switch their purchasing of toiletries to Tesco. A similar inducement might be given to those who appear to buy most of their wine elsewhere; alternatively, the wine buff may be invited to wine tasting events. In other cases, vouchers may be for what the customer already buys, and act as a reward. The database also reveals customers who have switched to competitors (they can differentiate this from going on holiday by the nature of the purchases before the customer leaves). Defecting customers can be sent vouchers in order to recover them. Customer purchase information also helps to sell items that never go through the stores, such as gardening equipment and baby buggies (certain other items purchased, together with a customer's age, can indicate when she may be pregnant). The customer database allows Tesco to launch financial products, such as credit cards and insurance, with less risk than its competitors. The pattern of demand in stores allows the management to tailor the inventories for different stores. Tesco can also sell data to manufacturers because the system shows the relative performance of brands.

This sophisticated operation has helped to expand Tesco's total business and, in the view of the company, it is the information rather than the direct incentive effect that justifies the scheme. However, researchers remain interested in the incentive effect of loyalty cards; this is difficult to measure because other factors may be involved. For example, Tesco took share from Sainsbury when the loyalty scheme was introduced in 1995 but much of this change might have happened in any case because Tesco built more stores, many of which were in Sainsbury territory (East and Hogg, 1997). Although Tesco gained market share, the firm's customers did not show a disproportionate increase in the share-of-category requirement (SCR). This is despite the fact that Tesco was targeting those with intermediate loyalty to the store in an effort to expand their SCR. The data in Table 11.3 from Taylor Nelson Sofres show that in 1996, a year after the introduction of the loyalty scheme, Tesco had a slightly greater market share than Sainsbury in 1994, but the same SCR. Thus, Tesco's loyalty scheme seems to have built the customer base by gaining new customers rather than by getting their existing customers to buy more. This seems to be the normal pattern for share gains that was noted in Chapter 4.

Table 11.3 Market share and share-of-category requirement for five UK store groups, 1994–7

Store group	1994		1996		1997	
	MS	SCR	MS	SCR	MS	SCR
Tesco	18	44	21	46	22	48
Sainsbury	20	46	19	45	20	48
Asda	11	42	12	42	13	44
Safeway	9	34	10	35	10	36
Somerfield	7	31	6	29	5	28

Source: Data from Taylor Nelson Sofres

Meyer-Waarden (2007) has reviewed studies of incentive effect. In general, there is little or no effect of SCR from loyalty schemes; for example, Sharp and Sharp (1997) found that the firms in the Fly Buys scheme in Australia did not show a significant increase in SCR compared with Dirichlet norms. Meyer-Waarden used panel data in his own research and found that customers who were holders of one card showed single-figure percentage increases in lifetime duration (retention) and more share of wallet but customers with several cards did not show these effects.

In these studies, loyalty membership may involve self-selection; if those who join a loyalty scheme are already highly loyal customers, it is difficult to attribute effects to the loyalty scheme. Leenheer et al. (2007) took account of self-selection effects in a study of loyalty schemes in Dutch supermarkets. They found that, if self-selection was ignored, loyalty schemes increased share of wallet by 30 percentage points but, when self-selection effects were taken into account, the increase in share of wallet attributable to loyalty programme membership averaged 4 per cent. The size of the effect varied slightly between schemes and reduced as the customers joined additional loyalty programmes. A four per cent gain in customer loyalty is probably not going to cover the cost of the scheme but it is a mistake to focus only on share of wallet since customer acquisition and retention may also give a return. Another study on the long-term effect of loyalty programmes by Liu (2007) found that these did not affect heavy buyers but low- and moderate-weight buyers increased spending. An influential early paper on loyalty schemes was quite sceptical about their benefits (Uncles, Dowling and Hammond, 2003). This review tends to support this verdict with regard to their incentive effect but it appears that loyalty schemes may be justified when the wider advantages derived from loyalty data are included.

SECTION 3: THE STORE ENVIRONMENT

Store Layout, Location and Space

Actions occur when the environment presents opportunities, stimuli and rewards. The store layout should therefore be designed to increase spending opportunities, present purchase cues and make the store an easy and pleasant place to be. These different considerations do not always coincide; for example, IKEA uses a layout that requires the customer to move through the whole store in order to reach the exit; this may raise spending opportunities but it can be a near-claustrophobic experience for some customers who find it difficult to get out.

In supermarkets, specific locations in the store are associated with different rates of purchase, probably because they provide a more powerful stimulus to shoppers. For example, the end-aisle position induces more purchase and eye-level shelves sell nearly twice as much as the lowest shelf. One of the applications of scanner technology, called direct product profitability (DPP), is to measure the profit from a given stock keeping unit (SKU) in a specific location. This technology identifies 'hot-spots' in the store and SKUs can be moved to optimize profit. However, sales gains for items given more space or better locations are offset by the lower sales of items that lose space or go to a worse location. Drèze, Hoch and Purk (1994) showed a potential profit difference of about 15 per cent when comparing the worst and best configurations of location and space but, in practice, the authors estimated that the feasible changes would produce a much smaller gain.

Early experimental studies on varying shelf space in grocery categories show that a doubling of space leads to sales increases in the region of 20 per cent (Cox, 1970; Curhan, 1972; Kotzan and Evanson, 1969; Krueckeberg, 1969). However, Drèze et al. found that more effect came from location than from the amount of space given to an SKU. The display of goods has been found to be important in supermarkets as a large proportion of grocery purchase decisions are made at the point of purchase (Dagnoli, 1987).

Atmospherics

Store Features

The store environment includes the amount of space employed, and the layout, fittings, colours, aromas, sound and density of customers present. There are some standard display features used by stores that affect the impression given by the store. For example, discount stores sell out of cases to emphasize low prices, shopping centres create central areas with entertaining features, and fashion shops use music that suits the age and taste of their clientele. These features help to define the store offering and to differentiate it from that of other stores (and from the sellers on the Internet). In this sense, store design and the display of goods have parallels with advertising and packaging.

Exercise 11.3   Assessing atmospheric features

Describe a shop which you find attractive *and* stimulating. What is the basis for this? How is space, colour, sound and odour used? Do these environmental features affect your spending in the store?

Kotler (1973) suggested that store features create an *atmosphere*, modifying the buyer's knowledge and mood and thus effect behaviour. Kotler also noted that atmospherics could be used to de-market; for example, State liquor stores in some countries are deliberately off-putting environments. There is no doubt that environmental features can have a strong effect on in-store behaviour. On colour, Bellizzi, Crowley and Hasty (1983) found that people were more aroused by red than blue or green and suggested that red will speed up behaviour and might be appropriate where quicker action is more profitable, e.g. in fast-food restaurants. Babin, Hardesty and Suter (2003) report that blue was associated with greater purchase intention, compared to orange, but this effect was much weaker under subdued lighting. Milliman (1982) found that fast-tempo music speeded up supermarket customers and this reduced their purchasing. When customers moved more slowly with slow-tempo music, they spent 38 per cent more. Areni and Kim (1993) conducted an experiment and showed that, compared with popular music, classical background music in a wine store led to the choice of more expensive wines. North, Hargreaves and McKendrick (1999) followed up Areni and Kim's study by using either French accordion music or German beer cellar music in a supermarket. More French wine was sold when the French music played and more German wine was sold when the German music played and customers were unaware of this influence on their behaviour.

Another study by Yalch and Spangenberg (2000) showed that music could raise sales in a departmental store. The music had to be appropriate for each department; for example, music in departments with younger customers had to be played at high volume. Other work has looked at the way different stimuli work together. For example, Mattila and Wirtz (2001) showed that, when music and scent were similar in terms of arousing properties, they worked together to increase the evaluation of the environment. Similarly, a 'Christmas' scent raised the evaluation of the store environment only when accompanied by Christmas music (Spangenberg, Grohmann and Sprott, 2005). Bosmans (2007) also found that scents that were congruent with the product had a powerful influence on

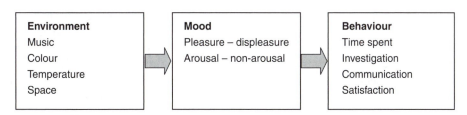

Figure 11.5   The role of moods in mediating atmospheric effects on shopping behaviour

evaluations. Intuitively, it seems reasonable that congruent stimuli will be more effective at raising evaluations.

Another explanation for atmospheric effects is that they affect mood which in turn affect purchasing. Donovan and Rossiter (1982) used a classification of mood states described by Mehrabian and Russell (1974). They found that a store's atmosphere produced mood effects in consumers which could affect the time and money spent in the store. Figure 11.5 shows this stimulus → organism → response (SOR) model with the intervening moods of pleasure and arousal. Donovan and Rossiter expected high arousal to act with pleasure to raise spending/time in store and with displeasure to reduce spending/time in store. The first was supported but there were too few unpleasant environments to test the second effect.

Smith and Sherman (1992) showed that store image was associated with mood, which then predicted the amount of time and money spent in the store. Mehrabian and Russell (1974) suggested that more novel and complex environments would raise interest and Gröppel (1993) observed that supermarkets with high novelty and complexity levels did give more pleasure, that customers spent more time and bought more in such stores. Swinyard (1993) argued that only the more elaborate processing of the highly involved consumer would be affected by mood and that this mood change would affect shopping intentions. This was supported in a scenario-based experiment, i.e. only the highly involved shoppers claimed that they would modify their shopping intentions. Sharma and Stafford (2000) showed that store design affected the persuasiveness of sales personnel, an effect that may be mediated by mood. Eroglu, Machleit and Davis (2003) even found support for mood effects in an online environment.

Donovan et al. (1994) reviewed research in this area. They noted weaknesses in their earlier paper and those of others. In particular, they suggested that it was necessary to distinguish moods induced by the environment from emotions associated with purchase. Donovan et al. conducted a further study which avoided these problems. They found that pleasure did contribute to time in the store and extra spending and that arousal did reduce spending in environments rated as unpleasant, but arousal did not increase spending when the environment was pleasant. The increase in time without increase in spending indicates more window shopping. In some retail sectors, window shoppers are as common as active shoppers (Nielsen, 2005) and we need to know how valuable window shoppers are: do they buy later or encourage others to buy through word of mouth?

While mood may act as an intervening variable to modify levels of spending, there are cases where this explanation is inadequate. In particular, the North et al. (1999) study indicates that behaviour can be modified directly by the French and German music cues (there are no French and German moods). Also, the effect of the tempo of music, observed by Milliman (1982), may be automatic and not mediated by mood. This fits a stimulus–response (SR) model rather than a SOR model. Many stimuli affect behaviour without much awareness; this is part of our low involvement response to the environment which helps us to cope with the wide variety of stimuli that impinge on our senses. By acting in this way, we leave ourselves free to concentrate on other features of the environment. One SR explanation comes from North et al. (2004) who looked at congruent elements in advertising; they suggest that one stimulus will activate or prime related processes so that a response occurs more easily when a second congruent stimulus is encountered. This priming process can be seen as readying an individual for certain types of stimulus but not others so that thought, feeling and action are channelled in particular directions. Such an account would explain the wine store results of Areni and Kim, and North et al., as well as the joint effect of congruent stimuli.

The work on atmospherics indicates powerful effects but limited explanation. Morin, Dubé and Chebat (2007) suggest a dual model whereby stimuli can affect shoppers' perceptions by two paths. Ambient environmental cues, such as smells, operate at an unconscious level – as pre-attentional signals – and induce limited processing, but focal cues with more value may be selected for conscious attention. The authors suggest that some stimuli, such as pleasant music, may influence behaviour through both channels. One route to influence, which involves conscious thought, is social. Some retail interiors may cause so much interest that these places are easily mentioned in conversations and lead more people to visit the store, for example, the vastness of the Mall of America and the aquarium and ski slope in the Dubai Mall. One other explanation for customer response to atmospheric effects comes from attribution theory. In this theory, an individual seeks to interpret and control his environment, and particularly to understand why and how things happen. The theory suggests some biases in reasoning of which the most important is fundamental attribution error. This is the tendency to find reasons for behaviour in the motivational dispositions of people rather than their environment. Attribution effects could guide inferences about the purpose of retail environments, and the behaviour of store staff and customers. Brown and Dant (2009) note a number of accounts of retail behaviour that fit this theory.

Crowding

A common problem in stores, banks, post offices, restaurants and other retail services is the level of congestion or crowding. People have a complex response to crowding and, in different contexts, may find it attractive or aversive. Hui and Bateson (1991) found that an important factor in determining whether crowding was liked or disliked is the control that customers feel that they have in the situation. In Hui and Bateson's study, high densities of people were associated with *increased* control in a bar and *reduced* control in a bank. People go to banks for instrumental reasons and bars for recreation and it seems likely that this different usage is associated with the way crowding affects perceived control since crowding is more likely to obstruct activity in banks than in bars. In shops, therefore, people are likely to dislike densities that impede action, and store designs should aim to reduce such congestion. However, there may be some recreational shoppers with little to buy who enjoy store congestion. It is also likely that people are put off when a store appears empty. Wicker (1984) has suggested that every setting has an optimal number of occupants. For example, some people feel reluctant to go into a near-empty restaurant. Here, people may attribute the emptiness of the restaurant to lack of quality. This may be true but other reasons could apply, for instance that the restaurant gets its custom mainly at a different time of day.

Milgram (1970) saw crowding as stressful, making people quicker, less exploratory and more inclined to omit purchases. The impact of stress is to narrow concentration so that central tasks may be performed better but more complex operations, which require more peripheral perceptions and memories for their completion, may be performed less efficiently. This means that the key functions of shopping may be done more efficiently under crowded conditions but shoppers may forget items that are peripheral to their needs. Anglin, Stuenkel and Lepisto (1994) found that shoppers who scored high on measures of stress engaged in more comparison shopping and were more price-sensitive; these behaviours might be seen as central to shopping. This is another reason why stress-reducing atmospheric factors may raise spending. Michon, Chebat and Turley (2005) found that scents made people more positive about their environment when the shopping density was at a medium level. This may be because scents tend to reduce stress. In psychology, it has been found that there is a preferred level of stimulation: people seek minimum arousal; they are more aroused when there are no stimuli (and they are bored) and also when there are many stimuli (and they cannot process them all). This model is shown in Figure 11.6. This suggests that store interiors, including the effects of crowding, can be too stimulating or not stimulating enough and that the optimum will vary across consumers and types of outlet.

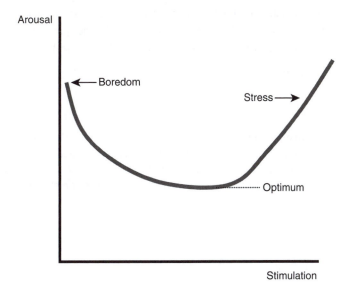

Figure 11.6   There is an optimum level of stimulation

SUMMARY

Retail use is explained at the aggregate level by gravity models and at the individual level by identifying the preferences of customers. Shoppers are mainly affected by convenience, price, range of choice and quality. In times of recession, price assumes more importance. Retail use varies by day, and time of day, and stores are under-used much of the time. Many of the reasons for use of stores at different times relate to the shopper's personal situation and this limits the scope for changing time of use. Fully employed people shop later in the day and later in the week compared with those who are not in full-time employment.

A number of typologies have been suggested for shoppers. One important group for retailers is high spenders. Among grocery shoppers these heavy buyers are found to be wealthier, have larger households and to use a car. A second group is high-loyalty customers. Store loyalty, like brand loyalty, has two basic behavioural forms: share-of-category-requirement loyalty is the proportion of patronage given to a store in the retail category, and retention is the duration of patronage. Early studies suggested that people were more loyal (measured as a proportion) when they lacked the time, money, transport resources or interest to spread their custom. A second theory, called discretionary loyalty, was that certain people, who had resources, used them to concentrate shopping. The latter are time poor and money rich and can afford to save time by spending a little more by shopping at one store. Evidence in the UK fitted a third theory, that store loyalty was a habit that was associated with other habits such as brand loyalty and regularity in time of shopping. Compulsive shoppers buy things that they do not need and may not use. This pattern of behaviour has raised concern because of the financial devastation that uncontrolled spending can produce. These people tend to have low self-esteem, which is temporarily alleviated by shopping.

In all types of store, spending may be affected by *atmospherics*, which is the impact of variations in space use, colour, sound, odour and crowding. Atmospheric changes produce quite strong effects on spending but the explanations for these effects need more development.

Additional Resources

There is a large literature in this area, as well as a major specialist journal, the *Journal of Retailing*. For particular topics, see Donovan et al. (1994) for store atmosphere, Morin, Dubé and Chebat (2007) for the effect of music, Meyer-Waarden (2007) on loyalty programmes, and Arce and Cebollada (2006) for work on online versus offline shopping behaviour.

12   Word-of-Mouth Influence

LEARNING OBJECTIVES

When you have completed this chapter, you should be able to:

1 Discuss the difficulty of conducting research on word of mouth (WOM).
2 Describe how product decisions in different categories are affected by WOM.
3 Report on the relative occurrence and impact of positive and negative WOM in familiar categories.
4 Describe variations in WOM that affect its impact.
5 Report how WOM relates to the current and past usage of brands and to market share.
6 Describe ways in which WOM may build up support for a product in social networks.
7 Suggest how marketers might apply knowledge about WOM.

OVERVIEW

Much of the evidence on WOM is quite recent and this new research focus has probably been stimulated by the growth of the Internet. Comment on the Internet is regarded as a form of WOM, which marketers are keen to use to promote products and predict sales.

In this chapter, we show how consumers use WOM to choose brands in different categories. We describe problems in researching this field and report findings on the relative frequency of positive and negative WOM (PWOM, NWOM) and the circumstances that stimulate people to give WOM. We provide evidence on the relative impact of PWOM and NWOM and we explain how different factors contribute to that impact. We describe how WOM production is related to market share, and review applications of WOM research.

SECTION 1: THE NATURE OF WORD OF MOUTH

In Chapter 5, we described the way in which innovations are adopted by consumers. At the centre of the adoption process is the communication of information. A person who adopts a new idea or product must find out about it, either through mass media (advertising, promotions, editorial content), through personal discovery (e.g. seeing it in a shop) or from other people (salespersons, other consumers). This chapter is concerned with the last way of finding out, through the influence of others. Sometimes, consumers just see what others do and copy them but often they receive advice as word of mouth (WOM). In addition to guiding the adoption of new products, WOM is involved in the switching from one brand to another in established markets. There are some specialized exchanges which differ from normal WOM. Sometimes compliments and complaints to a supplier are treated as WOM but we do not do this and have covered complaints separately in Chapter 9. WOM also sometimes occurs as rumour (see Box 12.1).

Box 12.1 | Rumour

Rumours are unverified topical beliefs that circulate between people. Early thinking about rumour was presented by Knapp (1944) and by Allport and Postman (1947). Rumours may be based on hope, fear or hatred and may involve claims about conspiracies or dangers. The Internet now provides a means for the rapid circulation of rumours and many companies have suffered from this hazard. The financial marketplace is particularly susceptible to rumour (Kimmel, 2004). Rosnow (2001) argues that uncertainty, credibility and personal relevance are the primary drivers of rumours, which will spread faster in contexts of high anxiety (for example when investments are at risk). Kimmel and Audrain-Pontevia (2007) found that roughly three-fifths of rumours were negative, one-fifth positive and one-fifth neutral. They confirmed that uncertainty, credibility and importance of the topic were the key factors in rumour transmission. For a recent review of research on rumours and their influence see Kimmel (2010).

WOM advice now covers direct face-to-face exchanges, telephone, text messages, mail, email, blogs, message boards and social networking websites. Much of this WOM is interactive so that a receiver can follow up and ask a sender further questions. When this applies, the advice can be tailored to and focused on the needs of the receiver, and this adds to its power.

WOM may be positive (PWOM – recommendation, advocacy) or negative (NWOM – advising against). Some exchanges contain both positive and negative comment and some are neutral. When it is about a brand, PWOM usually increases, and NWOM reduces, the receiver's probability of purchasing that brand. Some advice occurs in a commercial context, for example, from sales personnel and on sponsored websites. Commercial advice is different from consumer-to-consumer advice because it is potentially biased. However, Carl (2008) studied the responses of consumers to advice from BzzAgents (people who are given products by BzzAgent and asked to talk about these products to others); he found that three-quarters of respondents trusted the BzzAgent to give them good advice when they knew that he/she was a BzzAgent. In fact, the effect of the BzzAgent's advice was often greater when their affiliation was known. If such trust extends generally to sales personnel, their advice may be quite influential despite the potential for bias.

Many of the classic studies on WOM were concerned with innovations and new categories rather than established brands; for example, Whyte (1954) on air conditioners, Coleman, Katz and Menzel (1957) on the prescribing of new drugs by physicians, and Katz's (1961) work on new farming practices. These really new products may produce exceptional comment when compared with well-established products but there is clearly a gradation from the very novel to the familiar. Sometimes brands will have new features not offered by others and here, choice may be more like the adoption of a new product. For example, the widespread acceptance of smart phones was clearly driven by the new features that they offered. But, as the category matures and brands become more familiar, the reason for choice may not be an innovation but some simple advantage that can be drawn to a consumer's attention. For example, one person might advise another about the relative cost of mobile phone brands, or their performance in weak-signal areas. This is useful information to a prospective buyer but it is not an innovative feature of the product.

In this chapter, we focus less on the adoption of new categories and more on brands in mature categories. Research on WOM is limited because it is difficult to measure. Ideally, we would observe WOM as it occurs and then monitor its consequences. In practice, WOM occurs too rarely for it to be observed systematically, and usually any effect is delayed, so that direct observation of the outcomes of WOM may be impossible. As a result, other methods have to be used, which are reviewed below.

Text Mining on the Internet

Although we cannot observe WOM as it happens, we may be able to measure it as comments posted on the Internet. WOM is not hard to find in consumer-generated media, but there are two challenges. First, those who set up websites may encourage more PWOM or NWOM than is typical in everyday life and, second, those who post comments on the Internet, and those who read these comments, may be different from those who give and receive offline advice. Godes and Mayzlin (2004b) did not find that the volume of online comment about TV programmes was predictive of viewing but Liu (2006) was successful in predicting box office returns from the volume of online comment about movies, and Qin (2012) also found that the volume of the WOM predicted movie sales. Interestingly, Liu did not find that the valence of the WOM (i.e. whether it was positive or negative) was predictive of sales. However, a later paper by Liu (2012) on Twitter comments suggests that the valence is more predictive than the volume of comments. More work is required here.

Internet research usually deals with aggregate effects. We can count the posts and obtain data on box office receipts. We may be able to predict returns from such data but we do not know quite how individuals have used the online information. We want to understand as well as predict and, for this, we need individual-level data so that we can connect individual responses to individual experience. Individual-level data are obtained in experiments and surveys.

Box 12.2	Online advice

The predictive value of online comment depends, in part, on how much this medium is used, compared to other media. If it is only a small part of total advice on brands, it may not be a reliable guide to sales. Surveys show that online comment remains a modest part of the total. In 2006, Keller and Fay found that WOM was:

Face-to-face	70%
Phone	19%
Email	4%
Text message	3%
Online chat or blog	1%
Other	3%

Subsequently, the share of online WOM (eWOM) has not changed much. In 2010, the Keller Fay Group reported that 7 per cent of WOM was offline in the US, UK and Australia, though this rose to 15 per cent for the teen group in US measurements. In 2011, Keller Fay reported that, in the UK, 81 per cent of WOM was face-to-face, 10 per cent via phone and 9 per cent online

(including email, texting and social networking sites). Thus, the Internet is not the dominant channel for advice by any means. Even so, some categories like restaurants, holidays and hotels attract much more online comment and it is likely that, in these fields, the Internet is a more reliable guide to demand.

There are, however, some differences between Web and face-to-face advice. First, some online advice is one-way and not inter-active. Second, in many contexts, such as online reviews or on Twitter, online advice from one source may be received by many others, which is uncommon for offline advice. Third, the Web may allow a degree of deception – those reviews on Amazon may include some that are 'arranged'; because of this, people may be more suspicious of positive comment on the Web than they are when it occurs face-to-face. Fourth, offline WOM is more often between close ties but, on the Web, a larger amount of weak-tie contact is likely to occur (e.g. in discussion groups or anonymous product reviews).

Experiments

A number of experiments have examined the impact of positive and negative information (e.g. Ahluwalia, 2002; Herr, Kardes and Kim, 1991). The main problem here is that the artificiality of the laboratory situation restricts generalization to naturally occurring WOM. This artificiality has several aspects:

1 The stimulus is not like real WOM. In experiments, the 'WOM' is often prepared written information rather than spontaneous exchanges between people (e.g. Herr, Kardes and Kim, 1991). Such prepared advice cannot be asked for, which is often a feature of real WOM, and the advice is unlikely to be well tailored to the needs of the receiver.

2 The response measures may be inappropriate. Experimental studies of WOM have used attitude towards a product or brand and belief items to measure impact (e.g. Ahluwalia, 2002); marketers are generally more interested in the impact on purchase or purchase probability.

3 In experiments, each participant makes an equal contribution to the outcome; in everyday life, some people say nothing while others give a lot of WOM.

4 Experiments usually rush the process by taking measures of effect shortly after exposure to the stimulus. In natural settings, people who receive WOM may not act on it for months, as discussed by Christiansen and Tax (2000).

Some of these problems are evaded by the use of role-play experiments. In a role-play experiment, the subject may be asked what he or she would do in a specified situation, for example: 'If someone asked you about mobile phones, would you recommend/advise against …?' There is no guarantee that participants in such role plays would do as they claim; however, Christiansen and Tax succeeded in devising quite realistic WOM experiments, using pairs of participants, with one being required to give advice to the other about a real product. Another possibility is to use field experiments. In an early study, Arndt (1967) introduced a new brand into a community and measured sales and the reported PWOM and NWOM. More recently, Godes and Mayzlin (2004a) used a field experiment to compare the extra effect on sales of WOM from loyal and non-loyal customers. Unfortunately, field experiments are very resource-intensive and, to measure WOM, the experimenter may still have to ask participants to recall what advice they have given and/or received.

Retrospective Surveys

In retrospective surveys, respondents have to report on their experience and these reports may be systematically distorted by recall error. If NWOM is more easily recalled than PWOM, a measure of relative frequency will be biased in favour of NWOM. There may also be expectation effects; if NWOM is believed to generally have more impact than PWOM, this could affect the respondents' reports of impact.

Exercise 12.1 Questionnaire on word of mouth

Fill out this questionnaire:

1 Do you own a mobile phone?

No	[1]
Yes	[2]

2 Which make of mobile phone do you have?

Please write in (Nokia, iPhone, etc.) ……………

3 In the last six months, how many times have you *received positive* advice about any mobile phone handset?
Write in number (0, 1, 2, etc. ......)
If you answered 0, then please go to Q.9

4 The last time you received positive advice, did you ask for advice or was it just given?

Just given	[1]
Asked for it	[2]

5 What was your relationship to the person who last gave you positive advice?

Casual acquaintance	[1]
More distant family, friend or colleague	[2]
Close family, close friend or colleague	[3]

6 About which brand was the last positive advice received?

Please write in (Nokia, iPhone, etc.) ....

7 Did the last positive advice that you received affect your handset choice or intended handset choice?

No	[1]
Yes	[2]

8 How strongly expressed was the last negative advice?

Hardly at all strongly	[1]
Moderately strongly	[2]
Fairly strongly	[3]
Very strongly	[4]

9 In the last six months, how many times have you *received negative* advice about any mobile phone handset?
Write in number (0, 1, 2, etc. ....)
If you answered 0, then please go to Q.15

10 The last time you received negative advice, did you ask for advice or was it just given?

Just given	[1]
Asked for it	[2]

11 What was your relationship to the person who last gave you negative advice?

Casual acquaintance	[1]
More distant family, friend or colleague	[2]
Close family, close friend or colleague	[3]

12 About which brand was the last negative advice received?

Please write in (Nokia, iPhone, etc.) ....

13 Did the last negative advice received affect your handset choice or intended handset choice?

No	[1]
Yes	[2]

14 How strongly expressed was the last negative advice?

Hardly at all strongly	[1]
Moderately strongly	[2]
Fairly strongly	[3]
Very strongly	[4]

15 In the last six months, how many times have you *given negative* advice about any mobile phone handset?
Write in number (0, 1, 2, etc. ......)
If you answered 0, then please go to Q.17

16 About which brand did you last *give positive* advice?

Please write in (Nokia, iPhone, etc.) ....

17 In the last six months, how many times have you *given positive* advice about any mobile phone handset?
Write in number (0, 1, 2, etc. ......)

18 About which brand did you last *give negative* advice?

Please write in (Nokia, iPhone, etc.) ....

The purpose of this exercise is to show you how aspects of WOM may be measured in a retrospective survey. From the responses of a group of people it is possible to find out:

- How much PWOM is received compared with NWOM.
- How much PWOM is given compared with NWOM.
- Whether those who give more PWOM also give more NWOM.
- Whether people mostly give PWOM about their current brand.
- How much WOM comes from close ties.
- Whether most WOM is requested or not.
- What proportions of the sample claim to have had their choice affected by the PWOM and NWOM received.
- How different factors relate to impact; for example, are people more influenced by WOM when they have requested it and does WOM have more impact when it is about the currently owned brand?

A second concern about surveys relates to the recruitment of the sample, which is often based on convenience. However, problems about convenience sampling recede as more data are gathered. If we have 20 studies using diverse population samples and different categories, and these all show the same pattern, we can be more confident about the findings.

When no method is satisfactory, researchers may give up and investigate something else. This has probably led to a lack of research on WOM in the past. But this is something that we can ill afford. In many categories, WOM appears to be the most powerful influence on consumption and, outside the commercial arena, WOM assists in many social changes. In these circumstances, even weak findings should be put into the public domain.

To some extent, the problems that affect measurement in this area may be offset by using multiple methods and measures and a wide range of categories. A second strategy is to estimate measurement distortions so that errors can be corrected (Box 12.3).

Box 12.3	Measuring recall bias

East et al. (forthcoming) have tried to measure how the volume of WOM recalled is related to the time lapsed since the WOM was given. Respondents were asked about the volume of PWOM and NWOM that they gave in the week after using a service such as a hotel. Respondents were also asked how long ago the hotel was used. Data on six categories were collected. It was anticipated that people would forget more instances of WOM when the time lapse was longer. However, at an aggregate level, instead of the recalled volume declining with the time lapse since use, there was a tendency for it to increase for both PWOM and NWOM. When the ratio of PWOM to NWOM was measured in relation to time lapse, there was no significant trend.

This finding lacks explanation but suggests that ratios gathered over different periods may be comparable.

SECTION 2: THE OCCURRENCE OF WORD OF MOUTH

How Does Word of Mouth Affect Brand Choice in Different Categories?

When people lack experience, WOM from others provides helpful information and this is particularly true in the case of services that cannot be tested before a choice is made. For example, a person who has to find a new dentist has few sources of relevant information on a dentist's competence. Because of this, advice from other people is probably the best way of finding a good dentist. WOM will be less important in the case of goods that can be inspected and tested and when information can be gathered from advertising or online search before buying. This means that the need for WOM will vary between categories. It is often said that WOM reduces risk – and this is true – but risk is highest when there is a lack of information on a product and little opportunity to find out about it through direct experience.

In early work, WOM was credited with very large effects. Dichter (1966) claimed that advice figured in as many as 80 per cent of brand decisions. Katz and Lazarsfeld (1955) claimed to show that WOM was seven times as effective as newspapers and magazines, four times as effective as personal selling and twice as effective as radio advertising in influencing consumers to buy products. These early studies applied more to the adoption of new categories than to brand switching, so these claims may not tell us much about brand choice in familiar categories. However, WOM clearly has impact on brand choice; Keaveney (1995) found that about 50 per cent of service provider replacements occurred primarily through WOM.

East et al. (2005b) asked people about the *main* source of information influencing their choice when they changed brand or started using a service for the first time. Table 12.1 shows the results. The main source of information was divided into recommendation, personal search, advertising and 'other'. The 'other' category included non-commercial editorial advice in the mass media and situations where people had no choice because of contracts, gifts or other circumstances that were compelling. At the base of the table, we see that recommendation was the main influence in about one-third of the brand choices.

Two out of three customers come to us by word of mouth

In this research, each study involved asking respondents about two or three categories, and the data are grouped accordingly in Table 12.1. Within each survey grouping, you can see that categories differ in the way they get their customers. In the first grouping, coffee shops and mobile airtime providers are more often chosen on recommendation than credit cards. The evidence from Table 12.1 shows that WOM is less often a source of information for cars (13 per cent) and for retail services such as supermarkets (10 per cent and 9 per cent). This is not surprising since durables and supermarkets can be tried out and are the objects of substantial advertising.

By contrast, we might expect social networking sites to recruit largely via WOM and here Trusov, Bucklin and Pauwels (2009) showed a very substantial effect from referrals compared

Table 12.1 Choice of brand provider when switching buying a category for the first time (East et al., 2005b)

Category (country)	Main source when choosing new brand/provider (%)			
	Recommendation	Personal search	Advertising/ Promotion	Other
Coffee shop (UK)	65	20	1	14
Mobile phone airtime provider (UK)	50	24	6	20
Credit card (UK)	20	16	20	44
Car insurance (Mauritius)	60	16	6	18
Car servicing (Mauritius)	56	17	3	14
Dentist (UK)	59	3	9	30
Current car (UK)	13	42	13	33
Education institution (UK)	48	19	2	31
Mobile phone airtime provider (UK)	25	22	9	44
Optician (UK)	21	16	8	56
Bank (UK)	43	20	13	24
Mobile phone brand (UK)	21	26	16	37
House contents insurance (UK)	33	12	34	21
Car insurance (UK)	27	19	34	20
Car servicing (UK)	32	9	1	58
Dry cleaning (UK)	14	26	4	56
Hairdresser (Mexico)	32	29	5	34
Fashion store (Mexico)	13	27	43	17
Supermarket (Mexico)	10	36	33	21
Mobile phone airtime provider (UK)	29	13	21	37
Internet service provider (UK)	24	26	26	24
Fashion store (France)	15	47	9	29
Supermarket (France)	9	29	8	54
Means	31	22	14	32

with traditional marketing activity. Furthermore, both Trusov et al. and Villanueva, Yoo and Hanssens (2008) found that the customers derived from WOM were more valuable than those found by conventional marketing activity. Customers may be more valuable because they show greater retention and because they recommend the brand more to others.

How Does WOM Occur?

There is a widespread belief in marketing that PWOM comes from satisfied and NWOM from dissatisfied customers (see Box 12.4). But think back to the last advice that you gave. Was it driven by satisfaction or dissatisfaction, or were you trying to provide information that would help someone else with their decision? Our satisfaction or dissatisfaction with a product may be the main basis for giving advice but, often, we are influenced by other factors, such as the need for advice of the receiver.

Box 12.4	Comparing satisfied and dissatisfied consumers

Marketing textbooks such as Heskett, Sasser and Schlesinger (1997) and Hanna and Wosniak (2001) report NWOM to PWOM ratios of two or three to one *when comparing satisfied and dissatisfied customers*. The origin of these reports is work by a US agency, the Technical Assistance Research Program (TARP), which finds that NWOM from dissatisfied customers occurs about twice as frequently as PWOM from satisfied customers, though the ratio varies with the category (Goodman and Newman, 2003). Anderson's (1998) comprehensive study also showed greater WOM among those who were very dissatisfied compared with those who were very satisfied, but he commented: 'The widespread belief in a high degree of word of mouth by dissatisfied customers may be unwarranted. In fact, in a sizable proportion of cases, the difference between the two is probably not significant' (Anderson, 1998: 15).

People may confuse the WOM from dis/satisfied customers with WOM in general. This may be why Silverman (2001: 134) claims that studies have shown that most WOM is negative. In Figure 12.1, we see from Anderson (1998) that WOM is also produced by those who are neither satisfied nor dissatisfied and Mangold, Miller and Brockway (1999) found that only a small part of WOM is driven primarily by satisfaction and dissatisfaction (Table 12.2). To establish the ratio of all PWOM to NWOM, we need studies on the general occurrence of PWOM and NWOM, not just studies where the WOM is based on dis/satisfaction.

The fact that advice may be unrelated to satisfaction is indicated by a study conducted by Anderson (1998), who used the Swedish Customer Satisfaction Barometer and the American Customer Satisfaction Index, which cover many industries in each country. The results were very similar for the two countries and Figure 12.1 illustrates the data for Sweden. We see that there is a little more WOM when people are very satisfied or very dissatisfied, but that, when

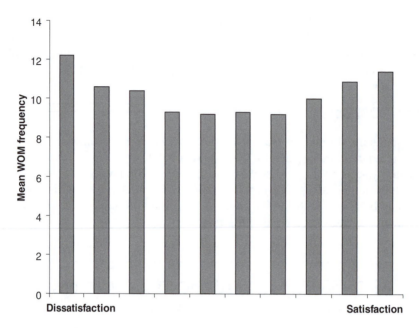

Figure 12.1 Frequency of word of mouth in relation to satisfaction and dissatisfaction in Sweden (adapted from Anderson, 1998)

they are neutral about an issue, WOM is still produced at about 80 per cent of the maximum level. This indicates that satisfaction and dissatisfaction need not be involved in the production of WOM and implies that other circumstances are relevant.

These other circumstances are illustrated by Mangold, Miller and Brockway (1999), who asked respondents to describe the last time they received positive or negative advice about a service. Mangold et al. identified ten catalysts that set off WOM, which are shown in Table 12.2. The most common catalyst was the receiver's felt need, which was either implicit in the situation or made explicit by a request for advice. Coincidental conversation occurred when a conversation led to advice, for example, when a discussion of weekend plans led to a destination recommendation. The communicator's dis/satisfaction with the service (as judged by the receiver) was the third catalyst and this made up 12 per cent of the total. The fourth catalyst occurred when the recipient made a comment that related to the service, for example, about the communicator's hair, which led the communicator to recommend her hairdresser. The fifth catalyst was the effort to make a joint decision, such as which restaurant to go to together. This work does *not* show that consumer satisfaction and dissatisfaction have little to do with WOM. What Mangold et al. found is that it is unusual to find that satisfaction and dissatisfaction are the main factors that cause WOM.

Mangold et al. only considered the catalysts from the standpoint of the receiver but Mazzarol, Sweeney and Soutar (2007) gathered data on both the giver and receiver of WOM, using focus groups, and found that 'felt need' was again the trigger for much of the WOM. This evidence means that researchers who have gathered evidence on WOM in

Table 12.2 Catalysts that stimulate word of mouth (adapted from Mangold, Miller and Brockway, 1999)

Stimulus	Positive communication (%)	Negative communication (%)	Total (%)
Receiver's felt need	54	47	50
Coincidental communication	16	21	18
Communicator's dis/satisfaction	5	13	9
Receiver's comment about effect of service	9	4	7
Joint decision on service	6	6	6
Marketing organization's promotion	2	5	3
Receiver's dis/satisfaction	3	3	3
Another's comment about the effect of service	4	1	2
Media exposure (not marketing organization)	1	1	1
Unsolicited comment	1	0	1

relation to dis/satisfaction have focused on only a part of the WOM that is produced. Richins (1983) treated NWOM in this way when she described NWOM as communication that *denigrated* the product. Halstead (2002) saw both NWOM and complaints as products of dissatisfaction. Similarly, Wetzer, Zeelenberg and Pieters (2007) concentrate on NWOM that arises from dissatisfaction and Goldenberg et al. (2007) also define NWOM in this way. In contrast to this, Asugman (1998) observed that NWOM was an everyday occurrence and need not be associated with dissatisfaction. It seems likely that dis/satisfaction is a condition for much WOM but the evidence from Mangold et al. suggests that it is not normally the main cause of it. However, there is a need for more research here; Mangold et al. used a method called critical incident technique and Mazzarol et al. used focus groups, but neither method is well designed for gathering frequencies.[1]

A feature of Mangold et al.'s study is the similarity of the catalyst frequencies for PWOM and NWOM; these have a correlation of 0.96. This shows that there is not much difference in the circumstances governing positive and negative advice. Clearly, PWOM makes the choice of a brand more likely and NWOM makes it less likely, but often they are both helpful advice.

Some products generate more WOM than others. Berger and Schwartz (2011) point out that some categories are more interesting than others – one would expect iPhones to get more comment than soap. However, they also observed that some products are more accessible than others; these may be cued by usage or be visible because they are frequently present in the environment. Such products (e.g. mobile phones) may stimulate more WOM than those that drop from sight after use, such as films. Berger and Schwartz found that the cued and visible products received more WOM than the interesting but short-term products. The latter were talked about a lot immediately after consumption but WOM then fell away. In a field experiment, they found that WOM could be increased by linking a product to a recurrent feature of the environment. The authors also suggest that advertising could be more effective when this sort of linkage is made.

Motives for Giving WOM

Mangold et al. researched catalysts to WOM; these relate to the situational circumstances as well as motives. Others have looked more narrowly at the motivation for WOM. There are circumstances in which people deliberately go out of their way to give advice, most notably when they write product assessments and give advice online, and it is worth understanding why they choose to do this. In an early study before online advice existed, Dichter (1966) reported on the motivation to talk about products. He analyzed interviews and found that people gave advice because this gave them standing with the receiver. The recommendations which people gave were based on experience with the product, involvement with the product, the needs of the receiver and public information (such as ads) on the product. Also using interviews, Sundaram, Mitra and Webster (1998) found that PWOM was motivated by altruism, product involvement, self-enhancement and assisting the company producing the product. The motives for giving NWOM were altruism, anxiety reduction, vengeance and as a response to others seeking advice. Hennig-Thurau et al. (2004) turned attention to online advice. Using an online questionnaire, they found that advice was motivated, as in offline, by wanting to vent negative feelings, concern for other consumers, social benefits, economic incentives, helping the company and advice seeking but there were two other factors related to the online environment; one was a form of self-enhancement coming from expressing positive feelings and a second was the assistance provided by the platform to express advice. Related to the second point, Berger and Iyengar (2012) found that more interesting topics are covered online because the medium gives more time to consider topics and to write reviews. One problem with online studies is that the research method may evoke particular forms of PWOM and NWOM that are atypical; a second problem is that the motives are likely to vary with the product category so that aggregate findings are of limited value; and a third problem is that, by asking about motives, researchers may miss important situational determinants of WOM such as the need of the receiver, revealed by Mangold et al.

Is there More PWOM than NWOM?

Naylor and Kleiser (2000) studied users of a health and fitness resort and found more positive comment than negative. Chevalier and Mayzlin (2003) found that the majority of book reviews on two websites were positive. Godes and Mayzlin (2004b) studied TV comment on websites and found that positive appraisals occurred nearly twice as often as negative appraisals. Romaniuk (2007) found four times as much PWOM as NWOM when assessing advice about television programmes. The Keller Fay Group conducts surveys of 'branded' conversations that have taken place over the last 24 hours in the USA and the Group has provided us with data for 2009. Sixty-five per cent of these conversations were mainly positive, 8 per cent mainly negative, 15 per cent mixed and 12 per cent neutral. If we assume that people hearing mixed comment on a brand state that they have received both PWOM and NWOM, these data indicate a ratio of 3.5 to 1. East, Hammond and Wright (2007b) examined the ratio of PWOM to NWOM in 15 different studies, covering all the brands in a range of widely used categories (mostly services). In every case, the PWOM incidence exceeded the NWOM incidence and the average ratio was 3.1 to 1. This work was conducted by asking respondents about the PWOM and NWOM that they had *given* in the last six months. In follow-up studies, respondents were asked about the WOM they had *received* in the last six months and the WOM they *would give, if asked*. These latter follow-up studies gave PWOM:NWOM ratios of of 2.4 to 1 and 3.4 to 1 respectively. From this evidence, it is clear that there is more PWOM than NWOM, though the ratio varies by category.

Why is there more PWOM? One explanation may be that there are not many negative things to say about goods and services. Mostly, people are satisfied with what they get according to Peterson and Wilson (1992), whose work suggested an average 10:1 ratio of satisfied to dissatisfied (Chapter 9). A second possibility is that PWOM is seen as more useful. Most consumer choices are about selecting one from many brands. NWOM may eliminate an option but this does not settle the choice if more than one option remains. By contrast, PWOM may be used by a receiver to make a final decision. Thus, if people are trying to help others with their advice, saying what is good may be more constructive than saying what is bad.

How much Do People Talk about Their Current Brand?

East, Romaniuk and Lomax (2011) investigated whether the brand that was referred to in PWOM and NWOM was currently used, previously used or never used (Table 12.3). Across 15 studies, they found that, on average, 71 per cent of PWOM was about the currently used brand, 22 per cent about a previously used brand and only 7 per cent about a never-used brand. For NWOM, 22 per cent was about the currently used brand, 55 per cent about a previously used brand and 22 per cent about a never-used brand. Wangenheim (2005) also found that NWOM was often about previously owned brands and Winchester and Romaniuk (2008) found that, when people expressed negative beliefs about brands, these were often about previously owned brands. Table 12.3 also shows that people are more willing to give NWOM than PWOM on brands they have not used and this suggests that, sometimes, brands become widely discussed because of their deficiencies. This is a serious worry for managers. Note that the previous work showing more PWOM than NWOM was about *all* the brands in a category. Individual brands could be the object of more NWOM than PWOM.

How Does the Occurrence of WOM Relate to the Market Share of the Brand?

Bigger brands, with more users, will get more recommendations because, as we see above, most recommendations are about the current main brand. As a result, the volume of recommendation will tend to relate to market share. WOM for previously owned brands will reflect the market share that applied at an earlier time and, if the market has not changed much, this will approximate to the current market share. This means that NWOM volume will also relate to market share, but less so than PWOM because it relates to an earlier market structure. This was tested by Uncles, East and Lomax (2010a). They analyzed data from 13 surveys and found an average correlation between market share and PWOM volume of 0.92. This was significantly greater than the corresponding correlation for NWOM which was 0.73.

This evidence shows that if one brand gets more PWOM than another, it is not necessarily performing better. To do well, a brand must get more PWOM and less NWOM than would

Table 12.3   The ownership of brands cited in given PWOM and NWOM (adapted from East, Romaniuk and Lomaz, 2011)

	PWOM			NWOM		
	Current main brand	A previous brand	Never owned	Current main brand	A previous brand	Never owned
Category (year data were collected)	%	%	%	%	%	%
Camera (2007)	88	12	0	33	34	33
Mobile phone handset (2005)	81	15	5	20	71	9
Mobile phone airtime supplier (2005)	79	9	12	19	56	26
Mobile phone handset (2007)	78	10	9	55	29	16
Main coffee shop (2008)	75	25	0	15	82	4
Mobile phone airtime supplier (2007)	73	20	7	33	44	23
Main coffee shop (2006)	72	27	1	18	71	12
Bank account (current) (2007)	72	22	6	30	39	30
Computers (2006)	70	19	12	24	19	58
Skin care products (2008)	70	25	6	4	96	0
Main credit card (2007)	67	29	4	18	54	24
Current bank account (2009)	64	26	10	11	45	44
Luxury leather goods (2006)	63	29	8	7	69	24
Main supermarket (2008)	63	36	1	28	69	4
Luxury brands (2006)	51	32	17	17	53	30
Means	71	22	7	22	55	22

be expected on the basis of the market-share norm. Sometimes, new brands may get much more PWOM than their market share warrants; for example, some unpublished evidence at Kingston showed that, when smart phones first arrived, iPhone was well above the norm for PWOM and its subsequent success has vindicated this early interest.

Factors Associated with Word-of-Mouth Production

In studies by researchers and students at Kingston University, we have found that the volume of recommendation is often related to:

- The relative attitude to the brand. Relative attitude is the rating of the brand compared with other available brands and, for practical purposes, this is the same as relative satisfaction.
- Whether a person was recruited to the brand by recommendation or not. In the main, those who are recruited by recommendation tend to give more recommendations themselves. This was also found by Wangenheim and Bayón (2004) when they investigated German utility customers. This effect is likely to depend on the size of a person's circle of friends. Those who interact more with others have more opportunity both to receive and to give advice. Related to this, Godes and Mayzlin (2004a) incentivized PWOM and found that the extra sales that resulted were related to the size of a person's social circle.

- Whether the communicator recommends other categories. This reflects a disposition, called *mavenism*, to give advice across a wide range of products (Feick and Price, 1987).
- Age. The pattern here is that people tend to give and receive less WOM as they age, particularly when they are over 65. This may depend on opportunity, since there is likely to be a loss of social contact as people age, stop work and their children leave home. This topic is covered in more detail in Chapter 6.
- Whether a brand owner has heard others recommend their brand. We discuss this in Section 4.

Other factors relating to WOM production depend on the categories:

- Customer tenure (duration of time as a customer of the brand). The relationship between tenure and PWOM was described in Chapter 2. In brief, East et al. (2005a) found that recommendations fell as tenure increased in the case of credit cards, bank accounts, motor insurance and supermarkets, but recommendation rose in the case of car servicing and fashion shops. In other categories there was no significant effect.
- Weight of purchase. Heavy buyers quite often give more WOM but not always. Perhaps, in some categories, they habituate to the brand and then become less interested in talking about it.

Interestingly, share-of-category requirement is not usually related to PWOM. High-share customers, by their nature, have more limited experience of brands other than their main one and this may limit their ability to give advice when this involves comparing brands.

SECTION 3: THE IMPACT OF WORD OF MOUTH

What Is the Impact of Positive and Negative Word of Mouth on Brand Choice?

NWOM may be less common than PWOM, but perhaps it has more impact when it does occur? There seems to be a belief among marketers that an instance of NWOM has more effect than an instance of PWOM, and there is some evidence suggesting that this might be true. Arndt (1967) showed twice as much impact on purchase from NWOM than from PWOM, but he studied only one brand. Also, a series of studies has shown a 'negativity effect' – that negative information has more impact on attitudes than positive information (Anderson, 1965; Chevalier and Mayzlin, 2003; Fiske, 1980; Herr, Kardes and Kim, 1991; Mittal, Ross and Baldasare, 1998; Mizerski, 1982). In these attitude studies, negative information is less common than positive information and Fiske (1980) has explained that the rarity of negative information makes it more useful than positive information because the latter is what most people already think. Thus, it is the gap between the position supported by the message and the position currently held by the receiver that is the basis for the negativity effect. For example, evidence that a brand is unreliable might be more useful than evidence that the brand is reliable because most people assume that modern products are reliable. Exceptionally, when the receiver's expectation is negative and the information received is positive, there could be a 'positivity effect'. Research on the negativity effect is reviewed in detail by Skowronski and Carlston (1989). However, some work has not supported the negativity effect. For example, Ahluwalia (2002) compared responses to written positive and negative information when participants were familiar or unfamiliar with the brand. When the brand was familiar, there were no significant differences in the impact of positive and negative information.

Much of this work has used measures of impact based on change in attitude or thinking. However, in marketing, impact may instead be measured in terms of change in purchase or purchase propensity. People might receive NWOM and change their attitude but not change their intention to purchase. This would happen if, prior to the NWOM, they had zero probability of purchase. East, Hammond and Lomax (2008) used the shift in purchase probability to measure the impact of WOM; they showed that positive advice will have more effect if the receiver has a low likelihood of purchase before the PWOM is received because this leaves more 'room for change'. Conversely, NWOM will have more effect when the initial probability of purchase is high. This applies the gap notion of the negativity effect to the intention measure of impact. In Table 12.4, we show East et al.'s average results from 19 studies. Respondents were asked what their probability of purchase was before and after hearing the WOM using the Juster (1966) scale, described in Chapter 7, to measure purchase probability.

The mean probability of purchase before WOM was 0.43 for those who received PWOM and 0.40 for those receiving NWOM so that there was slightly more 'room for change' in the purchasing probability for the receivers of PWOM (1 – 0.43 = 0.57) than NWOM (0.40). In addition, the impact of PWOM was correspondingly greater in magnitude than that of NWOM (0.20 versus –0.11). These findings suggest that PWOM usually has more impact on brand choice than NWOM when impact is measured as a change in intention. However, as we stated at the beginning of this chapter, it is difficult to study WOM effects, and estimates of past probabilities of purchase could easily be biased by selective recall. For this reason, we should be cautious about these research findings.[2]

What Variables Affect the Impact of WOM?

East et al. (2008) measured how six variables affected WOM impact, where impact was measured as change in the intention to buy. These were: the prior probability of purchase; how strongly expressed the WOM was; whether the WOM was about the main brand; the closeness of the communicator and receiver (that is, whether a close friend/relative, or not); whether the WOM was sought, or not; and how much advice the respondent reported *giving* on the category that was studied. These factors were used in a regression analysis to predict impact. Table 12.5 shows the output from the analysis. We see that the prior probability of choice is the most significant factor, supporting the argument in the previous section. For PWOM, the greater the prior probability, the less the change (and the reverse for NWOM). The strength of WOM expression, a variable noted by Mazzarol et al. (2007) as important, is a strong determinant of impact. Also, PWOM about the currently used main brand has more effect than PWOM on other brands, while NWOM on the main brand has less impact than NWOM on other brands. The closeness of the communicator and whether the advice was sought are only significant for PWOM, and the amount of WOM given by the respondent is only significant for NWOM. An interesting feature of Table 12.5 is the similarity in the magnitude of the different determinants, as shown by the beta coefficients. Remember that we have argued that PWOM and NWOM are similar in kind since they are often both intended to help the recipient. Table 12.5 supports this claim.

Table 12.4 The mean impact of PWOM and NWOM on brand choice probability (adapted from East, Hammond and Lomax, 2008)

Category	Probability of purchase before WOM %		Impact (shift in probability of purchase)	
	Prior to PWOM	Prior to NWOM	PWOM	NWOM
Supermarket	0.43	0.39	0.16	−0.16
Mobile phone airtime	0.40	0.41	0.16	−0.09
Mobile phone handset	0.50	0.42	0.08	−0.19
Current bank account	0.40	0.47	0.28	−0.11
Camera	0.45	0.38	0.01	−0.17
Computer	0.53	0.49	0.20	−0.20
Mobile phone airtime	0.32	0.41	0.19	−0.10
Main credit card	0.37	0.48	0.28	−0.17
Luxury brands	0.38	0.20	0.12	−0.06
Leather goods	0.48	0.46	0.23	−0.14
Camera	0.53	0.34	0.17	−0.12
Holiday destination	0.48	0.42	0.18	−0.19
Coffee shop	0.54	0.42	0.19	−0.11
Holiday destination	0.41	0.38	0.06	−0.06
Mobile phone handset	0.39	0.36	0.20	−0.07
Restaurant, favourite	0.35	0.59	0.39	−0.47
Restaurant, ethnic	0.36	0.41	0.34	−0.23
Luxury brands				
Hair colorant	0.51	0.28	0.19	−0.08
Restaurant, Iranian	0.44	0.22	0.31	−0.03
Means	**0.43**	**0.40**	**0.20**	**−0.11**

Table 12.5 Variables related to impact (multiple regression analysis) (adapted from East, Hammond and Lomax, 2008)

Variable	PWOM		NWOM	
	Beta	Sig.	Beta	Sig.
Prior probability of purchase	0.43	<.001	0.37	<.001
Strength of expression of WOM	0.22	<.001	0.22	<.001
WOM about main brand	0.16	<.001	−0.21	<.001
Closeness of communicator	0.10	<.001	0.06	0.06
Whether advice was sought	0.06	0.03	0.04	0.17
Amount of WOM given	0.04	0.13	0.08	0.01
Adjusted R²	0.23		0.21	

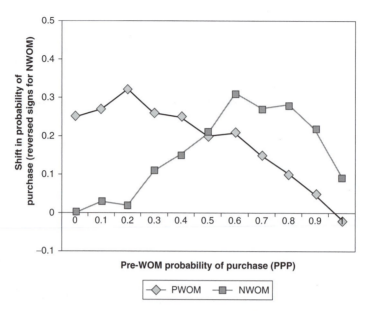

Figure 12.2   Shift in probability of purchase (impact) as a function of the probability of purchase before receiving WOM

Previous work has shown that close ties have more direct effect than distant ties (Brown and Reingen, 1987) and that sought advice is more influential than advice that is unsought (East et al., 2005a; Bansal and Voyer, 2000). The weak associations shown in Table 12.5 may relate to the method of analysis. When multiple regression is used, other variables that are associated with both the predictor and outcome variables can assume part of the explanation.

The Effect of Brand Commitment

East et al. (2008) analyzed the shift in purchase probability against the probability of purchase prior to receiving WOM. The result is shown in Figure 12.2. For most of the range, there is a close relationship between impact, measured as shift in purchase probability, and prior probability of purchase. However, people who are very likely to buy a brand give less weight to NWOM on that brand and people who are very unlikely to buy a brand give less weight to PWOM on the brand, perhaps because they intend to buy another brand. Thus, Figure 12.2 shows how commitment to brands can make people resistant to advice about alternatives. Figure 12.2 is useful because it helps us to see how consumers differ in their response to information, depending on their prior probability to purchase.

SECTION 4: WOM IN THE SOCIAL NETWORK

One stimulating development has been work by Watts and Dodds (2007), who cast a critical eye over the two-step flow model of mass media influence which was proposed by Lazarsfeld, Berelson, and Gaudet (1944) and refined by Katz and Lazarsfeld (1955). In this

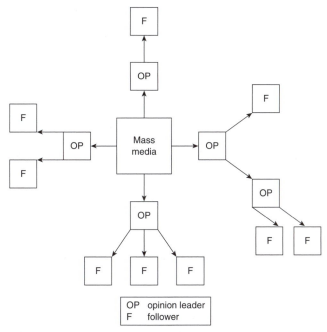

Figure 12.3   Flow of influence via opinion leaders

model, mass-media communications are processed by a small group of opinion leaders, who are well meshed into the mass media and, by interpreting, filtering and selectively passing on ideas, may promote or oppose change. Sometimes an opinion leader may recruit a further opinion leader to spread the word, as shown in Figure 12.3. Watts and Dodds suggest that the opinion leader is usually only modestly more influential than average. They argue that influence may flow in both directions in networks of individuals (unlike the two-step flow model). In the more fluid social network that they propose, their computer simulations suggest that innovations take off when a critical mass of easily influenced individuals has been reached. When this occurs, there is a large-scale cascade of adoption.

    If WOM is a lubricant to the adoption of innovations, how does it act in the social network? We have shown that most WOM is expressed by those who have already used a brand. How can this WOM be amplified? In some unpublished work at Kingston University, we asked respondents whether they had heard others recommending a service that they had recently used and we asked them how many times they had recommended the service themselves in the preceding four weeks. We found that, on average, those who had heard others recommend a service gave nearly twice as many recommendations compared with those who had not heard their brand recommended. Even after removing the effect of some co-variates, the effect remained. One explanation for this is that people can easily repeat recommendations that they hear. This provides a mechanism whereby influence can travel over the network of existing users in any direction. What is interesting about this mechanism is that it creates positive feedback. Suppose that, by some means, we induce extra recommendations in a social network; users who hear such recommendations will then produce more recommendations themselves and this will induce still more recommendations by other users, and so on. The amount of feedback will depend on the proportion of the population that are users and the extent to which hearing a recommendation raises the level of giving recommendations. It is possible that a process similar to this could underpin Watts and Dodds' cascade of influence.

Such ideas may also help us to understand how advertising can affect WOM. It is known that the level of WOM on a product rises in response to advertising (Bayus, 1985; Graham and Havlena, 2007). One mechanism that could cause this is that the ad increases the salience of the brand so that previously used PWOM scripts are more likely to be expressed after the ad has been seen. Brand salience may also be increased by conversations *about the ad*, since 20 per cent of WOM discussions refer to paid advertising content according to Keller and Fay (2009). In some cases the ad may supply a script that a receiver can repeat; this seems more likely for print and radio ads where information is already in a verbal form that can be passed on.

SECTION 5: APPLICATIONS OF WORD-OF-MOUTH RESEARCH

Net Promoter Score

The Net Promoter Score (NPS) is intended to measure the number of people who are positive about a brand/company (promoters) and the number who are negative (detractors) (Reichheld, 2003). The score is computed as shown in Figure 12.4. The NPS asks about future recommendation, but Romaniuk, Nguyen and East (2011) found that responses are usually influenced by the WOM that responders have given in the recent past; apparently, when asked what they will do, people check on what they have done. In these circumstances, it might be better to measure past WOM in the first place.

In the NPS, detractors are meant to give much of the NWOM on a brand. This seems doubtful; those who give little PWOM may just be disinclined to give WOM in any form. This

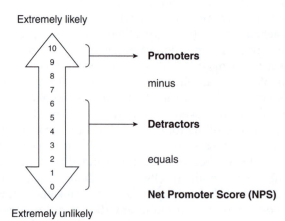

How likely is it you would recommend us to a friend?

Figure 12.4   Measuring the Net Promoter Score

was tested by East, Romaniuk and Lomax (2011a). They identified promoters and detractors in three categories and found out how much of the total PWOM and NWOM these groups had produced in the last six months. The detractors produced very little NWOM and, in two of the categories, they gave more PWOM than NWOM. Bear in mind that the NPS is based on *customers* and much of the NWOM on a brand is produced by *ex-customers* who were included in the East et al. study but are not included in the NPS measure. It appears that the NPS provides a good indication of PWOM but not NWOM because of the focus on current customers. Also, if we wish to evaluate the way that WOM supports a brand, it would be better to measure the amount of WOM received (the NPS is based on the amount of WOM *given*).

One of Reichheld's contentions is that the NPS is a better measure of company perfor-mance than satisfaction. The best-known measure of satisfaction is the American Customer Satisfaction Index (ACSI), first developed in Sweden by Fornell (1992) and discussed in Chapter 9. The predictions of the ACSI and the NPS have been compared (e.g. Morgan and Rego, 2006; Keiningham et al., 2007) and generally the ACSI has been superior. However, because both the NPS and the ACSI are restricted to recent customers, there is potential for a better WOM-based measure that covers all consumers.

Reichheld's thesis has recently been restated (Reichheld and Markey, 2011) but this book gives no answers to NPS critics. Instead, it emphasizes a corporate philosophy of designing management systems that deliver to customers the product that they like and will talk about. It is difficult to argue with this but what people like and dislike needs measurement and the NPS clearly could be improved as a measure.

Influentials or Current Users?

In the two-step flow model, advertising is relayed by a limited group of 'influentials' or opinion leaders who recommend widely. Thus, a popular strategy is to identify these influentials and direct communications to them. As we have seen, Watts and Dodds (2007) criticized the two-step flow model and suggested that influence was more widely spread in the network. Related to this, Balter and Butman (2005) argue that WOM is more effec-tive when it is delivered by ordinary people. Furthermore, research by Goodey and East (2008) showed that those who scored high on the mavenism index (Feick and Price, 1987) did not give much more WOM than those who scored low, so it may be difficult to identify truly influential people.

To some extent, the best strategy depends on cost. If costs are low (as when the Internet is used), it makes sense to target all those on a customer database. However, the messages need to differ between current users (responsible for most of the PWOM) and ex-users (responsible for most of the NWOM). If costs are high, it may pay to focus on the influentials; this is what happens when BzzAgents are given products to talk about. However, whether all users or just influentials are targeted, there is a need for research to find out what sort of information people pass on and what impact different forms of information have on receivers.

A popular method of using WOM from current customers is the referral programme. This is a managed intervention designed to add to naturally occurring PWOM. Often there is a reward for the person making a successful referral and sometimes an incentive for the person referred. There is evidence that the customers acquired through such campaigns are more valuable (Schmitt, Skiera and Van den Bulte, 2011).

Stopping Negative and Promoting Positive Comments

Suppliers may be able to use their customer databases to direct information to groups who could be criticizing the product. In Table 12.3, we showed that about one-fifth of negative advice relates to the communicator's main brand. Some of this negative advice is not because the brand is disliked but because the communicator thinks that it is unsuitable for another person and it is probably unrealistic to try to reduce this sort of NWOM. However, some of the NWOM about a currently used brand may reflect dissatisfaction with the brand and, where possible, this sort of WOM should be counteracted. Even if it is impossible to detect the minority who criticize their main brand, it may still be possible to deal with common complaints by communicating with all customers. By doing so, both NWOM and defection may be targeted.

Most cases of NWOM come from past customers, who are usually still on databases. Normally, past customers are contacted with a view to recovering them but there may also be value in contact designed to counteract NWOM. When products have improved, those who no longer buy them are unlikely to know about the improvement and may continue to criticize their previous brand offering on the assumption that it is unchanged. By sending past customers information about brand improvements, suppliers may be able to lessen NWOM. East et al. (2007) found that those who gave NWOM were much more likely to give PWOM (probably on another brand); this suggests that a person who stops giving NWOM could become a strong recommender.

Information, Not Hearsay

When there are widespread misunderstandings in research evidence, there is a danger that strategies will be misjudged. Many beliefs about WOM appear to have been mistaken. It is not true that NWOM is more common than PWOM according to the evidence that has now accumulated and it does not appear that there is much evidence that NWOM has more impact. The role of satisfaction or dissatisfaction in the genesis of WOM has probably been over-emphasized. Nor is it generally true that long-term customers usually recommend more than short-term customers. More research findings are needed to displace such hearsay and to inform well-based marketing strategies.

SUMMARY

PWOM and NWOM are powerful influences on consumer choice but they are difficult to study. Internet research deals with only a small fraction of those giving advice, experimental research lacks relevance to natural settings, and survey research is prone to bias. In the absence of good evidence, some misunderstanding has occurred. It now appears that much of WOM is given to help others, and dis/satisfaction, though relevant, may not be needed for WOM. Therefore, comparisons between satisfied and dissatisfied customers are inappropriate for determining the occurrence and impact of PWOM and NWOM.

PWOM tends to be about the communicator's current main brand and NWOM about previously owned brands. These patterns produce a strong association between the volume of PWOM and market share and a somewhat weaker association between NWOM volume and market share. Market share thus provides a norm for the amount of PWOM and NWOM that brands should receive on average and this allows measurement of better or worse performance for individual brands.

Research evidence shows that PWOM is more common than NWOM and that, in general, PWOM has somewhat more impact on the probability of purchase than NWOM. Impact is related to the probability of purchase before the WOM is received, the strength of expression of WOM, and whether the WOM is about the current main brand or not. Those people who are very likely to buy a brand give less weight to NWOM on this brand and those who are very unlikely to purchase the brand give less weight to PWOM on it.

There is uncertainty about the process whereby influence passes through the social structure. The two-step flow model (in which the mass media affect opinion leaders who then pass the message on to followers) has been criticized by Watts and Dodds (2007) who argue that influence is more dispersed and is bi-directional. One suggestion is that WOM production is increased by product users when they hear others recommend their brand, and this would make influence omni-directional and more dependent on ownership than opinion leadership. Managers, seeking to influence WOM, may target opinion leaders, if they can be identified, or they can seek to influence their whole customer base. The best strategy depends on costs; when these are low it is better to target the whole customer base.

The Net Promoter Score (Reichheld, 2003) is a measure of WOM, but this measure, along with the American Consumer Satisfaction Index, is based on customers and it is ex-customers who express most of the negative sentiment about brands. The Net Promoter Score measures PWOM but is a poor measure of NWOM.

Additional Resources

To see how word-of-mouth impact varies between categories and for a further review of the literature, see East, Hammond and Lomax (2008) and Mangold, Miller and Brockway (1999) who are concerned with the circumstances under which WOM is produced. It is worth checking the websites for the WOM agencies mentioned earlier, www.bzzagent. com, www.business.tremor.com and also www.womma.org. One marketing text has tried to apply the new thinking covered in this chapter, namely Allan Kimmel's (2010) *Connecting with Consumers*, Oxford: Oxford University Press. Some very interesting new work is coming from Wharton; check the Internet.

Note

1 However, some recent work, so far unpublished, suggests that Mangold et al.'s method (critical incident technique) may have affected his data. Using a survey method, satisfaction and dissatisfaction appear to be more common factors inducing WOM.

2 A critic might argue that a better measure of impact would relate the shift in probability to the movement necessary to reach certainty. On this basis, the effect of PWOM would average $0.20/0.57 = 0.35$ compared with $0.11/0.40 = 0.28$ so, even on this basis, PWOM has more effect. Note that this is an average effect; in some categories NWOM is clearly more influential as Table 12.4 indicates.

13   The Response to Advertising

LEARNING OBJECTIVES

When you have completed this chapter, you should be able to:

1   Describe what is meant by effective advertising, giving examples.
2   Discuss the issues relating to the effective frequency and concentration of ads.
3   Explain how advertising could have primary and secondary effects on sales.
4   Report evidence on the rate at which advertising effects decay.
5   Discuss which product fields and which customer segments are more responsive to advertising.
6   Consider how new media and changes to television viewing have changed advertising.

Exercise 13.1   What do you expect?

Go through the objectives above and decide what you think will be reported in the following pages. This helps you to take in the evidence presented in this chapter.

OVERVIEW

Advertising sometimes has a powerful impact on consumption, but its effect is variable and quite often there is no discernable outcome. We review research on the frequency and concentration of ad exposures, and how these affect the impact of advertising. There is evidence that high concentrations of ads may break through the resistance established by competitor brands.

Sales effects resulting from advertising appear to have two components: a short-term effect that is largely dissipated within a month and a long-term effect, which can last for more than a year, but which only occurs if there is a short-term effect. We discuss the bases for these effects.

Ads have more effect in certain product fields and more impact on certain consumer segments. We illustrate these effects, and consider which segments provide most extra sales volume. The Internet, mobile telephony and other developments are offering new ways of communicating with consumers.

SECTION 1: EFFECTIVE ADVERTISING

Ads may affect our beliefs and attitudes, but ultimately they must change or reinforce behaviour if they are to be useful. In social applications, ads can reduce accidents, increase voting rates, promote healthy eating, or get people to report suspicious behaviour that might indicate terrorist activity. In commercial applications, advertising can increase purchase and subscription, or maintain purchase rates when the price goes up. Sometimes the profit-making behaviour occurs at the end of a chain of prior actions, and the links in this chain may be strengthened by advertising, e.g. by getting consumers to go to a showroom or to check a product on the Internet.

Ambler and Broadbent (2000) discuss how advertising campaigns vary in effectiveness (how much change they achieve) and in efficiency (how much change they achieve for a given cost). Effectiveness depends in part on decisions about copy such as whether to write informative or emotional ads, the prominence given to the brand, whether to include a unique selling proposition, the use of a celebrity endorsement, the length of the ad, the creative idea and so forth. Efficiency depends on the quality of the ad and on media planning and buying, which should ensure that ads reach the target audience in a cost-effective manner. Decisions about content and media schedules depend on theories about how viewers consume media and how they process advertisements, so different theories will lead to different recommendations. The optimal approach may vary with the product category, whether the brand is already familiar to the consumer, and whether the purpose is to communicate an offer, remind people to keep buying the brand or to stimulate a substantial change in behaviour.

In the commercial arena, three particular outcomes may be derived from advertising, which we discuss in more detail in the following sections. These are:

- Price support: buyers pay more per unit and so the profit on a sale is increased.
- Sales support: buyers buy more than they would have done without the advertising. This is the most widely used criterion of ad effectiveness.
- Cost saving: costs are reduced as advertising stabilizes sales and makes intermediaries more compliant.

These outcomes can occur via a number of mechanisms. Advertising may:

- be based on a new analysis of the product range and consumer segments (a relaunch). For example, Virgin focused more on its younger customers when it relaunched the Australian service in 2004 (*Effective Advertising 8*, 2006).[1]

- induce word of mouth and media comment that eventually results in purchase. Murray-Burton, Dyke and Harrison (2007) report on a live Monopoly game, which could be played over the Internet and which generated measurable WOM.
- increase retailer stocking, raising the opportunity to purchase. The Felix cat food campaign (Broadbent, 2000) boosted distribution so that a third of the extra sales effect came from this source. In many cases, expanded distribution produces a sales gain without the help of advertising.
- raise demand for scarce items such as property and shares. In the case of the One2One (now T-Mobile) telephone company, ads lifted share values so that capital could be raised at lower cost (Kendall, 1998).

Price Support

Some ads make consumers aware of discounts and the possibility of saving money. This price-related advertising tends to be associated with increased price sensitivity on the part of the consumer (Bolton, 1989; Kaul and Wittink, 1995). When this occurs margins may be squeezed, so any benefits must come via increased sales. By contrast, most brand advertising is designed to raise perceptions of quality and thus increase appreciation of the brand. This tends to reduce price sensitivity, allowing the brand owner to raise margins. For example, Broadbent (2000) showed that price sensitivity about Lurpak butter dropped in regions that received more advertising for this brand. Hamilton, East and Kalafatis (1997) found that well-advertised brands usually had either slightly lower price elasticity or were more highly priced than others; brand leaders advertised twice as heavily as follower brands, and the main difference in price sensitivity occurred between these leader and follower brands. This combination of high adspend and high price is a common pattern for leading brands (Farris and Reibstein, 1991). Sometimes, it is suggested that the high level of advertising could be a consequence of the brand's success but several case histories provide quite good evidence that the reduction in price sensitivity *follows* the advertising. For example, in the Stella Artois case, the ads seemed to lead the sales (see Box 13.1). Binet and Field (2009) found that ad campaigns that tried to reduce price sensitivity were more effective than those that tried to increase sales.

Box 13.1	Stella Artois

Price support has been demonstrated by the success of Stella Artois advertising in Britain (Baker, 1993). Stella was advertised as 'reassuringly expensive', to imply high quality. It attracted a large proportion of lager drinkers despite a trade price premium of 7.5 per cent. Publicans more than recovered this premium when they sold Stella at its higher retail price. In 1999, Stella was priced 14 per cent above the premium lager average and the profit increment was estimated at six times the ad cost (Broadbent, 2000).

Mela, Gupta and Lehmann (1997) studied the impact of brand advertising and sales promotion on price sensitivity over an 8-year period. They focused on a mature product where life-cycle effects were minimal and found that *reductions* in brand advertising were associated with increased price sensitivity. Most of this effect occurred among the less brand-loyal customers, showing that price support from advertising occurs mainly because it affects low-loyalty buyers.

Squeezing the Retailer

Steiner (1973, 1993) found that advertising in the toy industry could both reduce the price to the customer and raise manufacturer margin. He showed that advertising created a consumer demand for products that compelled retailers to stock them, so they had to pay the manufacturer's asking price. At the same time, competition between retailers forced them to reduce the selling price. As a result, consumers and manufacturers did well at the expense of retailers. This effect is likely to be particularly strong when the product is a 'must have', such as the last Harry Potter book (see Box 13.2). Farris and Albion (1980) reviewed this subject and concluded that advertising exerted pressure on retailers' margins and that the net effect of such advertising often lowered the price to the consumer. When retailers have great power, as in the case of the leading UK supermarket groups, this effect may be less apparent but even in groceries there is evidence that manufacturers have adjusted production to emphasize the stronger brands where they have more leverage on price. In the 1990s, Procter & Gamble and Unilever dropped a large number of small brands and focused on the *power brands* which supermarkets had to stock.

Evidence from Hanssens (2009) and Ataman et al. (2010) shows that distribution has six to ten times the sales impact of advertising. Thus, to the extent that advertising promotes additional distribution of this sort, its effect is greatly multiplied. *Advertising Works 20* (Snow, 2011) gives the example of Marie Curie Cancer Cure changing their traditional annual advertising campaign to focus on distribution, and soliciting people to act as collectors rather than as donors. For an outlay of £184,000 they recruited an additional 5,219 collectors, who generated an extra £634,583 in donations.

Box 13.2	The trouble with Harry (from *The Guardian*, 4 May 2007)

Waterstone's owner HMV yesterday defended its decision to sacrifice profits and offer the forthcoming Harry Potter book at half price, suggesting a price war had left it with little choice.

HMV chief executive Simon Fox said the whole market for the final instalment of the boy wizard's tale would be at half price and cited Ottakar's, now owned by HMV, as an example of the price to be paid for not joining in a Harry Potter price battle. 'Not being price competitive on the book seemed to set a perception that the store was high price. There are very few books that have that level of publicity,' said Mr Fox. 'If we try to be anything other than half price we are setting the Waterstone's brand off as high price and that's something we are trying to change.

When Supply is Limited

When supply is relatively fixed – as in auctions, the services of top professionals and houses for sale – increased demand will result in an increase in price. In equity markets, where the available stock is fixed in the short term, corporate advertising may have a direct effect on the share price. Evidence for this effect is sketchy but Moraleda and Ferrer-Vidal (1991) showed that advertising raised the intention to apply for shares in the Spanish oil company, Repsol, in the run-up to privatization.

In monopoly situations, customers may feel their forced choice of a single product may be poor value. Here, advertising can be used to raise perceived value. Kendall (1998) showed how ads were used to raise the evaluation of North West Water in the United Kingdom (where water companies have monopolies). Before the advertising, customers were hostile to the company and objected to increases in their water costs. The advertising drew attention to the benefits offered by the company and raised the perceived value of the service.

Sales Support

The cases in the *Advertising Works* (UK) and *Effective Advertising* (Australia) series demonstrate that advertising can increase sales. On rare occasions the effect is large, as in the case of Levi 501 jeans in the UK. Here, campaigns from 1984 to 1987 raised sales 20 times (Feldwick, 1990). But the Levi 501 case was quite exceptional. Even when the best campaigns are reviewed, sales gains of 100 per cent or more are uncommon and tend to go to small brands, which can sometimes increase share substantially. In *Advertising Works 15* (Green, 2007), a small-volume brand, Actimel, secured a year-on-year sales gain of 426 per cent while the much bigger company O_2 gained about 35 per cent on contract customers and 100 per cent on pre-pay customers as a result of a very successful campaign in a rising market. The payback of a campaign can be very substantial when the brand is big. The O_2 payback was as much as 80 times the ad cost when all possible benefits were included. The Actimel payback was much lower at about 1.7 times because of the small size of the brand. Other examples from *Effective Advertising 8* (2006): the Sunbeam electric blanket brand gained 83 per cent but the return payback was only 1.8 because the market was relatively small. Compare this with a campaign for Australian lamb that raised sales by about 25 per cent over five years; the payback in this big market was 53 times the ad cost. So, ad campaigns can give very good returns for big brands but it is hard to show a large payback for small brands, even when market share is substantially increased.

Australian lamb was a generic campaign. Small brands may sometimes be able to band together and fund generic advertising for the whole industry. This works when suppliers are trying to overcome consumer inertia rather than displace each other. An example might be beds, where weak brand awareness makes individual brand advertising risky. Collectively, bed manufacturers might show a good return on advertising designed to get consumers to replace sagging beds and lumpy mattresses.

The Australian lamb advertising corrected a long-term decline in lamb sales, so the 25 per cent gain on sales at the start of the campaign was probably an underestimate of the advertising achievement. Sometimes, even static sales are an achievement if, without the advertising, there would have been a decline. In Australia, Hahn Premium light beer expected to lose its leading position because of a build-up of intense competition but its campaign successfully countered the attack and the brand even gained a little share (*Effective Advertising 8*, 2006).

One very successful campaign in the UK was conducted by the ad agency TBWA for Wonderbra. This ad probably drew attention because it was puzzling. The model was unconventionally provocative and the quote was mysterious to those unfamiliar with the work of the filmstar, Mae West. These ads featured a self-assured model (Eva Herzigova) and enigmatic captions. The cost of the initial four-month campaign was only £330,000 as billboards were the predominant medium used (Baker, 1995). Over a two-year period, a gain in sales of 120 per cent was achieved even though Wonderbra was selling above the price of many other brands. The key to this success was almost certainly the substantial editorial comment and word of mouth (WOM) that the advertising provoked, including discussion of how advertising could distract drivers and cause accidents (see Box 13.3). Although this is

Box 13.3	Successful ads

The wide variation in the effectiveness of ads has led to speculation among practitioners about which elements of an ad make it effective. It might be thought that copy tests would isolate the key factors but, although these tests differentiate between alternative ads once they have been prepared, they are not useful in helping create good ads. The supposed key elements of a good ad refer to rather obvious features of the ad. For example, Moldovan (1984) focused on ad credibility and Brown (1986) on the power of the ad to arrest attention. These claims are sensible but they are of limited value to those trying to create good copy.

By its nature, creativity cannot be anticipated. But, after its creation, we can see features of an ad that help to make it successful. For example, the Wonderbra campaign was noticed because it created curiosity at a number of levels. Among these were the enigmatic and challenging character of the model, the oddity of putting such ads on billboards and, in the ad shown, uncertainty about the origin of captions such as 'or are you just pleased to see me?'. This comes from a line Mae West says to Cary Grant in the film *She Done Him Wrong*. The full line is 'Is that a pistol in your pocket, or are you just glad to see me?'

an extreme example, WOM is an important secondary effect of advertising. Keller and Fay (2009) found that 32 per cent of online WOM and 21 per cent of offline WOM referred to paid advertising, and that this involved more recommendation than other WOM.

The *Advertising Works* and *Effective Advertising* cases are selected because they are successful. Most advertising for established brands produces far less sales response. This is illustrated by a report by Riskey (1997) on 23 Frito-Lay ad campaigns. This study compared brand sales when ads were running with a no-ad control condition. The study was conducted using the BehaviorScan method of Information Resources Inc. (IRI), which is described in more detail in Box 13.4. Twelve campaigns showed measurable effects, and these cases produced an average sales increase of 15 per cent.

Box 13.4 | BehaviorScan

Information Resources Inc. (now SymphonyIRI Group) uses cable TV in specific towns to test ads. Households are recruited to a panel and agree to receive television that may be modified by IRI. The BehaviorScan technology swaps commercials so that some households receive trial ads or extra exposures of normal ads when compared with other households. The former allows *copy* tests to be conducted, the latter *weight* tests. Members of the panel show an identification number when they buy groceries in town. IRI finances the scanners in the town's stores and downloads sales information each night from these scanners. This system allows sales to be tied to households receiving different frequencies of advertising. Malec (1982) describes the system in more detail. GfK has used the same technology in Germany (Litzenroth, 1991).

This system permits experimental tests but suffers from some weaknesses:

- Members of the household may not be watching a TV set when it is on.
- Out-of-town purchases (out-shopping) are missed.
- The tests exclude trade response. National advertising may generate more retailer stocking and competitor advertising than in the test communities.
- The brands that are tested are chosen for commercial reasons and this may bias the sampling.
- There may be a 'hothouse' effect if panellists guess that commercials are on test and, as a consequence, take more interest in them.

As a method of testing copy, the BehaviorScan procedure takes a long time and is expensive. The ARS Persuasion Measure is a cheaper, quicker but less reliable method; this uses the shift in intention to purchase after exposure to ads (Blair and Rabuck, 1998).

Armstrong (2010) offers guidelines for developing effective copy. He summarizes findings from 3,000 studies into around 200 normative principles on how to write effective ads. For example, Principle 3.1.1 notes 'Do not mix rational and emotional appeals', and Principle 6.9.2 notes 'Attack ads should employ objective information, not emotion'. Copy that follows his principles should be more effective. However, while all the principles are evidence based, their effectiveness when used to generate better ad copy has not yet been tested. Also, while these principles might help copywriters to avoid mistakes, creativity is still required to produce ads that gain attention and engagement from the audience.

Cost Saving

In some cases, advertising produces efficiencies that reduce cost. For example, Volkswagen saved on storage costs when extra demand meant that they had fewer cars unsold (Kendall, 1998). Costs may also be saved when advertising is accurately targeted so that irrelevant inquiries are avoided. Internet job advertising can get replies from anywhere in the world and such ads should be designed to cut out applicants who cannot be appointed by virtue of their location or nationality. Kendall (1998) showed the value of well-targeted advertising in the campaign to recruit personnel to the British Army. In 1994, one person from every 6.7 inquirers was enlisted. Following the advertising campaign, the conversion ratio improved to 1 in 3.4. In the analysis, it was estimated that this change in ratio saved the Army £16 million after deducting the cost of the advertising. In addition, it appeared that better recruits were enlisted since they were less likely to drop out during the period of initial training.

The Effects of Social Advertising

Large paybacks are quite often found in social applications of advertising. For example, a £31 million campaign to raise rear seat belt usage in the UK gave a directly quantifiable return of £18 million, and, when further assumptions were made about the costs of injury and death, the return was £73 million (Broadbent, 2000). Another campaign in Australia achieved a drop in smoking of over 7 per cent, equivalent to 190,000 fewer smokers. The healthcare saving was estimated at $24 million (*Effective Advertising 6*, 2001). Often, social advertising has no opposing advertising but has to work against consumer inertia (e.g. energy saving) or self-indulgence (e.g. eating less).

SECTION 2: ADVERTISING FREQUENCY AND CONCENTRATION

Schedules

Advertising is presented in media according to a schedule. Traditionally, for TV, radio or print media, ad exposures may be *continuous* (delivered at a steady frequency per month) or in *bursts* (e.g. one month on and two months off). When the bursts are short-interval (e.g. a week) this pattern may be called *pulsing*. Sometimes, a low level of advertising or *drip* is maintained in the gaps between bursts. The choice of schedule should be determined primarily by its sales impact on consumers. Continuous schedules spread the advertising across a larger number of people so that each person tends to see fewer

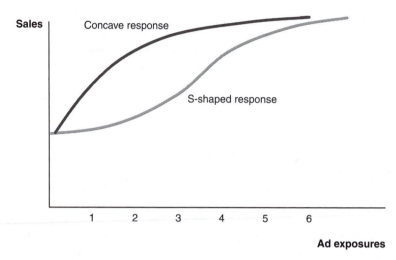

Figure 13.1   Concave and S-shaped responses to exposures

exposures compared with bursting. As the time for the burst is reduced, there is more *concentration* (the exposures occur over a shorter period).

In order to choose the most effective schedule, we need to know how individuals respond to each additional ad exposure and how they react to the same number of exposures when these are concentrated into different time intervals. Work in this field has been hampered in the past by the poor quality of the data available. Now, with actual sales data on individual respondents, the effect of each extra exposure can be measured. If each additional exposure produces a smaller sales effect than the last, the response is *concave to the x-axis* and is an example of *diminishing marginal returns* (see Figure 13.1). When this occurs, the most cost-effective number of exposures (known as the *effective frequency*) is *one per person* and it is best to use a continuous schedule that spreads the advertising across the target population as widely as possible. In this way, more people are reached at lower frequencies. But if additional exposures produce increasing and then decreasing increments in sales, which is an *S-shaped* response curve, then the best strategy is to use a schedule that takes the audience quickly to the point where their sales response is steepest. This strategy sacrifices ad penetration for ad frequency. It is achieved best by bursting and pulsing schedules.

S-Shaped or Concave Response?

Simon (1979) analyzed data from a study by Zielske (1959) and found that the second and later exposures gave a concave response (diminishing returns). In further evidence, Simon and Arndt (1980) reviewed 37 advertising studies and established that the great majority showed a concave response function. Roberts (1996) found that the response curve was concave in 15 out of 17 cases of mature brands. McDonald (1995) also argued that the true pattern of sales response to advertising exposures is concave for mature brands; his earlier work (McDonald, 1970) supported this when it was re-analyzed.[2] McDonald was influenced in part by work done by Jones on single-source data (Jones, 1995a, 1995b, 1995c), which showed little gain after the first exposure. In studies by Adams (1916) and by Burnkrant and Unnava (1987), three showings of different ads for a brand were compared with three showings of the same ad. There was more effect on purchase propensity when the ads were different. This indicates that the second and third exposures of the same ad had less effect than a new ad; the curve was concave.

Despite this evidence, there is practitioner support for the S-shaped response function. This is partly because the difficulties of research in this field make results uncertain. In particular, there is a problem posed by the decay of any ad effect as the period of time between exposure and measurement increases. Also, the time between exposures can vary, thus varying the concentration. Broadbent (1998) pointed out that there is very little agreement among researchers and practitioners on the period over which exposures should occur when frequency effects are studied; three exposures could occur in a day, a week or a month.

In addition, there are good reasons why the response to exposures *should be* S-shaped. An important argument is based on the idea of *breakthrough*, getting over a threshold of attention so that the audience cannot miss the message (Broadbent, 1998). This is discussed in more detail in the section below ('Explaining Breakthrough'). An S-shaped response is also implicit in Krugman's (1972) three-hit theory. Krugman argued that on first exposure, viewers are curious, on the second the meaning of the ad may become clear and they endorse or reject the message, and on the third and subsequent exposures they are reminded of the message again and may take action. In this account, the second and third exposures are more effective than the first. An influential book by Naples (1979) endorsed the three-hit theory.

Aggregate evidence supports an S-shaped response function. Lodish and Lubetkin (1992) analyzed IRI data and found that both new and established products did better when the advertising was initially concentrated, rather than spread over time. This suggests that exposures need to exceed some threshold level if they are to have optimum effect. This evidence has left considerable uncertainty, but this may be resolved by work on concentration, below.

Concentration

Roberts (1999) provided evidence on the way concentration affects the outcome of repeated exposures to ads. He used a UK data set on 750 households from Taylor Nelson Sofres' Superpanel, which was gathered by TVSpan. Each household was equipped with a TV 'setmeter' so that viewing could be recorded. Ad exposures were related to household purchases recorded through Superpanel. One hundred and thirteen brands from ten categories were studied. These were advertised over a two-year period from March 1996 to March 1998. This method does not produce data that controls for co-variates, and care must be taken to reduce the effects of such biases. Roberts controlled for two major co-variates: concurrent sales promotions and weight of television viewing. He compared respondents who had received exposures on a brand with *these same respondents* when, over another period, they had not received any ad exposures on the brand for 28 days.

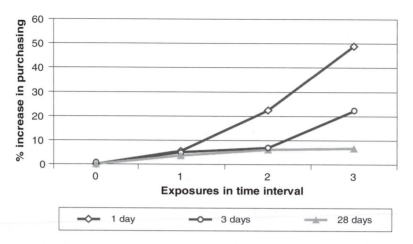

Figure 13.2   Percentage increase in sales for different frequencies and concentrations (from Roberts, 1999)

Roberts (1999) conducted a number of analyses. Here, we focus on the effects of three exposures in three different intervals: one day, three days and 28 days. Figure 13.2 shows the sales recorded after the end of the exposure interval. When the exposures occur over 28 days the additional effect of the second and third exposures is small and follows the familiar concave pattern. When all three exposures occur in the same day (and in practice this is often over a few hours) the effect of the second and third exposures is large and produces a convex sales response, which could be the lower part of an S-curve. Over three days, the pattern is more linear. There appears to be an interaction between exposures when these occur over a short period but not over a long period. Thus, multiple exposures, when close together, assist each other to achieve breakthrough. In further work, Roberts confirmed that the extra sales achieved by a high concentration decayed at the same rate as sales achieved by low concentration.

In a further unpublished analysis, Roberts calculated how concentration might affect sales under continuous, monthly burst and weekly pulse schedules. One-week pulsing had the most effect and continuous the least. The degree of superiority of pulsing over the continuous schedule was estimated to be from 4 to 13 per cent depending on the total weight of advertising employed.

Roberts' evidence, though persuasive, is still the main published evidence there is on ad concentration and it should be closely scrutinized. First, we note that the data are gathered in Britain where ad clutter is relatively low. This raises the possibility that stronger effects from ad concentration might be observed in high-clutter environments. Second, the study is restricted to groceries. Third, doubts may be felt about the effectiveness of the control comparison used in this work (the purchases made by the same respondents when they have not been exposed to the advertising for 28 days). However, in this study, control subjects had shown themselves to be in the market by making purchases in other categories and this limits the possible differences between control and test groups.

Explaining Breakthrough

Breakthrough relates to the psychological concept of interference, which occurs when a change in the strength of one concept affects the strength of another concept. In the competition between brands in a category, more recent ads for brand A tend to displace the propensity to buy brand B by retroactive interference, i.e. the new learning about brand A displaces the previously learned responses to buy brand B. Prior ads for brand B prevent this by proactive interference, i.e. previous learning makes it harder to acquire new learning that is similar to the previous learning. Breakthrough occurs when more concentrated exposure to ads for brand A overcomes the proactive interference set up by other brands.

A study by Burke and Srull (1988) showed proactive and retroactive interference effects in the recall of advertising. In their study, the target brand ad frequency was manipulated from 1 to 3 exposures while competitive advertising was manipulated from 0 to 3 exposures. The findings showed that, as competitive brand advertising was increased, the recall of target brand details decreased. This evidence of interference adds support to the argument that Roberts' results were obtained because the greater concentration overcame any interference from competitive brand ads. A weakness of this study is that it was based on recall and lacked any observation of sales effect but now the effect has been found in market data by Danaher, Bonfrer and Dhar (2008), who examined the impact on sales of a focal brand when competitors advertised within a week and found a substantial reduction compared with the sales that would have occurred without the competitor advertising. Practitioners have always been concerned to measure share of voice, the proportion of advertising exposure that a brand gets compared to its competitors. The research by Danaher et al. suggests that this simplifies the issue too much. Consider a situation in which two brands, A and B, which put out the same amount of advertising and have equal strength so that the ad for one always displaces the other brand from the minds of consumers. If the ads for brand A immediately follow those for brand B and then there is a delay before brand B advertises again, brand A's ad schedule will have more impact although the two brands have equal strength, advertise equally and their share of voice is the same.

Share of voice relates to the associative network discussed in Chapter 3. Interference should vary with the closeness and the linkage strength of competitive brands – some competitors are more of a threat than others. There is also a background level of interference set up by all the advertising received. This inhibits response to any ad and concentrated exposures may also help to overcome this clutter, thus increasing attention to the focal brand. These interference effects are more apparent when the content of the ad that is remembered is trivial, which fits most advertising.

SECTION 3: A MODEL OF ADVERTISING EFFECT

Some ads are aired a great number of times. This suggests some incremental effect after many exposures – probably, the brand name repetition helps to keep the brand salient relative to competitors. One mechanism for this is the effect of mere exposure, which was discussed in Chapter 8 (Zajonc, 1968; Zajonc and Rajecki, 1969). Therefore, we need a model

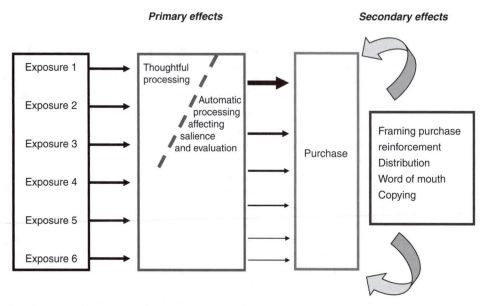

Figure 13.3   Primary and secondary responses to advertising

of advertising effect that describes the consequence of early exposures, as well as the continuing effect from what is often a large number of subsequent exposures. Figure 13.3
illustrates such a model in which advertising has two types of *primary* effect on an audience.

We suggest that the first few presentations of the ads may secure attention and may
sometimes modify thinking about a brand. It is likely that this thoughtful initial response
has a substantial sales effect when it occurs but that this response is not usually repeated
on later exposures when only the second primary effect occurs. This second primary
effect is produced by low-involvement automatic mechanisms that help to maintain brand
awareness. Mechanisms of this sort produce weak effects but may continue to work over
many repetitions. This dual-process account has some parallel in work on persuasion by
Fazio (1990) and Petty and Cacioppo (1985). Even if existing consumers of a brand do not
pay much attention to a new ad, they may still be affected by these passive low-involvement
processes.

Figure 13.3 also shows secondary processes that may occur later. These secondary
effects generally produce weak effects on sales but, because they are sustained over long
periods, may contribute substantially to the total sales benefit from advertising. Studies of
the connection between primary and secondary effects consistently show that a secondary
effect occurs only when there has been a primary effect on sales. Abraham and Lodish
(1990) reported that, if advertising tests do not show an effect after six months, they are
unlikely to show any effect later. Jones (1995a) found that no one-year ad effect was
observed if a short-term effect was not detected in the first seven days after exposure.
Riskey (1997) observed that longer-term effects in 12 ad campaigns occurred only when
there were shorter-term effects. Lodish et al. (1995b) found no delayed effects from ads

that were ineffective in their test year. This evidence shows that any secondary effect is an outcome of the primary effect; however, a primary effect does not guarantee a secondary effect because it could be countered by competitor communications.

The secondary effect could arise in a number of ways. There may be framing when ads modify thinking and produce a persistent change in the way that a product or brand is perceived. For example, ads may persuade customers to think of their phone as a replacement for their camera. Usually, the changes produced by advertising involve a more modest change in thinking that adjusts the positioning of the brand, rather than its categorization. For example, ads may establish that a car model is more economical than previously thought. These shifts in thinking, whether dealing with the category or the attribute, are likely to be first produced by the thoughtful primary processes rather than by automatic mechanisms.

Another process that could produce a secondary effect is *purchase reinforcement*. When the short-term effect of an ad is to induce extra purchase, this additional purchase experience may strengthen the propensity to buy the brand in the future. Purchase reinforcement could occur because, after buying a brand, it comes to mind more easily, as experience-based information is more easily recalled (Fazio, 1986; Fazio, Powell and Herr, 1983; Fazio and Zanna, 1981). Purchase reinforcement could also be based on knowledge of where to buy the brand – which store and the location in the store. One objection to the purchase reinforcement explanation for the secondary effect of advertising is that there can be no such effect in the case of consumer durables; people who have just bought a new cooker are not in the market for another one. Because of this, Givon and Horsky (1990) suggest that advertising induces a different effect for durables. They suggest that those who receive the advertising may become *potential* adopters and then may find out more about the product from others, particularly those who have already acquired it.

A third secondary effect occurs when advertising raises *distribution* and reduces *stock-outs* so that the product is more easily purchased. More efficient stocking may occur either because retailers anticipate demand and order more when they are advised about forthcoming ad campaigns, or because the extra demand from an ad campaign forces retailers to increase stock. Retailers may maintain the higher stock level after the advertising has finished, thus further boosting sales.

A fourth process is social influence, either as positive word of mouth when consumers recommend the product to others or as copying when publicly used products catch the attention of others, as with fashion goods. The idea that new usage and brand switching is often started by recommendation is undeniable. The role of social influence is implicit in the diffusion of new ideas and products (Chapter 5) and is often explicitly cited when people replace one brand with another. In Chapter 12, we reported evidence that word of mouth was increased by advertising (Bayus, 1985; Graham and Havlena, 2007) and discussed mechanisms that might bring this about.

How Long Do Advertising Effects Last?

Decay of advertising effect occurs when the extra propensity to buy declines over time. This decay process will affect both the primary and the secondary effects of advertising. Decay usually shows an exponential pattern, like that of radioactivity; the rate of decay is constant but, since it applies to a diminishing quantity, the change in the whole becomes less and less as it approaches some base level. Such patterns are usually described by their half-life, the period of time required for activity to decay to half its original level. Some of the decay may be due to forgetting and some to interference effects from competitive brands.

Short-Term Decay

To a large degree, the short-term decay relates to primary effects of advertising and the long-term decay to the secondary effects. Early studies estimated advertising half-lives on the assumption that there was a single process of ad decay. On this basis, Broadbent (1984) claimed that, for most brands, half-lives were in the region of 4–6 weeks and a meta-study of 70 brands by Clarke (1976) indicated half-lives in the range of 4–12 weeks. Subsequently, Broadbent and Fry (1995) suggested that ad decay had both short-term and long-term components and Roberts (1999) measured average short-term ad decay for frequently purchased brands. He found that this fitted an exponential curve with a half-life of 16 days. This means that, on average, an exposure loses 4.4 per cent of its sales effect each day and 72 per cent after 28 days. This rapid loss of effect has practical implications (see Exercise 13.2).

Exercise 13.2   Which day should you advertise?

Groceries have an uneven pattern of purchase over the week. Spending is heavier on Thursday, Friday and Saturday when compared with Sunday, Monday, Tuesday and Wednesday. The Nielsen figures are shown below.

Weekly supermarket sales by day of the week (percentage of total, Nielsen 2005):

Monday	Tuesday	Wednesday	Thursday	Friday	Saturday	Sunday
11.7	12.1	12.8	15.8	19.5	20.2	7.9

Which day should you advertise if the impact of your ads decays each day? What factors beside decay might affect your decision?

Long-Term Decay

Lodish and Lubetkin (1992) used IRI data on upweight tests to measure the persistence of ad-induced sales gains. In their study, 44 brands received 50–100 per cent extra advertising during a test year and sales of these brands were then followed for the ensuing two years when ad spending had returned to normal. These were compared with a control condition where there was no uplift in the test year. Approximately half of the brands showed a sales increase in the test year. Lodish and Lubetkin analyzed the extra sales for these brands and compared results with consumers who had not received extra advertising. Table 13.1 shows the extra sales in the upweight group over three years and shows that the extra sales that occurred in years 2 and 3, after the upweight had finished, were roughly equal

Table 13.1 Percentage gain in upweight group (adapted from Lodish and Lubetkin, 1992)

	Test year %	Year 2 %	Year 3 %
Sales gain	22	14	7

to the extra sales during the test year. This work was criticized for excluding cases where there was no sales impact from increased weight since these cases might have shown a response in later years but Lodish et al. (1995b) checked and found that there was no such later response.

Roberts (2000) divided customers into those who had – and those who had not – been exposed to advertising for grocery brands in the previous 28 days. His analysis took account of weight of viewing, concurrent promotions and brand size. He found that repeat purchase of the brand in the subsequent 12 months was higher if the ad had been seen. Roberts assessed the extra sales in the year as 5.6 times the short-term increase in sales over a month. When these extra sales are taken into account, advertising will often pay off over a year. Hanssens, Parsons and Schultz (2001) also find evidence of a substantial long-term ad effect.

Figure 13.4 shows both short- and long-term effects of advertising. In Figure 13.4, a burst of advertising produces a short-term primary effect. The long-term secondary effect is based on the extra sales generated by the short-term effect; it has a much smaller

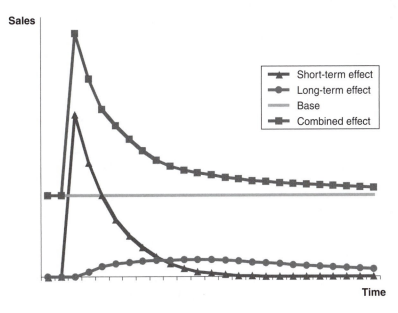

Figure 13.4 How primary and secondary effects of advertising may combine with base sales

amplitude but lasts much longer. The combined effect aggregates the base sales, long-term and short-term effects. Hanssens (2011) has reviewed evidence on the long-term effect of advertising.

SECTION 4: SPECIFIC EFFECTS

Segments

Advertising will have greater effect on some customer segments than others. Identifying such segments helps us to understand how advertising works and, more practically, how it may be profitably used.

Loyalty

Raj (1982) found the maximum sales response to advertising occurred among those with a share-of-category requirement (SCR) loyalty of 50–70 per cent. Raj found that the purchases of other brands were not much affected when the focal brand gained – the extra sales in the 50–70 per cent loyalty group came mainly from an increase in category volume. Tellis (1988a) studied one mature product category and also found that ads had more sales effect on loyal buyers with an SCR greater than 50 per cent. Those who had not bought the brand before showed only a small volume sales response to the advertising compared with loyal buyers.

Roberts (1999) looked at percentage increase rather than volume increase. He found that, on average, the low-loyalty segment (SCR less than 10 per cent) showed the greatest percentage increase and the high-loyalty group (SCR more than 50 per cent) the least. But the higher base purchase rate of the high-loyalty buyers means that the absolute volume increase among members of this group is large compared to the low-loyalty buyers. Baldinger and Rubinson (1996) found that there were three times as many buyers with an SCR of less than 10 per cent compared with buyers with an SCR greater than 10 per cent. Although the extra volume per individual low-loyalty buyer is small, the aggregate volume gain from the large segment of low-loyalty buyers can be very substantial when compared with the aggregate volume gain from the smaller number of buyers in the high-loyalty segment. Using the segment sizes found by Baldinger and Rubison, we calculate that the low-loyalty segment (SCR less than 10 per cent) gave a larger increment in volume than that from all the rest of the buyers.

This evidence helps us to understand the rather different roles performed by one-to-one direct marketing and media advertising. Media advertising provides access to the large number of low-loyalty buyers and non-buyers that can provide a large total of extra sales. Also, some low-loyalty buyers may evolve into high-loyalty buyers, and advertising can start this process. In direct marketing, it pays to focus on those with high initial loyalty if an approach to a buyer is expensive. If costs are low, this constraint does not apply. A sound marketing strategy needs to assess the likely outcomes and costs of both advertising and direct marketing before deciding on the appropriate mix.

Heavy and Light Buyers

Some of the previous discussion about low and high loyalty segments also applies to light and heavy buyers. In Chapter 4, we saw that the distribution of buyers' purchase frequencies follows a Gamma distribution. This means that there are many more light than heavy buyers so that the small volume changes made by many light buyers (and non-buyers) can aggregate to a much bigger increase in sales than the large volume changes made by few heavy buyers. This is what we see: sales growth comes principally from the light buyer/ non-buyer segment. Advertising can reach light buyers and non-buyers and is usually involved when a brand gains share. The parallel with high and low loyalty is not exact, as some light buyers are 100 per cent loyal – all those who buy only once, for example, must be 100 per cent loyal by definition. Nonetheless, a similar argument applies to both situations; sales growth principally comes from those who are not yet heavy buyers of the brand.

Heavy and Light Television Viewers

Heavy TV viewers have been found to be relatively less responsive to television ads. Roberts (1999) divided households into the 40 per cent with the lightest viewing pattern and the rest. When he compared these light and heavy viewers, the light viewers had over twice the sales response of the heavy viewers. Roberts suggests that the greater responsiveness of light viewers is a 'share-of-mind' effect, i.e. the light viewer experiences less clutter so that each ad has more effect. Light viewers tend to watch during the peak evening period – it is their extra viewing that makes it a peak period. Roberts compared off-peak-only and peak-only viewers and showed that peak-only viewers had three times the sales response of the off-peak-only viewers.

Do Some Brands Get More from Their Advertising?

Big Brands

Brands are big mainly because they have more buyers rather than because each buyer buys them more frequently (Ehrenberg, 1988). If the sales response from advertising depends mainly on the number of buyers, big brands will get more total volume uplift from an ad campaign, other things being equal. But the evidence often shows stronger gains for smaller brands. Riskey (1997) found that ads for small brands delivered greater volume increases than ads for big brands and suggested that this may be because the small-brand ads tend to report some advance in the brand and these 'newsy' ads were more effective. Sometimes, the buyer base of the small brand is actually quite large, even though purchases in a given period are relatively low; long-established small brands can have a large number of past buyers who may be activated by advertising. Another factor against big brands is that they may have reached a ceiling where there are few potential recruits; when this applies, advertising serves to retain buyers rather than to increase sales. In addition, the advertising of small brands is often infrequent and this may make it more effective when it does occur. An example of a small brand that benefited from advertising is the Co-operative Society (Broadbent, 2000). Here, an old and relatively small store brand, which was very well known and had not advertised for some time, did very well when it returned to advertising.

In summary, although big brands usually have more buyers, a small brand may get a good response from advertising if it has not advertised for a while, has something new to say and has a long history.

New Brands

New brands are often introduced by advertising. Unless the new brand can be directly marketed, it must use media advertising to let potential customers know that it exists. The responsiveness to ads, measured as advertising elasticity, is high for new brands. Advertising elasticity is the ratio of the proportional increase in sales to proportional increase in advertising. Lodish et al. (1995a) found an elasticity of 0.05 for established brands and 0.26 for new brands. The novelty of a product may help it to gain attention but, even though a new brand shows a high elasticity, the gain in volume can still be very modest because there are few base sales. Furthermore, buyers of new brands may not stay. If they are willing to try new brands, they may later move to try yet newer brands.

Elastic Categories

In some fields the boundaries between categories have little meaning to buyers. Consumers may replace Coca-Cola with beer and the cinema may replace the theatre. Thus, an increase in consumption of one brand may occur at the expense of other brands in the category *or* brands in another category. As a result, the whole category can grow and the sales of individual brands may be more responsive to advertising. Because of gains from other categories, food and drink brands are particularly responsive to advertising in comparison to toiletries and cleaners, where brands can usually only gain at the expense of other brands in the category. Supporting this effect, unpublished Unilever research shows a greater ad response among food and drink categories than among cleaning and toiletry products. However, the greater ad response of food and drink brands has its reverse side since, in these fields, gains in sales can be whittled away by same-category competitors *and* by brands in other categories.

SECTION 5: ADVERTISING, NEW MEDIA AND CHANGES TO TELEVISION VIEWING

The growth of the Internet is changing the face of advertising. Blogs, message boards, emails and personal websites allow large numbers of people to put ideas into the public domain with great ease. As a result, an increasing proportion of consumer choice is directed by consumer-generated media, over which suppliers have limited control. Because the Internet is used so widely, more and more of the ad budget goes to this medium. Much of this spending is related to search engines because of the exceptional precision of search-related advertising, and because the act of search pre-qualifies a customer as more likely to buy. Other major types of Internet activity include expenditure via display or banner ads and the use of websites, social media and other portals to promote customer engagement and interaction with the brand.

Digital marketing involves other new media as well. Smartphones offer search and web browsing, with associated opportunities for advertising. In addition, the geo-location of smartphones allows ads to be delivered in locations where consumption can occur. Smartphone apps enable companies to interact with customers through micro-website, games and other applications. *Advertising Works 20* (Snow, 2011) provides the example of a homeless charity, Depaul UK, developing the iHobo game app, allowing users to look after a virtual hobo and providing the opportunity to donate in-game. Their modest £6,000 budget was extended by seeding the app to two technology bloggers for a viral campaign, leading to 600,000 downloads, 95 times as many donors as in previous campaigns, and 1,021 young people added to their donor database.

The character of ads on new media may have altered audience expectations. The Internet can present material that would not be aired on commercial television. For example, the Trojan Games website shows risqué videos of sham sexual athleticism with voice-overs that are reminiscent of a darts match commentary. Visitors to the website who are amused can easily pass on the website link to others. As a result, people have become aware of the Trojan brand of condoms at a very low cost. A further case is a video of a suicide bomber detonating a bomb in a Volkswagen Polo. The bomb explodes but the Polo, 'small but tough', contains the explosion without breaking up. This ad, which may still be found on YouTube, was not made for Volkswagen but it probably enhanced the Polo's reputation for toughness.

Blogs and discussion sites have much of the character of personal communication, even though the communicators and receivers are usually not personally acquainted. Generally, comment on the Internet is treated as an electronic form of word of mouth (eWOM), which may be passed on from consumer to consumer, either as face-to-face WOM or by giving the link in emails. This emphasis on WOM seems to have refocused ad agencies on producing copy that people talk about. In the USA, some Burger King ads have been deliberately bizarre so that people discuss them. Public relations has always been concerned with creating comment, either between consumers or in editorial content. One example of this was the launch of the telephone directory inquiry number 118 118 in the UK. To emphasize the number, twins were used in the advertising. The twins were portrayed as runners and one technique was for them to run through public areas so that people saw them and talked about them to their friends. This case is reported by Hoad (2005).

Companies such as Facebook and Twitter now actively promote WOM through sharing functions within their online social networks. By seeking to make recommendation easy and relevant, they may increase the amount of WOM over time. More importantly, these companies create a forum for social engagement which they control, enabling them to inject advertising messages into personal interactions.

Exercise 13.3   Where are new media going to take us?

How is advertising on the Web and mobile phones going to develop? How is this going to affect other forms of advertising?

Television, as an advertising medium, faces competition from other media; with the growth of online/mobile media; there is fragmentation due to satellite and terrestrial digital television offering much more channel choice; and ad effectiveness may decline as viewers with digital video recorders zip through ads. Surprisingly, TV advertising has remained relatively unaffected. Average channel shares have dropped, due to the larger number of channels, but total viewing has not declined and viewer behaviour follows the same patterns it has for decades (Sharp, Beal and Collins, 2009). Nor has TV ad effectiveness declined – if anything it has increased (Rubinson, 2009). In addition, it has been found that fast-forwarding of ads does not seem to affect ad recall (du Plessis, 2009), perhaps because fast-forwarding requires that the viewer attend to the ad break, instead of engaging in ad avoidance behaviour.

Fulgoni and Morn (2009) examined how Internet advertising changed behaviour. Despite low click-through rates, they found that mere exposure to display ads and search marketing (such as Google Adwords) increased site visits, search behaviour and both online and offline purchasing. For now, Internet advertising seems to have simply added an additional medium that operates in a familiar manner.

SUMMARY

Commercial advertising targets behaviours that affect profit, such as purchase and rental. Social advertising may target behaviours such as smoking and dangerous driving. The benefit from commercial advertising may be via more sales, greater margins or lower costs. Ad campaigns usually have quite small effects on sales but, in large markets, the payback on advertising can be many times the expenditure.

We now understand better how individuals react to different frequencies and concentrations of advertising. Extra exposures tend to give increasing sales effects when these exposures are concentrated into a short interval; otherwise, extra ads have a diminishing effect. This is probably because concentrated exposures give better breakthrough. This evidence suggests that a schedule of short concentrated periods of advertising (pulsing) is the most effective.

We present a model in which ads may have two sorts of primary effect: one is thoughtful, and the effect is quite strong, if it occurs; the other is automatic and weak. Thoughtful processes occur early in the sequence of ad exposures if they occur at all; automatic mechanisms can occur at each exposure so ads can continue to have some effect for a long period.

When primary effects occur, there may be consequential secondary effects that include framing (persisting change in thinking about the brand), purchase reinforcement (later purchase is facilitated by the occurrence of the earlier purchase), better distribution, word of mouth and copying.

Corresponding to these primary and secondary effects, sales appear to have short-term and long-term decay rates. In one study, the short-term component had an average half-life of 16 days. The long-term component can persist for a year or more after the advertising has finished.

While low-loyalty and light buyers show less individual volume response to advertising, the large number of these buyers ensures that these segments provide more sales gain. Advertising is effective at reaching light and non-buyers and contrasts with direct marketing, which is better when there is a need to focus on the smaller number of high-loyalty or heavy buyers. In their reaction to television advertising, light viewers are more responsive than heavy viewers.

While the rise of new media and changes to television viewing present superficial challenges to traditional advertising methods, research shows that TV advertising continues to be effective and Internet advertising generates the kinds of offline sales lifts that have been traditionally expected from other media. However, the growth of recommendation on the Internet may create greater changes over time.

Additional Resources

You should read at least one of the cases in the *Advertising Works* series (or the equivalent in another country). These cases indicate the concerns of ad agencies and the difficulties of measuring advertising effects. If you are more interested in the decisions that have to be made in ad agencies, one textbook that is based on advertising research is Rossiter and Bellman (2005). If you are interested in Armstrong's rules, you can read his book or visit his site www.advertisingprinciples.com, where the rules can be downloaded free of charge.

Notes

1 The Advertising Federation of Australia (AFA) supports the publication *Effective Advertising* and, in the UK, the Institute of Practitioners in Advertising (IPA) supports *Advertising Works*. These publications are dedicated to showing how competent and creative advertising can bring returns to the advertiser.
2 There is more agreement between researchers and practitioners on ad frequency when the advertising or product is new or complex. It is widely held that a linear or S-shaped response may be expected under these conditions. Roberts (1996) found that the response was effectively linear in five out of seven cases where the brand was new or relaunched.

References

Aaker, D.A. (1991) *Managing Brand Equity: Capitalizing on the Value of a Brand Name*, New York: The Free Press.

Aaker, D.A. and Keller, K.L. (1990) Consumer evaluations of brand extensions, *Journal of Marketing*, 54(1), 27–41.

Aaker, J.L. and Williams, P. (1998) Empathy versus pride: the influence of emotional appeals across cultures, *Journal of Consumer Research*, 25(3), 241–261.

Abraham, M.M. and Lodish, L.M. (1990) Getting the most out of advertising and promotion, *Harvard Business Review*, 68(3), 50–60.

Adams, H.F. (1916) *Advertising and its Mental Laws*, New York: Macmillan.

AGB (1992) Revealed: the nation's shopping habits, *SuperMarketing*, 14 August.

Ahluwalia, R. (2002) How prevalent is the negativity effect in consumer environments?, *Journal of Consumer Research*, 29 (September), 270–279.

Ailawadi, K.L. and Neslin, S.A. (1998) The effect of promotion on consumption: buying more and consuming it faster, *Journal of Marketing Research*, 35(3), 390–398.

Ailawadi, K.L., Gedenk, K., Lutzky, C. and Neslin, S.A. (2007) Decomposition of the sales impact of promotion-induced stockpiling, *Journal of Marketing Research*, 44(3), 450–467.

Ailon, G. (2008) Mirror, mirror on the wall: culture's consequences in a value test of its own design, *Academy of Management Review*, 33(4), 885–904.

Ajzen, I. (1971) Attitude vs. normative messages: an investigation of the differential effects of persuasive communications on behavior, *Sociometry*, 34(2), 263–280.

Ajzen, I. (1985) From intentions to actions: a theory of planned behavior. In J. Kuhl and J. Beckmann (eds), *Action-Control: From Cognition to Behavior*, Heidelberg: Springer, 22–39.

Ajzen, I. (1991) The theory of planned behavior. In E.A. Locke (ed.), *Organizational Behavior and Human Decision Processes*, 50, 179–211.

Ajzen, I. (2002) Perceived behavioral control, self-efficacy, locus of control and the theory of planned behavior, *Journal of Applied Social Psychology*, 32(4), 665–683.

Ajzen, I. and Driver, B.L. (1992) Application of the theory of planned behavior to leisure choice, *Journal of Leisure Research*, 24(3), 207–224.

Ajzen, I. and Fishbein, M. (1969) The prediction of behavioral intentions in a choice situation, *Journal of Experimental Social Psychology*, 5(4), 400–416.

Ajzen, I. and Fishbein, M. (1972) Attitudinal and normative beliefs as factors influencing behavioral intentions, *Journal of Personality and Social Psychology*, 21(1), 1–9.

Ajzen, I. and Fishbein, M. (1977) Attitude–behavior relations: a theoretical analysis and review of empirical research, *Psychological Bulletin*, 84, 888–918.

Ajzen, I. and Fishbein, M. (1980) *Understanding Attitudes and Predicting Social Behavior*, Englewood Cliffs, NJ: Prentice-Hall.

Aksoy, L., Cooil, B., Groening, C., Keiningham, T. and Yalçın, A. (2008) The long-term stock market valuation of customer satisfaction, *Journal of Marketing*, 72(4), 105–122.

Ali, M. (1977) Probability and utility estimates for racetrack bettors, *Journal of Political Economy*, 85, 803–815.

Allais, M. (1953) Le comportement de l'homme rationel devant le risque: critique des postulats et axiomes de l'ecole americaine, *Econometrica*, 21(4), 503–546.

Allenby, G.M. and Ginter, J.L. (1995) The effects of in-store displays and feature advertising on consideration sets, *International Journal of Research in Marketing*, 12(1), 67–80.

Allport, G.W. (1935) Attitudes. In C. Murchison, (ed.), *A Handbook of Social Psychology*, Worcester, MA: Clark University Press, 798–844.

Allport, G.W. and Postman, L. (1947) *The Psychology of Rumor*, New York: Holt, Rinehart and Winston.

Ambler, T. and Broadbent, S. (2000) A dialogue on advertising effectiveness and efficiency, *Admap*, July/August, 29–31.

Anderson, E.I. and Simester, D. (2003) Effects of $9 price endings on retail sales: evidence from field experiments, *Qualitative Marketing and Economics*, 1(1), 93–110.

Anderson, E.W. and Mansi, S.A. (2009) Does customer satisfaction matter to investors? Findings from the bond market, *Journal of Marketing Research*, 46(5), 703–714.

Anderson, E.W. and Mittal, V. (2000) Strengthening the satisfaction–profit chain, *Journal of Service Research*, 3(2), 107–120.

Anderson, E.W., Fornell, C. and Lehmann, D.R. (1994) Customer satisfaction, market share and profitability, *Journal of Marketing*, 58(3), 53–66.

Anderson, E.W., Fornell, C. and Mazvancheryl, S.K. (2004) Customer satisfaction and shareholder value, *Journal of Marketing*, 68(4), 172–185.

Anderson, N.H. (1965) Averaging versus adding as a stimulus-combination rule in impression formation, *Journal of Experimental Psychology*, 70, 394–400.

Andreasen, A.R. (1985) Consumer responses to dissatisfaction in loose monopolies, *Journal of Consumer Research*, 12(2), 135–141.

Andreasen, A.R. (1988) Consumer complaints and redress: what we know and what we don't know. In E.S. Maynes (ed.), *The Frontier of Research in Consumer Interest*, Columbia: University of Columbia and American Council of Consumer Interest, 675–721.

Andreasen, A.R. and Manning, J. (1990) The dissatisfaction and complaining behavior of vulnerable consumers, *Journal of Consumer Satisfaction, Dissatisfaction and Complaining Behavior*, 3, 12–20.

Anglin, L.K., Stuenkel, J.K. and Lepisto, L.R. (1994) The effect of stress on price sensitivity and comparison shopping. In C.T. Allen and D.R. John (eds), *Advances in Consumer Research*, 21, 126–131.

Arce, M. and Cebollada, J. (2006) The role of loyalty in online and offline shopping behaviour: an empirical application to the grocery industry, *Conference Proceedings of the European Marketing Academy*, Athens.

Areni, C.S. and Kim, D. (1993) The influence of background music on shopping behavior: classical versus top-forty music in a wine store. In L. McAlister and M.L. Rothschild (eds), *Advances in Consumer Research*, 20, 336–340.

Armitage, C.J. and Conner, M. (2001) Efficacy of the theory of planned behaviour: a meta-analytic review, *British Journal of Social Psychology*, 40(4), 471–499.

Armstrong, J.S. (1985) *Long-range Forecasting: From Crystal Ball to Computer*, 2nd edition, London: Wiley.

Armstrong, J.S. (2010) *Persuasive Advertising: Evidence-Based Principles*, Basingstoke: Palgrave Macmillan.

Arndt, J. (1967) The role of product-related conversations in the diffusion of a new product, *Journal of Marketing Research*, 4 (August), 291–295.

Arthur, C. (1992) Fifteen million Americans are shopping addicts, *American Demographics*, March, 14–15.

Asugman, G. (1998) An evaluation of negative word-of-mouth research for extensions, *European Advances in Consumer Research*, 3, 70–75.

Ataman, M.B., Van Heerde, H.J. and Mela, C.F. (2010) The long-term effect of marketing strategy on brand sales, *Journal of Marketing Research*, 47(5), 866–882.

Babacus, E. and Boller, G.W. (1992) An empirical assessment of the SERVQUAL scale, *Journal of Business Research*, 24(3), 253–268.

Babin, B.J., Hardesty, D.M. and Suter, T.A. (2003) Color and shopping intentions: the intervening effect of price fairness and perceived affect, *Journal of Business Research*, 56(7), 541–551.

Bagozzi, R.P. (1981) Attitudes, intentions and behavior: a test of some key hypotheses, *Journal of Personality and Social Psychology*, 41(4), 607–627.

Bagozzi, R.P. (1984) Expectancy-value attitude models: an analysis of critical measurement issues, *International Journal of Research in Marketing*, 1(4), 295–310.

Bagozzi, R.P. (1992) The self-regulation of attitudes, intentions and behaviors, *Social Psychology Quarterly*, 55, 178–204.

Bagozzi, R.P. and Kimmel, S.K. (1995) A comparison of leading theories for the prediction of goal-directed behaviours, *British Journal of Social Psychology*, 34(4), 437–461.

Baker, C. (1993) *Advertising Works 7*, Henley-on-Thames: Institute of Practitioners in Advertising, NTC Publications.

Baker, C. (1995) *Advertising Works 8*, Henley-on-Thames: Institute of Practitioners in Advertising, NTC Publications.

Baldinger, A.L. and Rubinson, J. (1996) Brand loyalty: the link between attitude and behavior, *Journal of Advertising Research*, 36(6), 22–34.

Baldwin, M.W. and Holmes, J.G. (1987) Salient private audiences and awareness of the self, *Journal of Personality and Social Psychology*, 52(6), 1087–1098.

Balter, D. and Butman, J. (2005) *Grapevine: The New Art of Word-of-Mouth Marketing*, New York: Penguin Portfolio.

Bansal, H.S. and Voyer, P.A. (2000) Word-of-mouth processes within a services purchase decision context, *Journal of Service Research*, 2(3), 166–177.

Bargh, J.A., Chaiken, S., Govender, R. and Pratto, F. (1992) The generality of the automatic activation effect, *Journal of Personality and Social Psychology*, 62(6), 893–912.

Bartlett, F.C. (1932) *Remembering*, Cambridge: Cambridge University Press.

Bass, F.M. (1969) A new product growth model for consumer durables, *Management Science*, 15(5), 215–227.

Bass, F.M. (1995) Empirical generalizations and marketing science: a personal view, *Marketing Science*, 14(3), Part 2 of 2, G6–G18.

Bass, F.M., Jeuland, A.P. and Wright, G.P. (1976) Equilibrium stochastic choice and market penetration theories: derivation and comparisons, *Management Science*, 22(10), 1051–1063.

Bass, F.M., Givon, M.M., Kalwani, M.U., Reibstein, D. and Wright, G.P. (1984) An investigation into the order of the brand choice process, *Marketing Science*, 3(4), 267–287.

Batra, R., Lenk, P. and Wedel, M. (2010) Brand extensions strategy planning: empirical estimation of brand-category personality, *Journal of Marketing Research*, 47(2), 335–347.

Bayus, B.L. (1985) Word of mouth: the indirect effects of marketing efforts, *Journal of Advertising Research*, 25(3), 31–39.

Bayus, B.L. (1991) The consumer durable replacement buyer, *Journal of Marketing*, 55 (January), 42–51.

Beales, H.J., Mazis, M.B., Salop, S.C. and Staelin, R. (1981) Consumer search and public policy, *Journal of Consumer Research*, 8(1), 11–22.

Beatty, S.E. and Smith, S.M. (1987) External search effort: an investigation across several product categories, *Journal of Consumer Research*, 14(1), 83–95.

Bellizzi, J.A., Crowley, A.E. and Hasty, R.E. (1983) The effects of color in store design, *Journal of Retailing*, 59(1), 21–44.

Bemmaor, A.L. (1995) Predicting behavior from intention-to-buy measures: the parametric case, *Journal of Marketing Research*, 32(2), 176–191.

Benartzi, S. and Thaler, R.H. (1995) Myopic loss aversion and the equity premium puzzle, *Quarterly Journal of Economics*, 110(1), 73–92. Reprinted in Kahneman, D. and Tversky, A. (2000) *Choices, Values, and Frames*, New York: Russell Sage Foundation, Cambridge University Press, 301–316.

Bernoulli, D. (1738) Specimen Theoriae Novae de Mensura Sortis. *Comentarii Academiae Scientiarum Imperiales Petropolitanae*, 5, 175–92. Translated by L. Sommer in *Econometrica*, 1954, 22(1), 23–36.

Benterud, T. and Stø, E. (1993) TV shopping in Scandinavia: consumer satisfaction, dissatisfaction and complaining behavior, *Journal of Consumer Satisfaction, Dissatisfaction and Complaining Behavior*, 6, 196–203.

Bentler, P.M. and Speckart, G. (1979) Models of attitude–behavior relations, *Psychological Review*, 86(5), 452–464.

Bentler, P.M. and Speckart, G. (1981) Attitudes 'cause' behaviors: a structural equation analysis, *Journal of Personality and Social Psychology*, 40, 226–38.

Berger, J. and Iyengar, R. (2012) How interest shapes word of mouth over different channels, http://rady.ucsd.edu/faculty/seminars/papers/berger.pdf.

Berger, J. and Schwartz, E.M. (2011) What drives immediate and ongoing word of mouth?, *Journal of Marketing Research*, 48(October), 869–880.

Berlyne, D.E. (1965) *Structure and Direction in Thinking*, London: Wiley.

Berlyne, D.E. and McDonnell, P. (1965) Effects of stimulus complexity and incongruity on duration of EEG desynchronisation, *Electroencephalography and Clinical Neurophysiology*, 18(2), 156–161.

Berry, L.L. (1983) Relationship marketing. In L.L. Berry, G.L. Shostack, and G.D. Upah (eds), *Emerging Perspectives on Service Marketing*, Chicago: American Marketing Association, 25–28.

Bettman, J.R. (1979) *An Information Processing Theory of Consumer Choice*, Reading, MA: Addison-Wesley.

Biel, A.L. (1991) The brandscape: converting brand image into equity, *Admap*, Oct, 41–46.

Bijmolt, T.H.A., van Heerde, H.J. and Pieters, R.G.M. (2005) New empirical generalizations on the determinants of price elasticity, *Journal of Marketing Research*, 42(2), 141–156.

Binet, L. and Field, P. (2009) Empirical generalizations about advertising campaign success, *Journal of Advertising Research*, 49(2), 130–133.

Bird, M. and Ehrenburg, A.S.C. (1966) Intentions-to-buy and claimed brand usage, *Operational Research Quarterly*, 17, 27–46.

Bitner, M.J., Booms, B.H. and Tetreault, M.S. (1990) The service encounter: diagnosing favourable and unfavourable incidents, *Journal of Marketing*, 54(1), 71–84.

Black, D.W. (2007) A review of compulsive buying disorder, *World Psychiatry*, 6(1), 14–18.

Blair, M.H. and Rabuck, M.J. (1998) Advertising wearin and wearout: ten years later – more empirical evidence and successful practice, *Journal of Advertising Research*, 38(5), 7–18.

Blattberg, R.C., Briesch, R. and Fox, E.J. (1995) How promotions work, *Marketing Science*, 14(3), G122–G132.

Bogomolova, S. and Romaniuk, J. (2009) Brand defection in a business-to-business financial service, *Journal of Business Research*, 62(3), 291–296.

Bolton, L.E., Warlop, L. and Alba, J.W. (2003) Consumer perceptions of price (un)fairness, *Journal of Consumer Research*, 29(4), 474–491.

Bolton, R.N. (1989) The relationship between market characteristics and promotional price elasticities, *Marketing Science*, 8(2), 153–169.

Bolton, R.N. (1998) A dynamic model of the duration of the customer's relationship with a continuous service provider: the role of satisfaction, *Marketing Science*, 17(1), 45–65.

Bornemann, T. and Homburg, C. (2011) Psychological distance and the dual role of price, *Journal of Consumer Research*, 38(3), 490–504.

Bosmans, A. (2007) Scents and sensibility: when do (in)congruent ambient scents influence product evaluations?, *Journal of Marketing*, 71(3), 32–43.

Bottomley, P.A. and Holden, S.J.S. (2001) Do we really know how consumers evaluate brand extensions? Empirical generalizations based on secondary analysis of eight studies, *Journal of Marketing Research*, 38(4), 494–500.

Briesch, R.A., Krishnamurthy, L., Mazumdar, T. and Raj, S.P. (1997) A comparative analysis of reference price models, *Journal of Consumer Research*, 24 (September), 202–214.

Brislin, R.W. (1970) Back-translation for cross-cultural research, *Journal of Cross-Cultural Psychology*, 1(3), 185–216.

Broadbent, S. (1984) Modelling with Adstock, *Journal of the Market Research Society*, 26(4), 295–312.

Broadbent, S. (1989) *The Advertising Budget: The Advertiser's Guide to Budget Determination*, Henley-on-Thames: NTC Publications.

Broadbent, S. (1998) Effective frequency: there and back, *Admap*, May, 34–38.

Broadbent, S. and Fry, T. (1995) Adstock modelling for the long term, *Journal of the Market Research Society*, 37(4), 385–403.

Broadbent, T. (2000) *Advertising Works 11*, Henley-on-Thames: Institute of Practitioners in Advertising, World Advertising Research Centre (WARC).

Brown, G. (1986) Monitoring advertising performance, *Admap*, 22(3), 151–153.

Brown, G.H. (1953) Brand loyalty, *Advertising Age*, 24, 28–35. Reproduced in A.S.C. Ehrenberg and F.G. Pyatt (eds), *Consumer Behaviour*, Harmondsworth: Penguin Books, 28–35.

Brown, J.J. and Reingen, P.H. (1987) Social ties and word-of-mouth referral behavior, *Journal of Consumer Research*, 14(3), 350–362.

Brown, J.R. and Dant, R.P. (2009) The theoretical domains of retailing research: a retrospective, *Journal of Retailing*, 85(2), 113–128.

Buday, T. (1989) Capitalizing on brand extensions: lessons of success and failure, *Journal of Consumer Marketing*, 6(4), 27–30.

Budd, R. (1986) Predicting cigarette use: the need to incorporate measures of salience in the theory of reasoned action, *Journal of Applied Social Psychology*, 16, 663–685.

Burke, R.R. and Srull, T.K. (1988) Competitive interference and consumer memory for advertising, *Journal of Consumer Research*, 15(1), 55–68.

Burnkrant, R.E. and Unnava, H.R. (1987) Effects of variation in message execution on the learning of repeated brand information. In M. Wallendorf and P. Anderson (eds), *Advances in Consumer Research*, 14, 173–176.

Burns, D.J. and Perkins, D. (1996) Accounts in post-purchase behavior: excuses, justifications and meta-accounts, *Journal of Satisfaction, Dissatisfaction and Complaining Behavior*, 9, 144–157.

Buttle, F. (1996) SERVQUAL: review, critique, research agenda, *European Journal of Marketing*, 30(1), 8–32.

Buzzell, R.D. and Gale, B.T. (1987) *The PIMS Principles: Linking Strategy to Performance*, New York: The Free Press.

Buzzell, R.D., Quelch, J.A. and Salmon, W.J. (1991) The costly bargain of trade promotion, *Harvard Business Review*, 68(2), 141–149.

Camerer, C.F. (2000) Prospect theory in the wild. In D. Kahneman and A. Tversky (eds), *Choices, Values and Frames*, New York: Russell Sage Foundation, 288–300.

Campbell, M.C. (1999) Perceptions of price unfairness: antecedents and consequences, *Journal of Marketing Research*, 36(2), 187–199.

Caplovitz, D. (1967) *The Poor Pay More*, 2nd edition, New York: The Free Press.

Cardozo, R.N. (1965) An experimental study of consumer effort, expectation and satisfaction, *Journal of Marketing Research*, 2(3), 244–249.

Carl, W.J. (2008) The role of disclosure in organized word-of-mouth marketing programs, *Journal of Marketing Communications*, 14(3), 225–241.

Carman, J.M. (1970) Correlates of brand loyalty: some positive results, *Journal of Marketing Research*, 7(1), 67–76.

Carman, J.M. (1990) Consumer perceptions of service quality: an assessment of the SERVQUAL dimensions, *Journal of Retailing*, 66(1), 33–55.

Castensen, L.L., Isaakowitz, D.M. and Charles, S.T. (1999) Taking time seriously: a theory of socioemotional selectivity, *American Psychologist*, 54(March), 165–181.

Chan, H., Wan, L.C. and Sin, L.M. (2009) The contrasting effects of culture on consumer tolerance: interpersonal face and impersonal fate, *Journal of Consumer Research*, 36(2), 292–304.

Chandon, P., Wansink, B. and Laurent, G. (2000) A benefit congruency framework of sales promotion effectiveness, *Journal of Marketing*, 64(4), 65–81.

Chandon, P., Morwitz, V.G. and Reinartz, W.J. (2005) Do intentions really predict behavior? Self-generated validity effects in survey research, *Journal of Marketing*, 69(2), 1–14.

Chang-Hyeon, J., Arentze, T. and Timmermans, H. (2006) Characterisation and comparison of gender-specific utility functions of shopping duration episodes, *Journal of Retailing and Consumer Services*, 13(4), 249–259.

Channon, C. (1985) *Advertising Works 3*, London: Holt, Rinehart and Winston.

Charlton, P. (1973) A review of shop loyalty, *Journal of the Market Research Society*, 15(1), 35–51.

Chatfield, C. and Goodhardt, G. (1975) Results concerning brand choice, *Journal of Marketing Research*, 12(1), 110–113.

Chevalier, J.A. and Mayzlin, D. (2003) The effect of word of mouth on sales: online book reviews, *Journal of Marketing Research*, 44(3), 345–354.

Chintagunta, P.K. (1993) Investigating purchase incidence, brand choice and purchase quantity decisions of households, *Marketing Science*, 12(2), 184–208.

Christaller, W. (1933) *Central Places in Southern Germany*, translated by C.W. Baskin (1966), Englewood Cliffs, NJ: Prentice-Hall.

Christiansen, T. and Tax, S.S. (2000) Measuring word of mouth: the questions of who and when?, *Journal of Marketing Communications*, 6, 185–199.

Churcher, P.B. and Lawton, J.H. (1987) Predation by domestic cats in an English village, *Journal of Zoology*, 212, 439–455.

Churchill, G.A. Jr and Surprenant, C. (1982) An investigation into the determinants of customer satisfaction, *Journal of Marketing Research*, 19(4), 491–504.

Churchill, H. (1942) How to measure brand loyalty, *Advertising and Selling*, 35(24), 34–50.

Clare, J.E. and Kiser, C.V. (1951) Preference for children of a given sex in relation to fertility. In P.K. Whelpton and C.V. Kiser (eds), *Social and Psychological Factors Affecting Fertility*, New York: Milbank Memorial Fund, 621–673.

Clarke, D.G. (1976) Econometric measurement of the duration of advertising effect on sales, *Journal of Marketing Research*, 13(4), 345–357.

Clemmer, E.C. and Schneider, B. (1989) Towards understanding and controlling dissatisfaction with waiting during peak demand times. In M.J. Bitner and L.A. Crosby (eds), *Designing a Winning Service Strategy*, Chicago: American Marketing Association, 87–91.

Cole, C., Laurent, G., Drolet A., Ebert, J., Gutchess, A., Lambert-Pandraud, R., Mullet, E., Norton, M.I. and Peters, E. (2008) Decision making and brand choice by older consumers, *Marketing Letters*, 19(3/4), 355–365.

Cole, C.A. and Houston, M.J. (1987) Encoding and media effects on consumer learning deficiencies in the elderly, *Journal of Marketing Research*, 24(1), 55–63.

Coleman, J., Katz, E. and Menzel, H. (1957) The diffusion of an innovation among physicians, *Sociometry*, 20(4), 253–270.

Collins, M. (1971) Market segmentation – the realities of buyer behaviour, *Journal of the Market Research Society*, 13(3), 146–157.

Collins, M., Beal, V. and Barwise, P. (2003) Channel use among multi-channel viewers: patterns in TV viewing, *Report 15 for Corporate Sponsors*, Ehrenberg-Bass Institute for Marketing Science Adelaide Australia.

Conner, M., Lawton, R., Parker, D., Chorlton, K., Manstead, A.S.R. and Stradling, S. (2007) Application of the theory of planned behaviour to the prediction of objectively assessed breaking of posted speed limits, *British Journal of Psychology*, 98(3), 429–453.

Copeland, M.T. (1923) Relation of consumer's buying habits to marketing methods, *Harvard Business Review*, 1, 282–289.

Cox, K.K. (1970) The effect of shelf space upon sales of branded products, *Journal of Marketing Research*, 7(1), 55–58.

Crawford, C. and Di Benedetto, A. (2006) *New Products Management*, 8th edition, New York: McGraw-Hill/Irwin.

Crocker, J., Fiske, S.T. and Taylor, S.E. (1984) Schematic bases of belief change. In J.R. Eiser (ed.), *Attitudinal Judgement*, New York: Springer-Verlag.

Cronin, J.J., Jr and Taylor, S.A. (1992) Measuring service quality: a re-examination and extension, *Journal of Marketing*, 56(3), 55–68.

Crosby, L.A. and Stephens, N. (1987) Effects of relationship marketing on satisfaction, retention, and prices in the life insurance industry, *Journal of Marketing Research*, 24(4), 404–411.

Cross, S.E. and Madson, L. (1997) Models of the self: self-construals and gender, *Psychological Bulletin*, 122(1), 5–37.

Cunningham, R.M. (1956) Brand loyalty – what, where, how much?, *Harvard Business Review*, 34 (Jan./Feb.), 116–128.

Curhan, R.C. (1972) The relationship between shelf space and unit sales in supermarkets, *Journal of Marketing Research*, 9(4), 406–412.

D'Astous, A. (1990) An inquiry into the compulsive side of normal consumers, *Journal of Consumer Policy*, 13(1), 15–32.

Dabholkar, P.A., Thorpe, D.I. and Rentz, J.O. (1996) A measure of service quality for retail stores, *Journal of the Academy of Marketing Science*, 24(1), 3–16.

Dacin, P.A. and Smith, D.C. (1993) The effect of adding products to a brand on consumers' evaluations of new brand extensions. In L. McAlister and M.L. Rothschild (eds), *Advances in Consumer Research*, 20, 594–598.

Dagnoli, J. (1987) Impulse governs shoppers, *Advertising Age*, 5 October, 1993.

Dall'Olmo Riley, F.D. (2010) *Brand Management*, London: Sage.

Dall'Olmo Riley, F.D., Ehrenberg, A.S.C., Castleberry, S.B., Barwise, T.P. and Barnard, N.R. (1997) The variability of attitudinal repeat-rates, *International Journal of Research in Marketing*, 14(5), 437–450.

Dall'Olmo Riley, F., Pina, J.M., Bravo, R. (forthcoming) Step-down extensions: consumer evaluations and feedback effects, *Journal of Business Research*. http://dx.doi.org/10.1016/j.jbusres.2012.07.013

Danaher, P.J., Bonfrer, A. and Dhar, S. (2008) The effect of competitive advertising interference on sales for packaged goods, *Journal of Marketing Research*, 45(2), 211–225.

Davidson, A.R. and Jaccard, J.J. (1975) Population psychology: a new look at an old problem, *Journal of Personality and Social Psychology*, 31, 1073–1082.

Davis, F.D. (1989) Perceived usefulness, perceived ease of use, and user acceptance of information technology, *MIS Quarterly*, 13(3), 319–339.

Dawar, N. and Anderson, P.F. (1993) *Determining the Order and Direction of Multiple Brand Extensions*, INSEAD Working Paper 93/17/MKT.

Day, D., Gan, B., Gendall, P. and Esslemont, D. (1991) Predicting purchase behaviour, *Marketing Bulletin*, 2(May), 18–30.

Day, G.S. (1969) A two-dimensional concept of brand loyalty, *Journal of Advertising Research*, 9, 29–35.

Day, R.L. (1984) Modeling choices among alternative responses to dissatisfaction. In Kinnear, T.C. (ed.), *Advances in Consumer Research*, 11, 496–499.

Day, R.L. and Landon, E.L. (1976) Collecting comprehensive complaint data by survey research. In B.B. Anderson (ed.), *Advances in Consumer Research*, 3, 263–268.

De Matos, C.A., Henrique, J.L., Vargas, R. and Carlos, A. (2007) Service recovery paradox: a meta-analysis, *Journal of Service Research*, 10(1), 60–77.

de Mooij, M. (2010) *Global Marketing and Advertising, Understanding Cultural Paradoxes*, 3rd edition, London: Sage Publications Ltd.

de Mooij, M. (2011) *Consumer Behavior and Culture: Consequences for Global Marketing and Advertising*, 2nd edition, London: Sage Publications Ltd.

Degeratu, A.M., Rangaswamy, A. and Wu, J. (2001) Consumer choice behavior in online and traditional supermarkets: the effects of brand name, price, and other search attributes, *International Journal of Research in Marketing*, 17(1), 55–78.

Dekimpe, M.G., Hanssens, D.M. and Silva-Risso, J.M. (1999) Long-run effects of price promotions in scanner markets, *Journal of Econometrics*, 89(1/2), 269–291.

DelVecchio, D., Henard, D.H. and Freling, T.H. (2006) The effect of sales promotion on post-promotion brand preference: a meta-analysis, *Journal of Retailing*, 82(3), 203–214.

DeSarbo, W.S., Huff, L., Rolandelli, M.M. and Choi, J. (1994) On the measurement of perceived service quality. In R.T. Rust and R.L. Oliver (eds), *Service Quality: New Directions in Theory and Practice*, London: Sage, 201–222.

Deutsch, M. and Gerard, H.B. (1955) A study of the normative and informational influences upon individual judgment, *Journal of Abnormal and Social Psychology*, 51(3), 629–636.

DeWulf, K., Odekerken-Schroder, G. and Iacobucci, D. (2001) Investments in consumer relationships: a cross-country and cross-industry exploration, *Journal of Marketing*, 65 (October), 33–50.

Dichter, E. (1966) How word-of-mouth advertising works, *Harvard Business Review*, 44(6), 147–166.

Dick, A.S. and Basu, K. (1994) Customer loyalty: towards an integrated framework, *Journal of the Academy of Marketing Science*, 22(2), 99–113.

Dickson, P.R. and Sawyer, A.G. (1990) The price knowledge and search of supermarket shoppers, *Journal of Marketing*, 54(3), 42–54.

Dimson, E., Marsh, P. and Staunton, M. (2004) Low-cap and low-rated companies, *The Journal of Portfolio Management*, Summer, 1–12.

Dittmar, H. (2005) Compulsive buying – a growing concern? An examination of gender, age, and endorsement of materialistic values as predictors, *British Journal of Psychology*, 96(4), 467–491.

Dittmar, H., Beattie, J. and Friese, S. (1995) Gender identity and material symbols: objects and decision considerations in impulse purchases, *Journal of Economic Psychology*, 16(3), 491–512.

Donovan, R.J. and Rossiter, J.R. (1982) Store atmosphere: an environmental psychology approach, *Journal of Retailing*, 58(1), 34–56.

Donovan, R.J., Rossiter, J.R., Marcoolyn, G. and Nesdale, A. (1994) Store atmosphere and purchasing behaviour, *Journal of Retailing*, 70(3), 283–294.

Dowling, G.R. and Uncles, M.D. (1997) Do customer loyalty programs really work? *Sloan Management Review*, 38(Summer), 71–82.

Doyle, P. (1989) Building successful brands: the strategic options, *Journal of Marketing Management*, 5(1), 77–95.

Drèze, X. and Nunes J. C. (2009) Feeling superior: The impact of loyalty program structure on consumers' perception of status, *Journal of Consumer Research*, 35 (6), 890–905.

Drèze, X. and Nunes, J. (2011) Recurring goals and learning: the impact of successful reward attainment on purchase behavior, *Journal of Marketing Research*, 48(2), 268–281.

Drèze, X., Hoch, S.J. and Purk, M.E. (1994) Shelf management and space elasticity, *Journal of Retailing*, 70(4), 301–326.

Driesener, C. and Romaniuk, J. (2006) Comparing methods of brand image measurement, *International Journal of Market Research*, 48(6), 681–698.

Drolet, A., Schwarz, N. and Yoon, C. (2010) (eds). *The Aging Consumer: Perspectives from Psychology and Economics*, New York: Routledge, Taylor and Francis Group, ch. 4.

Du, R.Y. and Kamakura, W.A. (2011) Measuring contagion in the diffusion of consumer packaged goods, *Journal of Marketing Research*, 68(February), 28–47.

du Plessis, E. (2009) Digital video recorders and inadvertent advertising exposure, *Journal of Advertising Research*, 49(2), 236–239.

Dubé-Rioux, L., Schmitt, B.H. and Leclerc, F. (1989) Consumers' reactions to waiting: when delays affect the perception of service quality. In T.K. Srull (ed.), *Advances in Consumer Research*, 16, 59–63.

Dunn, R.S. and Wrigley, N. (1984) Store loyalty for grocery products: an empirical study, *Area*, 16(4), 307–314,

Dunn, R.S., Reader, S. and Wrigley, N. (1983) An investigation of the assumptions of the NBD model as applied to purchasing at individual stores, *Applied Statistics*, 32(3), 249–259.

Eagly, A.H. and Chaiken, S. (1993) *The Psychology of Attitudes*, Orlando, FL: Harcourt, Brace, Jovanovitch.

Eagly, A.H. and Chaiken, S. (2005) Attitude research in the 21st century: the current state of knowledge. In D. Albarracín, B.T. Johnson and M.P. Zanna (eds), *The Handbook of Attitudes*, Mahwah, NJ: Erlbaum, 743–767.

East, R. (1973) The duration of attention to alternatives and re-evaluation in choices with two and three alternatives, *European Journal of Social Psychology*, 3(2), 125–144.

East, R. (1992) The effects of experience on the decision making of expert and novice buyers, *Journal of Marketing Management*, 8(2), 167–176.

East, R. (1993) Investment decisions and the theory of planned behaviour, *Journal of Economic Psychology*, 14(2), 337–375.

East, R. (2000) Complaining as planned behavior, *Psychology and Marketing*, 17(12), 1077–1095.

East, R. and Hammond, K. (1996) The erosion of repeat-purchase loyalty, *Marketing Letters*, 7(2), 163–172.

East, R. and Hogg, A. (1997) The anatomy of conquest: Tesco versus Sainsbury, *Journal of Brand Management*, 5(1), 53–61.

East, R., Lomax, W. and Willson, G. (1991) Factors associated with service delay in supermarkets and post offices, *Journal of Consumer Satisfaction, Dissatisfaction and Complaining Behaviour*, 4, 123–128.

East, R., Lomax, W., Willson, G. and Harris, P. (1992) *Demand Over Time: Attitudes, Knowledge and Habits that Affect When Customers Use Banks and Building Societies*, Working Paper, Kingston Business School.

East, R., Lomax, W., Willson, G. and Harris, P. (1994) Decision making and habit in shopping times, *European Journal of Marketing*, 28(4), 56–71.

East, R., Harris, P., Willson, G. and Hammond, K. (1995) Correlates of first-brand loyalty, *Journal of Marketing Management*, 11(5), 487–497.

East, R., Uncles, M., Romaniuk, J. and Hand, C. (forthcoming) Distortions in retrospective word-of-mouth measurement, *International Journal of Market Research*.

East, R., Hammond, K., Harris, P. and Lomax, W. (2000) First-store loyalty and retention, *Journal of Marketing Management*, 16(4), 307–325.

East, R., Lomax, W. and Narain, R. (2001) Customer tenure, recommendation and switching, *Journal of Consumer Satisfaction, Dissatisfaction and Complaining Behavior*, 14, 46–54.

East, R., Eftichiadou, V. and Williamson, M. (2003) Point-of-purchase display and brand sales, *International Review of Retail, Distribution and Consumer Research*, 13(1), 127–134.

East, R., Gendall, P., Hammond, K. and Lomax, W. (2005a) Consumer loyalty: singular, additive or interactive?, *Australasian Marketing Journal*, 13(2), 10–26.

East, R., Hammond, K., Lomax, W. and Robinson, H. (2005b) What is the effect of a recommendation?, *Marketing Review*, 5(2), 145–157.

East, R., Hammond, K. and Gendall, P. (2006) Fact and fallacy in retention marketing, *Journal of Marketing Management*, 22(1–2), 5–23.

East, R., Hammond, K.A. and Wright, M. (2007) The relative incidence of positive and negative word of mouth: a multi-category study, *International Journal of Research in Marketing*, 24(2), 175–184.

East, R., Hammond, K. and Lomax, W. (2008) Measuring the impact of positive and negative word of mouth on brand purchase probability, *International Journal of Research in Marketing*, 25(3), 215–224.

East, R., Romaniuk, J. and Lomax, W. (2011) The NPS and the ACSI: a critique and an alternative metric, *International Journal of Market Research*, 53(3), 327–346.

East, R., Grandcolas, U., Dall'Olmo Riley, F.D. and Lomax, W. (2012) Reasons for switching service providers, *Australasian Marketing Journal*, 20(2), 164–170.

Edwards, W. (1954) The theory of decision making, *Psychological Bulletin*, 51(4), 380–417.

Effective Advertising 8 (2006) Sydney: Advertising Federation of Australia Advertising Effectiveness Awards.

Ehrenberg, A.S.C. (1959) The pattern of consumer purchases, *Applied Statistics*, 8, 26–41.

Ehrenberg, A.S.C. (1969) The discovery and use of laws of marketing, *Journal of Advertising Research*, 9(2), 11–17.

Ehrenberg, A.S.C. (1986) Pricing and brand differentiation, *Singapore Marketing Review*, 1, 5–15.

Ehrenberg, A.S.C. (1988) *Repeat Buying: Theory and Applications*, 2nd edition, London: Charles Griffin & Co. (first published in 1972 by North Holland).

Ehrenberg, A.S.C. (1993) If you're so strong, why aren't you bigger?, *Admap*, 28(1), 13–14.

Ehrenberg, A.S.C. and England, L.R. (1990) Generalising a pricing effect, *The Journal of Industrial Economics*, 39(1), 47–68.

Ehrenberg, A.S.C and Goodhardt, G.J. (1979) *Essays on Understanding Buyer Behavior*, New York: J. Walter Thompson Co. and Market Research Corporation of America.

Ehrenburg, A.S.C. and Goodhardt, G.J. (2001) New brands: near-instant loyalty, *Journal of Targeting, Measurement and Analysis in Marketing*, 10(1), 9–16.

Ehrenberg, A.S.C., Goodhardt, G.J. and Barwise, T.P. (1990) Double jeopardy revisited, *Journal of Marketing*, 54(3), 82–90.

Ehrenberg, A.S.C., Hammond, K.A. and Goodhardt, G.J. (1994a) The after-effects of price-related consumer promotions, *Journal of Advertising Research*, 34(4), 11–21.

Ehrenberg, A.S.C., Uncles, M.D. and Carrie, D. (1994b) *Armed to the Teeth: An Exercise in Brand Management*, Cranfield, UK: European Case Clearing House (reference M94-005:594-039-1/594-039-4/594-040-1/594-040-4).

Ehrenberg, A.S.C., Uncles, M.D. and Goodhardt, G.J. (2004) Understanding brand performance measures: using Dirichlet benchmarks, *Journal of Business Research*, 57(12), 1307–1325.

Elliott, R. (1993) Shopping addiction and mood repair. In M. Davies et al. (eds), *Emerging Issues in Marketing: Proceedings of the Marketing Education Group*, Loughborough: Loughborough University Press, 287–296.

Elliott, R. (1994) Addictive consumption: function and fragmentation in postmodernity, *Journal of Consumer Policy*, 17, 159–179.

Elliott, R. and Jobber, D. (1990) Understanding organizational buying behaviour: the role of cognitions, norms and attitudes, *Proceedings of the 23rd Marketing Education Group Conference*, Oxford Polytechnic, 402–423.

Elliott, R., Jobber, D. and Sharp, J. (1995) Using the theory of reasoned action to understand organizational behaviour: the role of belief salience, *British Journal of Social Psychology*, 34(2), 161–172.

Elliott, R., Eccles, S. and Gournay, K. (1996) Man management? Women and the use of debt to control personal relationships, *Proceedings of the XXnd Marketing Education Group Conference*, Strathclyde, available on compact disc, 'Buyer Behavior' track.

Enis, B.M. and Paul, G.W. (1970) Store loyalty as a basis for marketing segmentation, *Journal of Retailing*, 46(3), 42–56.

Ennew, C.T. and Binks, M.R. (1996) The impact of service quality and service characteristics on customer retention: small businesses and their banks in the UK, *British Journal of Management*, 7, 219–230.

Eroglu, S.A., Machleit, K.A. and Davis, L.M. (2003) Empirically testing a model of online store atmospherics and shopper responses, *Psychology and Marketing*, 20(2), 139–150.

Eskin, G. (1973) Dynamic forecasts of new product demands using a depth of repeat model, *Journal of Marketing Research*, 10(2), 115–129.

Euromonitor (2006) *Boomers: Now they are Sixty: Changing Consumption Habits of 40–60 Year-Olds to 2010*. Euromonitor, Global Report – Strategy Briefing.

Euromonitor (2011) *The World's Oldest Populations*. Euromonitor, Special Report.

Faber, R.J. and O'Guinn, T.C. (1988) Compulsive consumption and credit abuse, *Journal of Consumer Policy*, 11, 97–109.

Faber, R.J. and O'Guinn, T.C. (1992) A clinical screener for compulsive buying, *Journal of Consumer Research*, 19(3), 459–469.

Fader, P.S., Hardie, B.G.S. and Zeithammer, R. (2003) Forecasting new product trial in a controlled test market environment, *Journal of Forecasting*, 22(5), 391–410.

Fader, P.S., Hardie, B.G.S. and Huang, C.Y. (2004) A dynamic changepoint model for new product sales forecasting, *Marketing Science*, 23(1), 50–65.

Farris, P.W. and Albion, M.S. (1980) The impact of advertising on the price of consumer goods, *Journal of Marketing*, 44(3), 17–35.

Farris, P.W. and Reibstein, D.J. (1991) How prices, ad expenditures, and profits are linked, *Harvard Business Review*, 57(6), 173–184.

Fazio, R.H. (1986) How do attitudes guide behavior? In R.M. Sorrentino and E.T. Higgins (eds), *The Handbook of Motivation and Cognition: Foundations of Social Behavior*, New York: Guilford Press, 204–243.

Fazio, R.H. (1990) Multiple processes by which attitudes guide behavior: the mode model as an integrative framework. In M.P. Zanna (ed.), *Advances in Experimental Social Psychology*, 23, 75–109.

Fazio, R.H. and Zanna, M. (1981) Direct experience and attitude–behavior consistency. In L. Berkowitz (ed.), *Advances in Experimental Social Psychology*, 14, New York: Academic Press, 161–202.

Fazio, R.H., Powell, M.C. and Herr, P.M. (1983) Toward a process model of the attitude–behavior relation: accessing one's attitude upon mere observation of the attitude object, *Journal of Personality and Social Psychology*, 44, 723–735.

Feick, L.F. and Price, L.L. (1987) The market maven: a diffuser of marketplace information, *Journal of Marketing*, 51(1), 83–97.

Feinberg, R.A. and Smith, P. (1989) Misperceptions of time in the sales transaction. In T. Srull (ed.), *Advances in Consumer Research*, 16, 56–58.

Feinberg, R.A., Widdows, R., Hirsch-Wyncott, M. and Trappey, C. (1990) Myth and reality in customer service: good and bad service sometimes lead to repurchase, *Journal of Consumer Satisfaction, Dissatisfaction and Complaining Behavior*, 3, 112–113.

Feinberg, R.A., Widdows, R. and Steidle, R. (1996) Customer (dis)satisfaction and delays, *Journal of Consumer Satisfaction, Dissatisfaction and Complaining Behavior*, 9, 81–85.

Feldwick, P. (1990) *Advertising Works 5*, Institute of Practitioners in Advertising, London: Cassell Educational Ltd. 181–195.

Finn, D.W. and Lamb, C.W., Jr (1991) An evaluation of the SERVQUAL scale in a retail setting. In R.H. Holman and M.R. Solomon (eds), *Advances in Consumer Research*, 18, 483–490.

Fishbein, M. (1963) An investigation of the relationships between beliefs about an object and attitudes to that object, *Human Relations*, 16, 233–240.

Fishbein, M. and Ajzen, I. (1975) *Belief, Attitude, Intention and Behavior*, Reading, MA: Addison-Wesley.

Fishbein, M.F. and Ajzen, I. (1981) On construct validity: a critique of Miniard and Cohen's paper, *Journal of Experimental Social Psychology*, 17, 340–350.

Fisher, J.C. and Pry, R.H. (1971) A simple substitution model of technological change, *Technological Forecasting and Social Change*, 3, 75–88.

Fiske, S.T. (1980) Attention and weight in person perception: the impact of negative and extreme behavior, *Journal of Personality and Social Psychology*, 38(6), 889–906.

Flavián, C., Martínez, E. and Polo, Y. (2001) Loyalty to grocery stores in the Spanish market of the 1900s, *Journal of Retailing and Consumer Services*, 8(2), 85–93.

Folkes, V.S. (1984) Consumer reactions to product failure: an attributional approach, *Journal of Consumer Research*, 10(4), 398–409.

Folkes, V.S. (1988) The availability heuristic and perceived risk, *Journal of Consumer Research*, 15(1), 13–23.

Folkes, V.S., Koletsky, S. and Graham, J.L. (1987) A field study of causal inferences and consumer reaction: the view from the airport, *Journal of Consumer Research*, 13(4), 534–539.

Fornell, C. (1992) A national customer satisfaction barometer: the Swedish experience, *Journal of Marketing*, 56(1), 6–21.

Fornell, C. and Wernerfelt, B. (1987) Defensive marketing strategy by customer complaint management: a theoretical analysis, *Journal of Marketing Research*, 24(4), 337–346.

Fornell, C. and Wernerfelt, B. (1988) A model for customer complaining management, *Marketing Science*, 7(3), Summer, 187–198.

Fornell, C., Johnson, M.D., Anderson, E.W., Cha, J. and Bryant, B.E. (1996) The American Customer Satisfaction Index: nature, purpose, and findings, *Journal of Marketing*, 60(4), 7–18.

Fornell, C., Mithas, S., Morgeson, F.V., III and Krishnan, M.S. (2006) Customer satisfaction and stock prices: high returns, low risks, *Journal of Marketing*, 70(1), 3–14.

Forward, S.E. (2009) The theory of planned behaviour: the role of descriptive norms and past behaviour in the prediction of drivers' intentions to violate, *Transportation Research Part F: Traffic Psychology and Behaviour*, 12(3), 198–207.

Fournier, S. and Yao, J.L. (1997) Reviving brand loyalty: a reconceptualization within the framework of consumer-brand relationships, *International Journal of Research in Marketing*, 14(5), 451–472

Fournier, S., Dobscha, S. and Mick, D.G. (1998) Preventing the premature death of relationship marketing, *Harvard Business Review*, January/February, 42–51.

Fourt, L.A. and Woodlock, J.W. (1960) Early prediction of market success for new grocery products, *Journal of Marketing*, 25(2), 31–38.

Foxall, G. and Hackett, P.M.W. (1992) Consumers' perception of micro-retail location: wayfinding and cognitive mapping in planned and organic shopping environments, *International Review of Retail, Distribution and Consumer Research*, 2(3), 309–327.

Fredricks, A.J. and Dossett, K.L. (1983) Attitude–behavior relations: a comparison of the Fishbein–Ajzen and the Bentler–Speckart models, *Journal of Personality and Social Psychology*, 45, 501–512.

Frisbie, G.A., Jr (1980) Ehrenberg's negative binomial model applied to grocery store trips, *Journal of Marketing Research*, 17, 385–390.

Fulgoni, G.M. (1987) The role of advertising – is there one?, *Admap*, 262, 54–57.

Fulgoni, G. and Morn, M. (2009) Whither the click? How online advertising works, *Journal of Advertising Research*, 49(2), 134 –142.

Gabor, A. and Granger, C.W.J. (1961) On the price consciousness of consumers, *Applied Statistics*, 10, 170–188.

Gabor, A. and Granger, C.W.J. (1966) Price as an indicator of quality: report on an inquiry, *Economica*, 32, 43–70.

Gabor, A. and Granger, C.W.J. (1972) Ownership and acquisition of consumer durables: report on the Nottingham consumer durables project, *European Journal of Marketing*, 6(4), 234–248.

Gardner, A.G. and Levy, S.J. (1955) The product and the brand, *Harvard Business Review*, 33(March–April), 33–39.

Garretson, J.A. and Burton, S. (2003) Highly coupon and sale prone consumers: benefits beyond price savings, *Journal of Advertising Research*, 43(2), 162–172.

Gerard, H.B. (1967) Choice difficulty, dissonance and the decision sequence, *Journal of Personality and Social Psychology*, 35(1), 91–108.

Giebelhausen, M., Robinson, S. and Cronin, J. J. (2011) Worth waiting for: increasing satisfaction by making consumers wait, *Journal of the Academy Of Marketing Science*, 39(6), 889–905.

Gigerenzer, G. (1991) How to make cognitive illusions disappear: beyond 'heuristics and biases'. In W. Stroebe and M. Hewstone (eds), *European Review of Social Psychology*, 2, 83–115.

Gijsbrechts, E. (1993) Prices and pricing research in consumer marketing: some recent developments, *International Journal of Research in Marketing*, 10(2), 115–151.

Gilly, M. and Gelb, B. (1982) Post-purchase consumer processes and the complaining consumer, *Journal of Consumer Research*, 9(3), 323–328.

Givon, M. and Horsky, D. (1990) Untangling the effects of purchase reinforcement and advertising carryover, *Marketing Science*, 9(2), 171–187.

Godes, D. and Mayzlin, D. (2004a) *Firm-created Word-of-mouth Communication: a Field-based Quasi-Experiment*, Harvard Business School Marketing Research Papers No. 04–03.

Godes, D. and Mayzlin, D. (2004b) Using online conversations to study word-of-mouth communication, *Marketing Science*, 23(4), 545–560.

Goldenberg, J., Libai, B., Moldovan, S. and Muller E. (2007) The NPV of bad news, *International Journal of Research in Marketing*, 24(3), 186–200.

Goodey, C. and East, R. (2008) Testing the market maven concept, *Journal of Marketing Management*, 24(3/4), 265–282.

Goodhardt, G.J. and Ehrenberg, A.S.C. (1967) Conditional trend analysis: a breakdown by initial purchasing level, *Journal of Marketing Research*, 4(2), 155–161.

Goodhardt, G.J., Ehrenberg, A.S.C. and Collins, M.A. (1975) *The Television Audience: Patterns of Viewing*: Lexington, MA: Lexington Books.

Goodhardt, G.J., Ehrenberg, A.S.C. and Chatfield, C. (1984) The Dirichlet: a comprehensive model of buying behaviour, *Journal of the Royal Statistical Society*, A, 147, 621–655.

Goodhardt, G.J., Ehrenberg, A.S.C. and Collins, M.A. (1987) *The Television Audience: Patterns of Viewing: An Update*, Aldershot: Gower.

Goodman, J. and Newman, S. (2003) *Understanding customer behavior and complaints*. TARP (Technical Assistance Research Programs), available via www.asq.org.

Gourville, J.T. (1998) Pennies-a-day: the effect of temporal reframing on transaction evaluation, *Journal of Consumer Research*, 24(4), 395–409.

Graham, J. and Havlena, W.J. (2007) Finding the 'missing link': advertising's impact on word of mouth, Web searches, and site visits, *Journal of Advertising Research*, 47(4), 427–435.

Granbois, D., Summers, J.O. and Frazier, G.L. (1977) Correlates of consumer expectation and complaining behavior. In R.L. Day (ed.), *Consumer Satisfaction, Dissatisfaction and Complaining Behavior*, Bloomington, Indiana University, 18–25.

Granovetter, M.S. (1973) The strength of weak ties, *American Journal of Sociology*, 78(6), 1360–1380.

Green, L. (2007) *Advertising Works 15*, IPA Effectiveness Awards 2006, Henley-on-Thames: World Advertising Research Center (Warc).

Green, P.E. and Krieger, A.M. (2002) What's right with conjoint analysis?, *Marketing Research*, 14(1), 24–27.

Green, P.E., Krieger, A.M. and Wind, Y. (2001) Thirty years of conjoint analysis: reflections and prospects, *Interfaces*, 31(3), S56–S73.

Greenfield, S. (1997) *The Human Brain: A Guided Tour*, London: Phoenix.

Grewal, D., Kavanoor, S., Fern, E.F., Costley, C. and Barnes, J. (1997) Comparative versus noncomparative advertising: a meta-analysis, *Journal of Marketing*, 61(4), 1–15.

Grönroos, C. (1978) A service-oriented approach to marketing service, *European Journal of Marketing*, 12(8), 588–601.

Grönroos, C. (1994) From marketing mix to relationship marketing: towards a paradigm shift in marketing, *Management Decision*, 32(2), 4–20.

Gröppel, A. (1993) Store design and experience-orientated consumers in retailing: comparison between United States and Germany. In W.F. van Raaij and G.J. Bamossy (eds), *European Advances in Consumer Research*, 1, 99–109.

Grønhaug, K. (1977) Exploring complaining behavior: a model and some empirical results. In W.D., Perreault, Jr (ed.), *Advances in Consumer Research*, 4, 159–163.

Grønhaug, K. and Zaltman, G. (1981) Complainers and noncomplainers revisited: another look at the data. In K.B. Monroe (ed.), *Advances in Consumer Research*, 8, 83–87.

Gruca, T.S. and Rego, L.L. (2005) Customer satisfaction, cash flow and shareholder value, *Journal of Marketing*, 69(3), 115–130.

Guardian (2011, 16 August) Supermarkets changing market share, http://www.guardian.co.uk/business/2011/aug/16/supermarkets-market-share-kantar.

Gupta, S. (1988) Impact of sales promotions on when, what, and how much to buy, *Journal of Marketing Research*, 25(4), 342–355.

Gupta, S., Van Heerde, H.J. and Wittink, D.R. (2003) Is 75% of the sales promotion bump due to brand switching? No, only 33% is, *Journal of Marketing Research*, 40(4), 481–491.

Gupta, S., Lehmann, D.R. and Stuart, J.A. (2004) Valuing customers, *Journal of Marketing Research*, 41(1), 7–18.

Habel, C. and Rungie, C. (2005) Drawing a double jeopardy line, *Marketing Bulletin*, 16, Technical Note 1, 1–10.

Hallberg, G. (1996) *All Consumers Are Not Created Equal*, Hoboken, NJ: John Wiley & Sons.

Halstead, D. (2002) Negative word of mouth: substitute for or supplement to consumer complaints?, *Journal of Consumer Satisfaction, Dissatisfaction and Complaining Behavior*, 15, 1–12.

Hamilton, W., East, R. and Kalafatis, S. (1997) The measurement and utility of brand price elasticities, *Journal of Marketing Management*, 13(4), 285–298.

Hammond, K.A. and Ehrenberg, A.S.C. (1995) Heavy buyers: how many do you have? How important are they? In M. Bergardaà (ed.), *Marketing Today and for the 21st Century*. 24th EMAC Conference Proceedings, ESSEC, Paris, 1651–1656.

Hammond, K.A., Ehrenberg, A.S.C. and Goodhardt, G.J. (1996) Market segmentation for competitive brands, *European Journal of Marketing*, 30(12), 39–49.

Hanna, N. and Wosniak, R. (2001) *Consumer Behavior: An Applied Approach*, Englewood Cliffs, NJ: Prentice-Hall.

Hanssens, D.M. (2009) Advertising impact generalizations in a marketing mix context, *Journal of Advertising Research*, 49(2), 127–129.

Hanssens, D.M. (2011) What is known about the long-term impact of advertising. http:// www.anderson.ucla.edu/faculty/dominique.hanssens/Website/content/Long-Term%20PUP%202011%20-Hanssens.pdf.

Hanssens, D.M., Parsons, L.J. and Schultz, R.L. (2001) *Market Response Models: Econometric and Time Series Analysis*, 2nd edition, Dordrecht, The Netherlands: Kluwer Academic Publishers.

Hardie, B.G.S., Johnson, E.J. and Fader, P.S. (1993) Modeling loss aversion and reference dependence effects on brand choice, *Marketing Science*, 12(4), 378–395.

Harrison, A.A. (1968) Response competition, frequency, exploratory behavior and liking, *Journal of Personality and Social Psychology*, 9(4), 363–368.

Hartman, C.L., Price, L.L. and Duncan, C.P. (1990) Consumer evaluation of franchise extension products. In M.E. Goldberg, G. Gorn and R. Pollay (eds), *Advances in Consumer Research*, 17, 110–127.

Hartnett, M. (2006) Coupons still king, *Frozen Food Age*, 55(3) October.

Heath, T.B., DelVecchio, D. and McCarthy, M.S. (2011) The asymmetric effects of extending brands to lower and higher quality, *Journal of Marketing*, 75(4), 3–20.

Heilman, C.M., Nakamoto, K. and Rao, A.G. (2002) Pleasant surprises: consumer response to unexpected in-store coupons, *Journal of Marketing Research*, 39(2), 242–252.

Helson, H. (1964) *Adaptation Level Theory*, New York: Harper & Row.

Hennig-Thurau, T. and Klee, A. (1997) The impact of customer satisfaction and relationship quality on customer retention: a critical reassessment and model development, *Psychology and Marketing*, 14(8), 737–764.

Hennig-Thurau, T., Gwinner, K.P., Walsh, G. and Gremler, D.D. (2004) Electronic word-of-mouth via consumer-opinion platforms: what motivates consumers to articulate themselves on the Internet?, *Journal of Interactive Marketing*, 18(1), 38–52.

Herr, P.M., Kardes, F.R. and Kim, J. (1991) Effects of word-of-mouth and product-attribute information on persuasion: an accessibility-diagnosticity perspective, *Journal of Consumer Research*, 17(March), 454–462.

Heskett, J.L., Sasser, W.E., Jr and Schlesinger, L.A. (1997) *The Service Profit Chain*, New York: The Free Press.

Hirschman, A.O. (1970) *Exit, Voice and Loyalty: Responses to Decline in Firms, Organizations and States*, Cambridge, MA: Harvard University Press.

Hoad, A. (2005) *Advertising Works 13*, Henley-on-Thames: Institute of Practitioners in Advertising, World Advertising Research Center, 123–144.

Hoch, S.J., Drèze, X. and Purk, M.E. (1994) EDLP, Hi-Lo, and margin arithmetic, *Journal of Marketing*, 58(4), 16–28.

Hofstede, G. (1980) *Culture's Consequences: International Differences in Work-Related Values*, Beverly Hills, CA: Sage.

Hofstede, G. (2001) *Culture's Consequences: Comparing Values, Behaviors, Institutions, and Organizations across Nations*, 2nd edition, Thousand Oaks, CA: Sage.

Howard, J.A. and Sheth, J.N. (1969) *The Theory of Buyer Behavior*, New York: Wiley.

Huff, D.L. (1962) *Determination of Intra-Urban Retail Trade Areas*, Los Angeles: University of California, Real Estate Research Program.

Huff, D.L. (1981) Retail location theory. In R.W. Stampfl and E.C. Hirschman (eds), *Theory in Retailing: Traditional and Non-Traditional Sources*, Chigago: American Marketing Association, 108–121.

Hui, M.K. and Bateson, J.E.G. (1991) Perceived control and the effects of crowding and consumer choice on the service experience, *Journal of Consumer Research*, 18(2), 174–184.

Hunt, H.K., Hunt, D. and Hunt, T. (1988) Consumer grudge holding, *Journal of Consumer Satisfaction, Dissatisfaction and Complaining Behavior*, 1, 116–118.

Inman, J.J., McAlister, L. and Hoyer, W.D. (1990) Promotion signal: proxy for a price cut?, *Journal of Consumer Research*, 17(1), 74–82.

IRI (1989) Larger sample, stronger proof of P-O-P effectiveness. Reprinted from IRI which enlarges on a report that first appeared in *P-O-P Times*, March/April, 28–32, 1989.

Jaccard, J.J. and Davidson, A.R. (1972) Toward an understanding of family planning behaviors: an initial investigation, *Journal of Applied Social Psychology*, 2(3), 228–235.

Jacoby, J. and Olson, J.C. (1970) *An Attitudinal Model of Brand Loyalty: Conceptual Underpinnings and Instrumentation Research*. Purdue Papers in Consumer Psychology, No. 159, Purdue University, West Lafayette, IN.

Jones, E.E. and Nisbett, R.E. (1972) The actor and observer: divergent perceptions of the causes of behavior. In E.E. Jones, D.E. Kanouse, H.H. Kelley, R.E. Nisbett, S. Valins and B. Weiner (eds), *Attribution: Perceiving the Causes of Behavior*, Morristown, NJ: General Learning Press, 79–94.

Jones, J.P. (1995a) *When Ads Work: New Proof that Advertising Triggers Sales*, New York: Lexington Books.

Jones, J.P. (1995b) Single source research begins to fulfill its promise, *Journal of Advertising Research*, 35(3), 9–16.

Jones, J.P. (1995c) Advertising exposure effects under a microscope, *Admap*, February, 28–31.

Jones, T.O. and Sasser, W.E. (1995) Why satisfied customers defect, *Harvard Business Review*, Nov.–Dec., 88–99.

Juster, F.T. (1966) Consumer buying intentions and purchase probability: an experiment in survey design, *Journal of the American Statistical Association*, 61(September), 658–696.

Kahn, B.E. and McAlister, L. (1997) *Grocery Revolution: The New Focus on the Consumer*, Reading, MA: Addison-Wesley.

Kahn, B.E. and Schmittlein, D.C. (1989) Shopping trip behavior: an empirical investigation, *Marketing Letters*, 1(1), 55–69.

Kahn, B.E., Morrison, D.G. and Wright, G.P. (1986) Aggregating individual purchases to the household level, *Marketing Science*, 5(3), 260–268.

Kahneman, D. (2002) Presentation following the award of the Nobel Prize for Economics. http://nobelprize.org/nobel_prizes/economics/laureates/2002/kahneman-lecture.html.

Kahneman, D. (2012) *Thinking Fast and Thinking Slow*, London: Penguin Books.

Kahneman, D. and Tversky, A. (1979) Prospect theory: an analysis of decision under risk, *Econometrica*, 47, 263–291. Reprinted in D. Kahneman and A. Tversky (2000), *Choices, Values, and Frames*, New York: Russell Sage Foundation, Cambridge University Press, 17–43.

Kahneman, D. and Tversky, A. (1996) On the reality of cognitive illusions, *Psychological Review*, 103(3), 582–591. Also available at: http://psy.ucsd.edu/~mckenzie/KahnemanTversky1996 PsychRev.pdf.

Kahneman, D. and Tversky, A. (2000) *Choices, Values, and Frames*, New York: Russell Sage Foundation, Cambridge University Press.

Kahneman, D., Slovic, P. and Tversky, A. (1982) *Judgment under Uncertainty: Heuristics and Biases*, Cambridge: Cambridge University Press, 117–28.

Kahneman, D., Knetsch, J. and Thaler, R. (1991a) Anomalies: the endowment effect, loss aversion, and status quo bias, *Journal of Economic Perspectives*, 5(1), 193–206. Reprinted in D. Kahneman and A. Tversky (2000), *Choices, Values, and Frames*, New York: Russell Sage Foundation, Cambridge University Press, 159–170.

Kahneman, D., Knetsch, J.L. and Thaler, R.H. (1991b) Fairness as a constraint on profit seeking: entitlements in the market. In R.H. Thaler (ed.), *Quasi Rational Economics*, New York: Russell Sage Foundation, 199–219.

Kalwani, M.U. and Yim, C.K. (1990) A price expectations model of customer brand choice, *Journal of Marketing Research*, 27(3), 251–262.

Kalyanaram, G. and Little, J.D.C. (1994) An empirical analysis of latitude of price acceptance in consumer package goods, *Journal of Consumer Research*, 21(3), 408–419.

Kalyanaram, G. and Winer, R.S. (1995) Empirical generalizations from reference price research, *Marketing Science*, 14(3), G161–G170.

Kamakura, W.A. and Russell, G.J. (1991) *Measuring Consumer Perceptions of Brand Quality with Scanner Data: Implications for Brand Equity*, Report 91–122, Cambridge, MA: Marketing Science Institute.

Kardes, F.R., Cronley, M.L., Kellaris, J.J. and Posanac, S.S. (2004) The role of selective information processing in price-quality inference, *Journal of Consumer Research*, 31(2), 368–374.

Katz, E. and Lazarsfeld, P.F. (1955) *Personal Influence*, Glencoe, IL: The Free Press.

Katz, E. (1961) The social itinerary of technical change: two studies on the diffusion of innovation, *Human Organization*, 20(Summer), 70–82.

Katz, K., Larson, B. and Larson, R. (1991) Prescription for waiting-in-line blues: entertain, enlighten, and engage, *Sloan Management Review*, 32, 44–53.

Kau, A.K. and Ehrenberg, A.S.C. (1984) Patterns of store choice, *Journal of Marketing Research*, 21(4), 399–409.

Kaul, A. and Wittink, D.R. (1995) Empirical generalizations about the impact of advertising on price sensitivity and price, *Marketing Science*, 14(3, Part 2 of 2), G151–G160.

Keaveney, S.M. (1995) Customer switching behavior in service industries: an exploratory study, *Journal of Marketing*, 59(2), 71–82.

Keiningham, T.L., Cooil, B., Andreasson, T.W. and Aksoy, L. (2007) A longitudinal examination of 'net promoter' and firm revenue growth, *Journal of Marketing*, 71(3), 39–51.

Keller, E. and Fay, B. (2006) Single-source WOM measurement: bringing together senders' and receivers' inputs and outputs. In W.J. Carl (ed.), *Measuring Word of Mouth* (Vol. 2), Chicago: Word of Mouth Marketing Association, 31–41.

Keller, E. and Fay, B. (2009) The roles of advertising in word of mouth, *Journal of Advertising Research*, 49(2), 154–158.

Keller, K.L. (1993) Conceptualizing, measuring, and managing customer-based brand equity, *Journal of Marketing*, 57(1), 1–22.

Keller, K.L. (2002) Branding and brand equity. In B. Weitz and R. Wensley (eds), *Handbook of Marketing*, London: Sage Publications Ltd, 155–178.

Keller, K.L. and Aaker, D.A. (1992) The effects of sequential introduction of brand extensions, *Journal of Marketing Research*, 29(1), 35–52.

Keller, K.L. and Lehmann, D.R. (2006) Brands and branding: research findings and future priorities, *Marketing Science*, 25(6), 740–759.

Kendall, N. (1998) *Advertising Works 10*, Henley-on-Thames: NTC Publications.

Kimmel, A.J. (2004) Rumors and the financial marketplace, *Journal of Behavioral Finance*, 5, 232–239.

Kimmel, A. and Audrain-Pontevia, A.-F. (2007) Consumer Response to Marketplace Rumors: An Exploratory Cross-Cultural Analysis. *Proceedings of the 36th EMAC Conference*, Reykjavik University, Iceland.

Kimmel, A.J. (2010) *Connecting with Consumers*, Oxford: Oxford University Press.

Klein, G.A. (1989) Recognition-primed decisions. In W.B. Rouse (ed.), *Advances in Man–Machine System Research*, 5, Greenwich, CT: JAI Press, 47–92.

Knapp, A. (1944) A psychology of rumor, *Public Opinion Quarterly*, 8, 22–27.

Knox, S.D. and Denison, T.J. (2000) Store loyalty: its impact on retail revenue. An empirical study of purchasing behaviour in the UK, *Journal of Retailing and Consumer Services*, 7(1), 33–45.

Koelemeijer, K. (1992) Measuring perceived service quality in retailing: a comparison of methods. In K. Grunert (ed.), *Marketing for Europe – Marketing for the Future: Proceedings of the 21st Annual Conference of the European Marketing Academy*, Aarhus, Denmark, 729–744.

Kordupleski, R.E., Rust, R.T. and Zahoric, A.J. (1993) Why improving quality does not improve retention (or whatever happened to marketing?), *California Management Review*, Spring, 82–95.

Kotler, P. (1973) Atmosphere as a marketing tool, *Journal of Retailing*, 49(4), 48–63.

Kotzan, J.A. and Evanson, R.V. (1969) Responsiveness of drug stores sales to shelf space allocations, *Journal of Marketing Research*, 6(4), 465–469.

Krishnan, H.S. (1996) Characteristics of memory associations: a consumer-based brand equity perspective, *International Journal of Research in Marketing*, 13(4), 389–405.

Krueckeberg, H.F. (1969) The significance of consumer response to display space reallocation, *Proceedings of the American Marketing Association Fall Conference*, 30, 336–339.

Krugman, H.E. (1972) Why three exposures may be enough, *Journal of Advertising Research*, 12(6), 11–14.

Kuehn, A.A. (1962) Consumer brand choice as a learning process, *Journal of Advertising Research*, 2(December), 10–17.

Kumar, N., Scheer, L.K. and Steenkamp, J.-B.E.M. (1995) The effects of supplier fairness on vulnerable resellers, *Journal of Marketing Research*, 32(1), 54–65.

Kunst-Wilson, W.R. and Zajonc, R.B. (1980) Affective discrimination of stimuli that cannot be recognised, *Science*, 207, 557–558.

Lambert-Pandraud, R. and Laurent, G. (2010) Why do older consumers buy older brands? The role of attachment and declining innovativeness, *Journal of Marketing*, 74 (5), 104–121.

Lambert-Pandraud, R., Laurent, G. and Lapersonne, E. (2005) Repeat purchasing of new automobiles by older consumers: empirical evidence and interpretations, *Journal of Marketing*, 69(August), 97–113.

Lapersonne, E., Laurent, G. and Le Goff, J.-J. (1995) Consideration sets of size one: an empirical investigation of automobile purchases, *International Journal of Research in Marketing*, 12(1), 55–66.

LaTour, S.A. and Peat, N.C. (1979) Conceptual and methodological issues in consumer satisfaction research. In W.L. Wilkie (ed.), *Advances in Consumer Research*, 6, 431–437.

Le Boutillier, J., Le Boutillier, S.S. and Neslin, S.A. (1994) A replication and extension of the Dickson and Sawyer price-awareness study, *Marketing Letters*, 5(1), 31–42.

Leclerc, F., Schmitt, B.H. and Dubé, L. (1995) Waiting time and decision making: is time like money?, *Journal of Consumer Research*, 22(1), 110–119.

Lee, A.Y. (1994) The mere exposure effect: is it a mere case of misattribution? In C.T. Allen and D.R. John (eds), *Advances in Consumer Research*, 21, 270–275.

Leenheer, J., van Heerde, H.J., Bijmolt, T.H.A. and Smidts, A. (2007) Do loyalty programs really enhance behavioral loyalty? An empirical analysis accounting for self-selecting members, *International Journal of Research in Marketing*, 24(1), 31–47.

Lees, G. and Wright, M. (2012) Does the duplication of viewing law apply to radio listening?, *European Journal of Marketing*, in press.

Lees, G.J., Garland, B.R. and Wright, M.J. (2007) Switching banks: old bank gone but not forgotten, *Journal of Financial Services Marketing*, 12(2), 146–156.

Lemon, K.N. and Nowlis, S.M. (2002) Developing synergies between promotions and brands in different price-quality tiers, *Journal of Marketing Research*, 39(2), 171–185.

Les Échos (2004) Étendre sa marque, un pari souvent gagnat. No. 19301, 7 December, 15. http://archives.lesechos.fr/archives/2004/LesEchos/19301-50-ECH.htm (accessed 2012).

Lichtenstein, D.R. and Bearden, W.O. (1989) Contextual influences on perceptions of merchant-supplied reference prices, *Journal of Consumer Research*, 16(1), 55–67.

Lichtenstein, S., Slovic, P., Fischoff, B., Lyman, M. and Combs, B. (1978) Judged frequency of lethal events, *Journal of Experimental Psychology: Human Learning and Memory*, 4, 551–578.

Lilien, G.L. and Rangaswamy, A. (2002) *Marketing Engineering: Computer-assisted Marketing Analysis and Planning*, 2nd edition, Upper Saddle River, NJ: Prentice-Hall.

Litzenroth, H. (1991) A small town in Germany: single source data from a controlled micromarket, *Admap*, 26(5), 23–27.

Liu, H.-S. (2012) How does online word-of-mouth influence revenue? Evidence from Twitter. http://www.citi.uconn.edu/cist07/1a.pdf (draft).

Liu, Y. (2006) Word of mouth for movies: its dynamics and influence on box office revenue, *Journal of Marketing*, 70(3), 74–89.

Liu, Y. (2007) The long-term impact of loyalty programs on consumer purchase behavior and loyalty, *Journal of Marketing*, 71(4), 19–35.

Lodish, L.M. and Lubetkin, B. (1992) How advertising works. General truths? Nine key findings from IRI test data, *Admap*, February, 9–15.

Lodish, L.M., Abraham, M., Kalmansen, S., Livelsberger, J., Lubetkin, B., Richardson, B. and Stevens, M.E. (1995a) How TV advertising works: a meta-analysis of 389 real-world split cable TV advertising experiments, *Journal of Marketing Research*, 32(2), 125–139.

Lodish, L.M., Abraham, M., Livelsberger, J., Lubetkin, B., Richardson, B. and Stevens, M.E. (1995b) A summary of fifty-five in-market experiments on the long-term effect of TV advertising, *Marketing Science*, 14(Part 2 of 2), G133–G140.

Loken, B. (1983) The theory of reasoned action: examination of the sufficiency assumption for a television viewing behavior. In R.P. Bagozzi and A.M. Tybout (eds), *Advances in Consumer Research*, 10, Ann Arbor, MI: Association for Consumer Research, 100–105.

Lomax, W., Hammond, K., Clemente, M. and East, R. (1996) New entrants in a mature market: an empirical study of the detergent market, *Journal of Marketing Management*, 12(4), 281–295.

Losch, A. (1939) *The Economics of Location*, translated by W.H. Woglom and F. Stolper (1954), New Haven, CT: Yale University Press.

Luo, X., Homburg, C. and Wieseke, J. (2010) Customer satisfaction, analyst stock recommendations, and firm value, *Journal of Marketing Research*, 47(6), 1041–1058.

Macintosh, G. and Lockshin, L.S. (1997) Retail relationships and store loyalty: a multi-level perspective, *International Journal of Research in Marketing*, 14(5), 487–497.

Madden, T.J., Ellen, P.S. and Ajzen, I. (1992) A comparison of the theory of planned behavior and the theory of reasoned action, *Personality and Social Psychology Bulletin*, 18(1), 3–9.

Mägi, A.W. (2003) Share of wallet in retailing: the effects of customer satisfaction loyalty cards and shopper characteristics, *Journal of Retailing*, 79(2), 97–106.

Magnini, V.P., Ford, J.B., Markowski, E.P. and Honeycut, E.D., Jr (2007) The service recovery paradox: justifiable theory or smouldering myth, *Journal of Services Marketing*, 21(3), 213–224.

Mahajan, V., Muller, E. and Bass, F.M. (1990) New product diffusion models in marketing: a review and directions for research, *Journal of Marketing*, 54(1), 1–26.

Maister, D.H. (1985) The psychology of waiting lines. In J.A. Czepiel, M.R. Solomon and C.F. Surprenant (eds), *The Service Encounter*, Lexington, MA: D.C. Heath, 113–124.

Malafi, T.N., Cini, M.A., Taub, S.L. and Bertolami, J. (1993) Social influence and the decision to complain: investigations on the role of advice, *Journal of Consumer Satisfaction, Dissatisfaction and Complaining Behavior*, 6, 81–89.

Malec, J. (1982) Ad testing through the marriage of UPC scanning and targetable TV, *Admap*, May, 273–279.

Mangold, W.G., Miller, F. and Brockway, G.R. (1999) Word-of-mouth communication in the service marketplace, *Journal of Services Marketing*, 13(1), 73–89.

Manning, K.C. and Sprott, D.E. (2009) Price endings, left-digit effects, and choice, *Journal of Consumer Research*, 36(2), 328–335.

Marcel, J. (1976) Unconscious reading: experiments on people who do not know they are reading. Paper presented at the British Association for the Advancement of Science, Lancaster, UK.

Markus, H. and Kitayama, S. (1991) Culture and self: implications for cognition, emotion and motivation, *Psychological Review*, 98(2), 224–253

Markus, H. and Zajonc, R.B. (1985) The cognitive perspective in social psychology. In G. Lindzey and E. Aronson (eds), *Handbook of Social Psychology*, 3rd edition (Vol. 1), New York: Random House, 137–230.

Marsh, A. and Matheson, J. (1983) *Smoking Attitudes and Behaviour: An Enquiry Carried Out on Behalf of the Department of Health and Social Security*, London: HMSO.

Marsh, P., Barwise, P., Thomas, K. and Wensley, R. (1988) *Managing Strategic Investment Decisions in Large Diversified Companies*, Working Paper, London Business School, reviewed in *The Economist*, 9 July, 1988.

Marx, K. (1930) *Capital*, Vols 1, 2 and 3. London: J.M. Dent & Sons Ltd.

Mason, N. (1991) *An Investigation into Grocery Shopping Behaviour in Britain*, Headington, Oxford: Nielsen Consumer Research.

Mattila, A.S. and Wirtz, J. (2001) Congruency of scent and music as a driver of in-store evaluations and behavior, *Journal of Retailing*, 77(2), 273–289.

Mazumdar, T. and Papatla, P. (2000) An investigation of reference price segments, *Journal of Marketing Research*, 37(2), 246–258.

Mazumdar, T., Raj, S.P. and Sinha, I. (2005) Reference price research: review and propositions, *Journal of Marketing*, 69(4), 84–102.

Mazzarol, T., Sweeney, J. and Soutar, G.N. (2007) Conceptualizing word-of-mouth activity, triggers and conditions: an exploratory study, *European Journal of Marketing*, 41(11/12), 1475–1494.

McDonald, C. (1970) What is the short-term effect of advertising? *Proceedings of the ESOMAR Congress*, Barcelona, 463–485.

McDonald, C. (1995) *Advertising Reach and Frequency*, Chicago: NTC Business Books.

McKay, D.B. (1973) A spectral analysis of the frequency of supermarket visits, *Journal of Marketing Research*, 10(February), 84–90.

McPhee, W.N. (1963) *Formal Theories of Mass Behavior*, Glencoe, IL: The Free Press.

McQuarrie, E.F. (1988) An alternative to purchase intentions: the role of prior behaviour in consumer expenditure on computers, *Journal of the Market Research Society*, 30(4), 407–437.

McSweeney, B. (2002) Hofstede's model of national cultural differences and their consequences: a triumph of faith – a failure of analysis, *Human Relations*, 55, 89–118.

McWilliam, G. (1993) The effect of brand typology on the evaluation of brand extension fit: commercial and academic research findings. In W.F. Van Raaij and G.J. Bamossy (eds), *European Advances in Consumer Research*, 1, 485–91.

Mehrabian, A. and Russell, J.A. (1974) *An Approach to Environmental Psychology*, Cambridge, MA: Massachusetts Institute of Technology Press.

Mela, C.F., Gupta, S. and Lehmann, D.R. (1997) The long-term impact of promotion and advertising on consumer choice, *Journal of Marketing Research*, 34(2), 248–261.

Melnyk, V., van Osselaer, S.M.J. and Bijmolt, T.H.A. (2009) Are women more loyal customers than men? Gender differences in loyalty to firms and individual service providers, *Journal of Marketing*, 73(4), 82–96.

Meyer-Waarden, L. (2007) The effects of loyalty programs on customer lifetime duration and share of wallet, *Journal of Retailing*, 83(2), 223–236.

Meyers-Levy, J. and Tybout, A.M. (1989) Schema congruity as a basis for product evaluation, *Journal of Consumer Research*, 16 (1), 39–54.

Michon, R., Chebat, J.-C. and Turley, L.W. (2005) Mall atmospherics: the interaction effects of the mall environment on shopping behaviour, *Journal of Business Research*, 58(5), 576–583.

Milgram, S. (1970) The experience of living in cities, *Science*, 167, 1464–1468.

Milliman, R.E. (1982) Using background music to affect the behavior of supermarket shoppers, *Journal of Marketing*, 46(3), 86–91.

Mittal, V., Ross, W.T. and Baldasare, P.M. (1998) The asymmetric impact of negative and positive attribute-level performance on overall satisfaction and repurchase intentions, *Journal of Marketing*, 62(1), 33–47.

Mizerski, R.W. (1982) An attributional explanation of the disproportionate influence of unfavorable information, *Journal of Consumer Research*, 9(1), 301–310.

Moldovan, S.E. (1984) Copy factors related to persuasion scores, *Journal of Advertising Research*, 24(6), 16–22.

Monroe, K.B. (1973) Buyers' subjective perceptions of price, *Journal of Marketing Research*, 10(1), 70–80.

Monroe, K.B. and Lee, A.V. (1999) Remembering versus knowing: issues in buyers' processing of price information, *Journal of the Academy of Marketing Science*, 27(2), 207–225.

Moore, W.L. and Pessemier, E.A. (1993) *Product Planning and Management: Designing and Delivering Value*, Singapore: McGraw-Hill.

Moraleda, P. and Ferrer-Vidal, J. (eds) (1991) *Proceedings of the 1990 ESOMAR Conference*, Monte Carlo.

Morgan, N.A. and Rego, L.L. (2006) The value of different customer satisfaction and loyalty metrics in predicting business performance, *Marketing Science*, 25(5), 426–439.

Morin, S., Dubé, L. and Chebat, J.-C. (2007) The role of pleasant music in servicescapes: a test of the dual model of environmental perception, *Journal of Retailing*, 83(1), 115–130.

Morrison, D. and Schmittlein, D.C. (1981) Predicting future random events based on past performances, *Management Science*, 27(9), 1006–1023.

Morrison, D. and Schmittlein, D.C. (1988) Generalizing the NBD model for customer purchases: what are the implications and is it worth the effort?, *Journal of Business and Economic Statistics*, 6(2), 145–166.

Murray-Burton, G., Dyke, M. and Harrison, T. (2007) Monopoly here and now. In L. Green (ed.), *Advertising Works 15*, IPA Effectiveness Awards 2006, Henley-on-Thames: World Advertising Research Center (Warc).

Naples, M.J. (1979) *Effective Frequency: The Relationship Between Frequency and Advertising Effectiveness*, New York: Association of National Advertisers.

Narasimhan, C. (1984) A price discrimination theory of coupons, *Marketing Science*, 3(2), 128–148.

Narisetti, R. (1997) Move to drop coupons puts Procter & Gamble in sticky PR situation, *Wall Street Journal*, 17 April, 1, A10.

Naylor, G. and Kleiser, S.B. (2000) Negative versus positive word-of-mouth: an exception to the rule, *Journal of Satisfaction, Dissatisfaction and Complaining Behavior*, 13, 26–36.

Neslin, S.A. (1990) A market response model for coupon promotions, *Marketing Science*, 9(2), 125–146.

Neslin, S.A. (2002) *Sales Promotion*, Cambridge, MA: Marketing Science Institute.

Neslin, S.A. and Clarke, D.G. (1987) Relating the brand use profile of coupon redeemers to brand and coupon characteristics, *Journal of Advertising Research*, 27(1), 23–32.

Neslin, S.A. and Stone, L.G.S. (1996) Consumer inventory sensitivity and the postpromotion dip, *Marketing Letters*, 7(1), 77–94.

Nielsen (2005) *Retail Pocket Book, 2006*. Oxford: WARC and AC Nielsen.

Nielsen (2011a) Online Shopping, http://www.ukom.uk.net/media/Online%20Grocery %20Shopping_A4Final.pdf.

Nielsen (2011b) Phone usage, women v. men, http://www.marketingcharts.com/direct/ teens-sendreceive-3700-monthly-texts-15579/nielsen-phone-usage-women-v-men-jan11gif/.

Nijs, V.R., Dekimpe, M.G., Steenkamp, J.-B.E.M. and Hanssens, D.M. (2001) The category–demand effects of price promotions, *Marketing Science*, 20(1), 1–22.

Nitzan, I. and Libai, B. (2011) Social effects on customer retention, *Journal of Marketing*, 75(6), 24–38.

North, A.C., Hargreaves, D.J. and McKendrick, J. (1999) The influence of in-store music on wine selections, *Journal of Applied Social Psychology*, 84(2), 271–276.

North, A.C., Hargreaves, D.J. and Hargreaves, J.J. (2004) The uses of music in everyday life, *Music Perception*, 22(1), 41–77.

Nunes, J.C. and Drèze, X. (2006) The endowed progress effect: how artificial advancement increases effort, *Journal of Consumer Research*, 32(4), 504–512.

Odean, T. (1998) Are investors reluctant to realize their losses?, *Journal of Finance*, 53(5), 1775–1798. Reprinted in D. Kahneman and A. Tversky (2000) *Choices, Values, and Frames*, Cambridge: Russell Sage Foundation, Cambridge University Press, 371–392.

OECD (2000) *The Service Economy*. Business and Industry Policy Forum Series. Paris: Organization for Economic Cooperation and Development. http://www.oecd.org/ dataoecd/10/33/2090561.pdf.

Ogilvy, D. (1987) Sound an alarm!, *International Journal of Advertising*, 6, 81–4.

Oliver, R.L. (1980) Cognitive model of the antecedents and consequences of satisfaction decisions, *Journal of Marketing Research*, 17(4), 460–469.

Oliver, R.L. (1981) Measurement and evaluation of satisfaction processes in retail settings, *Journal of Retailing*, 57(3), 25–48.

Oliver, R.L. (1987) An investigation of the interrelationship between consumer (dis) satisfaction and complaint reports. In Wallendorf, M. and Anderson, P. (eds), *Advances in Consumer Research*, 14, 218–222.

Oliver, R.L. (1989) Processing of the satisfaction response in consumption: a suggested framework and research propositions, *Journal of Consumer Satisfaction, Dissatisfaction and Complaining Behavior*, 2, 1–16.

Oliver, R.L. (1999) Whence customer loyalty?, *Journal of Marketing*, 63(Special Issue), 33–44.

Oliver, R.L. and Swan, J.E. (1989) Consumer perceptions of interpersonal equity and satisfaction in transactions: a field survey approach, *Journal of Marketing*, 53(2), 21–35.

Olshavsky, R.W. and Granbois, D.H. (1979) Consumer decision making – fact or fiction?, *Journal of Consumer Research*, 6(2), 93–100.

Osgood, J.F., Suci, G.J. and Tannenbaum, P.H. (1957) *The Measurement of Meaning*, Urbana: University of Illinois Press.

Parasuraman, A., Zeithaml, V.A. and Berry, L.L. (1985) A conceptual model of service quality and its implications for future research, *Journal of Marketing*, 49(4), 41–50.

Parasuraman, A., Zeithaml, V.A. and Berry, L.L. (1988) SERVQUAL: a multiple-item scale for measuring consumer perceptions of service quality, *Journal of Retailing*, 64(1), 12–40.

Parasuraman, A., Berry, L.L. and Zeithaml, V.A. (1991) Refinement and reassessment of the SERVQUAL scale, *Journal of Retailing*, 67(4), 420–450.

Parasuraman, A., Zeithaml, V.A. and Berry, L.L. (1994) Reassessment of expectations as a comparison standard in measuring service quality, *Journal of Marketing*, 58(1), 111–124.

Partch, K. (1996) Still inching toward efficient promotion, *Supermarket Business*, 51, 16.

Pauwels, K., Hanssens, D.M. and Siddarth, S. (2002) The long-term effects of price promotions on category incidence, brand choice, and purchase quantity, *Journal of Marketing Research*, 39(4), 421–439.

Pavlov, I.P. (1927) *Conditioned Reflexes*, translated by G.V. Anrep, London: Oxford University Press.

Peterson, R.A. and Wilson, W.R. (1992) Measuring customer satisfaction: fact or artifact, *Journal of the Academy of Marketing Science*, 20(1), 61–71.

Petty, R.E. and Cacioppo, J.T. (1985) The elaboration likelihood model of persuasion. In L. Berkowitz (ed.), *Advances in Experimental Social Psychology*, 19, New York: Academic Press.

Pham, M., Goukens, C., Lehmann, D. and Stuart, J. (2010) Shaping customer satisfaction through self-awareness cues, *Journal of Marketing Research*, 47(5), 920–932.

Phillips, L.W. and Sternthal, B. (1977) Age differences in information processing: a perspective on the aged consumer, *Journal of Marketing Research*, 14(November), 744–757.

Pickering, J.F. (1975) Verbal explanations of consumer durable purchase decisions, *Journal of the Market Research Society*, 17(2), 107–113.

Pickering, J.F. and Isherwood, B.C. (1974) Purchase probabilities and consumer durable buying behaviour, *Journal of the Market Research Society*, 16(3), 203–226.

Pieters, R. and Warlop, L. (1999) Visual attention during brand choice: the impact of time pressure and task motivation, *International Journal of Research in Marketing*, 16(1), 1–16.

Plassmann, H., O'Doherty, J., Shiv, B. and Rangel, A. (2008) Marketing actions can modulate neural representations of experienced pleasantness, *Proceedings of the National Academy of Sciences of the United States of America* (published online).

Pritchard, M.P., Havitz, M.E. and Howard, D.R. (1999) Analyzing the commitment–loyalty link in service contexts, *Journal of the Academy of Marketing Science*, 27(3), 333–348.

Pruyn, A.Th.H. and Smidts, A. (1993) Customers' evaluations of queues: three exploratory studies. In W.F. Van Raaij and G.J. Bamossy (eds), *European Advances in Consumer Research*, 1, 371–382.

Putsis, W.M. and Srinivasan, V. (2000) Estimation techniques for macro diffusion models. In V. Mahajan, E. Muller and Y. Wind (eds), *New Product Diffusion Models*, Norwell, MA: Kluwer Academic Publishers, 263–291.

Qin, L. (2012) *An empirical investigation of online word-of-mouth dynamic in different online communities*, http://www.swdsi.org/swdsi2012/proceedings_2012/papers/Papers/PA104.pdf.

Raghubir, P. and Srivastava, J. (2002) Effect of face value on product valuation in foreign currencies, *Journal of Consumer Research*, 29(3), 335–347.

Raj, S.P. (1982) The effects of advertising on high and low loyalty segments, *Journal of Advertising Research*, 9(1), 77–89.

Raju, J.S. (1992) The effect of price promotions on variability in product category sales, *Marketing Science*, 11(3), 207–220.

Randall, D.M. and Wolff, J.A. (1994) The time interval in the intention–behaviour relationship, *British Journal of Social Psychology*, 33(4), 405–418.

Rao, A.R. and Monroe, K.R. (1989) The effect of price, brand name, and store name on buyers' perceptions of product quality: an integrative review, *Journal of Marketing Research*, 26(3), 351–358.

Rao, T.R. (1969) Consumer's purchase decision process: stochastic models, *Journal of Marketing Research*, 6(3), 321–329.

Reichheld, F.F. (1993) Loyalty-based management, *Harvard Business Review*, 71(2), 64–73.

Reichheld, F.F. (1996a) Learning from customer defections, *Harvard Business Review*, 74(2), 56–69.

Reichheld, F.F. (with Teal, T.) (1996b) *The Loyalty Effect*, Boston: Harvard Business School Publications.

Reichheld, F.F. (2003) The one number you need to grow, *Harvard Business Review*, 81(12), 46–54.

Reichheld, F.F. and Kenny, D.W. (1990) The hidden advantages of customer retention, *Journal of Retail Banking*, 12(4), 19–23.

Reichheld, F. and Markey, R. (2011) *The Ultimate Question 2.0*, Boston: Harvard Business Review Press.

Reichheld, F.F. and Sasser, W.E. (1990) Zero defections: quality comes to services, *Harvard Business Review*, 68(5), Sept.–Oct., 105–111.

Reilly, W.J. (1929) *Methods for the Study of Retail Relationships*, Austin, TX: Bureau of Business Research Studies in Marketing, No. 4.

Reinartz, W. and Kumar, V. (2000) On the profitability of long-life customers in a non-contractual setting: an empirical investigation and implications for marketing, *Journal of Marketing*, 64(4), 17–36.

Reinartz, W. and Kumar, V. (2002) The mismanagement of customer loyalty, *Harvard Business Review*, 80(7), July, 86–94.

Reinartz, W., Thomas, J.S. and Kumar, V. (2005) Balancing acquisition and retention resources to maximize customer profitability, *Journal of Marketing*, 69(1), 63–79.

Richins, M.L. (1981) An investigation of the consumer's attitudes towards complaining. In Mitchell, A. (ed.), *Advances in Consumer Research*, 9, 502–506.

Richins, M.L. (1983) Negative word of mouth by dissatisfied consumers, *Journal of Marketing*, 47(1), 68–78.

Richins, M.L. (1985) The role of product importance in complaint initiation, *Proceedings of the Eighth and Ninth Conferences on Consumer Satisfaction and Complaining Behavior*, Baton Rouge, Louisiana and Phoenix, Arizona, 50–53.

Richins, M.L. (1987) A multivariate analysis of responses to dissatisfaction, *Journal of the Academy of Marketing Science*, 15(3), 24–31.

Riebe, E., Sharp, B. and Stern, P. (2002) An empirical investigation of customer defection and acquisition rates for declining and growing pharmaceutical brands. *Australian and*

New Zealand Marketing Academy (ANZMAC) 2002 Conference Proceedings, available at: http://members.byronsharp.com/7716.pdf.

Riebe, E., Wright, M., Stern, P. and Sharp, B. Growing the base of loyal customers, acquisition versus retention, *Journal of Business Research*, forthcoming.

Riskey, D.R. (1997) How TV advertising works: an industry response, *Journal of Market Research*, 34(2), 292–293.

Rivis, A. and Sheeran, P. (2003) Descriptor norms as an additional predictor in the theory of planned behaviour: a meta-analysis, *Current Psychology: Developmental, Learning, Personality, Social*, 22(3), 218–233.

Roberts, A. (1996) What do we know about advertising's short-term effects?, *Admap*, February, 42–45.

Roberts, A. (1999) Recency, frequency and the sales effects of TV advertising, *Admap*, February, 40–44.

Roberts, A. (2000) tvSpan: the medium-term effects of TV advertising, *Admap*, November, 12–14.

Roedder-John, D. & Cole, C.A. (1986) Age differences in information processing: Understanding deficits in young and elderly consumers. Journal of Consumer Research, 13(3), 297–315.

Rogers, E.M. (1962) *Diffusion of Innovations*, 1st edition, New York: The Free Press.

Rogers, E.M. (2003) *Diffusion of Innovations*, 5th edition, New York: The Free Press.

Rokeach. M.J. (1973) *The Nature of Human Values*, New York: The Free Press.

Romaniuk, J. (2003) Brand attributes – 'distribution outlets' in the mind, *Journal of Marketing Communications*, 9(2), 73–92.

Romaniuk, J. (2007) Word of mouth and the viewing of television programs, *Journal of Advertising Research*, 47(4), 462–471.

Romaniuk, J. and Dawes, J. (2005) Loyalty to price tiers in purchases of bottled wine, *Journal of Product and Brand Management*, 14(1), 57–64.

Romaniuk, J. and Gaillard, E. (2007) The relationship between unique brand associations, brand usage and brand performance: analysis across eight categories, *Journal of Marketing Management*, 23(3–4), 267–284.

Romaniuk, J. and Sharp, B. (2003) Brand salience and customer defection in subscription markets, *Journal of Marketing Management*, 19(1–2), 25–44.

Romaniuk, J., Nguyen, C. and East, R. (2011) The accuracy of self-reported probabilities of giving recommendations, *International Journal of Market Research*, 53(4), 507–531.

Rosenberg, L.J. and Czepiel, J.A. (1984) A marketing approach to customer retention, *Journal of Consumer Marketing*, 1(2), 45–51.

Rosenberg, M. (2011) http://geography.about.com/od/obtainpopulationdata/a/india population.htm

Rosenberg, M.J. (1956) Cognitive structure and attitudinal affect, *Journal of Abnormal and Social Psychology*, 53, 367–372.

Rosnow, R.L. (2001) Rumor and gossip in interpersonal interaction and beyond: a social exchange perspective. In R.M. Kowalski (ed.), *Behaving Badly: Aversive Behaviors in Interpersonal Relationships*, Washington, DC: American Psychological Association, 203–232.

Rossiter, J. and Bellman, S. (2005) *Marketing Communications*, Sydney: Pearson Education.

Rubinson, J. (2009) Empirical evidence of TV advertising effectiveness, *Journal of Advertising Research*, 49(2), 220–226.

Russo, J.E. and Leclerc, F. (1994) An eye-fixation analysis of choice processes for consumer non-durables, *Journal of Consumer Research*, 21(2), 274–290.

Ryan, B. and Gross, N.C. (1943) The diffusion of hybrid seed corn in two Iowa communities, *Rural Sociology*, 8, 15–24, as cited in E.M. Rogers (2003) *Diffusion of Innovations*, 5th edition, New York: The Free Press.

Saegert, S.C. and Jellison, J.M. (1970) Effects of initial level of response competition and frequency of exposure on liking and exploratory behavior, *Journal of Personality and Social Psychology*, 16(3), 553–558.

Sandell, R. (1981) *The dynamic relationship between attitudes and choice behaviour in the light of cross-lagged panel correlations*, Dept. of Psychology, University of Stockholm, Report no. 581.

Sasser, W.E. (1976) Match supply and demand in the service industry, *Harvard Business Review*, 54(6), 133–138.

Sattler, H., Völckner, F., Riediger, C. and Ringle, C.M. (2010) The impact of brand extension success drivers on brand extension price premiums, *International Journal of Research in Marketing*, 27(4), 319–328.

Scherhorn, G., Reisch, L.A. and Raab, G. (1990) Addictive buying in West Germany: an empirical study, *Journal of Consumer Policy*, 13, 355–387.

Schindler, R.M. (2006) The 99 price ending as a signal of a low-price appeal, *Journal of Retailing*, 82(1), 71–77.

Schindler, R.M. and Kirby, P.N. (1997) Patterns of rightmost digits used in advertised prices: implications for nine-ending effects, *Journal of Consumer Research*, 24(2), 192–201.

Schmitt, P., Skiera, B. and Van den Bulte, C. (2011) Referral programs and customer value, *Journal of Marketing*, 75(1), 46–59.

Schmittlein, D.C., Bemmaor, A.C. and Morrison, D.G. (1985) Why does the NBD model work? Robustness in representing product purchases, brand purchases and imperfectly recorded purchases, *Marketing Science*, 4(3), 255–266.

Schmittlein, D.C., Cooper, L.G. and Morrison, D.G. (1993) Truth in concentration in the land of (80/20) laws, *Marketing Science*, 12(2), 167–183.

Schuman, H. and Johnson, M.P. (1976) Attitudes and behavior, *Annual Review of Sociology*, 2, 161–207.

Schwartz, S.H. (1992) Universals in value content and structure, *Advances in Experimental Social Psychology*, 25.

Schwartz, S.H. and Bilsky, W. (1987) Toward a universal psychological structure of human values, *Journal of Personality and Social Psychology*, 53(3), 550–562.

Schwartz, S.H. and Bilsky, W. (1990) Toward a theory of the universal content and structure of values: extensions and cross-cultural replications, *Journal of Personality and Social Psychology*, 58(5), 878–891.

Schwartz, S.H. and Sagiv, L. (1995) Identifying culture-specifics in the content and structure of values, *Journal of Cross-Cultural Psychology*, 26(1), 92–116.

Sharma, A. and Stafford, T.F. (2000) The effect of retail atmospherics on customers' perceptions of salespeople and customer persuasion: an empirical investigation, *Journal of Business Research*, 49(2), 183–191.

Sharp, B. (2010) *How Brands Grow*, Oxford: Oxford University Press.

Sharp, B. and Sharp, A. (1997) Loyalty programmes and their impact on repeat purchase loyalty patterns, *International Journal of Research in Marketing*, 14(5), 473–486.

Sharp, B., Wright, M.J. and Goodhardt, G.J. (2002) Purchase loyalty is polarised into either repertoire or subscription patterns, *Australasian Marketing Journal*, 10(3), 7–20.

Sharp, B., Beal, V. and Collins, M. (2009) Television: back to the future, *Journal of Advertising Research*, 49(2), 211–219.

Sheppard, B.H., Hartwick, J. and Warshaw, P.R. (1988) The theory of reasoned action: a meta-analysis of past research with recommendations for modifications and future research, *Journal of Consumer Research*, 15(3), 325–343.

Shiv, B., Carmon, Z. and Ariely, D. (2005) Placebo effects of marketing actions: consumers may get what they pay for, *Journal of Marketing Research*, 42(4), 383–393.

Shogren, J.F., Shin, S.Y., Hayes, D.J. and Kliebenstein, J.B. (1994) Resolving differences in willingness to pay and willingness to accept, *American Economic Review*, 84(1), 255–270.

Silverman, G. (2001) *The Secrets of Word-of-Mouth Marketing*, New York: AMACOM.

Simcock, P., Sudbury, L. Wright, G. (2006) Age, perceived risk and satisfaction in consumer decision making: A review and extension. *Journal of Marketing Management*, 22(3), 355–377.

Simmel, G. (1908) *The Sociology of Georg Simmel*, translated by Kurt H. Wolf, New York: The Free Press, 1964, as cited in E.M. Rogers (2003) *Diffusion of Innovations*, 5th edition, New York: The Free Press.

Simon, C.J. and Sullivan, M.W. (1993) The measurement and determinants of brand equity: a financial approach, *Marketing Science*, 12(1), 28–52.

Simon, H.A. (1957) *Administrative Behavior*, New York: Macmillan.

Simon, J.L. (1979) What do Zielske's real data show about pulsing?, *Journal of Marketing Research*, 16(3), 415–420.

Simon, J.L. and Arndt, J. (1980) The shape of the advertising response function, *Journal of Advertising Research*, 20(4), 11–28.

Singh, J. (1990) Voice, exit, and negative word-of-mouth behaviors: an investigation across three categories, *Journal of the Academy of Marketing Science*, 18, 1–15.

Singh, J. and Howell, R. (1985) Consumer complaining behaviour: a review and prospectus. In H.K. Hunt and R.L. Day (eds), *Consumer Satisfaction, Dissatisfaction and Complaining Behavior*, Bloomington: Indiana University Press, 41–9.

Singh, J., Ehrenberg, A. and Goodhardt, G. (2004) Loyalty to product variants – a pilot, *Journal of Customer Behaviour*, 3(2), 123–132.

Singh, J., Ehrenberg, A. and Goodhardt, G. (2008) Measuring loyalty to product variants, *International Journal of Market Research*, 50(4), 513–523.

Singh, J., Dall'Olmo Riley, F., Hand, C. and Maeda, M. (2012) Measuring brand choice in older customers in Japan, *International Journal of Market Research*, 54(3).

Skinner, B.F. (1938) *The Behaviour of Organisms*, New York: Appleton Century Crofts.

Skinner, B.F. (1953) *Scientific and Human Behavior*, New York: Macmillan.

Skowronski, J.J. and Carlston, D.E. (1989) Negativity and extremity biases in impression formation: a review of explanations, *Psychological Bulletin*, 105(1), 131–142.

Smith, A.M. (1995) Measuring service quality: is SERVQUAL now redundant?, *Journal of Marketing Management*, 11, 257–276.

Smith, D.C. and Park, C.W. (1992) The effects of brand extensions on market share and advertising efficiency, *Journal of Marketing Research*, 29(3), 296–313.

Smith, E.R. and Queller, S. (2001) Mental representations. In A. Tesser and N. Schwarz (eds), *Intra-individual Processes*, Oxford: Blackwell Publishing.

Smith, R.B. and Sherman, E. (1992) Effects of store image and mood on consumer behavior: a theoretical and empirical analysis. In L. McAlister and M.L. Rothschild (eds), *Advances in Consumer Research*, 20, 631.

Smith, W. and Higgins, M. (2000) Reconsidering the relationship analogy, *Journal of Marketing Management*, 16(1–3), 81–94.

Snow, C. (2011) *Advertising Works 20: Proving the Payback on Marketing Investment, Case Studies from the IPA Effectiveness Awards 2011*, London: Institute of Advertising Practitioners.

Solnick, S.J. and Hemenway, D. (1992) Complaints and disenrollment at a health maintenance organization, *Journal of Consumer Affairs*, 26(1), 90–103.

Spangenberg, E.R., Grohmann, B. and Sprott, D.E. (2005) It's beginning to smell (and sound) a lot like Christmas: the interactive effects of ambient scent and music in a retail setting, *Journal of Business Research*, 58(11), 1583–1589.

Steenkamp, J.M. and Geyskens, I. (2006) How country characteristics affect the perceived value of web sites, *Journal of Marketing*, 70(3), 136–150.

Steenkamp, J.M., Ter Hofstede, F. and Wedel, M. (1999) A cross-national investigation into the individual and national cultural antecedents of consumer innovativeness, *Journal of Marketing*, 63(2), 55–69.

Steiner, R.L. (1973) Does advertising lower consumer prices?, *Journal of Marketing*, 37(4), 19–27.

Steiner, R.L. (1993) The inverse association between the margins of manufacturers and retailers, *Review of Industrial Organisation*, 8, 717–740.

Stern, P. and Hammond, K. (2004) The relationship between customer loyalty and purchase incidence, *Marketing Letters*, 15(1), 5–19.

Stern, P. and Wright, M. (2007) *Predicting the Innovator*, European Marketing Academy Conference (EMAC).

Stø, E. and Glefjell, S. (1990) The complaining process in Norway: five steps to justice, *Journal of Consumer Satisfaction, Dissatisfaction and Complaining Behavior*, 3, 92–99.

Stiving, M. and Winer, R.S. (1997) An empirical analysis of price endings with scanner data, *Journal of Consumer Research*, 24(1), 57–67.

Sultan, F., Farley, J.U. and Lehmann, D.R. (1990) A meta-analysis of applications of diffusion models, *Journal of Marketing Research*, 27(1), 70–77.

Sundaram, D.S., Mitra, K. and Webster, C. (1998) Word-of-mouth communications: a motivational analysis. In Alba, J.W. and Hutchinson, J.W., *Advances in Consumer Research*, Vol. 25, 527–531.

Sunde, L. and Brodie, R.J. (1993) Consumer evaluation of brand extensions: further empirical results, *International Journal of Research in Marketing*, 10(1), 47–53.

Sutton, S., Marsh, A. and Matheson, J. (1990) Microanalysis of smokers' beliefs about the consequences of quitting: results from a large population sample, *Journal of Applied Social Psychology*, 20(22), 1847–1862.

Swan, J.E. and Trawick, I.F. (1980) Satisfaction related to predicted versus desired expectations. In H.K. Hunt and R.L. Day (eds), *Refining Concepts and Measures of Consumer Satisfaction and Complaining Behavior*, Bloomington: School of Business, Indiana University, 7–12.

Swan, J.E. and Trawick, I.F. (1981) Disconfirmation of expectations and satisfaction with a retail service, *Journal of Retailing*, 57(3), 49–67.

Swinyard, W.R. (1993) The effects of mood, involvement and quality of store experience on shopping intention, *Journal of Consumer Research*, 20(2), 271–280.

Tarde, G. (1903) *The Laws of Imitation*, translated by Elsie Clews Parson, New York: Holt (reprinted University of Chicago Press, 1969), first published in 1890 as *Les Lois de l'Imitation* and available on http://archive.org/details/lesloisdelimita00tarduoft.

TARP (Technical Assistance Research Programs) (1979) *Consumer Complaint Handling in America: A Summary of Findings and Recommendation*, Washington, DC: US Office of Consumer Affairs.

Tate, R.S. (1961) The supermarket battle for store loyalty, *Journal of Marketing*, 25(6), 8–13.

Tauber, E.M. (1981) Brand franchise extension: new product benefits from existing brand names, *Business Horizons*, 24, 36–41.

Tauber, E.M. (1988) Brand leverage: strategy for growth in a cost-conscious world, *Journal of Advertising Research*, 28(4), 26–30.

Taylor, J.W. (1977) A striking characteristic of innovators, *Journal of Marketing Research*, 14(1), 104–107.

Taylor, S. (1994) Waiting for service: the relationship between delays and evaluations of service, *Journal of Marketing*, 58(2), 56–69.

Taylor, S. (1995) The effects of filled waiting time and service provider control over the delay on evaluations of service, *Journal of the Academy of Marketing Science*, 23(1), 38–48.

Taylor, S.E. (1982) The availability bias in social perception and interaction. In D. Kahneman, P. Slovic and A. Tversky (eds), *Judgment under Uncertainty: Heuristics and Biases*, Cambridge: Cambridge University Press, 190–200.

Tellis, G.J. (1988a) Advertising exposure, loyalty and brand purchase: a two-stage model of choice, *Journal of Marketing Research*, 25(2), 134–144.

Tellis, G.J. (1988b) The price elasticity of selective demand: a meta-analysis of economic models of sales, *Journal of Marketing Research*, 25(4), 331–341.

Tellis, G.J. and Wernerfelt, B. (1987) Competitive price and quality under asymmetric information, *Marketing Science*, 6(3), 240–254.

Ter Hofstede, F., Steenkamp, J.-B. and Wedel, M. (1999) International market segmentation based on consumer-product relations, *Journal of Marketing Research*, 36(2), 1–17.

Thaler, R. (1980) Toward a positive theory of consumer choice, *Journal of Economic Behavior*, 1, 39–60. Reprinted in D. Kahneman and A. Tversky (2000), *Choices, Values, and Frames*, New York: Russell Sage Foundation, Cambridge University Press, 269–287.

Thaler, R. (1985) Mental accounting and consumer choice, *Marketing Science*, 4(3), 199–214.

Thaler, R. (1999) Mental accounting matters, *Journal of Behavioral Decision Making*, 12, 183–206. Reprinted in D. Kahneman and A. Tversky (2000), *Choices, Values, and Frames*, New York: Russell Sage Foundation, Cambridge University Press, 241–268.

Thaler, R. and Sunstein, C. (2008) *Nudge*, Yale: Yale University Press.

Theil, H. and Kosobud, R.F. (1968) How informative are consumer buying intentions surveys?, *Review of Economics and Statistics*, 50, 50–59.

Thøgersen, J. and Zhou, Y. (2012) Chinese consumers' adoption of a 'green' innovation – the case of organic food, *Journal of Marketing Management*, 8(3–4), 313–333.

Thomas, M. and Morwitz, V. (2005) Penny wise and pound foolish: the left-digit effect in price cognition, *Journal of Consumer Research*, 32(1), 54–64.

Thorndike, E.L. (1911) *Animal Intelligence*, New York: Macmillan.

Tobin, J. (1969) A general equilibrium approach to monetary theory, *Journal of Money, Credit, and Banking*, 1(1), 15–29.

Tom, G. and Lucey, S. (1995) Waiting time delays and customer satisfaction in supermarkets, *Journal of Services Marketing*, 9(5), 20–29.

Totten, J.C. and Block, M.P. (1987) *Analyzing Sales Promotion: Text and Cases*, Chicago: Commerce Communications Inc.

Treasure, J. (1975) How advertising works. In M. Barnes (ed.), *The Three Faces of Advertising*, London: The Advertising Association, 48, 52.

Triandis, H.C. (1977) *Interpersonal Behavior*, Monterey, CA: Brooks Cole.

Triandis, H.C. (1989) Self and social behavior in differing cultural contexts, *Psychological Review*, 96, 506–520.

Triandis, H.C. (2004) The many dimensions of culture, *Academy of Management Executive*, 18(1), 88–93.

Trusov, M., Bucklin R.E. and Pauwels, K. (2009) Effects of word-of-mouth versus traditional marketing: findings from an Internet social networking site, *Journal of Marketing*, 73(5), 90–102.

Tse, D.K. and Wilton, P.C. (1988) Models of consumer satisfaction formation: an extension, *Journal of Marketing Research*, 25(2), 204–212.

Tversky, A. and Kahneman, D. (1981) Causal schemas in judgements under uncertainty. In Tversky, A. and Kahneman, D. (1981) The framing of decisions and the psychology of choice, *Science*, 211, 453–458.

Tversky, A. and Kahneman, D. (1992) Advances in prospect theory: cumulative representation of uncertainty, *Journal of Risk and Uncertainty*, 5, 297–323. Reprinted in D. Kahneman and A. Tversky (2000), *Choices, Values, and Frames*, New York: Russell Sage Foundation, Cambridge University Press, 44–65.

Uncles, M.D. (2010) Retail change in China: retrospect and prospects, *International Review of Retail, Distribution and Consumer Research*, 20(1), 69–84.

Uncles, M.D. and Ehrenberg, A.S.C. (1990) The buying of packaged goods at US retail chains, *Journal of Retailing*, 66(3), 278–296.

Uncles, M.D. and Hammond, K.A. (1995) Grocery store patronage, *International Journal of Retail, Distribution and Consumer Research*, 5(3), 287–302.

Uncles, M.D. and Kwok, S. (2008) Generalizing patterns of store-type patronage, *International Review of Retail, Distribution and Consumer Research*, 18(5), 473–493.

Uncles, M.D. and Kwok, S. (2009) Patterns of store patronage in urban China, *Journal of Business Research*, 62(1), 68–81.

Uncles, M.D. and Lee, D. (2006) Brand purchasing by older consumers: an investigation using the Juster scale and the Dirichlet model, *Marketing Letters*, 17(1), 17–29.

Uncles, M.D., Dowling, G.R. and Hammond, K. (2003) Customer loyalty and customer loyalty programs, *Journal of Consumer Marketing*, 20(4), 294–316.

Uncles, M., East, R. and Lomax, W. (2010a) Market share is correlated with word-of-mouth volume, *Australasian Marketing Journal*, 18(3), 145–150.

Uncles, M.D., Wang, C., and Kwok, S. (2010b) A temporal analysis of behavioural brand loyalty among urban Chinese consumers, *Journal of Marketing Management*, 26(9–10), 921–942.

Uncles, M.D. et al. (2011) *Perspectives on Brand Management*, Tilde University Press.

United Nations (2002) *World Population Ageing: 1950–2050*, New York: United Nations, Department of Economic and Social Affairs, Population Division.

Usunier, J.C. and Lee J. (2011) *Marketing Across Cultures*, 5th edition, Harlow: Pearson.

Van der Plight, J. and van Schie, E.C.M. (1990) Frames of reference, judgement and preference. In W. Stroebe and M. Hewstone (eds), *European Review of Social Psychology*, 1, Chichester: Wiley and Sons, 61–80.

van Heerde, H.J., Leeflang, P.S.H. and Wittink, D.R. (2004) Decomposing the sales promotion bump with store data, *Marketing Science*, 23(3), 317–334.

Vanhuele, M. (1994) Mere exposure and the cognitive-affective debate revisited. In C.T. Allen and D.R. John (eds), *Advances in Consumer Research*, 21, 264–269.

Vanhuele, M. and Drèze, X. (2002) Measuring the price knowledge shoppers bring to the store, *Journal of Marketing*, 66(4), 72–85.

Vanhuele, M., Laurent, G. and Drèze, X. (2006) Consumers' immediate memory for prices, *Journal of Consumer Research*, 33(2), 163–172.

Vargo, S.L. and Lusch, R.F. (2004) Evolving to a new dominant logic for marketing, *Journal of Marketing*, 68(1), 1–17.

Venkatesh, V. and Davis, F.D. (2000) A theoretical extension of the technology acceptance model: four longitudinal field studies, *Management Science*, 46(2), 186–204.

Venkatraman, M.P. and Price, L.L. (1990) Differentiating between cognitive and sensory innovativeness: concepts, measurement, and implications, *Journal of Business Research*, 20(4), 293–315.

Verhoef, P.C. (2003) Understanding the effect of customer relationship management efforts on customer retention and customer share development, *Journal of Marketing*, 67(October), 30–45.

Verhoef, P.C., Franses, P.H. and Hoekstra, J.C. (2002) The effect of relational constructs on customer referrals and number of services purchased from a multiservice provider: does age of relationship matter?, *Journal of the Academy of Marketing Science*, 30(3), 202–216.

Villanueva, J., Yoo, S. and Hanssens, D.M. (2008) The impact of marketing-induced versus word-of-mouth customer acquisition on customer equity growth, *Journal of Marketing Research*, 45(1), 48–59.

Viscusi, W.K. (1984) The lulling effect: the impact of child resistant packaging on aspirin and analgesic ingestions, *American Economic Review*, 74(2), 324–327.

Völckner, F. and Sattler, H. (2006) Drivers of brand extension success, *Journal of Marketing*, 70(2), 18–34.

Wakefield, K.L. and Inman, J.J. (1993) Who are the price vigilantes? An investigation of differentiating characteristics influencing price information processing, *Journal of Retailing*, 69(2), 216–234.

Wallach, M.A. and Kogan, N. (1961) Aspects of judgment and decision making: interrelationships and changes with age, *Behavioral Science*, 6(1), 23–36.

Wangenheim, F. v. and Bayón, T. (2004) Satisfaction, loyalty and word of mouth within the customer base of a utility provider: differences between stayers, switchers and referral switchers, *Journal of Consumer Behaviour*, 3(1), 211–220.

Wangenheim, F. v. (2005) Postswitching negative word of mouth, *Journal of Service Research*, 8(1), 67–78.

Wangenheim, F. and Bayón, T. (2007) Behavioral consequences of overbooking service capacity, *Journal of Marketing*, 71(4), 36–47.

Warland, R.H., Herrmann, R.O. and Willits, J. (1975) Dissatisfied customers: who gets upset and what they do about it, *Journal of Consumer Affairs*, 9(Winter), 152–162.

Watts, D.J. and Dodds, P.S. (2007) Influentials, networks, and public opinion formation, *Journal of Consumer Research*, 34(December), 441–458.

Weber, M. and Camerer, C.F. (1998) The disposition effect in securities trading: an experimental analysis, *Journal of Economic Behavior and Organization*, 33, 167–184.

Wedel, M. and Leeflang, P.S.H. (1998) A model for the effects of psychological pricing in Gabor–Granger price studies, *Journal of Economic Psychology*, 19(2), 237–261.

Wee, C.H. and Pearce, M.R. (1985) Patronage behavior toward shopping areas: a proposed model based on Huff's model of retail gravitation. In E.C. Hirschman and M.B. Holbrook (eds), *Advances in Consumer Research*, 12, 592–597.

Weigel, R.H. and Newman, L.S. (1976) Increasing attitude–behavior correspondence by broadening the scope of the behavioral measure, *Journal of Personality and Social Psychology*, 33, 793–802.

Weiner, B. (1980) *Human Motivation*, New York: Holt, Rinehart and Winston.

Weiner, B. (1990) Searching for the roots of applied attribution theory. In S. Graham and V.S. Folkes (eds), *Attribution Theory: Application to Achievement, Mental Health and Interpersonal Conflict*, Hillsdale, NJ: Lawrence Erlbaum Associates, 1–16.

Wellan, D.M. and Ehrenberg, A.S.C. (1988) A successful new brand: shield, *Journal of the Market Research Society*, 30(1), 35–44.

Wellan, D.M. and Ehrenberg, A.S.C. (1990) A case of seasonal segmentation, *Marketing Research*, 1, 11–13.

Westbrook, R.A. (1980) Intrapersonal affective influences upon consumer satisfaction, *Journal of Consumer Research*, 7(1), 49–54.

Wetzer, I., Zeelenberg, M. and Pieters, R. (2007) 'Never eat in that restaurant, I did': exploring why people engage in negative word-of-mouth communication, *Psychology and Marketing*, 24(8), 661–680.

White, K.M., Smith, J.K., Terry, D.J., Greenslade, J.H. and McKimmie, B.M. (2009) Social influence in the theory of planned behaviour: the role of descriptive, injunctive, and ingroup norms, *British Journal of Social Psychology*, 48(1), 135–158.

Whyte, W.H. (1954) The web of word of mouth, *Fortune*, 50(November), 140.

Wicker, A.W. (1969) Attitude vs actions: the relationship of verbal and overt behavioral responses to attitude objects, *Journal of Social Issues*, 25, 41–78.

Wicker, A.W. (1984) *An Introduction to Ecological Psychology*, Monterey, CA: Brooks/Cole.

Wilkie, W.L. and Dickson, P.R. (1985) *Shopping for Appliances: Consumers' Strategies and Patterns of Information Search*, Cambridge, MA: Marketing Science Institute Research Report No. 85–108.

Williams, L.G. (1966) The effect of target specification on objects fixed during visual search, *Perception and Psychophysics*, 1, 315–318.

Winchester, M. and Romaniuk, J. (2008) Negative brand beliefs and brand usage, *International Journal of Market Research*, 50(3), 1–20.

Winchester, M., Romaniuk, J. and Bogomolova, S. (2008) Positive and negative brand beliefs and brand defection/uptake, *European Journal of Marketing*, 42(5/6), 553–570.

Winer, R.S. (1986) A reference price model of brand choice for frequently purchased products, *Journal of Consumer Research*, 13(2), 250–256.

Winer, R.S. (1988) Behavioral perspectives on pricing: buyers' subjective perceptions of price revisited. In T.M. Divinney (ed.), *Issues in Pricing*, Lexington, MA: Lexington Books, 35–57.

Wittink, D.R., Vriens, M. and Burhenne, W. (1994) Commercial use of conjoint analysis in Europe: results and critical reflections, *International Journal of Research in Marketing*, 11(1), 41–52.

Wright, M.J. and Charlett, D. (1995) New product diffusion models in marketing: an assessment of two approaches, *Marketing Bulletin*, 6, 32–41.

Wright, M.J. and MacRae, M. (2007) Bias and variability in purchase intention scales, *Journal of the Academy of Marketing Science*, 35(4), 617–624.

Wright, M. and Riebe, E. (2010) Double jeopardy in brand defection, *European Journal of Marketing*, 44(6), 860–873.

Wright, M. and Sharp, A. (2001) The effects of a new brand entrant on a market, *Journal of Empirical Generalisations in Marketing Science*, 6, 15–29.

Wright, M.J. and Stern, P. (2006) *Extending consumer trial models to national panel data*, Working Paper, Victoria University of Wellington, New Zealand.

Wright, M.J., Upritchard, C. and Lewis, A. (1997) A validation of the Bass new product diffusion model in New Zealand, *Marketing Bulletin*, 8, 15–29.

Wright, M., Sharp, A. and Sharp, B. (1998) Are Australasian brands different?, *Journal of Product and Brand Management*, 7 (6), 465–480.

Xia, L., Monroe, K.B. and Cox, J.L. (2004) The price is unfair! A conceptual framework of price fairness perceptions, *Journal of Marketing*, 68(4), 1–15.

Yalch, R. and Spangenberg, E. (2000) Using store music for retail zoning: a field experiment. In L. McAlister and M.L. Rothschild (eds), *Advances in Consumer Research*, 20, 632–636.

Yi, Y. (1990) A critical review of consumer satisfaction. In V.A. Zeithaml (ed.), *Review of Marketing*, Chicago: American Marketing Association, 68–113.

Zajonc, R.B. (1968) Attitudinal effects of mere exposure, *Journal of Personality and Social Psychology Monograph Supplement*, 9(2, Part 2), 1–27.

Zajonc, R.B. (1980) Feeling and thinking: preferences need no inferences, *American Psychologist*, 35, 151–175.

Zajonc, R.B. and Rajecki, D.W. (1969) Exposure and affect: a field experiment, *Psychonomic Science*, 17, 216–217.

Zeithaml, V.A. (1988) Consumer perceptions of price, quality, and value: a means–end model and synthesis of evidence, *Journal of Marketing*, 52(3), 2–21.

Zeithaml, V.A. (2000) Service quality, profitability, and the economic worth of customers: what we know and what we need to learn, *Journal of the Academy of Marketing Science*, 28(1), 67–85.

Zettelmeyer, F., Morton, F.S. and Silva-Risso, J. (2006) How the Internet lowers prices: evidence from matched survey and auto transaction data, *Journal of Marketing Research*, 43(2), 168–181.

Zhang, J. (2006) An integrated choice model incorporating alternative mechanisms for consumers' reactions to in-store display and feature advertising, *Marketing Science*, 25(3), 278–290.

Zhang, J. and Wedel, M. (2009) The effectiveness of customized promotions in online and offline stores, *Journal of Marketing Research*, 46(2), 190–206.

Zhang, J., Beatty, S.E. and Walsh, G. (2008) Review and future directions of cross-cultural consumer services research, *Journal of Business Research*, 61(3), 211–224.

Zielske, H. (1959) The remembering and forgetting of advertising, *Journal of Marketing*, 23(3), 239–243.

Zufryden, F.S. (1996) Multibrand transition probabilities as a function of explanatory variables: estimation by a least squares approach, *Journal of Marketing Research*, 23(2), 177–183.

Author Index

Subject Index